Leading a Human Life

Leading a Human Life

Wittgenstein, Intentionality, and Romanticism § § § § § § §

Richard Eldridge

The University of Chicago Press   *Chicago & London*

Richard Eldridge is professor and chair of the Department of Philosophy at Swarthmore College. He is the author of *On Moral Personhood: Philosophy, Literature, Criticism, and Self-Understanding* (1989), also published by the University of Chicago Press.

The University of Chicago Press, Chicago 60637
The University of Chicago Press, Ltd., London

© 1997 by The University of Chicago
All rights reserved. Published 1997

Printed in the United States of America
06 05 04 03 02 01 00 99 98 97   1 2 3 4 5

ISBN: 0-226-20312-3 (cloth)
ISBN: 0-226-20313-1 (paper)

Library of Congress Cataloging-in-Publication Data

Eldridge, Richard Thomas, 1953–
    Leading a human life : Wittgenstein, intentionality, and
romanticism / Richard Eldridge.
        p.   cm.
    Includes bibliographical references and index.
    ISBN 0-226-20312-3 (cloth : alk. paper). — ISBN 0-226-20313-1
(pbk. : alk. paper)
    1. Wittgenstein, Ludwig, 1889–1951.   Philosophische
Untersuchungen.   2. Intentionality (Philosophy).   3. Romanticism.
I. Title.
B3376.W563P53   1997
192—dc21   97-7998
                                                            CIP

For although I cannot prove to them that my confessions are true, at least I shall be believed by those whose ears are opened to me by charity.

          —Augustine, *Confessions*, X, 3

Nearly all my writings are private conversation with myself. Things that I say to myself tête-à-tête. [Ich schreibe beinahe immer Selbstgespräche mit mir selbst. Sachen, die ich mir unter vier Augen sage.]

     —Ludwig Wittgenstein, *Culture and Value*, 77, 77e

The hour arrived. Kraft was there, the philosophers were there—but no Wittgenstein. Afterward, Elizabeth told me how difficult it had been for Wittgenstein to negotiate this particular event. Should he come at the correct time, sit down, and just listen? Should he come a little late and enter with a flourish? Should he come very late, simply walk in, and sit down as if nothing had happened? Should he come very late and make a joke?

       —Paul Feyerabend, *Killing Time*, 76

The blissful oneness, Being, in the singular sense of the word, is lost to us, and we had to lose it so that we should be able to strive for it and attain it. We tear ourselves loose from the peaceful *Hen Kai Pan* of the world in order to erect it as our own. We've become estranged from nature, and what, as one can believe, was once One, now stands in discord with itself and lordship and bondage alternate by changing places. It is often as if the world were everything and we nothing, but it is often too as if we were everything and the world nothing.

      —Friedrich Hölderlin, preface to *Hyperion*

Contents

Acknowledgments

Some of my thoughts about Wittgenstein surfaced in my first reading of *Philosophical Investigations* roughly twenty years ago, and they then developed and grew throughout my dissertation and my later teaching of Wittgenstein. I was able to cast these thoughts into a book-length draft that began to satisfy me, however, only when I came to hold a Humanities Forum Fellowship at the Stanford Humanities Center during a sabbatical year in 1993–94. I am grateful to the Humanities Center—especially to Director Wanda Corn, Associate Director Charles Junkerman, and its extremely helpful staff—for providing a very congenial environment in which to live, think, and write. I am indebted to Swarthmore College and to its provost, Jennie Keith, for further support during this sabbatical year.

The students to whom I taught Wittgenstein at Swarthmore, at the University of Essex, and at Stanford, in ways that were to them often unexpected, were happily encouraging in their responses, both oral and written, to that teaching. It is difficult for me to imagine going on with my work on Wittgenstein in the absence of those responses.

My debts to the writing of Stanley Cavell go well beyond the points that are already evident in my citations of his work. I have found regular inspiration in his cultivation of a style of thinking that seemed otherwise little present in contemporary philosophy.

It would have been impossible for me to have completed the kind of close reading of *Philosophical Investigations* that I have undertaken without the immense labors and example, textual and philosophical, of Peter Hacker and Gordon Baker, not only in their volumes of commentary but also in their various topical works. The aid and influence of their writings, individual and joint, was augmented by Peter Hacker's having spent a six-week term teaching at Swarthmore, where I was able to rehearse with him my own approaches to Wittgenstein and to issues in the philosophies of mind and language. These rehearsals were later fruitfully continued with his then student, now colleague, John Hyman. I share many of their stances toward contemporary intellectual culture, and I have been helped by their examples to articulate those stances in my engagements with Wittgenstein, even while my own engagements with the text of *Philosophical Investigations* are more elaborately literary and romantic than theirs.

A number of conversations contributed immediately to the shaping of this manuscript, even though my interlocutors may not always have been aware of that result. I am grateful to Jay Bernstein for remarks about conscience and impersonality, and especially about Adorno (Wittgenstein's almost contemporary) and his responses to modernity. These conversations persuaded me that what one critic has called Adorno's fragmentary "ciphers of a possible redemption,"[1] themselves aimed at continuously holding open a space for thoughts about expressive freedom in culture, without idle or forced utopianism and without a grounding in the properties of material substances, lie strand by strand alongside Wittgenstein's. This discovery in turn confirmed my sense of the depth of Wittgenstein's writings about conceptual consciousness and the pertinence of that depth to thoughts about the prospects for expressive freedom within antagonized cultures. I reported my progress in thinking and writing, sometimes daily, to my Humanities Center colleague Morris Kaplan, whose responses were unfailingly supportive. While writing, I often had in mind conversations with him about identity formation, Hegel, and the relations between identity, style, and expressive power. Conversations with Annette Richards about imagination, originality, expressive power, and anxieties of reception, mostly though not always having to do with music, and often particularly with Schubert's *Impromptus,* Beethoven's *Bagatelles,* and C. P. E. Bach's *Fantasias,* also found their ways into my writing, as well as making my year at Stanford happier than it would otherwise have been. Peter Baumann, Peter Winch, Adrian Slobin, Hugh Lacey, and Hilary Putnam read various chapters in late drafts; through their comments they helped me see how to formulate some of my stances about Wittgenstein and intentionality more persuasively than I would otherwise have been able to do.

As a late student of English and German romanticism and German idealism, I have often had to try out my formulations on those better educated than I

1. Martin Jay, *Adorno* (Cambridge: Harvard University Press, 1984), p. 62.

am. My gratitude extends to the critical comments and encouragement in these regions, in conversation and in correspondence, of M. H. Abrams, Charles Altieri, Daniel Breazale, Anthony J. Cascardi, Michael Fischer, Kenneth Johnston, Theresa Kelley, Salim Kemal, Richard Velkley, Allen Wood, and especially my Swarthmore German Studies colleague Hans-Jakob Werlen, with whom I co-taught texts in German romanticism to my enormous profit. At Stanford, Eckhart Förster usefully directed me to Hölderlin's essays and to recent work on Wittgenstein and Goethe, while also generously showing me his own writing on Hölderlin.

Throughout my thinking and writing, I have been instructed about romanticism—and expression and form—by my work in music with my teachers Barbara Devin, Kris Yenney, David Szepessy, and especially Barbara Scherer, without whom I would have had no hope of understanding what sense it makes that Schubert was Wittgenstein's favorite composer.

Despite these influences and encouragements, and the generosities of those who have provided them, I have often felt isolated in my thinking and writing about Wittgenstein, and uncertain and anxious about its destinations and significances. One of this book's arguments is that such feelings, and with patience and luck their redemption, naturally inhabit the development of a life in culture. My sense of what a life in culture is—of how one may take to, or resist, or begin to reshape the ways of culture as it stands, and of the risks, and costs, and rewards of doing this—has been deeply shaped by my life with my children, Hannah, Sarah, and Jonathan, as they have been growing up. Figuring out how to aid in that growing up, and how much of it can't be figured out, as personality must test its own powers, has made an enormous difference to my thinking about expression and freedom and to what I do every day. This life with them in turn has led me to new appreciation of and gratitude for my own parents' encouragement and cultivation of my powers and sensibility. Woven everywhere throughout these relations with parents, children, music teachers, colleagues, Wordsworth, and the novel is my life with Joan Vandegrift, with whom I feel such assurances as there can be of sharing certain aspirations, and anxieties, and ways of going on in culture, as well as the fun of sometimes getting the counting to come out right.

1

Introduction: Philosophical Thinking beyond Dogmatism and Nihilism

Wittgenstein's *Philosophical Investigations* has proved uncannily attractive as both philosophy and writing for many of those who have entered it, as though no other thought or writing could count as serious if not somehow in its orbit or image. It has also put off many others as unprofessional, or unreasoned, or grandiose, albeit possessed of some odd aperçus about qualia or proper names. Why? What are the sources and natures of both its attractiveness and its difficulty?

The answers to these questions have largely to do with the character of the writing in *Philosophical Investigations*. The text does not present a single definite philosophical theory of mind and understanding that is supported by a single definite course of argument. Instead we find an internal dialogue of proposal and criticism that nowhere ends in the assured announcement of a discovery. The problems of understanding language, thought, sensations, and our lives as conceptually conscious beings persist. No doctrine to guide us in subsequent scientific theoretical research into these phenomena is laid down. We are not, for example, told what it is to think or what thinking consists in. The internal dialogue trails off, as though it could be continued indefinitely, but without any definite direction having been established.

Wittgenstein himself noted that his post-*Tractatus* thinking and writing have the character of an ongoing effort. Rush Rhees reports that Wittgenstein "said to me roughly this: 'In my book I say that I am able to leave off with a problem in philosophy when I want to. But that's a lie; I can't.'"[1] (In fact, in *Philosophical Investigations* the claim is only the weaker one that "the real discovery" to be made in philosophy "is the one that makes me able to break off

---

1. Cited in Garth Hallett, *A Companion to Wittgenstein's Philosophical Investigations* (Ithaca: Cornell University Press, 1977), p. 230.

from doing philosophy when I want to,"[2] *not* that this discovery has been achieved.) Wittgenstein further held that the problems that beset him were not peculiar to him but natural in human life. For example, the effort to describe the putatively private contents of immediate perceptual experience "is a significant dead end, for it tempts everyone to go down it as though the final solution to the problems of philosophy were to be found there."[3] If Wittgenstein is right about this, then the philosophical problems about understanding and mind that mostly occupy him are not optional intellectual curiosities. They are instead somehow woven into our sense of our conceptual and agentive powers and our worries about how to exercise them. (This is so even if we often repress such worries, and for good reason: rejecting narcissistic lingering in one's worries in favor of modest and decent persistence in doing what one can do can itself be an exemplary response to the problem of leading a human life.) In going down dead ends in philosophy and then in coming back to himself still in the grip of philosophical problems, Wittgenstein, as David G. Stern puts it, "acts out the tension [between essentialism and conventionalism] in dialogues" in ways that display to us who we are.[4]

To the extent that we are drawn into the course of internal dialogical reflection in *Philosophical Investigations,* we then find ourselves to be shown to ourselves. This showing, so far as it occurs, supports a new sense of human life that runs counter to the theses of Cartesianism, behaviorism, cognitive psychology, and materialist naturalism. It is, further, achieved dramatically and critically rather than through the characterization of processes or substances that are independent of this course of reflection. Mindedness reveals itself to itself in and through the protagonist's internal dialogical reflections on it. Impersonal mindedness in a particular reflecting individual is here both the object of the investigation and the power that conducts it.

Very schematically, the structure of the mind's showing of itself to itself in a particular course of reflection that is continually reenacted in the text is as follows. Various theses about the nature of conceptual consciousness, as opposed to mere sensory responsiveness, are brought forward in the course of internal reflection. It is alternately suggested that conceptual consciousness

---

2. Ludwig Wittgenstein, *Philosophical Investigations,* 3d ed., trans. G. E. M. Anscombe (New York: Macmillan, 1958), §133, pp. 51e, 51.

3. Wittgenstein, MS 105, cited in David G. Stern, *Wittgenstein on Mind and Language* (Oxford: Oxford University Press, 1994), p. 149.

4. Stern, *Wittgenstein on Mind and Language,* p. 116.

consists in neural processes, or that it is a matter of conformity to social practices, or that it originates in private awareness of a private object. Various
considerations are adduced in support of these quite different theses. Each of
these considerations, however, is philosophically inconclusive. None of them
succeeds in making the bearing of conceptual consciousness transparent to
itself. This fact is continually registered in the text, as the protagonist's reflections lead to reminders of incoherencies and of problems that seem not even
to admit of solution that trouble each position. For example, talk of brain
processes scants the normativity of the application of a concept; talk of compli-
ance with social practices scants the natural, species-specific powers that we
bring to language acquisition and diachronic language development. Yet in
this continual rehearsal and rejection of positions, none of which is supported
by conclusive considerations, the problem of understanding the nature of conceptual consciousness is neither solved nor dismissed. There is no triumphant
philosophical discovery, and yet no reversion to skepticism or materialist naturalism. Instead, the protagonist stops to ask himself: Why do I wish to know
about this? What might such knowledge, if I should come to possess it, have
to do with my life? What peace might it bring? This knowledge remains elusive,
yet the wish for it does not lapse. In this way we are shown what it is like to
live with an unappeasable wish to have an account of the nature of conceptual
consciousness, as this life is dramatized in the protagonist's course of reflections. It is in this drama that the teachings of *Philosophical Investigations* are
finally to be found.

It may easily seem more than a little obscurantist or recherché to focus on
this drama as the substance of the text's showings. After all, don't we know
that Wittgenstein simply wished to bring words back from metaphysical to
ordinary usages? Isn't his teaching rather quite straightforwardly that metaphysical investigations are altogether misbegotten, in arising out of surface
similarities between expressions—such as "I have a coin in my pocket" and
"I have a pain in my shoulder"—that mask deep differences in use? Once we
note the enormous varieties of appropriate uses of expressions in different
circumstances, shouldn't we just stop? Shouldn't our wish for a unified account
of the natures of meaning and understanding just go away?[5]

But no. Why are we tempted in the first place to build a theory of under-

5. I am grateful to an anonymous reader for the University of Chicago Press for pressing this
objection on me in just this way, including the "coin-pain" example.

standing and meaning on surface similarities between expressions, and what happens to that temptation once differences in uses are noted? It does not go away. It is not true that everything becomes clear. There is the puzzling apparent species-specificity of language and conceptual consciousness. There are diachronic meaning shifts. It is difficult to draw principled distinctions between literal and figurative meaning. Above all, there is this brute wonder: How do I have a world of objects that are there for me as a judging consciousness, and how and to what extent do others also have such a world?[6] How might I best develop a character and display it in practice? How am I to lead my life? All these phenomena and wonders are noted in the course of reflection in the text without any final settling in any doctrine of the priority of ordinary life. We are continually drawn into the drama of reflection and self-interrogation, as the protagonist is unable to break off doing philosophy.

Reading a text to trace this kind of drama and its showings presents difficulties on which philosophers, oriented toward the truth of sentences, are not much accustomed to dwell. This way of reading does not readily yield any thematizable truth about the nature of mindedness or conceptual consciousness that is other than banal (mindedness is a problem for us) or torturously baroque. Since it does not prescind from dramas of self-interrogation in which we are entangled, it does not support any spectatorial-theoretical program of research into how inert things or processes yield mind. Hence it points to no transcendent hero story about how a resolute detached investigator might see into the heart of things. It does not support a fantasy of control of mindedness as an independent object of theoretical understanding. The way of reading that the drama of *Philosophical Investigations* requires asks more for the recognition of wishes and entanglements than for the acceptance of theses. Hence this way of reading resembles the activity of the critic of the arts who, in Arnold Isenberg's formulation, "*gets us to see*" by offering us "directions for perceiving" something that cannot be wholly described but must be experienced. "It is a function of criticism," Isenberg tells us, and here of this way of reading, "to induce a sameness of vision, of experienced content." Through following the drama of *Philosophical Investigations,* human life may come to look different to

---

6. Stern points to the depth of Wittgenstein's engagement with phenomenalism in 1930–31 and suggests that the sort of wonder at experience that captivated Wittgenstein is natural (*Wittgenstein on Mind and Language,* chap. 5, "The Description of Immediate Experience," pp. 128–59).

us as we experience the content of this drama. Or it may not: Isenberg adds that an experience of artistic content "may or may not be followed by agreement, or what is called 'communion.' "[7] Stanley Cavell echoes this thought in remarking that a certain kind of critical philosophy, "like art, is, and should be, powerless to *prove* its relevance; and that says something about the kind of relevance it wishes to have. All the philosopher, this kind of philosopher, can do is to express, as fully as he can, his world, and attract our undivided attention to our own."[8] By following the drama that is played out in *Philosophical Investigations,* we shall at least have the chance to see whether our attentions might therein have been called to our own world.

Wittgenstein himself noted the existence of a way of reading out loud that might serve strikingly to bring a poem into connection with one's life:

> Take the question: "How should poetry be read? What is the correct way of reading it?" If you are talking about blank verse the right way of reading it might be stressing it correctly—you discuss how far you should stress the rhythm and how far you should hide it. A man says it ought to be read *this* way and reads it out to you. You say: "Oh yes. Now it makes sense." There are cases of poetry which should almost be scanned—where the metre is as clear as crystal—others where the metre is entirely in the background. I had an experience with the 18th century poet Klopstock. I found that the way to read him was to stress his metre abnormally. Klopstock put ∪–∪ (etc.) in front of his poems. When I read his poems in this new way, I said: "Ah-ha, now I know why he did this." What had happened? I had read this kind of stuff and had been moderately bored, but when I read it in this particular way, intensely, I smiled, said: "This is *grand,*" etc. But I might not have said anything. The important fact was that I read it again and again. When I read these poems I made gestures and facial expressions which were what would be called gestures of approval. But the important thing was that I read the poems entirely differently, more intensely, and said to others: "Look! This is how they should be read."[9]

7. Arnold Isenberg, "Critical Communication," in *The Philosophy of Art: Readings Ancient and Modern,* ed. Alex Neill and Aaron Ridley (New York: McGraw-Hill, 1995), p. 367; first published in *Philosophical Review* 58 (1949): 330–44.

8. Stanley Cavell, "Aesthetic Problems of Modern Philosophy," in *Must We Mean What We Say?* (New York: Charles Scribner's Sons, 1969), p. 96.

9. Wittgenstein, "Lectures on Aesthetics I," in *Lectures on Aesthetics, Psychology, and Religious Belief,* ed. Cyril Barrett (Berkeley: University of California Press, 1967), §12, pp. 4–5.

What is here true of reading aloud is also true of reading with a certain critical attention to a text's drama. It can attract us, intensely, to a new sense of the stuff of our own lives.

A central organizing motif of the drama of *Philosophical Investigations* as I trace it is the idea that the protagonist continually imagines and then criticizes routes toward the achievement of *expressive freedom*. To a considerable extent, what is meant by this phrase will have to be unfolded through the tracing of the text's drama and of the Kantian-Hegelian background of a critical philosophy of the expression of reason that *Philosophical Investigations* takes up. It may help, however, in beginning to follow this unfolding to note that Wittgenstein remarked that there "is a phenomenon, being certain of yourself," in presenting yourself to others as reading with understanding, and by extension in presenting yourself to yourself and to others generally.[10] The sort of sureness in self-presentation that is in question here is—for Wittgenstein and I think in popular imagination—most fully realized in the composition and virtuoso performance of absolute music. One might think of how J. S. Bach, in the Prelude to the first cello suite (G major, c. 1720) arrives, after a strenuous struggle involving intervals over a pedal point D increasing by half-steps from a minor second to a major tenth, four measures from the end of the piece at a triumphant arpeggiated G major chord, and then rests in the center of the key of G major, cadenzalike, in a straightforward progression of arpeggios from G to D^6 to D^7 to a final G chord, as though the piece were accepting its own achievement. Or one might think of what Patricia Herzog hears in what she calls the "precarious balance" of Beethoven's *Diabelli Variations* (C major, op. 120, 1819–23), as they display "the dynamic tension between necessity and contingency [in character and commitment] that is the inescapable paradox of our human being."[11] Or one might think of the similar balance that is achieved in Schubert's *Impromptus* (D. 899, op. 90, 1827; D. 935, op. post. 142, 1827), in which lyrical cantabile melody lines and sometimes surprising modulations are played off against quite regular rhythmic patterns and carefully prepared resolutions, as though the thought were always both of self-sustaining lyricism and of finitude. Or one might think of the power and re-

10. Wittgenstein, "From a Lecture Belonging to a Course of Lectures on Description," in *Lectures on Aesthetics,* ed. Barrett, p. 40.

11. Patricia Herzog, "The Practical Wisdom of Beethoven's *Diabelli* Variations," *Musical Quarterly,* 79, no. 1 (Spring 1995): 36, 47.

straint of Gil Shaham's performances of the Prokofiev violin concertos or of Claudio Arrau's of the Schumann piano sonatas. (Or one might think of Suzanne Farrell's clarity of line or of the grace and economy of Ozzie Smith's play at shortstop.) All that is needed here is the thought that there is something like this to be thought of and that it might both figure in the self-interrogations of the protagonist of *Philosophical Investigations* and somehow, dimly, matter for us, no matter how elusive it might be.

One could of course just deny that any of this makes sense and hold instead that we are altogether creatures of our biology or our social practices, rather than being open to such imaginings of our performances. But there is at least an issue here: What is it to be honest in acknowledging the conditions of human life? If genuine acknowledgment includes the recognition of such imaginings for ourselves and their possibilities of finite realization, then a philosophical understanding of human life must consist more of overlapping readings of finite performances than of the announcement of the truth of realism or antirealism, naturalism or conventionalism, or representationalism or connectionism.

The drama of *Philosophical Investigations,* as it will be read here, thus presents a protagonist seeking to articulate the terms for full human self-command and self-expression. The protagonist imagines at times that this might be achieved through grasping the nature of human intentionality and conceptual consciousness, but then continually finds that no formulation of the nature of conceptual consciousness in fact yields this command. The governing problem of human life that is played out in this drama is how to avoid all at once dogmatism, nihilist skepticism, and simple indifferentism, a problem first posed by Kant and taken up powerfully by his immediate successors. The moral—a more or less typical romantic one—is that a certain continuousness of aspiration and self-revision in culture, against the commands of dogma, must be accepted, even embraced. In Kantian-Hegelian terms, our powers of *Willkür,* or arbitrary choice, must be accepted, even embraced, as being open to continuous re-information by *Wille,* or norms of rational willing and expression, against and within changing cultural backgrounds. Leading a life will be always something like trying to write a poem or a novel or a sonata or a liturgy. Only through such an embrace will it be possible to avoid the reductions of philosophical thinking to either complacent dogmatism or empty, self-congratulatory nihilism, and of human life to subservience to either

stale, external powers or wayward desires. *Philosophical Investigations* dramatizes persistence in such an embrace against other easier, but finally less human, ways of going on.

Hence *Philosophical Investigations* resists by example the underdescription
of human thought and action and life. It is a piece of writing about philosophical ideas, especially about thinking and understanding, that is not only wide
ranging in what it considers but also continuously dramatic in its structure.
Through its drama, it aims at making it impossible for us to forget the entanglement of conceptual consciousness with memory, desire, social relations, and
aspirations to expressive freedom.

Having such a remembrance of the character of a human life put before
one is not always a comfortable experience. It may fly in the face of present
repressions, preoccupations, considered beliefs about human psychology, and
natural interests in understanding things by taking them apart, whether in fact
or in analytical imagination. Computational linguistics, cognitive and behav-
ioral psychology, game theory, and economic analysis have achieved powerful
partial results by abstracting from the possibility of changes in thought and
action that might result from sudden artistic or moral insight. The power of
these partial results is in turn partly sustained by a sense of ourselves, often
taken for granted in modern life and by no means always maleficent in its
effects, as having a free, meaning-constructing, internal subjectivity, responsible to nothing and standing over and against a physical nature that it seeks
to understand and control.

The drama of *Philosophical Investigations* in part shares in a commitment to
the value of freedom or autonomy, but less as the exercise of arbitrary choice
than as the achievement of a way of being in which resonances to nature and
artistic achievements and moral possibilities are taken seriously, even felt to
be unavoidable. In asking how we think conceptually or how we go on to
follow a rule—both how we in fact do that at all and how we might do it
with assurance and human expressiveness and self-command—in the face of
the mischaracterizations of that ability that are urged on us by modern, scientifically oriented philosophy and psychology, Wittgenstein in *Philosophical Investigations* develops a sense of human intentionality as both entangled with,
and yet capable of significant departures from, social life, artistic accomplish-
ments, and religious and moral traditions. The implied protagonist of the text
continuously introduces one or another master account of the nature of conceptual consciousness and explores ways to persist in it effectively, with au-

thority and command. Such accounts offer the tempting promise of being able to control one's performances in engaging with culture. By knowing how we in fact think conceptually, and how then to exercise that ability well, we might, it seems, adjust our concepts and thoughts to the world as it is and thereby make the cultural performances that seem to flow from them necessarily in order. We might, it seems, free ourselves from anxieties about how we engage with the affordances of culture. But each account of conceptual consciousness that is introduced is then criticized as partial or one-sided, as emphasizing only that it is sometimes possible to think of things as having parts (but sometimes not), or as emphasizing only that sensations and thoughts are in some senses inner (but in other senses not), or as emphasizing only that in certain circumstances rules do not guide us in understanding (while in others they do). No formula or doctrine of the nature of consciousness succeeds in controlling our performances in cultural practice and in freeing us from anxiety. The text is strikingly incomplete and inconclusive doctrinally, as it traces skeins of intentionality's entanglements in various directions. Throughout these tracings what is most present is the protagonist who is engaged in an ongoing effort to grasp the conditions of perfect self-command by grasping the nature of thought.

To read *Philosophical Investigations* by focusing on the itinerary of this protagonist, and to regard that itinerary as exemplary, is to arrive at a stance in which ethics and aesthetics and the philosophy of mind are all one, insofar as the very existence of intentional consciousness is dramatized as bound up with moral and artistic powers, aspirations, and self-imaginations. In contrast, other ways of reading, associated with other conceptions of persons and mind (and often dismissive of *Philosophical Investigations*), will then seem characteristically to underdescribe their objects: human persons, thought, action, and life. If we find ourselves caught up in the drama of the protagonist's development in *Philosophical Investigations,* then it will seem that much contemporary philosophy of mind errs in treating qualia, for example, as isolable phenomena of mind, distinct from memory or from the recognition of grammatical sentences, not to mention from artistic imagination or moral aspiration or friendship (phenomena that are typically ignored altogether, seen as the province of a separate and often secondary part of philosophy). *Philosophical Investigations* suggests that it is a mistake to strip these phenomena out of their connections with one another within the life of a human person, possessed of wide-ranging, structurally complicated, intentional consciousness, itself entangled dramatically with culture. Hermeneutic thought about *Verstehen,* or internal, sympathetic understanding, as a method for comprehending human beings, though somewhat wider ranging, likewise will seem to underdescribe its object. In urging a *method* on us, it sees a human life as something of a capturable whole internally related to that method rather than as something continuously in dramatic flux and revision.

Against these stances in contemporary philosophy, taking *Philosophical Investigations* seriously will involve holding in mind simultaneously at least the following problems and phenomena:

1. issues in the philosophy of logic, the philosophy of mind, and the philosophy of language that are interwoven with issues about the nature of intentional consciousness (positions or theses or stances with respect to these issues will appear in *Philosophical Investigations* as tempting dogmas that would absolutize and control possibilities of expression in culture);

2. linguistic expression, artistic expression, and human action generally as internally related, as potential vehicles for the articulation and embodiment of free humanity in culture;

3. the character of *Philosophical Investigations* as a literary form, a dramatic text of fragments, in which elegy, expressing a sense of lost or never quite fully realizable human possibilities, is blended with quest romance, expressing a sense of movement toward these possibilities, of continuing aspiration;

4. the philosophical significance of the presence of that form and the way that form itself helps to articulate and argue by exemplification for a picture of human beings as continuous self-interrogators and bearers of aspiration;

5. the cultural history, particularly of modernity, in which the vicissitudes of various literary forms are imbricated as both causes and effects of other developments in material, political, and imaginative culture; and

6. the particular Kantian and post-Kantian senses of the possibilities of expressive freedom in culture.

It is not easy to read with all these problems and phenomena in mind. It requires a certain slowness and patience with imagery, the voicing of motivations, and dramatic structure. Once these problems and phenomena are held in mind, however, *Philosophical Investigations* then begins to emerge as a dramatic text on the character of human life that has few equals as an expression of our condition as intentionally conscious beings, freighted with aspirations and anxieties that attach to fitful possibilities of expressive power.

✳

Philosophical Investigations is notoriously not finished to Wittgenstein's satisfaction. There are a number of reasons for this, some having to do with his wish at times to integrate remarks on the philosophy of mathematics more fully and smoothly into the text, some having to do with the emergence, especially after 1946, of new thoughts in the philosophy of psychology, which Wittgenstein may have planned to incorporate into *Philosophical Investigations*.[12] But when we look closely at the text that we have, one thing is especially striking—a lapse in dramatic intensity around section 308. The section itself has an air of summing up: "How does the philosophical problem about mental processes and states and about behaviourism arise?—The first step is the one that altogether escapes notice. We talk of processes and states and leave their nature undecided. Sometime perhaps we shall know more about them—we think. But that is just what commits us to a particular way of looking at the matter. For we have a definite concept of what it means to learn to know a process better. (The decisive move in the conjuring trick has been made, and it was the very one we thought quite innocent.)"[13] Prior to section 308, the remarks are held together dramatically by their being rehearsals and rejections of philosophical views, where we experience those rehearsals and rejections as occurring within the consciousness of a single protagonist who is tempted by these views but who cannot believe in them when they are articulated further and imagined as brought into engagement with conversational and cognitive practice. There is a sense of continuous involvement of this protagonist with the temptations that these views embody, of a continuous and dramatically coherent play within the protagonist of temptation and its resistance or partial overcoming. Around section 308, this sense of involvement in temp-

12. G. H. von Wright, "The Origin and Composition of the *Philosophical Investigations*," in *Wittgenstein* (Minneapolis: University of Minnesota Press, 1982), pp. 111–36, offers a detailed composition history of *Philosophical Investigations* based on examination of Wittgenstein's typescripts and correspondence and on inquiries to his friends. He supplements this with some useful conjectures about Wittgenstein's plans at various stages of composition.

13. Wittgenstein, *Philosophical Investigations,* trans. Anscombe, §308. Subsequent references to this edition appear in the text by section number, or, for Part II, by part number, section number, and page number (e.g., II, xi, 217).

tation lapses. There are a number of striking remarks, about the nature of persons, about expectation and its fulfillment, about orders, and about grammar, that occur after section 308. But they do not give the sense of being housed in the consciousness of a protagonist caught between temptation and its overcoming. To some extent this sense of a protagonist reenters fitfully in Part II and again in passages in *Zettel* and in *Remarks on the Philosophy of Psychology*. But it is less intense and sustained there than in sections 1–308 of *Philosophical Investigations*.

In light of this shift, it is not unreasonable to suppose that the particular problem of integrating these later works into *Philosophical Investigations,* and of therein modifying principally the sections after 308, was that of trying to sustain the dramatic intensity of the protagonist's itinerary of temptation and resistance, while still moving forward into further regions of thought and toward some sort of resulting conclusions or general philosophical stances. How might the sense of someone *working through* various possible philosophical stances and trying to live them out be balanced against a sense of something in general to be said about human life, a conclusion to be reached, whose discovery and announcement would conclude the protagonist's journey and redeem it as progress, not mere wandering?[14] The effort to balance these two senses is the main problem of romantic poetics, which seeks to marry a partly self-constructing, meaning-making, modern individual with an individual in need of integration into the ways of culture as they stand or might stand, yet where those ways of culture are themselves riven by antagonisms. It is not difficult to see this leading problem of romantic poetics, and behind it of serious philosophical thinking in modernity about culture and value, attaching to Wittgenstein's continual recomposing and reordering of *Philosophical Investigations* and its possible associated quarry works.

One unplanned resolution to this problem that is often reached in romantic texts is the production of the fragment, that which, as Lacoue-Labarthe and Nancy put it, "figures . . . the outside-the-work that is essential to the work."[15] With fragments, the work of critical thinking, of self-interrogation and the

14. I describe this leading problem of romantic poetics in "Internal Transcendentalism: Wordsworth and 'A New Condition of Philosophy,'" *Philosophy and Literature* 18, no. 1 (April 1994): 50–71.

15. Philippe Lacoue-Labarthe and Jean-Luc Nancy, *The Literary Absolute: The Theory of Literature in German Romanticism,* trans. Philip Barnard and Cheryl Lester (Albany: State University of New York Press, 1988), p. 48.

interrogation of possibilities for culture, seems to go on outside them, the self never finding itself fully present to itself, never fully at home and ratified in its place with others in culture. Part of the uncanny but problematic attractiveness of *Philosophical Investigations* is due to its having the form of the fragment. It consists of short sections; it is unfinished; and it does not have a clear border between its inside and its outside. These features contribute to a sense that Wittgenstein's thinking and criticism go on outside the text, perhaps in his life, addressing every problem of mind and culture and value. No doubt this sense is also due to the fundamental character of the topics that Wittgenstein did explicitly investigate in a sustained way: the natures of mind, meaning, and conceptual consciousness. But the way in which his investigations seem to go on beyond the text and to bear on everything in culture is surely also in part a function of the text's fragmentariness.

This fragmentariness further helps to explain the reader's sense that the text and its thoughts are somehow specially Wittgenstein's. As Lacoue-Labarthe and Nancy put it, in a fragmentary work "the unity of the ensemble [is] constituted in a certain way outside the work, in the subject that is seen in it."[16] The persona that is developed within the fragments as their composer, arranger, and thinker is more immediately present to us than any doctrine or dogma, the formulation of which is resisted by the form of the fragment. This underlies the sense of discipleship to the persona in the text that overcomes some of its readers and that puts off others for whom discipleship is not a happy social role.

Suppose we think about the lapse in dramatic intensity in *Philosophical Investigations* around section 308 as well as about the poetics of the romantic fragment. When we further discover that sections 1–308 correspond roughly to what von Wright conjectures to have been "an intermediate version of the *Investigations*,"[17] completed around January 1945 but subjected to continuous later supplementation and revision, then the structure and mode of appeal to us of *Philosophical Investigations* as we have it begin to make more sense. That intermediate version almost concludes around section 308. The dramatic intensity does lapse; there is a pronounced move toward explicit philosophical generality, almost toward a thesis. To some extent, Wittgenstein began to give way to the temptation to announce a discovery, roughly of the truth of what

16. Ibid. p. 40.
17. von Wright, "Origin and Composition," p. 127.

David Stern calls "practical holism" or Baker and Hacker call "the autonomy of grammar."[18] The comparative flatness of the text after the early 300s is due to its now being more fully controlled by that thought. Yet, as the protagonist has already recognized, the leading thought of practical holism—nothing is hidden; meaning is what shows itself in our uses of language—is not really convincing in the face of demands to know how we do what we do. Instead of wholeheartedly endorsing this thought as a discovery, the text trails off, not quite reaching a conclusion, but not quite sustaining its drama either, and remaining in need of supplementation and revision. What then survives this trailing off is the sense of a protagonist caught up in this problem of how both continuously to enact, and yet also to conclude, criticism of human personhood and its best possibilities of life in a divided culture, that protagonist's interrogations then seeming somehow to outweigh the later attenuation of its presence in the text.

✻

It is the dramatic itinerary of this protagonist in sections 1–308, the crucial, most intense, "intermediate version" of the text, that I herein trace. I have sometimes cited remarks from later sections of *Philosophical Investigations,* but not in any way that differs from occasional citations of *Culture and Value* or the *Tractatus.* These citations sometimes illuminate a thought, but the focus is always on the thinking in its dramatic context, not on a thesis or argument taken on its own. I have sometimes made small modifications in the translation to bring out certain images or senses of direction that are specific to German idioms. Whenever I have done this, I have shown the German as well as the English, and the German is sometimes shown in other places as well in order to lend a certain emphasis or perspective to the English of the translation as it stands.

This focus on the thinking in its dramatic context lends a certain gestural and exegetical quality to my way of reading the text. While I am impressed by the cogency of the arguments against cognitivist, behaviorist, and naturalist stances in the philosophy of mind that are present in the text's interior dialogue, I am even more impressed with the continuousness of critical energy,

18. Stern, *Wittgenstein on Mind and Language,* pp. 106–8, 120–27; and Stern, "The 'Middle Wittgenstein': From Logical Atomism to Practical Holism," *Synthese* 87 (1991): 203–26, esp. 218–21. G. P. Baker and P. M. S. Hacker, *Wittgenstein: Rules, Grammar, and Necessity* (Oxford: Basil Blackwell, 1985), pp. 329–37.

never itself quite housed within theses or doctrines, that is also present there. The mobilization of this energy within the protagonist and its dramatic rendering in interior dialogue strike me as about as exemplary an enactment and expression of human intentionality in culture as there can be.

One of the pains of bearing this sense is that, holding it, I have very little way of arguing that it must be so, that Wittgenstein must be right about the nature of human life, or even that Wittgenstein's writing must be taken seriously. The protagonist's self-imaginations and interrogations move at a level that is deeper than that of arguing about theses, as the basis of the possibility of holding any view about anything at all is continually queried and requeried.

But if it is painful not to be able here to put forward proofs and authoritatively to announce results, bearing this sense of the text as an enactment also has its own peculiar pleasures. It returns to us whole ranges of philosophical texts as readable, dramatic enactments of aspiration and anxiety in cultural circumstances so that philosophy and literature—at least in the regions of matters of culture, mind, and value—are then not always so clearly separable. Receiving texts in this way seems to me to be a useful and apt way of reading, and then also of writing and thinking, for both philosophy and literature. Aspiration and anxiety in culture and its criticism—Wittgenstein's example shows, but cannot prove—may be natural to us as human bearers of intentionality. It is as though humanity could sometimes find itself written in its expressions, not always alone or apart or within, if only they are attended to and acknowledged and read aright.

2

Intentionality and Idealism:
Hegel, Kant, and Freedom

It is widely recognized that *Philosophical Investigations* is a book in the philosophy of consciousness or the theory of intentionality. It asks, insistently, how human beings are able to recognize objects under concepts. What is the nature of that ability? What makes ordinary, adult, human consciousness discursive, or conceptual, or propositional, in a way that goes beyond the mere sensory awareness that is possessed by at least vertebrate mammals generally? Other topics that come up in *Philosophical Investigations*—the nature of linguistic meaning, the relation between order and execution, the criteria for ascribing an ability to read, and the nature of justification—either derive from or are woven into the central topic of the nature of conceptual consciousness. A grasp of linguistic meaning, for example, informs conceptual consciousness, and conceptual consciousness is evinced, among other things, in knowing the meaning of a word. The ability to read presupposes the ability to identify words and objects, and it reciprocally structures and extends that ability. Everywhere the topic of the nature of conceptual consciousness is central.

It is also widely recognized that one strain of the book's thought about this topic is largely negative. Conceptual consciousness is *not* Cartesian-Humean. The recognition of public objects is *not* the result of an inference from a prior and primitive recognition of private objects or sensibilia. Nor does it arise naturalistically out of biologically innate classification propensities and subsequent causal processes. Instead, training in linguistic and recognitive practice is crucially important for the development of conceptual consciousness.

In this negative stance, particularly against Cartesianism, *Philosophical Investigations* stands in a nineteenth- and twentieth-century tradition of thought about conceptual consciousness. Charles Taylor has identified what he calls a common "argument from transcendental conditions" present in one way or another in the writings of Hegel, Heidegger, Merleau-Ponty, and Wittgenstein, designed to show that conceptual consciousness cannot be Cartesian Humean.[1] This argument suggests that the picture of conceptual consciousness as rooted in primitive recognitions of the inner, whether in its Cartesian-rationalist or Humean-empiricist version, makes no sense. That picture is "an ultimately incoherent amalgam of two features: (a) these [primitive] states [of private recognition] (the ideas) are self-enclosed, in the sense that they can be accurately identified and described in abstraction from the 'outside' world; . . . and (b) they nevertheless point toward and represent things in that outside world."[2] Instead, then, of taking the existence of a primitive and private conceptual-recognitive consciousness for granted, these thinkers instead ask how we come to have ideas or the ability to represent objects to ourselves under concepts at all. What are the necessary conditions of conceptual consciousness, or, in a slightly different idiom, what are the transcendental necessities of thought—the things that must be the case if we are to be able to think conceptually or recognize objects under concepts at all?

These critical writers do not, however, limit themselves only to the criticism of earlier views in epistemology or the philosophy of mind. They recognize how the Cartesian-Humean picture is woven through a set of moral aspirations and self-images of the possibilities of value that are open to persons in culture. They typically aim further to unseat those moral aspirations by showing that the picture of human, conceptual consciousness on which they are based is misbegotten. As Taylor puts it,

> the connection between the scientific and the moral is generally made more evident in their work than in that of mainstream supporters of the epistemological standpoint. But an important feature of all these critiques is that they establish a new moral outlook *through* overturning the modern conception of knowledge. They do not just register their dissidence from the anthropological beliefs associated with this conception, but show the foundations of these beliefs to be unsound, based as they are in an untenable construal of knowledge.[3]

Here, in seeing conceptions of the nature of consciousness—epistemological stances—as indissolubly welded to moral aspirations, Hegel, Heidegger,

1. Charles Taylor, "Overcoming Epistemology," in *After Philosophy: End or Transformation?* ed. Kenneth Baynes, James Bohman, and Thomas McCarthy (Cambridge: MIT Press, 1987), p. 473.
2. Ibid., p. 474.
3. Ibid., p. 473.

Merleau-Ponty, and Wittgenstein are themselves at one with their great precursors whom they criticize. There is a long tradition of philosophers attempting to outline the nature of conceptual consciousness. For Plato, our ability to recognize objects is rooted in our innate ability, capable of flowering under provocation, to grasp or recollect eternal forms, patterns, as it were, of things. For Aristotle, divine Noûs thinking itself in and through us and things brings about a fit between the categories of recognition that we have and the categories that are present in nature. For Aquinas, this job is done by God in his Providence. Descartes follows Aquinas in this, but restricts the fit between categories of recognition and categories of reality to mathematical quantities. Hume sees no alternative but to trust to what we naturally do anyway in recognizing objects and to hope that our categories of recognition will continue to have survival value.

Crucially, these sketches of the nature of conceptual consciousness are not matters for epistemology or the philosophy of mind alone. Each of them is powerfully associated with a moral ideal of comportment in culture. The favored account of conceptual consciousness in each case fits, supports, and helps to articulate that associated ideal. For Plato, our ability to recollect forms is due to the higher, rational part of the soul, the part that ought to rule desire. In developing his picture of the rational control of desire, he puts forward an ideal of integrity, stability of character, well-orderedness, and rational self-control against the disturbing temptations of the senses, the body, and the market. Knowledge, a grasp of the forms, and justice, the well-ordering of the soul, are one. For Aristotle, the moral ideal of *eudaimonia,* a moderate, skill-exercising happiness, is revealed to us by exercises of thought, surveying and assessing comparatively the various embodiments of human nature that are presented to us in different forms of cultural practice. The content and value of *eudaimonia* as an ideal are made evident to us through a rational, Noûs-guided survey of manners of human life. For Aquinas, divinely created human rationality is the root of *synderesis,* or conscience, the ability to grasp and follow the will of God, first to achieve happiness and rightness in life and thence blessedness and beatitude. For Descartes, the appropriate exercise of intellect both gives us the power to ameliorate our material condition, to understand and control nature, and enjoins and fulfills the Stoic ideal of refusing to speculate about matters that are beyond one's control. One is to remain humbly confident that in exercising intellect appropriately one has done one's best as a human being. "Thus we see that the repose of mind and inner satisfaction felt by those who know they never fail to do their best is a pleasure incomparably sweeter, more lasting and more solid than all those which come from elsewhere."[4] For Hume, following one's natural inclinations, undistorted by false intellectualism, frees one from hubris and makes one's life more humanly expressive of one's sentiments. The unfruitful agonies of struggling for purely intellectual self-command are to be given up in favor of the graceful and self-conscious leading of a life that is naturally one's own, and in favor of a science that traces nature's presentations but remains silent about its possible secret powers. In each case, the picture of what it is to be conceptually conscious underlies a further picture of what it is to be fully and fitly conceptually conscious so that, knowing this, one might arrive at a way of being that is seen as preeminently valuable.

This connection between the philosophy of mind and the articulation of moral ideals is then also held in place, Taylor suggests, in the writings of Hegel, Heidegger, Merleau-Ponty, and Wittgenstein. This is clear enough in the cases of Hegel, with his accounts of freedom, reason, and right, Heidegger, with his talk of responsiveness to the call of Being, and Merleau-Ponty, with his talk of resonance with the possibilities of lived embodiment in concrete, historical circumstances.

But with Wittgenstein the connection between the philosophy of mind and the articulation of a moral ideal is both powerfully intense and yet elusive. The moral ideal that seems to be forwarded in the text of *Philosophical Investigations* is scarcely articulable as a state or condition at all. Instead, as Stanley Cavell has put it, *Philosophical Investigations* exhibits "a struggle with the contrary depths of oneself."[5] The writing in *Philosophical Investigations* displays a "spiritual fervor" that suggests a conception of "humanity as a form of life, or a level of life, standing in need of something like transfiguration— some radical change, but as it were from inside, not *by* anything." Yet the terms of this transfiguration are never quite made evident, are never laid down by appeal to the properties of a substance or agency that is external to us and to which we might resonate. Instead, a sense of continuing energies of aspiration and anxiety predominates. The ceaseless investigation of the nature of conceptual consciousness remains central. The "moral or religious demand in

4. René Descartes, "Letter to Queen Christina of Sweden, 20 November 1647," in *Philosophical Letters*, trans. and ed. Anthony Kenny (Oxford: Clarendon Press, 1970), p. 228.
5. Stanley Cavell, *This New Yet Unapproachable America* (Albuquerque: Living Batch Press, 1989), p. 37.

the *Investigations* . . . is not the subject of a *separate* study within it, call it Ethics."[6]

✳

All this can sound both tantalizing and obscure. If *Philosophical Investigations* is in fact as deep as its philosophical predecessors in refusing to separate moral philosophy from the philosophy of mind, and if the moral fervor of the text is really so evident, then why isn't a moral ideal more clearly and explicitly articulated? Why isn't it argued directly that this ideal is compelling for us because of *something*—practical reason, or the will of God, or natural sympathies, or a common human nature, or whatever it may be? Why aren't any routes toward the achievement of that moral ideal sketched? Why instead is there so much indirection, so much turning back over the ground of the nature of conceptual consciousness?

One way to elaborate and elucidate these tantalizing obscurities is to compare the ambitions and strategies of *Philosophical Investigations* explicitly with a range of texts in immediately post-Kantian romantic and idealist philosophy, literature, and criticism. Like Wittgenstein in criticizing the Cartesian-Humean picture of the mind, these texts react against the picture of human subjectivity and its possibilities of fulfillment that emerges in modern culture and in modern philosophy. These texts bear a countersense that modern subjectivity—a sense of oneself as having a private, inner life of thoughts and desires that are immediately present to one—is both in part inevitable and desirable, and yet also in part a curse that we must escape.

In modern culture a sense of the self as private or inner predominates. The self is seen as not entirely bound up in rite and ritual, but instead as having various possibilities of expressing itself, where these varieties of available possibilities themselves enforce a sense of the self's distance from any particular public practice. This sense of the self is a fact of modern cultural life, connected with developments in technology and in the economics of daily life. And not only is this sense of the self a fact, it is also something that we deeply value. Autonomy, or the expression of one's inner subjectivity and will, achieved through taking up some particular strand of public practice in a particular way, is among our highest values. Throughout modern philosophy the construal of the nature of autonomy varies somewhat, depending on what is seen as most

6. Ibid., pp. 30, 44, 40.

deeply present in interior subjectivity—practical reason, or desire, or sympathy, as may be. But the values of autonomy and of the modern cultural practices under which it might be achieved are rarely abandoned. When these values are abandoned, the resulting commitments often seem to us either authoritarian or quixotic (or both).

At the same time, however, this modern sense of the self has been experienced as a difficulty or burden, particularly in post-Kantian romantic and idealist writing. In being connected by nature with no routes of public practice (other than those perhaps legislated within), the self and its will are sometimes seen as capable of tyrannizing over everything, capable of finding meaning and content only through furies of the negation of everything the self encounters as opposite to it. Or, more modestly, the sense of the self as private is seen as enforcing an excessive detachment and reserve, a continuing failure of intimacy. The very varieties of available possibilities of practice seem to inhibit commitment to anything. The commitments of others, and hence their minds, come to seem inscrutable. Autonomy seems to yield anomie.

Yet there seems to be no way back. Modern culture is in place, and the value of autonomy continues to be accepted. How, then, might autonomy and intimacy be blended? How might one retain a sense of oneself as subjectively capable of directing one's own commitments yet combine it with a sense of oneself as engaging, stably and with sureness, in cooperative, meaningful projects of human life? To take these questions seriously is already very nearly to be forced into a condition of a continuous longing for meaningfulness, a condition of moral fervor or intensity, but without articulate shape, since the value of autonomy remains in place, yet without any cosmological order to house, embrace, and guide its achievement. These are the questions that preoccupy the immediately post-Kantian writers. Tracing their threads of response to these questions, and in particular the contortions of writing into which they sometimes find themselves forced, can help to open up the obscurities of *Philosophical Investigations* and to reveal its interest and power as it moves through a similar field of concerns.

✳

The story of the emergence of the post-Kantian romantic and idealist concern to blend autonomy with intimacy begins with the Copernican turn away from writing about external natures and powers and toward writing about things as they appear to us. A sense of the self as a locus for the reality of things—

that against which and through which they appear as things—comes to predominate. This sense is not entirely absent in earlier thought and writing; modern philosophy and culture are not simply the products of an inscrutable rupture with what precedes them. Protagoras notoriously seems to articulate a sense of things as coming to be what they are through their interactions with human beings. But the sense of the self as inner, and of things as in their nature appearing to it, gains a particular intensity and is woven through a particular set of cultural practices with the rise of modernity.

Northrop Frye usefully contrasts the medieval-Renaissance and modern-romantic senses of the self and its world as those senses are made evident in their distinct styles of poetic expression. In medieval and Renaissance poetry, he notes, there is a sense of four distinct levels of reality surrounding the self: heaven, human culture, physical nature, and hell. This sense of reality contrasts with what he calls "the internalizing of reality in Romanticism proper," which itself arises out of the modern sense of "the constructive power of the mind to make culture out of its own resources."[7] Interior subjectivity steps back from its surroundings and regards itself as capable of making its own world. In Hegel's formulation, describing the relation of interior subjectivity to forms of government and, by implication, to culture generally, "the principle of the modern world is freedom of subjectivity. . . . We may only say that all constitutional forms are one-sided unless they can sustain in themselves the principle of free subjectivity and know how to correspond with a matured rationality."[8] Instead of being surrounded by fixities to which it must adapt itself, the inner is now to construct and judge the outer. The self and its powers are more present to it than are the externalities that it is able to refashion. Once this modern sense of the self and its central powers to make culture and to understand and control nature are in place, then the immediately natural drift of philosophical thought is toward an exploration of these central powers of the self. As Frye puts it, in modernity and in romanticism "the natural metaphorical direction of the inside world is downward, into the profounder depths of consciousness," as articulation and release of these central powers are sought.[9]

---

7. Northrop Frye, "The Drunken Boat," in *Romanticism Reconsidered*, ed. Frye (New York: Columbia University Press, 1963), pp. 12, 11.

8. G. W. F. Hegel, *Philosophy of Right*, trans. T. M. Knox (Oxford: Clarendon Press, 1952), addition to paragraph 273, p. 286.

9. Frye, "The Drunken Boat," p. 8.

Descartes notoriously expresses this modern sense of the mind's constructive power to make and judge culture against its own internal standards.
Cartesian meditation is just such a project of internal descent, aimed at uncovering and articulating these internal standards. This is powerfully evident in
the preface to Descartes' unfinished dialogue *The Search after Truth*.

> *The Search after Truth by means of the Light of Nature which alone, and
> without the assistance of Religion or Philosophy, determines what are the opinions
> which a good man should hold on all matters which may occupy his thoughts, and
> which penetrate into the secrets of the most curious of the sciences.*

A good man has no need to have read every book, nor to have carefully
learned all that which is taught in the Schools; it would even be a defect in
his education were he to have devoted too much of his time to the study of
letters. There are many other things to do in life, and he has to direct that
life in such a manner that the greater part of it shall remain to him for the
performance of good actions which his own reason ought to teach him, even
supposing that he were to receive his lessons from it alone. But he comes
into the world in ignorance, and as the knowledge of his earliest years rests
only on the weakness of the senses and the authority of masters, he can
scarcely avoid his imagination being filled with an infinite number of false
ideas, before his reason has the power of taking his conduct into its own
hands; in consequence he requires to have good natural endowments or else
instruction from a wise man, both in order to rid himself of the false doctrines
with which his mind is filled, and for building the first foundations of a
solid knowledge, and discovering all the means by which he may carry his
knowledge to the highest point to which it can possibly attain.

In this work I propose to show what these means are, and to bring to
light the true riches of our souls, by opening to each one the road by which
he can find in himself, and without borrowing from any, the whole knowledge which is essential to him in the direction of his life, and then by his
study succeed in acquiring the most curious forms of knowledge that the
human reason is capable of possessing.

But in order that the greatness of my scheme may not to begin with seize
your minds with an astonishment so great that confidence in my words can
no longer find therein a place, I warn you that what I undertake is not as
difficult as might be imagined. Those branches of knowledge which do not
extend beyond the capacities of the human mind are, as a matter of fact,
united by a bond so marvelous, they are capable of being deduced from one
another by sequences so necessary, that it is not essential to possess much
art or address in order to discover them, provided that by commencing with

those that are most simple we learn gradually to raise ourselves to the most sublime. That is what I shall try to show you here by a system of reasoning so clear and yet so simple, that every one will be able to judge for himself that if he has not observed the same things, it is solely because he has not cast his eyes in the right direction, nor fixed his thoughts on the same considerations as I, and that no more glory is due to me for having discovered them, than is due to a casual passer-by for having accidentally discovered under his feet a rich treasure which had for long successfully eluded the searches of many.[10]

Here we see all the central motifs of the modern conception of the subject displayed in their interconnectedness. The search for truth is to be carried out in the sciences, including intellect-generated epistemology and metaphysics, but separated from text-based and liturgical religion. Scholarship is rejected as a route to truth ("a good man has no need to have read every book . . . ; it would even be a defect in his education"). There are slight overtones of a fear of judgment by history and culture and a wish to transcend them: a man's "own reason *ought* to teach him" good actions, but if it doesn't, is the teaching of this text then still receivable by anyone, corrupted as that person may be? A strong cognitive individualism is asserted. The dignity of the person as capable of carrying out methodological reflections and substantive investigations without assistance is upheld; resonance to the ways of culture as they stand is construed as submission to baseless authority. Again the certainty about how to make progress is accompanied by a slight overtone of anxiety ("everyone will be able to judge for himself" what the routes to truth are and what is its substance; but what if they do not replicate the writer's results?). Imagination and the senses are held suspect as sources of falsity. There is an analytical impulse to seek truth by breaking ideas up into their simplest, most reliable components and to understand the motions and behaviors of things by decomposing them into their simple atomic parts. A strong distinction between subject and object is held in place. The subject out of its own resources voluntarily carries out an investigation of its own powers and of the surrounding physical things that those powers, if used rightly, can discern. The surrounding physical things themselves are the passive objects of the investigation. Above all, the

10. René Descartes, *The Search after Truth,* trans. E. S. Haldane and G. R. T. Ross, in *The Philosophical Works of Descartes,* ed. E. S. Haldane and G. R. T. Ross (Cambridge: Cambridge University Press, 1911), 1:305–6.

philosophy of mind, epistemology, metaphysics, and ethics are held together. Through a motion of internal descent into an exploration of our own cognitive powers, we are, each of us, to discover not only how to discover truth but also how to live ("the performance of good actions which his own reason ought to teach him"; "A good man has no need to have read every book").

This modern conception of the subject, its place in nature, and its possibilities of living well through its cognitive achievements, themselves glimpsed as possible through internal descent, is far from independent of other wide-ranging developments in the history of culture. The growth of technological power, in metallurgy, hydraulics, optics, and so forth, through tinkering throughout the late medieval period; improved transportation and communication systems; a resultant increasing awareness of cultural-religious diversity; the rise of market economies; a general attenuation of the predominance of ritual in daily life, as both the market and technology make available more multiform modes of social relationship; the sense of the spiritual dignity of the individual person that is developed under Christianity—all these accompany and contribute to the growth of the modern understanding of subjectivity.

It is not clear, however, which of these developments is cause and which is effect. While changes in material practice can often reveal, and are even necessary for, new possibilities of self-understanding and the pursuit of value, it is also the case that self-understanding and the pursuit of value can drive changes in material practice. As Charles Taylor observes in "A Digression on Historical Explanation,"

> To understand wherein the force of certain ideas consists is to know something relevant to how they come to be central to a society in history. . . . One reason why vulgar Marxism is so implausible is that its reductive accounts of, say, religious or moral or legal-political ideas seem to give no weight at all to their intrinsic power.
>
>   . . . [M]oral ideals, understandings of the human predicament, [and] concepts of the self . . . for the most part exist in our lives through being embedded in practices. . . . By "practice," I mean something extremely vague and general: more or less any stable configuration of shared activity, whose shape is defined by a certain pattern of dos and don'ts, can be a practice for my purpose. The way we discipline our children, greet each other in the street, determine group decisions through voting in elections, and exchange things

through markets, are all practices. And there are practices at all levels of human social life: family, village, national politics, rituals of religious communities, and so on.

It is clear that change can come about in both directions, as it were: through mutations and developments in the ideas, including new visions and insights, bringing about alterations, ruptures, reforms, revolutions in practices; and also through drift, change, constrictions or flourishings of practices, bringing about the alteration, flourishing, or decline of ideas. But even this is too abstract. It is better to say that in any concrete development in history, change is occurring both ways. The real skein of events is interwoven with threads running in both directions. . . . The skein of causes in inextricable.[11]

The rise of the modern conception of the subject and the emergence of various, manifold regions of practice are inextricably interwoven with one another. The modern conception of the subject and modern cultural practices are both powerfully with us.

Yet another complication is that the emergence of new forms of cultural practice and associated new forms of self-understanding may itself be necessary in order for new, but genuine, human interests to become articulate and show themselves. It is well to avoid any form of primitivist, materialist reductionism that assumes that the only genuine and general human interests are those which show themselves nearly universally at the most primitive stages of material and cultural development—interests in food, clothing, and shelter, say. While these interests are surely genuine and while technologically advanced cultures have no monopoly on the clear articulation of higher but genuine interests—indeed, they may themselves foster various characteristic distortions of the human—we need not, and should not, assume that only what is very basic and nearly universally pursued counts as a genuinely human interest. Our lives with culture, in all its dimensions, can sometimes reveal to us what we might be, in ways that may come close to commanding our allegiances.

But then it is also not easy to see how any such command to allegiance to a particular form of practice could readily be articulated and received in modernity. Enormous varieties of practice are present in modernity and present to reflective consciousness, which can scarcely help but feel some privacy,

11. Charles Taylor, *Sources of the Self: The Making of the Modern Identity* (Cambridge: Harvard University Press, 1989), pp. 203, 204, 205–6.

some reserve from attachment to any of them, however much commitment it seeks to will in order to hold on to meaning. Modernity confers some technological benefits, and it supports and embodies an ideal of autonomy that, in some form or other, we continue to find compelling. How then might the content of autonomy as an ideal be more fully and fitly articulated, in such a way as to break down our reserve, by attaching us in rational solidarity to specific modes of cultural practice? This question is inevitable for any reflective consciousness concerned with culture and value in modernity, as it confronts modernity's varieties and its achievements and failures in articulating the substance of autonomy. Responding to this question is a project at once in epistemology/philosophy of mind and ethics/political philosophy. We must ask what the powers of persons are to grasp nature and to guide cognitive practice, on the one hand, and to fashion the moral, political, religious, and artistic practices that further autonomy and solidarity, on the other.

✳

A sense that modern subjectivity and its epistemological project, aimed (as in Descartes) at rationalizing cultural life in accordance with the demands of free interior subjectivity, but now coupled with the further sense that carrying out that project is *not* a purely intellectual affair, defines Hegel's sense of his enterprise. In *Phenomenology of Spirit,* near the beginning of part B ("Self-Consciousness") and at the end of the general introductory section to chapter IV ("The Truth of Self-Certainty"), Hegel announces that consciousness, in its reflections on itself and its powers to know things, has reached "its turning point, where it leaves behind it the colourful show of the sensuous here-and-now and the nightlike void of the supersensible beyond, and steps out into the spiritual daylight of the present."[12]

What this turning point amounts to, roughly, is the absorption and transfiguration of the modern epistemological project into a more explicitly cultural and political project. Pure epistemology, Hegel argues, has exhausted itself in frustration and incoherence. Pure epistemology attempts to articulate a criterion of unproblematic, certain, and stable consciousness of an object, inner or outer. In seeking such a criterion, it considers various forms of putative primitive and basic experience: the experience of bare particulars, or the expe-

12. Hegel, *Phenomenology of Spirit,* trans. A. V. Miller (Oxford: Clarendon Press, 1977), paragraph 177, pp. 110–11.

rience of sensible qualities, or conscious experience simply as having a character in relation to objects that is determined by laws governing successions of sensible qualia. Each of these construals of experience as a basis for certain knowledge proves inadequate. The bare particular is insignificant for us, fails to fall into any kinds we might grasp. Sensible qualities alone afford us no experience of a thing in which they inhere, no awareness of an object. The laws that might govern our experiences of changing sensible qualities of things are obscure and conjectural. Consciousness of any object at all seems problematic. Intentionality—the object-directedness of our consciousness under concepts—seems undeniable but inscrutable.

The way out of this impasse is then to move beyond pure epistemology. We are now to see our desire to know things, and to know the nature of our consciousness as knowing things, no longer as simply self-standing and given but instead as part of, a distorted version of, a desire or demand that is satisfiable—a desire or demand that Hegel calls bringing one's self-certainty to truth. Satisfying this latter desire is not simply a matter of arriving at a self-certifying consciousness of an object, but also a matter of the actualization and ratification of who one is—a free subjectivity coherently and meaningfully manifested in a distinctive social role. To be a conceptually conscious being, aware of objects as falling under concepts, even problematically, is also to be a self-conscious being, committed to a practical project of securing recognition of oneself within a social role. The desire to know how we are conceptually conscious of objects at all, and further to know which concepts genuinely fit their objects, emerges as part of this larger practical project.

As self-conscious beings, we are not only aware of objects, we are also aware of ourselves as aware of objects—aware, that is, of ourselves as subjectivities or loci of experience. This awareness of oneself has a complex structure. It implies both recalling a past and envisioning a future. In order to have self-awareness, one must be aware that moments of experience not only succeed one another but are also moments of one's own life.

> In point of fact, self-consciousness is the reflection out of the being of the world of sense and perception, and is essentially the return from *otherness*. . . . Hence otherness is for [self-consciousness] in the form of *a being,* or as a *distinct moment;* but there is also for consciousness the unity of itself with this difference as a *second distinct moment.* With that first moment, self-consciousness is in the form of a *consciousness,* and the whole expanse of the

sensuous world is preserved for it, but at the same time only as connected with the second moment, the unity of self-consciousness with itself.[13]

Even the most primitive and basic conceptual consciousness of an object, Hegel suggests, is in fact a form of self-consciousness. There is no properly conceptual awareness of things without also self-awareness. Though self-awareness may be repressed or ignored while within a particular moment of awareness, it must be structurally present if that simpler awareness of an object is itself genuinely conceptual.

But what, then, about this unity of self-consciousness with itself? What does that mean? How, in particular, is it achieved and sustained? Surely I did not have it when I was an infant. I was not conscious of myself as conscious. Nor did I actively recall my past experiences or envision my future ones. Even now I recall only some things and envision some others. Just how unified is my self-consciousness? The truth of my self-consciousness, as Hegel puts it, is unity, something to be achieved, but then there are all these changing experiences. Might they not simply overwhelm and fragment my unity, which in any case was not simply given from birth?

The crucial moves in Hegel's criticism and supplantation of modern epistemology are, first, to see conceptual consciousness *simpliciter* as already caught up in self-consciousness and, second, to see the epistemological enterprise of characterizing and certifying knowledge of an object as already caught up in self-consciousness's practical problem of achieving and sustaining unity with itself. For self-consciousness, Hegel tells us, "This antithesis of its appearance and its truth has, however, for its essence only the truth, viz. the unity of self-consciousness with itself." Here the term "essence" (*Wesen*) carries the sense of a plan or pattern of development, waiting to be manifested or realized in actual historical time. Though it initially appears in historical time as fragmented, not yet unified, and close to the merely sensory, self-consciousness (and the conceptual consciousness of objects that it implicitly structures) must become a stable unity, must achieve a sense of itself as continuing across various changing moments of experience. "This unity," Hegel goes on, "must become essential to self-consciousness; i.e. self-consciousness is *Desire* in general."[14]

13. Ibid., paragraph 167, p. 105.
14. Ibid.

This is a definition of desire, something that only a self-conscious being has, in contrast with want and need. The achievement of a unity of self-consciousness turns out crucially to involve the satisfaction of desire. Desire, unlike want and need, requires recalling and envisioning. It involves seeing oneself, thinking of oneself, as satisfiable by a kind of thing, some *F*. It consists in an articulate envisioning of oneself as thus satisfied by *F*. Desire, unlike want and need, is necessarily satisfied by having and carrying out a plan directed at *F*.

Having and carrying out a plan for the satisfaction of desire reciprocally involves articulating and sustaining a consciousness of oneself over a period of time. In desiring, one reasons: "I want *F*. Doing *G* will bring about *F*. So I will do *G*." One then acts: "I do *G*. I take satisfaction in *F*." So having desire, and satisfying it by carrying out a plan, is part of what it is to achieve a unity of self-consciousness. Satisfying desire embodies the envisioning of oneself as a continuing locus of experience and of plans and their fulfillment over time. It is the most primitive and central form of this envisioning. To be capable of a unity of self-consciousness, achieved through successful recalling and envisioning, and to be capable of the satisfaction of desire are two sides of the same ability. Hence the definition of desire is also, reciprocally, a definition of self-consciousness. "Self-consciousness is desire in general." It is through the satisfaction of desire, via plan formation and execution, that unity of self-consciousness will be achieved, that self-consciousness will be fully actualized. "In this sphere," says Hegel, "self-consciousness exhibits itself as the movement in which this antithesis [i.e., first between itself and the objects it would grasp, but now also understood as an antithesis between successor moments or versions of itself] is removed, and the identity of itself with itself becomes explicit for it [*wird*—becomes, comes about]. . . . The satisfaction of Desire is . . . the reflection of self-consciousness into itself."[15]

If, however, the project of the satisfaction of desire *is* the project of the achievement of a unity of self-consciousness, we do not yet know what it is to form and execute a plan that might structure and inform the whole of one's life. Unless we discover how to do that, the problem of achieving a unity of self-consciousness and of satisfying desire will receive only fitful and evanescent partial solutions. Hegel thinks that he can describe how we can do better than that, how we are already coming to learn to do better than that.

15. Ibid., paragraph 167, p. 105; paragraph 176, p. 110.

Here we encounter the fact that the necessary practical and conceptual arena for our forming and executing of plans is human society. "A self-consciousness exists *for a self-consciousness.*" This is clear already in the sense that the unity of my self-consciousness with itself is a project *for me.* But this formula, by a pun, leads Hegel to note the multiplicity of self-consciousnesses, all bearing this project, that confront one another. This fact of confrontation, both actual-practical and conceptually necessary, then informs and structures the project of achieving a unity of self-consciousness and satisfying desire. "What still lies ahead for consciousness is the experience of what Spirit is— this absolute substance which is the unity [in all bearing the same project] of the different independent self-consciousnesses which, in their opposition, enjoy perfect freedom and independence: 'I' that is 'We' and 'We' that is 'I.'"[16]

Conceptual consciousness involves not only self-consciousness and the pursuit of its unity via the satisfaction of desire, but also undertaking this pursuit amidst other pursuers of unity and satisfaction, with whom one will have relations that are both competitive and cooperative. Two facts make the presence of others not only a matter of actual, historical fact, but also necessary for us as conceptually conscious, self-conscious, and desiring beings. First, one's ability to form and execute any plan at all for the satisfaction of desire requires both a language and a pattern of actions or ways of doing things, a practice. One must be able to articulate what *F* is and to see that *G* is a reasonable means to it. This is something that one comes to be able to do only as one discerns, takes up, and modifies patterns of conceptualization, responses to objects, and actions that are already laid down before one by others. Second, one's ability to form and execute a plan for the satisfaction of desire that structures one's whole life in historical time requires that others also have that ability. It requires that competitiveness in satisfying desires not be ultimate, but rather always housed within deeper mutualities of interest and commitment. One must come to stand with another in relations of reciprocity, not use. One must be related to others who freely recognize oneself, without themselves being consumed and tossed aside. Mere things cannot confer such free recognition. They are objects of use. Incurably antagonistic relations with others fracture one's sense of self-identity and unity, insofar as one finds oneself incapable of dealing with others except through use and violence. Both simple consumption and violence represent a failure of self-unity. For actualized self-

16. Ibid., paragraph 177, p. 110.

unity, mutual self-recognition of all as bearers of free personality is required. "Self-consciousness exists in and for itself when, and by the fact that, it so exists for another; that is it exists only in being acknowledged [es ist nur als Anerkenntnes]. . . . The detailed exposition of the Notion of this spiritual unity in its duplication will present us with the process of Recognition [Anerkennung]."[17] Fully self-conscious self-unity is achieved, and is no longer a project, only when each person is recognized by all others as an expresser of free spontaneity and rationality within the particular social role and empirical identity that the person inhabits. And, Hegel argues, this achievement is already underway, is coming to be, in and through the forms of partial self-consciousness, attained through partial recognitions and partial satisfactions of desires that we already possess.

All this is an enormous story, without even beginning to elaborate Hegel's detailed account of how progress in self-consciousness, reason, and freedom is being achieved, through historical changes in both social life and self-understanding. What is immediately striking—ignoring the claims about progress—is how this story reconstrues the aims of epistemology and the philosophy of mind, and their satisfaction, as part of the acculturated project of a desiring being who seeks self-unity through the expression and acknowledgment of a free personality housed in a social role. The philosophy of consciousness—the investigation of how we are conceptually conscious of any object at all—inaugurates, is part of, and leads into the investigation of the possibilities of achieving expressive freedom in culture.

But not only is this story striking in itself, it is also accurate as an elaboration of Kant's investigations into the existence of a spontaneity at the heart of conceptual consciousness and into the possibilities of expression of that spontaneity in culture and history. Hegel's more progressivist and more explicitly social and political version of the expression of free personality in history helps us to see that a similar project of the expression of free personality is already attributed to human beings by Kant. It then further helps us to see how that project of expression was taken up, and its pursuit variously re-envisioned, by Kant's more immediate romantic and idealist successors. In seeing that this sense of a human project of the achievement of freedom is already in place in Kant, and then in their own re-envisioning of the pursuit of that project, Hegel, Fichte, Schiller, Schelling, Coleridge, Hölderlin, and Schlegel are strik-

17. Ibid., paragraph 178, p. 111.

ingly perceptive readers of Kant and of human interests and possibilities—
more so than Kant's purely epistemologically oriented interpreters and more
so than anyone who divides Kant's philosophy of consciousness entirely from
his moral philosophy and philosophy of history. Even where these later figures
diverge markedly and deliberately from Kant, they nonetheless do so in an
effort to envision how freedom might be achieved, expressed, and acknowledged in actual human life and history. They vary a Kantian theme by accom-
panying it with differing senses of how human action and personality formation actually take place in historical time. But it is, above all, Kant's texts and
their sense of a human project of expressive freedom that set the terms for
the later, more hyperbolically anxious, and tentative romantic and idealist investigations of freedom that themselves prefigure Wittgenstein's writing. Moreover, it is Kant's texts, with their curious blend of a sense of continuing aspiration and internal command toward expressive freedom with a sense of standing
antagonisms in culture, that more directly and deeply prefigure both romantic
and idealist anxieties and Wittgenstein's ongoing interrogations of human
powers. In Kant, desires are not so readily satisfied, self-unities not so readily
achieved, ideals not so readily fulfilled as in Hegel, even while these projects
remain part of the human. Having been alerted by Hegel's more explicit development of it to the theme of the achievement of expressive freedom as a human
project, it is now possible to turn to the more complicated and self-crossed
developments of that theme in Kant, Fichte, Schiller, Schlegel, and, ultimately,
Wittgenstein.

✳

Kant's investigations of the nature of consciousness, of its relation to objects,
and of the demands and possibilities of freedom begin, notoriously, in just
the way that Frye suggests is typical of investigations of consciousness in modernity: with a Copernican turn toward the spectator, prescinding from any
assumed cosmology and instead, through internal descent, considering how
any objects come to appear in consciousness at all. By investigating consciousness and its powers to receive objects, it should, Kant tells us, be possible to
determine

> something in regard to them prior to their being given. We should then be
> proceeding precisely on the lines of Copernicus' primary hypothesis. Failing
> of satisfactory progress in explaining the movements of the heavenly bodies
> on the supposition that they all revolved round the spectator, he tried

> whether he might not have better success if he made the spectator to revolve
> and the stars to remain at rest. A similar experiment can be tried in metaphys-
> ics, as regards the *intuition* of objects.[18]

This amounts, as Michael Morton has usefully noted, to a rejection of the
medieval conception of truth as consisting in an "*adaequatio intellectus ad rem.*"
According to the *adaequatio* model, "the attainment of knowledge consists in
having brought our minds in some way into correspondence with an object
of knowledge, itself understood to exist prior to and independently of both
the knower and the act of cognition."[19] It is not that Kant adopts an uncritical
idealism, constructivism, or relativism; he upholds the existence of an element
of givenness, through sense, in consciousness of an object, and he further
defends the ultimate adequacy of some of our concepts—even such pure,
nonempirical, and abstract concepts as substance and causality—to the reality
of the objects that are presented to us in intuition. But this adequacy is never
assumed or taken for granted. It is not assumed that there is an ordering of
things into kinds, an ordering that the mind can unproblematically replicate.
Instead, the starting point is an investigation of the energies and powers of
mind that figure in the construction of conceptual consciousness. We are, as
Kant puts it, "to seek the observed movements, not in the heavenly bodies,
but in the spectator" (Bxxiii, note a). It is the functions of the mind through
which conceptual consciousness is achieved, and not an independent ordering
of substances, that are the immediate object of investigation of the Critical
Philosophy. This prohibition on the direct investigation of substances extends
to the investigation of the mind as a substance. We are to ask not what the
mind as a substance is, but instead what functions must be in operation if
there is to be conceptual consciousness. "My soul, viewed from the latter standpoint [of freedom, and, it will emerge, as a source of spontaneity], cannot
indeed be known by means of speculative reason (and still less through empirical observation)" (Bxxviii). It is not the thing that is the mind that we are first
of all to seek to know, but the functions that enable consciousness of an object

18. Immanuel Kant, *Critique of Pure Reason,* 2d ed., trans. Norman Kemp Smith, (London:
Macmillan, 1933), Bxvi–xvii. Subsequent references to this edition appear parenthetically in the
text by page number of the Prussian Akademie edition, A for first edition and B for second edition,
as indicated in the margins in the Kemp Smith translation.
19. Michael Morton, *The Critical Turn: Studies in Kant, Herder, Wittgenstein, and Contemporary
Theory* (Detroit: Wayne State University Press, 1993), p. 152.

and are logically presupposed in it—functions which in turn will obscurely commit us to the project of expressive freedom.

In undertaking to investigate these functions, Kant is not, however, pointing toward a Humean or naturalistic conception of consciousness or mind. The functions under which conceptual consciousness is possible are not determined by natural processes (or by any describable supernatural processes either); the laws that describe them are not laws of material nature. As in contemporary functionalism, the functions that enable conceptual consciousness are to be described in ways that are specific to that consciousness. Unlike contemporary functionalism, however, it is not a constraint on the descriptions of these functions that they should be consistent with naturalized biology or psychology as they stand. Instead, appropriate description may have to leave room for—will leave room for—the attribution to us of a spontaneity that resists any explanation, whether material-natural or spiritual-supernatural. To adopt either naturalism or supernaturalism as a constraint on the description of the functions of consciousness, in order to arrive at an explanation of those functions as determined by the properties of some conceptual-consciousness-independent substance, would be to fall back into some version of metaphysical dogmatism. (Contemporary functionalism and connectionism fall into such dogmatisms in accepting metaphysical constraints on the description of consciousness.)

Instead, then, of assuming any metaphysical standpoint on consciousness, we are—so Kant invites us—simply to trace the functions or powers that there must be if there is any conceptual consciousness at all, from the inside, without seeking immediately to explain metaphysically or scientifically how these functions or powers have arisen. This tracing, Kant claims, will yield unexpected riches. We will become able legitimately to regard ourselves as articulators and pursuers of ideals, both cognitive and moral, out of our own resources, rather than in response to any external command of God or nature. By carrying out such a tracing, we can avoid all at once dogmatism with its submissions to an external authority, skepticism about ideals with its consequent anomie, and an indifferentism that professes nothing and yet collapses back into metaphysical dogmatism. "Criticism alone can sever the root of *materialism, fatalism, atheism, free-thinking, fanaticism* and *superstition* . . . ; as well as of *idealism* and *scepticism*" (Bxxxiv; cf. Aix–x; Bxxxv–xxxvi). Through the critical investigation of the functions that are presupposed in conceptual consciousness, prescinding from any metaphysics or cosmology, we will be able, Kant claims, to find a way between Lockean metaphysical enthusiasm and Humean scepticism and into a kind of self-assured and principled sense of ourselves as self-responsible agents, both cognitive and moral.

> While the former of these two illustrious men [Locke] opened a wide door to *enthusiasm*—for if reason once be allowed such rights, it will no longer allow itself to be kept within bounds by vaguely defined recommendations of moderation—the other [Hume] gave himself over entirely to *scepticism*, having, as he believed, discovered that what had hitherto been regarded as reason was but an all-prevalent illusion infecting our faculty of knowledge. We now propose to make trial whether it be not possible to find for human reason safe conduct between these two rocks, assigning to her determinate limits, and yet keeping open for her the whole field of her appropriate activities.
>
> (B128)

The connection in the Critical Philosophy between the cognitive ideals and the moral ideals that are legitimated from within, not by appeal to anything exterior, lies in the unity of apperception. That unity—the fact that all my representations are mine—which is itself a nonempirical fact, a necessary presupposition of any conceptual consciousness, grounds both a cognitive entitlement and a moral command.

Cognitively, Kant's aim, notoriously, is to answer—without dogmatic appeal to present natures, either material-external or one's own-spiritual—the *quid juris:* by what right do we claim to know that there are substances existing independently of consciousness and suffering alterations only as a result of causal interactions (A84=B116)? The establishment of our entitlement to claim this knowledge begins by noting a certain connectedness among our representations—among, that is, our concepts and our intuitions of objects. The intentionality or directedness toward an object of our representations entails a further connectedness among our representations. As Taylor puts it, "Their being of an object entails a certain 'relatedness' among our 'representations.'"[20] That is, our experience of conceptual consciousness is of objects as bearing properties. It is propositional or judgmental in structure. It has the form of one saying to oneself, "This X is F"—e.g., "This apple (the apple) is sour." But that intentionality, aboutness, or directedness toward an object

20. Taylor, "Overcoming Epistemology," p. 475.

(whether or not the judgment is true, whether or not the object exists independently of us) is in turn possible only if the representations—Kant's portmanteau term for concepts, intuitions, and ideas—are themselves held together within my consciousness, combinable by me to form a judgment. They must be mine; I must be able to attach "sour" to "the apple," to predicate sourness of the apple. Were there not this relatedness, were these representations not one and all mine, then my conscious experience "would be without an object, merely a blind play of representations, less even than a dream" (A112). It would not be what it evidently is—intentional, judgmental, or object-directed.

Thus my representations do not subsist on their own, in a free play, but instead belong to me. They fall within "the combination (*conjunctio*) of a manifold in general" (B129) that is the unity of my consciousness. In virtue of the intentional, object-directed, conceptual character of my conscious experience, I know that this is true of me, that there is such a combination in me. Kant makes this point by saying that the intentionality of my conscious experiences means that I must be able to *think* my representations, to recognize that they are all connected with one another as mine.

> It must be possible for the "I think" to accompany all my representations; for otherwise something would be represented in me which could not be thought of at all, and this is equivalent to saying that the representation would be impossible, or at least would be nothing to me. . . . I call [the fact that I can think my representations; recognize them as connected with one another as mine] *pure apperception,* to distinguish it from empirical apperception [e.g., actually hearing myself saying "the apple is sour"—something I might or might not do], or again, *original apperception,* because it is that self-consciousness which, while generating the representation "*I think*" (a representation which must be capable of accompanying all other representations, and which in all consciousness is one and the same), cannot itself be accompanied by any further representation. The unity of this apperception I likewise entitle the *transcendental* unity of self-consciousness, in order to indicate the possibility of *a priori* knowledge arising from it.
>
> (B131–32)

Why is there this connectedness? How is it that, as conceptually and intentionally conscious, I have come to have the ability to think all my representations? There is remarkably little that can be said about this. It is not something that can be explained by appeal to independently existing substances and processes, at least not without metaphysical dogmatism. But what little there is that can be said is crucial to Kant's enterprise. The connectedness or *conjunctio* among my representations "is an act of spontaneity of the faculty of representation" (B129–30). My thinking my representations as mine "is an act of *spontaneity,* that is, it cannot be regarded as belonging to sensibility" (B132). It is, one might say, something that I *do or can do,* not something that forces itself on me in the way that unconceptualized sense experience does. That I *can* do it—can be aware of my experience as mine—or not do it, shows, Kant thinks, that this ability is simply there in me as conceptual intelligence, not something that is given in nonconscious natural processes. It is, in his words, the result of a *spontaneity* in me that I have conceptual, object-directed consciousness and that my consciousness is therein apperceptively unified, that my representations are mine.

Another way to put the nonnatural, nonempirical character of apperceptive unity is to note that its existence is itself known a priori, through reflection on the basic character of intentional consciousness rather than through any specific experience of an object. A *synthesis,* a connectedness of representations, is achieved through spontaneity within my consciousness, of which I am not myself aware through my senses, but which I rather know through reflection must be there. Only a spontaneous synthetic activity could make my conceptual consciousness what it is—object-directed and mine. "The thought that the representations given in intuition one and all belong to me, is therefore equivalent to the thought that I unite them in one self-consciousness, or can at least so unite them; and although this thought is not itself the consciousness of the *synthesis* of the representations, it presupposes the possibility of that synthesis" (B134). That is, the actual, spontaneously generated synthetic activity that makes my consciousness both intentional and apperceptively unified is not itself something I experience empirically. Rather, I know it must exist insofar as its existence is presupposed by the way my consciousness is. Hence "I am conscious to myself *a priori* [rather than through any specific experience] of a necessary synthesis of representations—to be entitled the original synthetic unity of apperception—under which all representations that are given to me must stand, but under which they have also first to be brought by means of a synthesis" (B135).

This spontaneously effected synthesis, this something-we-know-not-how-or-what that must nonetheless be there, is then the ground of our cognitive entitlements and moral duties. Cognitively, the unity of apperception that is brought about in this synthesis is a *"transcendental* unity of self-consciousness" (B132)—transcendental in the sense that this unity pertains to the possibility of knowledge; its existence and operations will establish our cognitive entitlements. The implications of the existence and nature of this original, spontaneous, synthetic activity are then traced so as to show how we are able to know that substances exist independently of us and suffer alterations as a result of causal interactions. Or, as Kant prefigures the argument, "From this original combination many consequences follow" (B133). Roughly and without argument: the fact that I synthesize or connect my representations with one another within my consciousness so that my conceptual consciousness is judgmental and so that I can think all my representations as mine implies, Kant claims, that there is an objective ordering of the representations themselves. My representations themselves must have properties that make them identifiable and recallable by me. Otherwise I could not combine these representations to form a judgment. Without an objective ordering of representations, these representations would be one and all fleeting and insignificant, would be as nothing to me. But now the objective ordering of representations that makes them identifiable and recallable must in turn be content-related, for my representations are used by me to form judgments, not in virtue of their pure syntax but in virtue of what they represent or present. I am able to recall and combine the representations "sour" and "this apple" to form the judgment "this apple is sour," not because of how those representations "look" within my consciousness, but because they are representations that have specific content, that present something specific to me. (Compare: there is no natural connection between sign and signifier; what makes a signifier meaningful is not its shape alone but also its content as laid down in use—however that happens.) Finally, this objective and content-related ordering of my representations must then in turn be borrowed from an ordering that is present in what is represented, an ordering in things that exist apart from me but are presented to my consciousness in intuitions of them. If *no* purely formal or structural features of my representations could order them and give them specific content, then that order and content must be there in the things that my representations represent. As a result—and after further specific investigation of the fundamental contents and modes of ordering of my representations—we may conclude, justifiably, that there exist independently of my consciousness various substances that affect one another causally. "In all change of appearances substance is permanent; its quantum in nature is neither increased nor diminished" (A182=B224). "All alterations take place in conformity with the law of cause and effect" (A189=B232). I may be wrong about some specific judgments—the light may always be bad, or my attention may be distracted—but my entitlement to make judgments about substances apart from me and about their causal interactions is secure. It is a consequence of the "original combination," the spontaneously achieved synthesis that is present, that must be present, beneath my conceptual consciousness, given its character.

All this is very compressed and relatively unassessed. (What, for example, is the nature of "logical presupposition" involved in the claim that the intentionality of our consciousness *presupposes* a unity of apperception? Can we be confident of that presupposition in the absence of either a natural scientific or a metaphysical explanation of what makes it true? Just why must the modes of synthesis that make for apperceptive unity mirror and reveal the modes of synthesis of an intuition out of manifold nonrepresentational sensory buzzings? Just what are the relevant modes of synthesis in each case? And so on.) But the general character and direction of the effort are clear. Kant has sought to establish epistemological claims, to ground some entitlements to know, without claiming direct awareness of the existence and nature of any substance. The starting point is only the basic character of conceptual consciousness and whatever that basic character implies about spontaneities of synthesis within. It is this avoidance of claims about substances, but instead the appeal to a general character of intentional consciousness, that enables the move between dogmatism and skepticism.

Crucially and strikingly, the very spontaneity that Kant centrally appeals to in his epistemological project of upholding our cognitive entitlements is then also legislative for morality. That spontaneity is the source of moral commands that are not external directives. It is not only the source or locus of apperceptively unified conceptual consciousness but also the seat of practical reason. This connection is often little noted or dwelt upon, as epistemology is kept separate from moral and political philosophy, but it is powerfully insisted on in Kant's discussions of the nature of freedom.

Within conceptual consciousness of objects, Kant tells us, the spontaneity that must be present is a locus of freedom and, ultimately, of moral intelligibility and duty.

> Appearances [intuitions of objects as having properties, falling under concepts] themselves have grounds which are not appearances. The effects of

such an intelligible cause appear, and accordingly can be determined through other appearances, but its causality is not so determined. . . . [T]he intelligible cause, together with its causality, is outside the series. . . . [Appearances] must rest upon a transcendental object which determines them as mere representations; and consequently there is nothing to prevent us from ascribing to this transcendental object [this nonintuitable spontaneity that makes knowledge possible] . . . a *causality* which is not appearance.

(A537=B565; A538–39=B566–67)

The fact of this spontaneity in us, itself exercised in the construction of conceptually conscious experience as we have it, in turn makes us free and bound by the demands of morality. This inscrutable spontaneity is the intelligible cause of our perceptions, the ground of our agency, and the source of our duties, through the intelligible laws of reason. Kant connects the functions of spontaneity—cognitive and moral—with one another in a crucial passage in the Solution to the Third Antinomy, as he seeks to explain how freedom is possible and compatible with a comprehensive causal ordering of events in nature. The key is that an intelligible, free action—this spontaneity—is already present in the construction of conceptually conscious experience.

Man, . . . who knows all the rest of nature solely through the senses, knows himself also through pure apperception; and this, indeed, in acts and inner determinations which he cannot regard as impressions of the senses. He is thus to himself, on the one hand phenomenon, and on the other hand, in respect of certain faculties the action of which cannot be ascribed to the receptivity of sensibility, a purely intelligible object. We entitle these faculties understanding and reason. The latter, in particular, we distinguish in a quite peculiar and especial way from all empirically conditioned powers. For it views objects exclusively in the light of ideas, and in accordance with them determines the understanding, which then proceeds to make an empirical use of its own similarly pure concepts.

That our reason has causality, or that we at least represent it to ourselves as having causality, is evident from the *imperatives* which in all matters of conduct we impose as rules upon our active powers. "*Ought*" expresses a kind of necessity and of connection with grounds which is found nowhere else in the whole of nature.

. . . Reason does not here follow the order of things as they present themselves in appearance, but frames for itself with perfect spontaneity an order of its own according to ideas, to which it adapts the empirical conditions, and according to which it declares actions to be necessary, even although they have never taken place, and perhaps never will take place. And at the same time reason also presupposes that it can have causality in regard to all these actions, since otherwise no empirical effects could be expected from its ideas.

Now, in view of these considerations, let us take our stand, and regard it as at least possible for reason to have causality with respect to appearances.
(A546–47=B574–75; A548–49=B576–77)

The character of conceptual consciousness presupposes, and discloses, a spontaneity, free of the order of natural causes, that is effective in the construction of conscious experience. And that spontaneity, in turn, as Reason, acting under the rules "we impose . . . upon our active powers," makes our actions free and determines our moral duties, no matter how the empirical world may happen to go. As Kant similarly puts the point in the *Critique of Practical Reason,* in the section entitled "Of the Right of Pure Reason to an Extension in Its Practical Use Which Is Not Possible to It in Its Speculative Use," "I have this right [to assume a causality of freedom] by virtue of the pure nonempirical origin [viz., in inner spontaneity] of the concept of cause."[21]

So we have this *ought,* a categorical imperative laid down by a spontaneity within, Reason, whose substantial nature is we know not what. We are aware of this spontaneity of Reason not directly, through experience of it, but instead as a presupposition of the kind of conceptual consciousness that we have and through the formula of duty that it hands down to us. The moral law is "the *ratio cognoscendi* [that through which we know] of freedom."[22] We do not know how we have this spontaneity. Since it is not given to us by being present in a substance that we know, following its commands is not enabled by the self-development of an order of substances of which it is a part. The commands of this spontaneity that enables our conceptual consciousness are given to us, but we do not know how they are given, and we do not know how, in engaging with things, to follow them in specific detail. Our moral life becomes a kind of standing problem to be solved, a problem forced on us by this insubstantial inner spontaneity. As Lacoue-Labarthe and Nancy observe,

> As is well known, the Kantian "cogito" is empty. . . . This weakening of the subject is accompanied by an apparently compensatory "promotion" of the *moral subject* which, as we know, launches a variety of philosophical careers.

21. Immanuel Kant, *Critique of Practical Reason,* trans. Lewis White Beck (Indianapolis: Bobbs-Merrill, 1956), pp. 57–58.
22. Ibid., p. 4 n. 1.

> One must set out from this problematic of the subject unpresentable to itself and from this eradication of all substantialism in order to understand what romanticism will receive, not as a bequest but as its "own" most difficult and perhaps insoluble question.[23]

In Kant's own moral philosophy and philosophy of culture, this eradication of substantialism along with the promotion of our sense of moral duty lead to a sharp and ever-present sense of moral anxiety. There are standing constraints on what we may *not* do. We may not violate perfect duties to others or to ourselves; we may not, for example, lie or commit fraud. There are also standing conditions of political relationship—liberal freedoms and rights to equal political citizenship—that serve to hold equally open to all the public space for leading a moral life.

But these standing constraints and political conditions do not tell us *how* to lead a life affirmatively, how to follow out our internally legislated command to ourselves to cultivate our talents or to achieve a comprehensive and fulfilling moral community. There are affirmative, imperfect duties to self and others. Shall I play the cello or read to my children? Shall I work an extra two hours in order to earn a better wage or cook and enjoy a fine dinner? Shall I attend a town zoning board meeting or write a letter to my state representative? Shall I take up tennis or bridge? Shall I have another child or go into social work? Shall I marry? Nothing in the commands to cultivate our talents and to achieve a moral community that we lay down to ourselves tells us how to answer these questions. Nor does any metaphysical ordering of things tell us this.

No doubt habit and critical reflection typically step in to fill the gap between the commands of moral principle and what we actually do in specific circumstances. But nothing tells us how therein to achieve an appropriate, reason-expressive and free-personality-expressive mixture of habit and critical reflection. Nothing tells us in any specific detail how to reflect about our habits of practice in specific circumstances. We have open-ended, unspecifiable, imperfect duties of self-cultivation and the cultivation of moral community, duties commanded by an obscure, insubstantial spontaneity within. How to fulfill these duties remains a problem for us. There is no fixed plot for carrying them out, no independent ordering of substances to whose development we must resonate. It is up to us. As Charles Taylor usefully observes, Kant, along with Rousseau, here puts forward "an anti-levelling objection" against both Panglos-

---

23. Lacoue-Labarthe and Nancy, *The Literary Absolute,* pp. 30, 31.

sian optimism and "a too simple view of the human will, intent simply on happiness, . . . [wherein] good [is simply] a matter of training, knowledge, enlightenment."[24] There is, instead, always a conflict within the will about how to act, no matter what training, knowledge, and enlightenment we have.

Kant's moral philosophy and psychology thus help to recover an Augustinian-Pauline sense of the will in conflict with itself, torn between good and evil and torn also between various routes of freedom-cultivating action. It is not even just that we are afflicted with base desires and inclinations that must be repressed and denied expression in action (though that is true). It is also that we do not know how to release or express our affirmative, freedom-cultivating, rational personality in culture. We are torn between various ways of doing this, all of which seem at best to work only partially, in that they seem to leave standing the antagonisms and problems that they would confront and overcome in the interest of harmonious moral community and full wholeness of free personality. Playing the cello and attending a zoning board meeting are good things, are partial expressions of free personality and cultivations of freedom in community. But they do not readily speak to or engage with the equally significant efforts to express and cultivate freedom of those who practice performance art or those who live in different towns, states, or nations. Only sectarian recognitions and ratifications of the worth of any of these efforts at the expression of freedom are to be expected.

Nor can the internally, but obscurely, self-legislated project of the cultivation and expression of rational freedom be completed in any obvious way. There is no clear end-state to be achieved. Instead, the cultivation and expression of rational freedom is to suffuse a life—and a life with others. The cultivation and expression of rational freedom is more like a modality of action or being with others throughout a life than it is like the achievement of a state, so that it is quite unlike other moral ideals of an achieved state, such as harmony of soul or beatitude or happiness or *eudaimonia*.

Always, then, there is a conflict within, a conflict about how to release, or express, or sustain, or cultivate thoughtfulness, or rational autonomy, or integrity and wholeness of self-consciousness, or free personality as a conceptually conscious being. This conflict within is both cause and effect of conflicts without—in a culture, between persons—as varying routes of the expression and cultivation of freedom are tried out and as varying, sectarian circles of recogni-

24. Taylor, *Sources of the Self,* p. 355.

tion and ratification are achieved. Individual moral personalities grow up within these sectarian circles and hence are shaped by them in the routes of expression and cultivation that they find salient; they then in turn contribute to these sectarian circles, which remain in both complementarity and yet tension with one another.

In more explicitly Kantian-Hegelian terms, the standing problem for any moral subject, and for any culture of moral subjects, is that of passing from a life dominated by *Willkür* to a life informed by *Wille*. *Willkür* is simple volitional freedom, an *arbitrium liberum*. It is "the power to choose between alternatives . . . according to the strength of the pleasures or displeasures it anticipates in connection with the alternatives open to it."[25] This power of choice is not, however, a matter of the strongest inclination or desire forcing an action on a passive subject. Rather, it is *Willkür* itself that determines which inclination or desire is strongest for it and hence decisive for action. For Kant, "Freedom of the will [*Willkür*] is of a wholly unique nature in that an incentive can determine the will [*Willkür*] to an action *only so far as an individual has incorporated it into his maxim;* . . . only thus can an incentive, whatever it may be, co-exist with the absolute spontaneity of the will [*Willkür*]."[26] As John Silber observes, "No impulse or desire can be a determining incentive for the *Willkür* until the *Willkür* chooses to make it so."[27]

Wille, in contrast, is not a power or spontaneity but rather the law or normative content of free willing. Silber notes that "[*Wille*] is the source of a strong and ever present incentive in *Willkür.* . . . *Wille* is . . . the law of freedom, the normative aspect of will, which as a norm is neither free nor unfree. Having no freedom of action, *Wille* is under no constraint or pressure. It exerts, instead, the pressure of its own normative rational nature upon *Willkür.*"[28] Because this rational norm of *Wille* is present within us, capable of informing *Willkür* and providing its most powerful incentives, coming to lead a rational, free, and fully human life is hence a matter of *Wille,* this rational norm or law, coming to have effect in *Willkür.* Becoming affirmatively free is, for Kant, a matter of "the establishment of the *purity* of this [moral] law as the supreme

25. John Silber, "The Ethical Significance of Kant's *Religion,*" introduction to *Religion within the Limits of Reason Alone,* by Immanuel Kant, trans. T. M. Greene and H. H. Hudson (New York: Harper and Brothers, 1960), p. xcv.
26. Kant, *Religion within the Limits of Reason Alone,* p. 19.
27. Silber, "The Ethical Significance of Kant's *Religion,*" p. xcv.
28. Ibid., p. civ.

ground of all our maxims, whereby it is not merely associated with other incentives, and certainly is not subordinated to any such (to inclinations) as its conditions, but instead must be adopted, in its entire purity as an incentive *adequate* in itself for the determination of the will [*Willkür*]."[29]

Hegel both adopts Kant's terminology and explicitly locates the process through which *Willkür* comes to be informed by *Wille* within psychological and sociohistorical courses of development. "At this [early] stage [of development], the freedom of the will is arbitrariness (*Willkür*) and this involves two factors: (a) free reflection, abstracting from everything, and (b) dependence on a content and material given either from within or from without."[30] In possessing *Willkür*—arbitrariness or spontaneity or the power of choice—one is aware of oneself as a detached person, the initiator of one's actions, but also dependent on the contents thrown up by inclination and desire that the *Willkür* incorporates as its incentives. If *Willkür*, or the power of choice, seeks to refuse all dependence on any content and instead to provide its content for itself, then

> we have negative freedom, . . . the freedom of the void which rises to a
> passion and takes shape in the world. . . . [W]hen it turns to actual practice,
> it takes shape in religion and politics alike as the fanaticism of destruction—
> the destruction of the whole subsisting social order—as the elimination of
> individuals who are objects of suspicion to any social order, and the annihila-
> tion of any organization which tries to rise anew from the ruins. Only in
> destroying something does this negative will possess the feeling of itself as
> existent. . . . [I]t is precisely out of the annihilation of particularity and objec-
> tive characterization that the self-consciousness of this negative freedom pro-
> ceeds. Consequently, what negative freedom intends to will can never be
> anything in itself but an abstract idea, and giving effect to this idea can only
> be the fury of destruction.[31]

Instead, then, of refusing all dependence on norms, *Willkür* must come to be informed by a rational normative content. Yet in arriving at this mode of willing, we are also not simply to accept any content that is given; we are not slavishly to conform to any norms of action or life that happen to be pursued by those around us. Rather, rational freedom, or *Wille*, must bring about "the

---

29. Kant, *Religion within the Limits of Reason Alone*, p. 42.
30. Hegel, *Philosophy of Right*, paragraph. 15, p. 27.
31. Ibid., paragraph 5, remark, p. 22.

engendering of its determinations" as effective incentives in and for *Willkür*. As it progressively comes to find rational norms in place around it, which it then accepts as its specifically determined incentives and contents, *Willkür* itself increasingly comes to be rational will in the world. Through this process, rational freedom "comes to have *itself* as its content and aim." As Hegel acknowledges, the view that this is our task and aim—*Willkür's* coming to be informed by *Wille* so as to achieve and express rational freedom in the world—is already present in Kant and Fichte, albeit that they imagine the completion of this aim in a way that is, for Hegel, too individualist, subjectivist, and hence negativity-engendering: "The determination and differentiation of the two moments which have been mentioned [i.e., negative freedom or mere arbitrary voluntariness, choice, as well as the critical acceptance of norms in place, the 'positing of a determinacy as content and object'] is to be found in the philosophies of Fichte, Kant, and others."[32]

In explicitly Kantian terms, this process of *Willkür's* coming to have a rational content or to embrace the norms of rational freedom [*Wille*] is less a gift of history than it is a matter of the formation of a character or disposition (*Gesinnung*). *Willkür* must come to have the habit or general character of responsiveness in context to the demands of *Wille,* of making expressive conformity to *Wille's* commands its continuous aim. Kant emphasizes that acquiring and sustaining this character or disposition is a continuous and difficult task, involving inner transformation.

> Man's moral growth of necessity begins not in the improvement of his practices but rather in the transforming of his cast of mind and in the grounding of a character; though customarily man goes about the matter otherwise and fights against vices one by one, leaving undisturbed their common root. . . . [A man's becoming morally good and affirmatively free] cannot be brought about through gradual *reformation* so long as the basis of the maxims remains impure, but must be effected through a *revolution* in the man's disposition (a going over to the maxim of the holiness of the disposition). He can become a new man only by a kind of rebirth, as it were a new creation (John III, 5; compare also Genesis I, 2), and a change of heart.[33]

This Kantian picture of the achievement of affirmative freedom and moral goodness through inner transformation of disposition can sometimes seem

32. Ibid., paragraph 31, p. 34; paragraph 15, remark, p. 27; paragraph 6, remark, p. 23.
33. Kant, *Religion within the Limits of Reason Alone*, pp. 43–44.

excessively voluntaristic, rigoristic, and scornful of existing institutions and modes of social relationship. Hegel notoriously judged it in this way, finding Kant's exhortations toward inner transformation to alternate between urging a vapid, concretely impotent, and merely inner hopefulness, an uncritical acquiescence in the standing ways of culture, and a narcissistic, baseless pride in an inner character that one is unable to express with others. The Hegelian project is to accept the Kantian picture of the transformation of arbitrary action into affirmatively free, *Wille*-expressive action as our task, but to find in historical time more specific, more adequate, and less predominantly inner ways of carrying out that task. Where the project of achieving expressive freedom is taken seriously, rather than ignored, dismissed, or simply reduced to utilitarian considerations about material satisfaction, Hegel's criticisms of Kant have largely been authoritative. Yet their authority has often blocked attention to the sketches of the achievement of expressive freedom in and through historical life that Kant does put forward, fitfully, in his historical essays and in the *Critique of Judgment*. These sketches are all at once more careful, more nuanced, more influential for Kant's successors—not only idealists and romantics but also such self-crossed, self-criticizing later writers, suspicious of theodicies, as Nietzsche, Freud, and Wittgenstein—and more compelling in their darkened optimism than Hegel's *Bildungsroman* of Spirit in history.

How, then, without invoking a theodicy might expressive freedom come to be achieved, fitfully, in the world in historical time? Kant announces his interest in how we might achieve expressive freedom in the world near the beginning of the *Critique of Judgment*. Previously he has uncovered analytically an inner spontaneity that is responsible for the apperceptive unity of consciousness and for self-conscious conceptual experience. The fact that our consciousness is conceptual and apperceptively unified has served as the starting point for an argument that the objects presented to us in our conscious conceptual experience display a mathematical nature and a causal ordering that we can know. The spontaneity that makes for apperceptive unity and self-conscious conceptual experience is not itself, however, an object of empirical investigation. It is noumenal, outside the bounds of experience. That this noumenal spontaneity then further legislates a moral command is likewise a mystery for empirical investigation. The nature of morality cannot be derived from any study of how people act that ignores the reason-expressive character of human action and instead looks only at how actions rearrange objects and seek satisfaction. But now if moral commands come from outside the world of empirical objects that we experience and in which we act, come from a noumenal spontaneity, then how are they to be effective within the world of experience? Kant's leading question in the *Critique of Judgment* is now no longer this: What power or agency in me enables me to have conceptually conscious, apperceptively unified experience, and what cognitive and moral ideals and practices does that power or agency support? Those questions have been settled by the first and second *Critiques*. Instead Kant now asks: How might I specifically express my spontaneity, free personality, rationality, and dignity in human, historical, temporal, life? Our noumenal spontaneity and rationality are not supposed to be vapid, impotent, merely inner, idly hopeful, uncritical, or supportive of narcissism or tyranny. Legitimate moral commands must not be any of these things. But if it is initially inner and noumenal, exactly how is rational freedom to be expressed in the world? Our freedom and rationality are "meant to influence" the empirical and historical world; "the concept of freedom is meant to actualize in the sensible world the end proposed by its laws."[34] Kant continues, "So much indeed is implied in the concept of a causality by freedom, the *operation* of which, in conformity with the formal laws of freedom, is to take effect in the world."[35] But how? Just what might the achievement of rational, personality-manifesting, expressive freedom look like?

Kant addresses this question most directly in his historical and anthropological essays as he puts forward a conjectural history of human culture.[36] According to this conjectural history, human beings are originally creatures of sensation and animal instinct. A given but latent capacity of reason then comes to be articulately used, comes to life, as human beings begin to make comparisons among things, preferring some foods to others and distinguishing between pleasures and perils. In doing this they further acquire new, artificial desires, through imaginatively conceiving of pleasures or satisfactions they have recognized rather than merely pursuing satisfaction instinctively. Having multiple, explicitly conceived and articulated desires, they therein "become

---

34. Immanuel Kant, *Critique of Judgment*, trans. J. C. Meredith (Oxford: Clarendon Press, 1952), p. 14.

35. Ibid., p. 37.

36. In developing Kant's conjectural history, I draw on Allen Wood's elegant and insightful reading of Kant's historical and anthropological essays in his "Unsociable Sociability: The Anthropological Basis of Kantian Ethics," *Philosophical Topics* 19, no. 1 (Spring 1991), pp. 325–51.

aware of what it means to choose," conscious of and effective exercisers of at least a negative freedom from domination by immediate inclination.[37] Nearer pleasures can be foregone in favor of pleasures in prospect that promise to be more intense, or deeply satisfying, or longer lasting. Insofar as one exercises and is conscious of one's negative freedom, one is aware of oneself as leading a life in time. One comes to be aware of a need to work and to plan in pursuing the satisfactions one has articulately conceived, and one comes to be aware of one's own death as putting an end to this pursuit.

But articulate exercise and awareness of negative freedom in the rational pursuit of satisfaction is not the end of the story. Human beings, expelled from the paradise of animal instinct, become aware of and committed to the project of developing their natures and talents so as to express their rational freedom. Their reasoning comes to be no longer merely instrumental to simply given propensities for taking satisfaction in states of affairs, but further to impose an affirmative ideal on them. One comes to be aware of oneself, of one's rational nature, as an end in itself.

> So far as natural gifts are concerned, other beings may surpass man beyond all comparison. Nevertheless, man is without qualification equal even to higher beings in that none has the right to use him according to pleasure. This is because of his reason—reason considered not insofar as it is a tool to the satisfaction of his inclinations, but insofar as it makes him an end in himself. Hence this last step of reason is at the same time man's *release* from the womb of nature, an alteration of condition which is honorable, to be sure, but also fraught with danger. For nature had now driven him from the safe and harmless state of childhood—a garden, as it were, which looked after his needs without any trouble on his part ([Gen.] 3:23)—into the wide world, where so many cares, troubles, and unforeseen ills awaited him. In the future, the wretchedness of his condition would often arouse in him the wish for a paradise, the creation of his imagination, where he could dream or while away his existence in quiet inactivity and permanent peace. But between him and that imagined place of bliss, restless reason would interpose itself, irresistibly impelling him to develop the faculties in him. It would not permit him to return to that crude and simple place from which it had driven him to begin with ([Gen.] 3:24). It would make him take up patiently the toil which he yet hates, and pursue the frippery which he despises. It would make him

37. Ibid., p. 330.

forget even death itself which he dreads, because of all those trifles which he is even more afraid to lose.[38]

Here reason as a source of an affirmative command to achieve expressive freedom through the development of one's talents has made human beings, in a certain way, interesting animals, capable of articulate desires, repressions, the development of talents, and the pursuit of commands and ideals.

Once awareness of oneself as an end and as affirmatively commanded by reason to develop one's talents has begun first to dawn, there are then two further developments that serve to complete and perfect this awareness. We are to establish a rational state, "a universal civic society which administers law among men," to serve as the public, political framework for the project of developing talents and achieving expressive freedom.[39] The full achievement of expressive freedom is then the final work of the setting up of a harmonious moral culture, a kingdom of ends, a rational community in which our ends "are brought systematically into harmony by reason as reciprocal end and means, like the interdependent organs of a living thing."[40] One's individual pursuit of the satisfaction of desire is no longer either haphazard or antagonistically competitive. Instead, that pursuit now expresses who one is along with others—a joint developer of talents in such a way that free, rational, human personality is achieved and expressed. Kant here regards his own philosophical writing as contributing to that development, both by characterizing the form of political relationship—the liberal state—that is rationally and humanly appropriate and by articulating the further work of reason's development in and through culture that we have already begun dimly to undertake.

The development of self-consciousness and of rational, expressive freedom is not only—is not even primarily—a political or a philosophico-theoretical project. It is instead art or *poesis* that serves as the crucial expressive vehicle through which our talents are developed, as we move from our first awareness of ourselves as time-conscious, instrumental reasoners toward our conjectured, final, articulate awareness of ourselves as ends in ourselves, rationally

38. Immanuel Kant, "Conjectural Beginning of Human History," trans. Emil L. Fackenheim, in *On History,* ed. Lewis White Beck (Indianapolis: Bobbs-Merrill, 1963), p. 59.
39. Immanuel Kant, "Idea for a Universal History from a Cosmopolitan Point of View," trans. Lewis White Beck, in *On History,* Fifth Thesis, p. 16.
40. Wood, "Unsociable Sociability," p. 343.

free beings with a free personality fitly housed in a social role, under which it is reciprocally recognized and ratified. "Fine art," Kant writes in the *Critique of Judgment*, "has the effect of advancing the culture of the mental powers in the interests of social communication."[41] The work of making art does this by blending sublime, natural spontaneity and originality—the "primary property" of genius, "the innate mental aptitude *through which* nature gives the rule to art"[42]—with sense, intelligibility, and the crafting of material. Works of art achieve and embody a kind of unpredictable, free intelligibility in *following after* predecessor works, forming coherent series, but without *imitating* their predecessors.[43] Each predecessor work inspires and provokes successors, as each successor refigures the sense of its predecessors. Art's achievement of original sense serves both as an emblem and spur for the development of expressive freedom in a specific personality in society and as an actual vehicle for this latter achievement. In taking up "something of a compulsory character . . . or, as it is called, a *mechanism*"—that is, in responding to the demand to craft material not only originally, but also intelligibly, in a way that admits of recognition and ratification—artists therein embody the soul, which otherwise "would be bodiless and evanescent" ("gar keinen Körper haben und ganzlich verdunsten würde").[44] The artist achieves in the work "a play which is self-maintaining and which strengthens [the] powers [of the soul—*Geist*] for such activity." In fitting free originality to the demands of intelligibility, the artist seeks a "form [that] is not, as it were, a matter of inspiration, or of a free swing of the mental powers, but rather of a slow and even painful process of improvement, directed to making the form adequate to his thought without prejudice to the freedom in the play of those powers."[45] That is to say, in the production of art and in its reception, which makes similar demands on critical intelligence to appreciate new sense, rational, free personality finds itself articulated and embodied in the world. By embodying both the rational, free personality of its maker and rational, intelligible ideas, which otherwise would be as nothing to sense, the work of art engenders in us a "feeling . . . which quickens the cognitive faculties and which binds up language, which otherwise

41. Kant, *Critique of Judgment*, p. 166.
42. Ibid., p. 168.
43. See ibid., pp. 171, 181.
44. Ibid., p. 164; Kant, *Kritik der Urteilskraft* (Frankfurt: Suhrkamp, 1974), p. 238.
45. Kant, *Critique of Judgment*, pp. 175, 174.

would be mere letters, with spirit" ("mit der Sprache, als bloßem Buchstaben, Geist verbindet").[46] Through and in this quickening of our powers, rational expressive freedom comes to be, in the world.

*

This sketch of human history and of art's place in it is a wonderful story of the growth of expressive freedom in the world, full of psychological acuity and independent of the assumption of any metaphysical cosmology that would guarantee its coming true. But does it win our allegiance by reflecting genuine possibilities of development to us? It is by no means clear that any such story is coming true, or that it succeeds in revealing to us our powers and possibilities.[47] Bitterness, antagonism, envy, competitiveness, violence, and domination are conspicuously more the stuff of our lives than reciprocity and harmonious rational freedom. Nor did Kant fail to notice this. The ideal narrative of our progress in realizing our capacities that he produces is merely conjectural, elaborated out of the reading of Genesis. Such "conjectures cannot make too high a claim on one's assent. They cannot announce themselves as serious business, but at best only as a permissible exercise of the imagination guided by reason."[48] A conjectural narrative does not aim at any verifiable historical truth, nor does it permit any justification of our ascription to ourselves of rational capacities and self-legislated moral principles that we are learning to fulfill. Against the background of what history is actually like, Kant's conjectures are a story of long ago and far away that may well seem to have little to do with us here and now.

And Kant is himself fully aware of the actual course of historical developments. Recall that in Kant's story commitment to an affirmative ideal of expressive freedom and of living as an end in itself suddenly emerges out of instrumental reasoning. The moment of this emergence is, Kant notes, a moment of competitiveness and envy. One is suddenly overwhelmed, struck by the wealth or force of personality or expressive power of another in that other's way of occupying a role in social life. Therein one is moved to envy, resent-

---

46. Ibid., p. 179, translation modified; Kant, *Kritik der Urteilskraft*, p. 253.

47. The next few paragraphs closely paraphrase passages in my "Kant, Hölderlin, and the Experience of Longing," in *Beyond Representation: Philosophy and Poesis*, ed. Richard Eldridge (Cambridge: Cambridge University Press, 1996), pp. 175–96.

48. Kant, "Conjectural Beginning," p. 53.

ment, and competitiveness, moved to develop one's own talents so as to emulate, compete with, and displace this commanding precursor. Commitment to that affirmative ideal to develop one's own talents is bound up with a reactivity and opposition to others that Kant calls "antagonism."

> The means employed by Nature to bring about the development of all the capacities of men is their antagonism in society, so far as this is, in the end, the cause of a lawful order among men. By "antagonism" I mean the unsocial sociability of men, i.e. their propensity to enter into society, together with a mutual opposition which constantly threatens to break up the society. . . . This opposition it is which awakens all [man's] powers, brings him to conquer his inclination to laziness, and, propelled by vainglory, lust for power, and avarice, to achieve a rank among his fellows whom he cannot tolerate but from whom he cannot withdraw.[49]

Thus art, while embodying our soul and articulating and expressing rational freedom, will also embody conflict, vainglory, lust for power, and avarice. Every exercise of rational power or virtue, every act of originality or courage or kindness or justice or love, whether in art or elsewhere, that might advance us toward a moral culture of expressive freedom will be at the same time marked by vainglory and antagonism. Actual, as opposed to ideal or conjectural, history is the record of the exercise of powers and virtues under and often contributing to antagonisms and relations of domination. The coming to be of rational expressive freedom in the world is not underwritten by any metaphysics of human nature and history. "Nature," Kant tells us, "reveals something, but very little" of the path toward a kingdom of ends.[50]

Yet somehow—perhaps in the affirmative moment of our reaction to certain exemplary achievements—we are nonetheless to believe, or hope, that movement toward a kingdom of ends is possible. We are to believe that it is at least in principle possible, *deo volente,* that the virtues are fully compossible—expressive power coexisting with love, justice coexisting with intimacy, all without envy and vainglory—both within the individual psyche and within an achieved moral culture. The condition in which conformity to our moral duties is fully and harmoniously compossible with, even effective for, the exercise of our powers to win satisfaction is, Kant tells us, not necessarily impossible to achieve, even if history provides little concrete indication of the possibil-

49. Kant, "Idea for a Universal History," p. 15.
50. Ibid., p. 22.

ity of that achievement. That virtue is crowned with happiness is pervasively but "only *conditionally* false."[51] It might, somehow, be otherwise.

Unattached, then, to any metaphysical cosmology that might underwrite the realization of Kant's hopes for humanity in culture, we are left with what Lacoue-Labarthe and Nancy call a "view of history that refers its telos to infinity."[52] There is an ideal of the achievement of rational, expressive freedom in the setting up and maintaining of an expressive identity in culture in a way that is recognized and ratified by others in and through their similar efforts. That ideal is present for us, dimly housed within the power or spontaneity that makes our consciousness conceptual and apperceptively unified at all. There are certain exemplary intimations or prefigurings, in art and elsewhere in expressive social life, of its coming to be present in the world. But no clear route to the achievement of that ideal presents itself. Any course of expressive action in social life seems marked by antagonism and opposition. Yet there seems to be no ready way to return to a conception of ourselves as having a more nearly animal existence, free of an aspiration to expressive freedom and power and harmony in our social roles, concerned instead only with duller, more material satisfactions and ready to accept the pervasiveness of trade-offs in human social life.

How present for us, then, is the ideal of expressive freedom, blending full self-consciousness and self-unity with the satisfaction of desire with reciprocal recognition, when no secure route toward that ideal seems present? In what way is that ideal present? How might it be pursued, through what sorts of activities and with what critical attitudes toward culture and its antagonisms? These are the questions that would preoccupy Kant's successors—from Fichte, Schiller, and Schlegel to Kierkegaard, Nietzsche, and Wittgenstein—as they struggled to articulate how to live with a sense of oneself as bearing, obscurely within one's conceptual consciousness, a spontaneity and a possibility of free expressive power in a divided and increasingly routinized culture.

51. Kant, *Critique of Practical Reason,* p. 119.
52. Lacoue-Labarthe and Nancy, *The Literary Absolute,* p. 32.

3
Toward a Critique of Critique: Fichte, Schiller, Schlegel, and *Poesis*

Kant begins his critical philosophical project by prescinding from any cosmology. He undertakes instead to investigate the logically necessary presuppositions of conceptual consciousness and self-consciousness, and then further to elaborate the ideal of affirmative, reason-expressive freedom to which we are, he argues, committed. As he begins this critical project, he comments on the epoch and kind of culture in which it has arisen: "Our age is, in especial degree, the age of criticism [*Kritik*], and to criticism everything must submit. Religion through its sanctity, and law-giving through its majesty, may seek to exempt themselves from it. But they awaken just suspicion, and cannot claim the sincere respect which reason accords only to that which has been able to sustain the test of free and open examination" (Axi, note a). Nothing may be withheld from reason's tests. Authority over and within practices—cognitive or moral, political or religious—is supportable only insofar as its commands conform to principles that critical reason can certify of itself. Reversion to dogma, whether political or moral or religious or cosmological, only deepens the critical demand, only awakens a "just suspicion" that the content of that dogma is insupportable in the light of reason. We live, Kant suggests, in an age in which dogmatism is evidently unreasonable and in which the demand for criticism is evidently natural and congenial.

But how exactly has such a demand for criticism arisen? What happens when this demand is made of the Critical Philosophy itself? That is, why must critical reasoning begin with an examination of the logically necessary presuppositions of conceptual consciousness and self-consciousness? Why exactly there? Most pointedly, exactly how does that critical examination of conceptual consciousness then point us to the existence of a genuine, concretely livable moral ideal of expressive freedom? Perhaps if one accepts the Kantian starting point and begins from an examination of conceptual consciousness, one then arrives at some notion about the existence of a power or spontaneity in us that makes our conceptual consciousness apperceptively unified and propositionally structured. But, again, why should one begin there? And, more pressingly, why isn't that power or spontaneity a subject of biology or neuroscience or functional psychology? Exactly how does it commit us to the project of expressive freedom?

These questions were immediately raised by Kant's readers. As Frederick C. Beiser observes,

> Kant's solution to the meta-critical problem [of how to find a way between dogmatism and skepticism] left one unanswered question in its wake. Namely, how do we know the necessary conditions of any possible experience? This question is legitimate, pressing, and important; but Kant did not have any clear or explicit answer to it. The sad truth of the matter is that he never developed a meta-critical theory about how to acquire knowledge of the first principles of criticism. If self-knowledge was the most difficult of all reason's tasks, Kant still was not forthcoming with any advice about how this was to be achieved. But Kant's failure to address the meta-critical problem in any sustained and explicit manner had a very serious consequence: it left the authority of reason hanging in the balance. Although Kant taught that the authority of reason depended upon the possibility of criticism, he had no clear explanation or justification of the possibility of criticism itself.[1]

If criticism and critical philosophy as Kant undertook them could not be justified, then both dogmatism and skepticism again threaten us. Kant insists, in Beiser's formulation, that "nothing [is] sacred before the criticism of reason, not even the state in its majesty or religion in its holiness. Nothing, that is, except of course the tribunal of critique itself, which was somehow sacred, holy, and sublime."[2] But why? Is the holiness of reason itself anything more than either a piece of dogma or a disguised injunction to continuing critical skepticism and nihilism?

From one natural point of view, the demand for a critique of critique, raised by Kant's successors, seems impossibly metaphysical and foundational in spirit. How, without circularity, could critical reasoning establish the authority of critical reasoning? Instead of making the vain demand that it do so, why

1. Frederick C. Beiser, *The Fate of Reason: German Philosophy from Kant to Fichte* (Cambridge: Harvard University Press, 1987), p. 7.
2. Ibid., p. 6.

not instead just get on with the business of critical reasoning, letting its powers show themselves in the course of the activity so that readers are simply drawn into it? Why not give up the metacritical demand to find something that *makes* us reason critically, and makes us justly suspicious of dogmatic authorities? Why not think instead that this is just the way we are, perhaps as a result of a natural biology or psychology? Such a stance seems to be the right way to move into holistic, "internal" criticism, beyond metaphysical foundationalism. As J. S. Beck remarks in a letter to Kant, scorning Fichte's metaphysical system as "a stupid idea! Anyone who talks like that must never have mastered the critical principles," the right thing to do seems to be not to hunt for a metaphysical foundation for critical reasoning, but instead simply to "get to feel at home with the whole system; then it is easy to show anyone who has interest and a bit of talent how to arrive at the true critical principles."[3] To a considerable extent, and for some good reasons, the spirit of this reply dominates Anglo-American philosophy today, after Quine and Davidson. Epistemology and metaphysics cannot be first philosophy; there is no metaphysics that is either sounder than the categorical schemes of the natural sciences or immune from revision. At best, epistemology and metaphysics can be immanent reflection on categories-as-they-are-developing within the sciences, handmaidens of the sciences, not their queen.

Kant himself famously endorses this antimetaphysical, antifoundationalist, critical holist line in his "Open Letter on Fichte's *Wissenschaftslehre*."

> I hereby declare that I regard Fichte's *Theory of Science* as a totally indefensible system. For the pure theory of science is nothing more or less than mere logic, and the principles of logic cannot lead to any material knowledge. Since logic, that is to say, *pure logic*, abstracts from the content of knowledge, the attempt to cull a real object out of logic is a vain effort and therefore a thing that no one has ever done. If the transcendental philosophy is correct, such a task would involve metaphysics rather than logic. But I am so opposed to metaphysics, as defined according to Fichtean principles, that I have advised him, in a letter, to turn his fine literary gifts to the problem of applying the *Critique of Pure Reason,* rather than squander them in cultivating fruitless sophistries.[4]

3. J. S. Beck, "Letter to Kant, June 24, 1797," in *Philosophical Correspondence, 1795–99*, ed. and trans. Arnulf Zweig (Chicago: University of Chicago Press, 1967), pp. 234, 233.

4. Kant, "Open Letter on Fichte's *Wissenschaftslehre*, August 7, 1799," in *Philosophical Correspondence,* ed. and trans. Zweig, p. 253.

That is to say, we must simply begin with transcendental logic, with the investigation of the logically necessary presuppositions of conceptual consciousness, *without* having any warrant for this investigation given to us by any metaphysical substance, spiritual or natural. We must begin in *media res,* in our conceptual consciousness and schemes and practices as we happen to have them, and then just keep going, critically. The best, indeed the only, assurance that our critical investigations thus begun are in order is their *completeness,* their addressing and answering any questions about cognitive or moral or political or religious principles that our curiosity may happen to raise. "I took," Kant writes, "the completeness of pure philosophy within the *Critique of Pure Reason* to be the best indication of the truth of my work."[5] Though it possesses no warrant from without, Critical Philosophy may at least promise, in its examination of cognitive, moral, political, and religious principles, "such completion as will leave no task to our successors save that of adapting it in a *didactic* manner according to their own preferences, without their being able to add anything whatever to its content" (Axx). That warrant from within is all that the Critical Philosophy needs; any appeal to a metaphysical scheme to warrant its critical reasoning would undermine it.

This antifoundationalist reply to the demand for a metaphysical critique of critique is both modest and extraordinarily appealing. It is even more appealing when it is softened a bit by being combined with a decent respect for the open-ended ways of natural science—when, that is, the claim to completeness is dropped in favor of a simple resoluteness to continue to examine and reflect upon achievements in various regions of practice and upon their principles. Who would now claim, against this appealing modesty, pure and privileged rational or intellectual awareness of a metaphysical substance that commands and controls our critical reflections? Philosophy, at best, seems to be continuous, open-ended, critical activity, without any final or grounding commitment to any metaphysical scheme or system.

Yet there is a difficulty with this line of thought. If we are to begin doing criticism in *media res,* in the middle of our practices and forms of consciousness as we have them, then exactly where is that? One natural way of beginning is to take seriously our cognitive achievements in the practices of the natural sciences as we have them. Insofar as one assumes a form of Kantian, critical antifoundationalism and then begins critical activity from and within the natu-

5. Ibid., p. 254.

ral sciences, one will be tempted toward a strongly naturalistic point of view. It will be natural to concede that there must be a power or spontaneity within us in order for there to be conceptual consciousness and apperceptively unified self-consciousness as we take ourselves to have them. But then it will be natural further to take this power or spontaneity to be a matter of the occurrence of natural processes—chemical or neurological—within us, natural processes thence to be investigated not through transcendental deduction, but instead through biochemistry or neurology or artificial intelligence theory. Why, after all, should we assume that we have some privileged standpoint, more advantaged than the standpoint of the natural sciences, for saying what is going on within us? If there is a spontaneity in us, then why not instead take it to be a natural something to be investigated, open-endedly? Some naturalist model of mind—cognitivist or connectionist or immediately biochemical, as may be—will press upon us as offering the most plausible, critically revisable account of the nature of that spontaneity. Epistemology becomes transmuted into the philosophy of the natural sciences; the philosophy of mind becomes cognitive science or some other form of a revisable naturalist theory of mind.

The trouble with this naturalist line of reasoning is that we therein abandon our sense of ourselves as free subjectivities, seeking to make meaning and evince free personality in action in culture. The very notion of free personality to be evinced or expressed becomes suspect. While from a scientific point of view, this may not seem to be much of a loss, it seems also to betray a sense of ourselves as free, meaning-making agents that we both inherit from modernity and live out in our day-to-day nonscientific practices—and in our scientific practices, considered as congeries of projects we undertake, assess, and revise. Naturalist philosophy of mind does not immediately sit easily with our legal, moral, artistic, and scientific practices. It is forced to offer a number of promissory notes about how we will, sooner or later, understand scientifically the spontaneity that is in us, and in so doing also to undermine equally natural and immediate senses of ourselves as critically reasoning agents that figure throughout our lives.

If we now conclude that the task of the critical philosophy of mind is simply to balance these two perspectives on our spontaneity—the naturalist and the voluntarist-ethical—against one another, so as to show how we can be both wholly natural beings and free, then we find that this is not a conclusion easily persisted in. The demand to know how we are free does not lapse. Talk of two standpoints on action—natural and legal-moral—evades rather than meets this demand to know how we are what we are. As a result, the plausibility of a wholly naturalist analysis of our power or spontaneity reasserts itself. Antinaturalist views of human powers then seem somewhat vague and tendentious, and they present themselves as alternatives or challenges to a naturalist standpoint, not as readily and intelligibly compatible with it. We tend to waver between a sense of ourselves as wholly natural beings to be understood through the natural sciences and a vaguer but equally powerful sense of ourselves as free subjectivities. Promissory notes about scientific progress are played off *against* reminders of our practices of ascribing responsibility, and we seem not quite to be critically at home with ourselves.

To insist now in this critical situation, as Kant does, that, yes, nature is a course of determined causal processes of interaction among substances, but also, yes, we are free and morally responsible (because there are two standpoints on action, phenomenal and noumenal) seems to evade the demand to know *how* we are what we are—how there is some spontaneity within us and how it can be expressed and expressed well in various practices. To say, with Kant, that there is no problem, that the field of human life has been completely surveyed critically and that human action simply has both these aspects—natural and free—seems more a piece of insistence, a dogmatism of completeness, than a full response to our uncertainties and anxieties about the nature of our powers and how to express them. It seems to betray the initial imperative to submit everything to criticism. The claim to completeness of the Critical Philosophy seems a bit of a cheat.

Kantian antidogmatism begins by pointing us toward a sense of ourselves both as free and rational inquirers and agents—criticizers capable of following out the arguments of the Critical Philosophy from the inside—and as beings bound up in a causally determined course of nature. But it then fails to show us how quite to live out these two senses with or against one another. And now to say, "but these senses have been critically surveyed and upheld," seems not to say very much. Kant seems to revert to dogmatism and to leave us disappointed. The claim to completeness of the Critical Philosophy seems to be hollow or to miss the point. Friedrich Schlegel sharply expresses this sense of disappointment in the Critical Philosophy, a sense of it as, in the end, a house of words. "In vain do the orthodox Kantians seek the principle of their philosophy in Kant. It's to be found in Bürger's poems, and reads: 'The words of the Emperor shouldn't be twisted and turned.' "[6]

6. Friedrich Schlegel, "Athenaeum Fragments," in *Friedrich Schlegel's "Lucinde" and the Fragments,* trans. Peter Firchow (Minneapolis: University of Minnesota Press, 1971), Fragment 298, p. 204.

There seem then to be three options for an account of our powers: orthodox Kantianism (taking up and repeating Kant's insistence on completeness), consistent naturalism (putting off or issuing promissory notes about our sense of ourselves as free subjectivities), or insistence on the autonomy from explanation of our practices as agents (ignoring the achievements of naturalism and its project of explaining our spontaneity). None of them seems terribly appealing. As Schlegel goes on to observe, after criticizing orthodox Kantianism, "I rather doubt if the philosophers are very far behind the poets in their sublime lack of awareness."[7] Each strategy seems to embody a forgetfulness of one or another side of the sense of ourselves as rational powers in nature that inaugurated the Critical Philosophy.

✳

But is there then any strategy of pursuing an understanding of our powers and possibilities that does not involve one or another form of forgetfulness of our multiple senses of ourselves? How might we seek to understand ourselves as at once natural beings and also beings possessed of rational powers to articulate and act on ideals of freedom? How might we do this without simply falling into the equivocations and anxieties of expression that are involved in simply stipulating that there are two incommensurable ways of looking at human action? These are the questions that Fichte takes up in putting forward a demand for a critique of critique. In pursuing this demand, Fichte falls, almost inadvertently, into new modes of writerly self-interrogation, as his thought continually turns back to question its own grounds of development, refusing to settle in any fixed thematics or doctrine of freedom. These swerves are then taken up and themselves thematized by subsequent writers on expressive freedom.

A critique of critique, as Fichte conceives of it, must satisfy two conditions. First, it must furnish a new principle of conceptual consciousness. It must explain how it is that we are conceptually conscious of objects—how objects are, as Fichte puts it, presented to us in an orderly way. "The system of presentations accompanied by the feeling of necessity is also called *experience,* both internal and external. Philosophy . . . must therefore furnish the ground of all experience."[8] The requirement here is that philosophy shall begin from a

7. Ibid., Fragment 299, p. 204.
8. J. G. Fichte, *The Science of Knowledge,* trans. Peter Heath and John Lachs (Cambridge: Cambridge University Press, 1982), First Introduction, p. 6.

new first principle, replacing the problematic Kantian principle of a mysteriously spontaneous unity of apperception. The apperceptive unity that Kant describes is instead to be derived from this more fundamental—more inescapable, more self-evident—principle of consciousness.[9] This principle shall be, like the Kantian principle of the unity of apperception, descriptive of what is immanently present in conceptual consciousness of objects as we have it, but—Fichte hopes—without the obscurities of talk of a mysterious spontaneity that is always presupposed but never present to us. Second, this principle shall account for the reality of freedom. That is, we appear to ourselves to be free in at least two senses. Sometimes we apparently bring certain images and ideas into our consciousness spontaneously and voluntarily; "some of them appear to us as completely dependent on our freedom."[10] And, more important, we appear to ourselves, or in our practices we think of ourselves, as having a positive capacity for rational, moral culture, for aiming at a culture of expressive freedom in conformity with moral principle. Philosophy must show not only how we are conceptually conscious but also how we are in fact free, in both these two senses, within a rational system of nature. In carrying out these tasks, Fichte's system will unify Kantian theoretical and practical philosophy, overcoming the *aporiae* and dogmatisms attaching to Kant's insistence on the two standpoints. Fichte sums up his ambitions for philosophy in a strange and marvelous passage in his 1794 essay "Concerning Human Dignity" as he modulates smoothly from an account of human beings as conceptually conscious observers to an account of human beings as capable of moral culture.

> *Regularity* comes from man alone, surrounding him and extending as far as he can see, and as he expands the sphere of his observations, order and harmony are further extended as well. His observation assigns to each of the infinitely many and varied things its proper place, so that none may displace any other. It brings unity into infinite diversity. Human observation holds together the planets, which, thanks to it, constitute just *one* organized body. Thanks to it, the suns move in their allotted paths. From the lichen to the seraphim, this immense hierarchy owes its existence to the I. The system of

9. Daniel Breazale, "Fichte's *Aenesidemus* Review and the Transformation of German Idealism," *Review of Metaphysics* 34 (1981): 545–68, usefully describes the emergence of Fichte's project out of reflections on Kant's, by way of Schulze and Reinhold, particularly the latter's efforts, unsatisfactory to Fichte, to develop a new "principle of consciousness."

10. Fichte, *The Science of Knowledge,* First Introduction, p. 6.

the entire spiritual world lies in *it*, and man justifiably expects that the law
he gives to himself and to this world must hold for this world. The I contains
the sure guarantee that order and harmony will spread outward from it into
infinity, where there is neither order nor harmony, the guarantee that the
culture of the universe will advance with the culture of man. Through man,
all that is still unformed and unordered will dissolve into the most beautiful
order, and what is already harmonious will become still more harmonious,
in accordance with still undeveloped laws. Into turmoil, man will bring order,
and into universal devastation, design. Thanks to him, decay will create and
death will summon to a new and splendid life.[11]

No doubt the thought here is, to contemporary ears, grandiose. Fichte shifts,
apparently without awareness, from an account of what must be *presupposed*
in order for there to be conceptual consciousness as we have it—a certain
regularity or ordering of conscious experience, as Kant argued—to an account
of that regularity as causally *produced* by consciousness and then further to
an account of consciousness as spreading this regularity throughout the natural
and cultural worlds. The final lines about order—and design out of devastation, life out of death—are chilling. It is an astonishing vision of the powers
that make for self-conscious, conceptual experience of objects, an incredible
metaphysical idealism of those powers ultimately and productively informing
the development of everything that is.

Despite its grandiosity, however, this vision, as Fichte develops it, has two
features that may hold our interest and that point to the emergence of new
modalities of self-conscious, critical philosophical writing beyond doctrinal
thesis-mongering. This vision promises, again, to unify theoretical and practical philosophy, to restore to us a sense of how we can be both observing beings
of and within a world that has a knowable order ("man justifiably expects that
the law he gives to himself and to this world must hold for this world") and
also active moral agents within culture ("the culture of man . . . will advance").
It promises to overcome—through an account of the powers of our self-
consciousness coming to effect in culture—the antinomies and associated anxieties attaching to Kant's talk of the two standpoints. More important, we are
to arrive at this vision—to take it up and further its truth—from a Copernican
standpoint, without dogmatism, from within consciousness as we have it. "At-

---

11. Fichte, "Concerning Human Dignity," trans. Daniel Breazale, in *Early Philosophical Writings,* ed. Breazale (Ithaca: Cornell University Press, 1988), pp. 83–84.

tend to yourself: turn your attention away from everything that surrounds you and toward your inner life; this is the first demand that philosophy makes of its disciple. Our concern is not with anything that lies outside you, but only with yourself."[12] We are to begin from where we are, critically, without dogmatism, but yet we are to get further than Kant in the direction of upholding both our cognitive and moral powers.

These two features—the promise to unify our senses of ourselves as both natural and free beings; the Copernican starting point from within consciousness and its structures—then lead to astonishing waverings on Fichte's part between confident announcements of the powers of free ego activity to shape the world and anxious worrying about how ever to get started in explaining experience at all, without dogmatism. Our progress in and through culture is to rest on powers of free activity that are effective in structuring consciousness itself, yet we are confined in thinking about our powers and possibilities initially within consciousness. How, then, shall we get started? How shall the powers of free activity that are hidden within consciousness be uncovered and unleashed?

Two strategies naturally suggest themselves. One might seek to establish our possibilities of developing a moral culture of freedom by first examining the powers that are latent within our conceptual consciousness of objects. Or, conversely, one might try to uncover and articulate the powers within conceptual consciousness by first making progress in the development of a moral culture, wherein these powers might show themselves more clearly. Yet neither strategy has a secure ground. The powers to be uncovered within consciousness are not clearly effective and present in any intuition of them; progress in moral culture is not so readily apparent. As a result of these difficulties, Fichte persistently wavers between these two strategies. He writes introduction after introduction, essay after essay, in an effort to explain his system, establish its starting point clearly, and quell his own anxiety about its intelligibility and receivability. It is this wavering that is Fichte's peculiar writerliness, a writerliness that is far more interesting and absorbing, in its swervings through self-criticism, than the lineaments of the philosophical system that he seeks ever anew to outline and justify.

Thus, in numerous passages Fichte claims to find a starting point for his system of freedom in a transparent fact of consciousness. Awareness of one's

12. Fichte, *The Science of Knowledge,* First Introduction, p. 6.

freedom is, he suggests, built into what we do or are able to do as beings who are conceptually conscious of objects. I sometimes think freely and actively, he claims, so that I am forced through awareness of this free activity in me to accept the ultimate existence of free activity, realizing itself in the world.

> I can freely determine myself to think this or that . . . . If I now abstract from what is thought and observe only myself, I become to myself in this object the content of a specific presentation. . . . [In doing this] I am compelled to presuppose myself as that which is to be determined by self-determination [rather than as something determined through material processes]. . . . Thus the object of idealism [the free activity of self-determination; the "self-in-itself"] has this advantage over the object of dogmatism [the material "thing-in-itself"], that it may be demonstrated . . . in consciousness; whereas the latter object cannot be looked upon as anything other than a pure invention, which expects its conversion into reality only from the success of the system.[13]

There is a claim here that free activity is present in the structure of ordinary conceptual consciousness and that we can further become aware of this free activity by turning our consciousness on it, abstracting from any particular object of thought. "For not only the necessity of presentations, but also their freedom is present in consciousness."[14] A system that will describe our emerging possibilities of the free development of a moral culture can get started by simply noting these facts of conscious activity.

But in other passages, often within a page or two of the announcement of a starting point in consciousness, Fichte's confidence falters. He worries that consciousness of free activity within oneself may itself be an illusion. There is no direct and certain intuition of a substance here, only a problematic awareness of free activity within. What makes this awareness reliable? Why can't material science show it to be a causally determined phenomenon? There seems then to be no rational ground, no justification, for preferring an idealist system of freedom to a dogmatist system.

> [In the dispute between the idealist and the materialist dogmatist] Reason provides no principle of choice; for we deal here not with the addition of a link in the chain of reasoning, which is all that rational grounds extend to, but with the beginning of the whole chain, which, as an absolutely primary

13. Ibid., pp. 10, 11.
14. Ibid., p. 28.

act, depends solely upon the freedom of thought. Hence the choice is governed by caprice, and since even a capricious decision must have some source, it is governed by *inclination* and *interest.* The ultimate basis of the difference between idealists and dogmatists is thus the difference of their interests.[15]

That is to say, if we accept the fact that we do reason, do recognize logically valid inferences, freely and rationally, then we can always find reasons in the principles of logic for accepting or rejecting a new inference. But if we do not to begin with accept that we reason freely and rationally, then reason is impotent to show that we do. It might be that all our free reasonings, and all our free imaginings and idealizings and self-projections too, are nothing more at bottom than ineffective and illusory epiphenomena of material processes. Hence, "neither of these two systems [idealism and materialist dogmatism] can directly refute its opposite, for their quarrel is about the first principle, which admits of no derivation from anything beyond it; each of the two, if only its first principle is granted, refutes that of the other; each denies everything in its opposite, and they have no point at all in common from which they could arrive at mutual understanding and unity." Once we realize this—that "idealism is, therefore, unproved and unprovable"—then the only thing to be said in favor of idealism is that it is the system preferred by someone who sustains a higher, finer, better way of life, more bound up with the project of forming a moral culture of free self-determination. "What sort of philosophy one chooses depends, therefore, on what sort of man one is; for a philosophical system is not a dead piece of furniture that we can reject or accept as we wish; it is rather animated by the soul of the person who holds it. A person indolent by nature or dulled and distorted by mental servitude, learned luxury, and vanity will never raise himself to the level of idealism."[16]

But what sort of being one is—a locus of only material processes or a being capable of free activity and self-determination in culture—was precisely what was initially to be proved through an examination of the structures and powers of conceptual consciousness. Whether we are in fact capable of free activity was precisely the point at issue. To say now that those who are capable of free activity will prefer a system of free activity is to beg the question: What can we freely do? Thus Fichte reverts to the first argumentative strategy, the

15. Ibid., pp. 14–15.
16. Ibid., pp. 12, 17, 24, 18, 16.

attempt to display the existence of genuinely free activity within conceptual
consciousness. But this effort again founders. Dogmatism might be true; nothing proves it false, so the only thing that supports idealism is that it is preferred
by better, more self-determining, freer people. But then, again, how are we to
know what it is to be better, freer, or more self-determining? Of what are we
capable?

    Embodied in this desperate wavering on Fichte's part between two ways
of getting started in thinking about human thought and life is an overwhelming
anxiety about how we are to know our consciousness and our capabilities at all.
What goes on in conceptual consciousness? What possibilities of development
within and of culture are laid down there? How are inclinations and interests
formed? The way of addressing these questions that finally emerges in Fichte's
writing, holding together, fitfully, the moments of direct argumentation from
consciousness with the moments of appeals to character, is poetic narrative.
Fichte puts forward a story about how universal (he hopes) capabilities of
development evince themselves in and through his particular consciousness.
This story is a narrative, in that this evincing comes in stages. It is poetic, in
that it points to the presence of the universal in the particular. And it is writerly, displacing direct philosophical argumentation and the textual form of the
treatise, in that it is inconclusive, circular, and self-devouring.

    There is in Fichte's writing a continuing cycle of assertions of metaphysical
accomplishment, followed by doubt, followed by survival, followed again by
assertion, a continual cycle of what M. H. Abrams calls procession, or fall, and
epistrophe, or return.[17] Romantic texts often employ the Neoplatonic figure
of the circle as a figuration of evil and its overcoming in historical time through
procession and epistrophe. "The self-moving circle," Abrams comments,
"fuses the idea of the circular return with the idea of linear progress, to describe
a distinctive figure of Romantic thought and imagination."[18] In Fichte, and in
the most writerly of the romantics, the motif of circular return is always com-
peting with the motif of linear progress, and this competition is never quite
resolved. There is a continual return to narration of a course of development
that enables direct philosophical understanding and argumentation, a continual return required by persisting doubt, as the philosophical understanding

    17. M. H. Abrams, "The Great Circle: Pagan and Christian Neoplatonism," in *Natural Super-
naturalism* (New York: W. W. Norton, 1971), pp. 146–54, describes the romantic use of the
Neoplatonic figure of the circle as a figuration of evil and its overcoming, through procession
and epistrophe, now occurring in historical time, and often repeatedly, inconclusively.
    18. Ibid., p. 184.

and argumentation never quite become self-certifying. A brighter, transcendental self, capable of free philosophical thought and full self-command, is presented as emerging out of a darker, empirical self and its troubling historical contingencies. This emergence is never quite complete, for a moral culture of freedom, embodying and certifying this understanding, never quite emerges. Thus the narrative of emergence is repeated, both in the hope that it will be taken up and in an effort to confront and still the doubt and anxiety that persist in the writer, as a result of the failure of a culture of philosophical understanding and moral freedom to emerge.[19]

In Fichte, then, we see the following pattern:[20]

1. A claim to incarnate an exemplary, free, and rational character, possessed of philosophical understanding. This philosophical persona presents itself as at home, or almost at home, in nature and culture and in possession of a standpoint, either through intuition or inclination, for thinking about and pursuing freedom in culture. This persona assumes rational authority for itself over the development of culture, and it takes its task to be that of introducing to the public the system of freedom it has discovered that may guide culture. The development of this persona is taken to be proleptic for the development of those who are to follow it. Having achieved this understanding, the remaining tasks for it are the apparently simple ones of introduction and exposition.

2. The emergence of metaphysical doubt and anxiety. The philosophical system that the persona is to present is not certified by any self-certain intuition or argument. That materialism is false cannot be proved. Yet, more pressingly, the public fails to take up the system and to conduct its cultural life in its terms; the system is received as ill formed or unintelligible or baseless. Skepticism about our powers of free activity forces itself on the philosophical persona; the claims of materialism stand undismissed.

3. The confrontation of metaphysical doubt and anxiety through an effort to write a new introduction to the system, or to articulate the system more clearly, in a way that will make it receivable by a public.

19. For an account of this continual competition—between direct philosophical argumentation and narrative and the continual return to narrative to confront anxiety and certify the possibility of progress—in Wordsworth's *Prelude*, see my "Internal Transcendalism."

20. This structure of the narration of the achievement of philosophical understanding, followed by doubt, followed by survival, followed by a renewed claim to understanding that is again subjected to doubt, and so on, is especially explicit in the intermediate, dialogical section of *The Vocation of Man*.

4. The philosophical persona survives and reestablishes itself through the act of confronting metaphysical doubt and anxiety and through the act of writing. (Wordsworth: "For now a trouble came into my mind / From unknown causes. I was left alone / Seeking the visible world, nor knowing why. / The props of my affections were removed, / And yet the building stood, as if sustained / By its own spirit!")[21] A certain sense of oneself as capable of writing, of onwardness, of understanding, emerges in and through the writing that confronts the fall into doubt.

5. Through reflection, these possibilities of survival and power are generalized until a philosophical standpoint on our possibilities of freedom in culture is achieved.

6. Return to the first stage and begin again.

In this movement, present in Fichte and in other post-Kantian writers about freedom in and through culture, we see what Lacoue-Labarthe and Nancy describe as the sublation—the preserving and/through canceling—of philosophy into *poesis*. It is the continuing effort to grasp and figure oneself as a possessor of rational power and possibilities of freedom that is fundamental. It is this writerly, poetic effort, more than its results in a system, that is the movement of thought and that presents us to ourselves as thinking, conceptually conscious and self-conscious beings. From now on, Lacoue-Labarthe and Nancy explain, "programmatically, the philosophical *organon* is thought as the product or *effect* of a *poiesis*, as work (*Werk*) or as poetical *opus* . . . . Philosophy must effectuate itself—complete, fulfill, and realize itself—as poetry."[22] The way toward philosophical authority and toward freedom in culture, indeed the very life of philosophical thinking, must be through a continuing poetic effort to grasp and incarnate the emergence of free, rational authority, of power, in the development of a concretely situated persona. In this movement into *poesis*, philosophical thinking has recognized itself as a situated, endlessly complex and interesting human activity, rather than as an act of recognition of some external intellectual or spiritual realm or agency that might govern us. As Abrams puts it, within this movement of *poesis* "the course of human life . . . is no longer a *Heilsgeschichte* but a *Bildungsgeschichte;* or more precisely, it is a *Heilsgeschichte* translated into the secular mode of a *Bildungsgeschichte*."[23]

21. William Wordsworth, *The Prelude Or, Growth of a Poet's Mind: An Autobiographical Poem,* in Wordsworth, *Selected Poems and Prefaces,* ed. Jack Stillinger (Boston: Houghton Mifflin Company, 1965), Book II, ll. 276–81, p. 213.

22. Lacoue-Labarthe and Nancy, *The Literary Absolute,* p. 36.

23. Abrams, *Natural Supernaturalism,* p. 188.

The central issue responded to in the movement of *poesis* is how, if at all, we might grasp, articulate, and realize the powers of expressive freedom within us that we seem dimly to sense. How can philosophical thinking even begin? In what vehicles can it sustain itself?

✳

Responsiveness to these questions, issuing in a movement toward *poesis* as the site and inconclusive vehicle of philosophical thinking about our powers, is the central thematic thread of post-Kantian German romanticism. This thematic thread is especially prominent in the theoretical writings of Schiller, where it is literalized in being coupled with explicit meditation on the powers of various textual forms to embody human thinking. As Schiller sees human life, "all [people caught up in the process of civilization], without exception, must fall away from Nature by the abuse of Reason before they can return to her by the use of Reason."[24] There is a kind of procession or fall that is built into the development of increasing powers of comparative, instrumental reason and dawning self-conscious awareness of those powers, as Kant had already noted in his own historical writings.

For Schiller, the fall away from naturalness, simplicity, and quasi animality and into Reason and self-consciousness further involves a variety of complex social developments that are interwoven with this fall as both its causes and its effects. Once upon a time, Schiller supposes, labor was predominantly handicraft and agricultural labor; in "the early republics" people lived under "the simplicity of early manners and conditions" wherein an individual could still "when need arose, grow into the whole organism."[25] Now there has instead arisen, Schiller notes, in a passage that deeply anticipates and is directly influential upon Marx and Nietzsche,

> an ingenious clock-work, in which, out of the piecing together of innumerable but lifeless parts, a mechanical kind of collective life ensued. State and Church, laws and customs, were now torn asunder; enjoyment was divorced from labor, the means from the end, the effort from the reward. Everlastingly chained to a single little fragment of the Whole, man develops himself into nothing but a fragment; everlastingly in his ear the monotonous sound of the wheel that he turns, he never develops the harmony of his being, and

24. Friedrich Schiller, *On the Aesthetic Education of Man in a Series of Letters*, trans. Elizabeth M. Wilkinson and L. A. Willoughby, in *The Origins of Modern Critical Thought*, ed. David Simpson (Cambridge: Cambridge University Press, 1988), Sixth Letter, p. 129.
25. Ibid., p. 131.

instead of putting the stamp of humanity upon his own nature, he becomes nothing more than the imprint of his occupation or of his specialized knowledge. . . . The dead letter takes the place of living understanding, and a good memory is a safer guide than imagination and feeling.[26]

Human activity here becomes opaque to itself. Antagonisms abound. Social life becomes deritualized and atomistic, as no one can any longer readily recognize expressive power and intelligibility in what anyone does. The arts become aestheticized. Poetizing is marked off from the investigation of nature through experimentation, measurement, and theorization, to the impoverishment of each.

> The intuitive and the speculative understanding now withdrew in hostility to take up positions in their respective fields, whose frontiers they now began to guard with jealous mistrust; and with this confining of our activity to a particular sphere we have given ourselves a master within, who not infrequently ends by suppressing the rest of our potentialities. While in the one a riotous imagination ravages the hard-won fruits of the intellect, in another the spirit of abstraction stifles the fire at which the heart should have warmed itself and the imagination been kindled.[27]

Philosophy and the arts become distinguished from engineering and economics, the former amounting to nothing but "empty subtilties," the latter to "narrow pedantry." Nowhere are human beings present to themselves, or to one another, as bearers of powers of expressive freedom, capable of creating and sustaining an intelligible moral culture. Instead, one-sidedness in human activity everywhere predominates, as human beings, within classes and coteries, develop skills and pursue the satisfaction of desires that they just happen to have, without anywhere becoming expressively free, to themselves or to one another. "One-sidedness in the exercise of [our] powers" is our present lot.[28]

Yet, according to Schiller, not all is lost. The "antagonism of faculties and functions is the great instrument of civilization"; this antagonism has served to develop our skills and powers. Now, once these skills and powers have been developed, "it must," Schiller writes, "be possible to restore by means of a higher Art the totality of our nature which the arts themselves have destroyed." Whether this is the expression of a confidently sensed possibility or a desperate

26. Ibid.
27. Ibid., p. 130.
28. Ibid., pp. 132, 133.

wish on Schiller's part is unclear. That restoration blended with elevation *must* be possible seems to be a remark made more out of anxiety at a lack of reception and recognition that one knows oneself somewhere to face than out of simple confidence. It is difficult to know how even to get started, given the pervasiveness of the dilemma of revolutionary politics that Schiller notes: Which is to be changed first, human character or sociopolitical institutions? Change in human character and change in sociopolitical institutions presuppose one another, with no evident way to break into this circle of presuppositions. One will fail in trying directly to educate and elevate the human beings who are formed under sociopolitical institutions, and one will fail in trying directly to change the sociopolitical institutions that express human character. "All improvement in the political sphere is to proceed from the ennobling of character—but how under the influence of a barbarous constitution is character ever to become ennobled?"[29]

No matter whether one hears predominantly hope or anxiety in Schiller's claim that restoration blended with elevation must be possible, it is clear that the vehicle for the achievement of expressive freedom is for Schiller art, *poesis*. It is art that will solve the dilemma of revolutionary politics. Art is the "instrument not corrupted by the State," itself able "to open up the living springs which, whatever the political corruption, would remain clear and pure."[30] It is art that will bring about the information of *Willkür* by *Wille* and lead us to uncover and exercise the rational, expressive power within us. Artistic production is the paradigm of free, self-determining, intelligible activity.

> Art, like Science, is absolved from all positive constraints and from all conventions introduced by man; both rejoice in absolute *immunity* from human arbitrariness. The political legislator may put their territory out of bounds; he cannot rule within it. He can proscribe the lover of truth; Truth itself will prevail. He can humiliate the artist, but Art he cannot falsify.
>
> . . . Humanity has lost its dignity, but Art has rescued it and preserved it in significant stone. Truth lives on in the illusion of Art, and it is from this copy, or after-image, that the original image will once again be restored.[31]

In a kind of unending quest-romance of reason coming to be embodied in artistic activity, self-conscious self-identity may at last be achieved. "The Direc-

29. Ibid., pp. 133, 134; Ninth Letter, p. 134.
30. Ibid., pp. 134–35.
31. Ibid., p. 135.

tion is at once the Destination, and the Way is completed from the moment it is trodden."[32] On this way, we will know who we are, become legible to ourselves and to one another as bearers of an expressive power to form and sustain a moral culture.

Despite these ringing pronouncements about the powers of art—or even legible within these pronouncements themselves, which seem to claim too much, as though to mask an underlying anxiety—Schiller's sketch of art as the instrument of the formation of a higher human culture has little immediate promise of coming true. That sketch is troubled with a number of significant difficulties.

Schiller's claims about art indulge an extreme aesthetic subjectivism and escapism. Pleasurable feeling remains both the only criterion for art and its principal aim and social product. "Beauty alone makes the whole world happy, and each and every being forgets its limitations while under its spell. . . . [T]he aesthetic alone leads to the absence of all limitation."[33] Aesthetic feeling is never specified either phenomenologically or functionally, in such a way that particular works could be identified as provokers of its peculiarities as a feeling. While absorption in art's formal organization of expressive powers may be a genuine and important phenomenon in human life, it is also unlikely by itself to make very many human beings forget the limitations of poverty or lack of respect or lack of democratic equality for very long. However important art may be socially and politically as inspiration, emblem, and route of social practice, failures of social effect are even more likely when the aesthetic feeling that art produces is left underspecified and its place in the economies of human psychological and social life is left untraced. In refusing to elaborate art's powers for social life in anything other than the vaguest terms (art "leads to the absence of all limitations"), Schiller's claims about the powers of art amount to little more than an idle, apolitical, aesthetic utopianism.

This impression is reinforced by Schiller's implicit acknowledgment of his failure to confront the dilemma of revolutionary politics, his failure to show how art can in fact break through the mutual information of corrupt human character and corrupt political constitution. "I shall," he writes in the first paragraph of the First Letter, "be pleading the cause of Beauty before a heart

---

32. Ibid., p. 136.
33. Ibid., Twenty-Seventh Letter, p. 147; Twenty-Second Letter, p. 142.

that perceives and exercises her whole power, and, in an enquiry where one is compelled to appeal as often to feelings as to principles, [that] will take upon itself the heaviest part of my labour."[34] But this effort to write from and to a heart with a feeling for art presupposes that this feeling is already in place in the human character. It presupposes that the corruption of human character under a barbarous political constitution has already been sufficiently undone that this feeling shall express itself and inform human life. Yet it was precisely this task that was to be undertaken by art.

Schiller's lack of specificity about art's powers and his uncritical reliance on the human heart also lead him into inconsistent treatments of human freedom and of art's relation to morality. Sometimes freedom is depicted as the absence of constraint, as limitlessness in the ecstatic artistic expression of one's powers—"the aesthetic alone leads to the absence of all limitation." Sometimes, in contrast, freedom is depicted as Kantian autonomy, as conformity to a moral law that is self-legislated out of practical reason, and art is depicted as raising us up to this condition of conformity to moral self-legislation. "Reason is to be a power, and a logical or moral necessity to take the place of that physical necessity."[35] Hence, torn between these two conceptions of freedom, Schiller alternates between moral didacticism and pure aestheticism. Sometimes he describes human development as involving a series of stages in which domination of human action by a sensuous animal drive (ein sinnlicher Stofftrieb) will be succeeded by domination by abstract intellect and a drive for form and law (ein Formtrieb), which in turn will be succeeded by action within a moral culture, dominated by a fulfilled drive for form and law (ein erfüllter Formtrieb). Within this course of development, it is unclear whether artistic activity is to be the means of raising us from the second to the third level or is rather itself the end. Sometimes the aesthetic is presented as a "middle disposition" between the physical and the moral, raising us from the first to the second. Sometimes, in contrast, artistic activity seems to be an end in itself, as Schiller seems to advocate an ecstatic, aestheticist Kunstmoralität. "In the midst of the fearful kingdom of forces, and in the midst of the sacred kingdom of laws, the aesthetic impulse to form is at work, unnoticed, on the build-

---

34. Schiller, On the Aesthetic Education of Man in a Series of Letters, trans. Reginald Snell (New York: Frederick Ungar, 1965), p. 23.

35. Schiller, On the Aesthetic Education of Man, trans. Wilkinson and Willoughby, Twentieth Letter, p. 141.

ing of a third joyous kingdom of play and of semblance, in which man is relieved of the shackles of circumstance, and released from all that might be called constraint, alike in the physical and in the moral sphere."[36]

Schiller's subjectivist, aesthetic escapism and his inconsistencies in describing the powers of art have a number of causes. Perhaps he might have thought more deeply, and more politically, about the powers of art. Perhaps, as Hegel charged, Schiller's aesthetics, like Kant's, ought to have focused more on the objective life of forms in art—a life bound up with the evolution of sociopolitical institutions. Perhaps, as Hölderlin charged, Schiller's account of aesthetic activity errs by being too individualist-activist in emphasizing play within the individual rather than receptivity and a measure of passivity. Emphasizing the importance in the artist of unlimited activity too easily encourages the artist's further alienation from both nature and social life.

Yet it is not entirely clear that these other programs for thinking about art's powers will work either. Psychological and social life may simply be more resistant to revolutionary transformation through artistic activity than any of these programs supposes. It may be that no optimistic plan for developing our present powers can readily bring about the information of *Willkür* by *Wille,* that no such plan can readily overcome deep and long-standing social antagonisms of talent and interest. Self-conscious subjectivity's place in the modern world is not so readily perfected or cured.

Hence Schiller's very difficulties and inconsistencies in articulating the social powers of art to form a moral culture are themselves the sign of his deeper, implicit awareness of the enduring difficulties of achieving expressive freedom in and through culture. This awareness comes to the fore in Schiller's essay "On Naive and Sentimental Poetry," a far darker piece than the *Aesthetic Letters,* dominated by the figure of the sentimental poet as the one who writes anyway, despite awareness of the persistence of antagonisms.

In this essay, as in the *Aesthetic Letters,* the general aim of poetry is to lead us toward expressive, moral freedom. "The faculty of poetic composition comes to the aid of reason in order to render that [rational] idea [of freedom] palpable to intuition and to realise it in individual cases." In order to achieve this aim, Schiller calls for an idyll of the future, a poetic work that will present a model of the full overcoming of antagonisms and motivate its own embodiment. "The concept of this idyll is the concept of a conflict fully reconciled

36. Ibid., Twentieth Letter, p. 141.; Twenty-Seventh Letter, p. 146.

not only in the individual, but in society, of a free uniting of inclination with the law, of a nature illuminated by the highest moral dignity, briefly, none other than the ideal of beauty applied to actual life. Its character thus subsists in the complete reconciliation of *all opposition between actuality and the ideal.*"[37]

Yet Schiller acknowledges that such an idyll is destined to be culturally impotent, reduced to a mere vehicle of escapism that in fact deepens the very oppositions it is designed to confront. Antagonisms, psychological and social, are too strong for art to do its work. *Willkür* in part resists *Wille;* human identities are formed in and through oppositions to one another in talent and interest. In a remarkable passage, Schiller notes these facts and draws the conclusion that defeat is the inevitable fate of anyone who would seek to overcome antagonisms and inaugurate a culture of expressive freedom.

> This leads me to a very remarkable psychological antagonism among men in a century that is civilising itself: an antagonism that because it is radical and based on inner mental dispositions is the cause of a worse division among men than any fortuitous clash of interests could ever provoke; one that deprives the artist and poet of all hope of pleasing and affecting universally, as is their task; which makes it impossible for the philosopher, even when he has done his utmost, to convince universally: yet the very concept of philosophy demands this; which, finally, will never permit a man in practical life to see his course of action universally approved—in a word, an antithesis that is to blame that no work of the spirit and no action of the heart can decisively satisfy one class without for that very reason bringing upon itself the damning judgment of the other. This antithesis is without doubt as old as the beginnings of civilisation and is scarcely to be overcome before its end other than in a few rare individuals who, it is to be hoped, always existed and always will; but among its effects is also this one, that it defeats every effort to overcome it because neither side can be induced to admit that there is any shortcoming on its part and any reality on the other.[38]

As a result of these antagonisms, which are central to the very life of human subjectivity in and through culture, no culture can be fully perfected. "All actuality, we know, falls short of the ideal."[39] Since it cannot succeed in per-

37. Friedrich Schiller, "On Naive and Sentimental Poetry," trans. Julius A. Elias, in *The Origins of Modern Critical Thought,* ed. Simpson, p. 166.
38. Ibid., p. 171.
39. Ibid., p. 167.

fecting culture, art tends to be reduced to escapist entertainment. Its audiences, formed in the culture that resists perfection, come to expect nothing else.

> Those who are divided in themselves by abstract thought, hemmed in by petty business formalities, or exhausted by strenuous concentration . . . yearn indeed for sensuous matter, not in order to continue the play of their intellectual powers, but in order to stop it. . . . They expected recreation from [art], but a recreation to meet their need and in accordance with their feeble notion. . . . Here [in the writers who pander to them] they are at once relieved of the burden of thought; and nature relaxed can indulge itself upon the downy pillow of *platitude* in blessed enjoyment of nothingness. In the temple of Thalia and Melpomene [the Muses of comedy and tragedy], as it is established among us, the beloved goddess sits enthroned receiving in her ample bosom the dull pedant and the tired businessman, and lulls the mind into mesmeric sleep, thawing out the frigid senses and rocking the imagination in gentle motion.[40]

Given that art is established as it is, against this background of expectations reinforced by social and psychological antagonisms, it is by no means clear what social powers art might have, what it might be other than entertainment. How are these antagonisms to be cured? How is art to uncover and articulate its own nature as the instrument of such a cure? The depth and pervasiveness of the antagonisms that Schiller notes block any ready answer to these questions.

Yet, despite his awareness of these antagonisms, Schiller does not altogether abandon hope for the powers of art. He does not conclude that there can be only coterie art, either narcissist-exclusivist high culture art or popular-escapist entertainment art. Instead, he sketches a figure who, in the face of these antagonisms, writes anyway and finds a form to preserve a dim memory of the possible powers of art. This figure is the sentimental poet.

Such a poet lives in a world of antagonisms, within a culture which, like the city of luxury that succeeds the city of pigs in the *Republic,* has "fallen from simplicity of manners" into complexity and the division of labor and competitive individuality. Unlike the naive poet whom Schiller imagines, who, living within a more homogeneous culture, "only follows simple nature and feeling, and limits himself solely to imitation of actuality," the sentimental poet is aware of divergent energies of competitive individuality that are expressed

40. Ibid., p. 168.

along divergent routes within culture. There is, for the sentimental poet, no one way that objects are experienced, no one way in which our powers to grasp objects coherently express themselves. As a result, instead of imitating either objects or lived plots of human achievement within culture, the sentimental poet "*reflects* upon the impression that objects make upon him, and only in that reflection is the emotion grounded which he himself experiences and which he excites in us."[41] The sentimental poet's emotional absorption in the articulation and expression of free personality under social roles, within conventions, has no one fixed object. Instead of imitating either nature or human action, the sentimental poet writes out of an awareness of an internal expressive power whose full exercise is blocked. Opposed ways of articulating spontaneity into personality present themselves to the sentimental poet. Awareness of the existence within the human person of a spontaneity or power to be expressed in and through cultural practices is present. That ideal retains its force, is not foregone. But the sentimental poet is aware of the existence within culture of multiple, antagonized modes of pursuit of that ideal. As a result, the sentimental poet's imagination of the realization of that ideal can never be complete, must always be haunted by some lack of resolution.[42] In attempting to imagine the realization of the ideal of expressive freedom within a moral culture, the sentimental poet "indeed does not fulfill his [task], but his task is an infinite one."[43]

This failure to carry out the task of imagining the embodiment of the ideal of expressive freedom in and through moral culture then commits the sentimental poet to a specific textual form: *elegy*, a work of mourning for our inability fully to exercise powers of rational spontaneity whose existence within we nonetheless continue dimly to apprehend.[44] "Either nature and the ideal are

41. Ibid., pp. 157, 161.
42. Cf. Herbert Marcuse, *The Aesthetic Dimension* (Boston: Beacon Press, 1978), p. 47: "Authentic works of art are aware of [the triumph of evil and unfreedom]; they reject the promise made too easily; they refuse the unburdened happy end. . . . The happy ending is 'the other' of art. Where it nevertheless appears, as in Shakespeare, as in Goethe's *Iphigenie,* as in the finale of *Figaro* or *Falstaff,* as in Proust, it seems to be denied by the work as a whole. In *Faust* the happy end is only and merely in heaven, and the great comedy cannot free itself from the tragedy which it attempts to banish."
43. Schiller, "On Naive and Sentimental Poetry," p. 167.
44. J. M. Bernstein, *The Fate of Art: Aesthetic Alienation from Kant to Derrida and Adorno* (University Park: Pennsylvania State University Press, 1992), usefully and powerfully describes the conception of the work of art in Kant, Heidegger, Adorno, and Derrida as in various ways that of a site of mourning for art's inability to fulfill its task in and through culture. "In modernity

an object of sadness if the first is treated as lost and the second as unattained. Or both are an object of joy represented as actual. The first yields the *elegy* in the narrower sense, and the second the idyll in the broader sense."[45] Given that the antagonisms within culture are so pervasive as to make the achievement of the ideal unimaginable realistically, elegy will be the primary mode of serious poetic expression, wherein our powers are still sensed but their frustration acknowledged.

Within the form of the elegy, there will be a prominent typology of development, seen as playing itself out on the levels of both the individual and the culture. At the first stage, there will be childhood, in the individual or in the culture, seen as an archaic time of unity, naturalness, and lack of competitive differentiation. "The feeling by which we are attached to nature is . . . closely related to the feeling with which we mourn the lost age of childhood and childlike innocence. Our childhood is the only undisfigured nature that we still encounter in civilised mankind, hence it is no wonder if every trace of the nature outside us leads us back to our childhood." Set against our present divided condition, cultural-social and individual-psychological, the child is capable of "revealing more closely the unnatural in us." We see "the unlimited *determinability* of the child and . . . its pure innocence."[46]

Out of this initial stage of childhood, there will emerge, inevitably, under no one's control and with astonishing force, a stage of complexity and contradiction, under which self-consciousness will be formed. Spontaneity within us becomes wedded to specific routines of discipline and identity articulation. *Willkür* comes to be partially informed by *Wille,* but in specific, competitive ways. We attain what Schiller calls a "determination" of character and identity.[47]

And then a third stage, projected and longed for, never quite emerges. We remain caught within the antagonisms of culture. There is a persistent tension between the movement of *Willkür* into modes of *Wille* as though into its expres-

---

beauty is not only alienated from truth, but grieves its loss; modernity is the site of beauty bereaved—bereaved of truth" (p. 4). Bernstein himself is perhaps slightly more hopeful—than Schiller, Kant, or Wittgenstein—that these elegies might point us beyond themselves, toward a more successful work of inaugurating a culture of moral freedom and thence toward new modes of artistic expression.

45. Schiller, "On Naive and Sentimental Poetry," p. 163.
46. Ibid., pp. 155, 150.
47. Ibid., p. 150.

sive house or home and a sense that, in being partial and opposed to other modes, this movement at the same time reinforces *Willkür* against the demands of rational, expressive freedom and social harmony. The child now becomes an uncanny figure of both ideal possibility, in its unselfconscious naturalness, and horror, insofar as in its spontaneity it is already on the way into competitive antagonisms.

Elegy tracks the persistence of this tension, as *Wille*'s appeal for and demands on *Willkür* play off against *Willkür*'s waywardness and against the competitive partiality of any modes of *Wille*, any ways of life. Elegy, the mode of writing of the sentimental poet, represents the ideal as unattained.

❋

It is possible to imagine two sharply opposed reactions to Kantian-Schillerian elegiac consciousness of unattainable ideals, reactions that accept the existence of a dim spontaneity or power within us but construe its possibilities of expression differently. One might, with Hegel, try to trace emerging routes for the full, fit, and harmonious housing in social roles of human self-consciousness, conceptual consciousness, and rationality. To be sure, Hegel noted the "widespread upheaval in various forms of culture" through which new social roles emerge. Fit, expressive homes for self-consciousness and rationality are not to be won without "the suffering, the patience, and the labour of the negative." Death and devastation are part of the life of Spirit, part of rational freedom's coming to be.[48] But nonetheless, through tracing the ways of history in playing out the demands of conceptual consciousness, self-consciousness, rationality, and freedom, Hegel projects the fulfillment of rational freedom in a moral culture. Spirit in the end "wins its truth," knows itself and its rational freedom in and through our achievement of rational freedom in a moral culture.[49] At the end of the *Phenomenology*, Hegel announces that the self-conscious self-identity of Spirit with itself, in and through our rational freedom, "is now a fact." "In this knowing then, Spirit has concluded the movement in which it has shaped itself, in so far as this shaping was burdened with the difference of consciousness, a difference now overcome." At the end of this movement, in the continuing movement of confession and forgiveness, we find "God man-

48. Hegel, *Phenomenology of Spirit*, paragraph 12, p. 7.; paragraph 19, p. 10; paragraph 32, p. 19.
49. Ibid., paragraph 32, p. 19. See also paragraphs 25–27, pp. 14–16.

ifested in the midst of those who know themselves in the form of pure knowledge."[50]

Even if one takes this completion more notionally and less actually (which seems false to Hegel's details of historical development), as merely sketching the ideal modes of life under which we might always acknowledge and ratify one another as rational and free beings, this seems too optimistic a picture of history. What makes these modes of acknowledgement available, either in actuality or as available ideals to be lived? What might lead us to make use of them? If the answer to these questions is "Spirit, in and through its social institutions and its self-consciousness in art, religion, and philosophy," that answer seems to overlook a number of difficulties, as Hegel's successors were not slow to see. With Marx, we might wonder who will pay for these social institutions, and hence whether they will transcend social antagonisms or rather serve as instruments of class domination. With Freud and Nietzsche, Sartre and Lacan, we might wonder whether, given what is done to us antagonistically, as we come to enter into social roles, we can ever transcend our resentments and wishes for vengeance. Perhaps dynamics of power—one partial, competitive mode of *Wille* facing off against another, with subjects coming to be within these competitions—are omnipresent and inescapable. With Kierkegaard, we might wonder whether, given that all available modes of the formation and expression of personality seem partial and opposed, it would even be a good thing were social harmony under the authority of reason to be achieved. Perhaps a putative rational culture would betray the very energies of subjectivity that in part make us what we are.

Alternatively, one might seek to liberate spontaneity and *Willkür* altogether from the demands of reason and *Wille*. This, notoriously, is Friedrich Schlegel's response to the problem of how spontaneity might best confront antagonisms. Poetry, according to Schlegel, articulates and expresses spontaneity or power, and poetry should follow only its own impulses, should be what Schlegel calls romantic. Romantic poetry "can . . . —more than any other form—hover at the midpoint between the portrayed and the portrayer, free of all real and ideal self-interest, on the wings of poetic reflection, and can raise that reflection again to a higher power, can multiply it in an endless succession of mirrors."[51] This poetry that articulates and expresses our spontaneity should be law only

---

50. Ibid., paragraph 798, p. 485; paragraph 805, p. 490.; paragraph 671, p. 409.
51. Schlegel, "Athenaeum Fragments," Fragment 116, p. 175.

unto itself, free from bondage either to the imitation of nature or to a rational ideal for culture.

> The romantic kind of poetry is still in the state of becoming; that, in fact, is its real essence: that it should forever be becoming and never be perfected. It can be exhausted by no theory and only a divinatory criticism would dare to try to characterize its ideal. It alone is infinite, just as it alone is free; and it recognizes as its first commandment that the will of the poet can tolerate no law above itself. The romantic kind of poetry is the only one that is more than a kind, that is, as it were, poetry itself: for in a certain sense all poetry is or should be romantic.[52]

Poesis is Schlegel's name for the process through which spontaneity or energy or *Willkür* comes to articulate and express itself. This process works itself out best, and we articulate and express ourselves as well as we can, when it goes its own way, in freedom from the demands of imitation, from the demands of the ideal, which is in any case unattainable, and from the narrow and irrational demands of conventional social roles. Energy and its onwardness are all.

This view about the importance of the imperatives of spontaneity and *poesis*, independent of reason, nature, and standing culture, extends as well to philosophy, which, according to Schlegel, should likewise be poetic, should participate in spontaneity's expressive efforts. As a result, philosophy should resist and refuse all doctrines, in favor of irony, its real essence, insofar as philosophy itself participates in the ongoing movement of *poesis*. "Philosophy is the real homeland of irony, which one would like to define as logical beauty: for wherever philosophy appears in oral or written dialogues—and is not simply confined into rigid systems—there irony should be asked for and provided."[53]

Irony's importance as a mode of resistance to doctrine, dogmatism, and cold rationalism is a matter of the undecidability that it sets up in the oral or written text. In contrast with Swiftian irony, which is a figure of speech that forcefully leads the reader to the opposite of the surface message, Schlegel praises Socratic irony, in which undecidability is emphasized. Does Socrates know (that he knows nothing), or does he know nothing? Socratic irony functions as a kind of provocation rather than as a transmission of a message. It is an act of *poesis* that stimulates new acts of *poesis* in its readers through its

---

52. Ibid., pp. 175–76.
53. Schlegel, "Critical Fragments," in *"Lucinde" and the Fragments,* trans. Firchow, Fragment 42, p. 148.

very undecidability. It is pure *poesis* that refuses all semantic or doctrinal or truth-value constraint.

> Socratic irony is the only involuntary and yet completely deliberate dissimulation. It is equally impossible to feign it or divulge it. To a person who hasn't got it, it will remain a riddle even after it is openly confessed. It is meant to deceive no one except those who consider it a deception and who either take pleasure in the delightful roguery of making fools of the whole world or else become angry when they get an inkling they themselves might be included. In this sort of irony, everything should be playful and serious, guilelessly open and deeply hidden. It originates in the union of *savoir vivre* and scientific spirit, in the conjunction of a perfectly instinctive and a perfectly conscious philosophy. It contains and arouses a feeling of indissoluble antagonism between the absolute and the relative, between the impossibility and the necessity of complete communication. It is the freest of all licenses, for by its means one transcends oneself; and yet it is also the most lawful, for it is absolutely necessary. It is a very good sign when the harmonious bores are at a loss about how they should react to this continuous self-parody, when they fluctuate endlessly between belief and disbelief until they get dizzy and take what is meant as a joke seriously and what is meant seriously as a joke.[54]

As the freest of all licenses, an instrument of eternal self-transcendence rooted in wayward spontaneity, irony hence involves the cultivation, in writing and in life, of eternal agility. "Irony is the clear consciousness of eternal agility, of an infinitely teeming chaos."[55] Cultivating this eternal agility, which Schlegel elsewhere calls incomprehensibility, is the only route to a human life, one that does not betray our spontaneity, which is our sole strength.

> Yes, even man's most precious possession, his own inner happiness, depends in the last analysis, as anybody can easily verify, on some such point of strength that must be left in the dark, but that nonetheless shores up and supports the whole burden and would crumble the moment one subjected it to rational analysis. Verily, it would fare badly with you if, as you demand, the whole world were ever to become wholly comprehensible in earnest. And isn't this entire, unending world constructed by the understanding out of incomprehensibility or chaos?[56]

54. Ibid., Fragment 108, pp. 155–56.
55. Schlegel, "Ideas," in *"Lucinde" and the Fragments,* trans. Firchow, Fragment 69, p. 247.
56. Schlegel, "On Incomprehensibility," in *"Lucinde" and the Fragments,* trans. Firchow, p. 268.

Whatever the merits of this view in resisting dogmatism, narrow conventionalism, and stale rationalism and in holding out nothing other than resistance itself as an eternal ideal, in the end it seems idle and empty. In casting our spontaneity as a sheer power of agility and resistance, against the claims of reason, Schlegel in fact empties that spontaneity of content, reducing it to something more nearly resembling an animal function in the manner of Nietzsche. No remembrance of an aspiration to expressive freedom is any longer bound up with our spontaneity in this view. All there is is reactivity and restlessness.

But is a Hegelian solution, presenting the closure of spontaneity's struggles under perfected, rational forms of social life, any better, any more plausible? Hegel's rationalism seems equally inhuman. Hegelian theodicism faces off against Schlegelian nihilism, and both stances undo or deny our senses of ourselves as groping, imperfect bearers of possibilities of expressive freedom.

Between them lies the Kantian consciousness of consciousness, which sees us, in our conceptual consciousness and self-consciousness, as possessors of a spontaneity that articulates an ideal of expressive freedom, but which, caught up in antagonisms of its own making that reciprocally inform its operations, finds no ready way forward toward the achievement of that ideal. Remembrance, articulation, and projection of an ideal of expressive moral freedom play off within us against a consciousness of the antagonisms that surround our spontaneity and inform the culture in which that spontaneity might express itself. A temptation to claim rational freedom and expressiveness, a claim simply to know what the spontaneity underlying our conceptual consciousness demands of us and enables, a claim to know the specific cultural modalities and identities under which *Willkür* would be at last fully informed by *Wille*, plays off against consciousness of the impossibility of living out that temptation. Thus crossed by temptation and by its frustration, human intentionality finds itself to be at once more than merely natural and endlessly interesting.

4
Wittgenstein's Writerliness
and Its Repressions

In the Kantian conception of the mind in culture, it is impossible to forego efforts at criticism. The repertoires of culture express our understandings of value. We are able to some extent to change or modify cultural routines as those understandings change. A wish to know what our spontaneity enables and demands of us, and to know how in our lives in culture *Willkür* may at last be fully informed by *Wille*, inhabits our humanity. Even the repression of that wish is legible as itself an act of spontaneity, in lending one or another quality—brittleness, or overprotestation, or dulled self-defeat, or chill humorlessness—to the ways of dogmatism and skepticism.

Yet it remains unclear, always, how that wish is to be fully realized. Culture affords different, opposed modalities of the expression of our spontaneity and of the achievement of expressive freedom. These oppositions block our full and universal recognition and ratification of one another. Our very identities, as self-conscious, desiring beings, involved in one or another modality of envisioning and pursuing expressive freedom, are bound up with these antagonisms. "This opposition it is which awakens all [man's] powers, brings him to conquer his inclination to laziness and, propelled by vainglory, lust for power, and avarice, to achieve a rank among his fellows whom he cannot tolerate but from whom he cannot withdraw."

There seems to be no way forward toward universal, rational, expressive freedom. Culture-independent, autonomous practical reason is empty on its own; it can be exercised only within the opposed modalities of expressive freedom afforded within culture. Contrary to the claims of Cartesianism and the Enlightenment, our sociality is too strong for practical reason to assert itself with full autonomy. Our identities are bound up with our specific, antagonized cultural positions. Yet there is no way back toward mere unselfconscious naturalness, free of self-conscious desire, and envisioning, and a wish for expressive freedom. Contrary to the claims of behaviorism and naturalism, culture is more than a dispositive source of conditioning according to naturally laid down similarity spaces and pleasure/pain propensities. It is a source of possibilities of partial expressive power. Culture is shaped by our aspirations, and it calls to them. In living in culture, as self-conscious, desiring, envisioning beings, we are beyond mere naturalness but before full, universal, reciprocal expressive freedom.

The central texts of romanticism acknowledge this ongoing tension between aspiration and its defeat in and through humanity's life in culture. In Yuval Lurie's useful formulation,

> Romanticism strove to formulate a view of human life emerging through culture as a powerful, expressive, *natural* force, which, in turn, is constrained and refined by means of communal forces. In this way, culture was seen to furnish human beings with a mode of existence which does not drive a wedge between human existence and nature, but which enables human beings to join nature in a powerful, creative, effort. The view of culture which emerged thereby (through the joining together of both these forces) was that of a (joint) spiritual effort: one that unfolds in an aesthetical fashion. From a Romantic point of view, the life pursued and achieved by human beings was judged similar in kind to the creation of a work of art.[1]

Romanticism *strove* to formulate such a view, never quite arriving at conclusiveness. Romantic texts depict—often dramatically in their self-revising, self-questioning swerves in and out of doctrine and commitment—an effort to live with expressive freedom as both an enduring aspiration and an insuperable problem. They are dances of simultaneous efforts first to articulate and attach oneself to emerging modalities of more fully human, self-conscious, thought-embodying culture, but then also to cope with, even to preserve, one's alienation or estrangement from any consolidated form of cultural life—to claim independence or what Emerson will call self-reliance—as awareness of the antagonistic foundering of universal, reciprocal expressive freedom returns. Felt and partially achieved expressive power and its affirmation contend with doubt and anxiety and defeat. ("These beauteous forms, / Through a long absence, have not been to me / As is a landscape to a blind man's eye . . . feelings too / Of unremembered pleasure: such, *perhaps*, / As have no slight

---

1. Yuval Lurie, "Culture as a Form of Life: A Romantic Reading of Wittgenstein," *International Philosophical Quarterly* 32, no. 2 (June 1992): 195.

or trivial influence / On that best portion of a good man's life . . . While with
an eye made quiet by the power / Of harmony, and the deep power of joy, /
We see into the life of things. / *If this* / *Be but a vain belief* . . . other gifts / Have
followed; for such loss, *I would believe* / Abundant recompense. . . Therefore am
I still / A lover of the meadows and the woods . . . *Nor perchance,* / *If I were
not thus taught* . . . with what healing thoughts / Of tender joy wilt thou remember me, / And these my exhortations!")[2] There is in these romantic texts a
combination of a hunger for rational authority to express itself doctrinally and
a kind of aversiveness, a swerving away from doctrine and community. These
texts depict us dramatically as convention-transforming animals, acting always
out of and against a cultural background, capable of changing it but never of
fully grounding its life in reason. We are depicted as responding, fitfully, to
possibilities of rational humanity and expressive freedom. A sense of delayed
or suspended conversion—conversion sought and always about to be but also
conversion defeated and resisted—dominates these texts.

Living within these tensions between aspiration and its defeat, with a sense
of conversion into full expressiveness both sought and always already blocked,
one will experience cultural life as it stands, the ordinary, as *uncanny*. The
ordinary presents itself as a home for our humanity and its aspirations, a set
of repertoires of self-conscious expressiveness, but also as dead and decayed,
a site of the defeat of those aspirations, something to be departed from. Cavell
memorably registers this sense of the ordinary, therein accepting his own identification as romantic.

> I might describe my philosophical task as one of outlining the necessity, and
> the lack of necessity, in the sense of the human as inherently strange, say
> unstable, its quotidian as forever fantastic. . . . [Within this task] the ordinary
> is subject at once to autopsy and to augury, facing at once its end and its
> anticipation. The everyday is ordinary because, after all, it is our habit, or
> habitat; but since that very habitation is from time to time perceptible to
> us—we who have constructed it—as extraordinary, we conceive that some
> place elsewhere, or this place otherwise constructed, must be what is ordinary
> to us, must be what romantics . . . call 'home.' . . . Romantics are brave in
> noting the possibility of life-in-death and what you might call death-in-life.
> My favorite romantics are the ones (I think the bravest ones) who do not

2. William Wordsworth, "Lines Composed a Few Miles Above Tintern Abbey, On Revisiting
the Banks of the Wye During a Tour, July 13, 1798," in *Selected Poems and Prefaces,* ed. Stillinger,
pp. 103–11; emphasis added.

attempt to escape these conditions by taking revenge on existence. But this means willing to continue to be born, to be natal, hence mortal.[3]

How, on earth or anywhere else, does one do this? Accepting the uncanniness of the ordinary, refusing to take revenge on existence, and consenting to be natal and mortal will require persisting in what Cavell has called the argument of the ordinary. Affirmation and continuance of one's culture's modalities of expression and ways of thinking of things—its criteria—must be mixed with disappointment or repudiation or an effort to fashion something better. "The human capacity—and the drive—both to affirm and to deny our criteria constitutes the argument of the ordinary."[4] That capacity and drive persist, in and through the argument of the ordinary that they conduct. Onwardness and self-revision, not doctrine and self-completion, are pervasive.

In carrying on this argument, within this search for elevation into expressive freedom that Cavell calls perfectionism, various stylistic and thematic motifs will be prominent. The protagonist will be presented as seeking orientation within culture and of culture, within the self and of the self. There will be particular scenes of partial reorientation, accomplished through the influence of a friend, precursor, or instructor, who symbolizes certain possibilities of expressiveness to the protagonist. As Cavell puts it, "Perfectionism's emphasis on culture or cultivation is . . . to be understood in connection with this search for intelligibility [to oneself], or say this search for direction in what seems a scene of moral chaos, the scene of the dark place in which one has lost one's way. Here also is the importance to perfectionism of the friend, the figure, let us say, whose conviction in one's moral intelligibility draws one to discover it, to find words and deeds in which to express it, in which to enter the conversation of justice."[5] Waiting and responding to others and to modalities of expression that are present or emerging within one's culture will be blended with active criticism and refiguration of those modalities. The protagonist seeking expressiveness will live out its search between pure active ego identity and pure passive victimization by fortune. "It is the same self that is active and passive."[6] Persisting in the search for elevation, and refusing to take revenge

---

3. Stanley Cavell, *In Quest of the Ordinary: Lines of Skepticism and Romanticism* (Chicago: University of Chicago Press, 1988), pp. 154, 9, 143.

4. Stanley Cavell, *Conditions Handsome and Unhandsome: The Constitution of Emersonian Perfectionism* (Chicago: University of Chicago Press, 1990), p. 92.

5. Ibid., p. xxxii.

6. Ibid., p. xxxvi.

on the human existence that both enables and frustrates this quest, there will arise, in the romantic text that dramatizes this pursuit, a standing "irreconcilability . . . between our dissatisfaction with the ordinary and our satisfaction in it, between speaking outside and inside language games"[7]—a feature of thought or style that Cavell takes as part of the signature of *Philosophical Investigations*. "We are struggling," Wittgenstein says of himself, "with language. We are engaged in a struggle with language. [Wir kämpfen mit der Sprache. Wir stehen—we stand—im Kampf mit der Sprache]."[8] Proleptic achievements of expressive power are followed by doubt and despair; direction is sought without the guidance of doctrine; the line between original expressive power and chaotically wayward spontaneity wavers, and antinomianism threatens. The protagonist swerves between acceptance of attunement in concepts, criteria, and culture—a moment or figure of the experience of beauty or harmony— and a wish for a new ground, a will to step outside culture, an assertion of independence in spontanteity—a moment or figure of sublimity.

Philosophical Investigations above all dramatizes such swerves, carried out within the protagonist-persona's philosophical imagination, in self-interrogation. The drama of the text enacts these swerves. The movement through them is one of *poesis, not theoria*. The self's continuing efforts to bring *Willkür* to full information by *Wille*, to full expressive power in and through culture, are enacted, as they are crossed by doubt and despair. A sense of oneself as potentially achieving expressive freedom under certain modalities of culture—a self-certainty—is never quite wholly filled in, never quite wholly brought to truth, but never quite foregone. Wittgenstein himself characterizes his own efforts in philosophy as having just such a structure of *poesis*, a structure of continuing struggle.

> I think I summed up my attitude to philosophy when I said: philosophy ought really to be written only as a *poetic composition*. [Philosophie dürfte man eigentlich nur *dichten*.] It must, as it seems to me, be possible to gather from this how far my thinking belongs to the present, future or past. For I was thereby revealing myself as someone who cannot quite do what he would like to be able to do [der nicht ganz kann, was er zu können wünscht— who cannot do wholly that which he wishes to do].[9]

7. Ibid., p. 83.
8. Wittgenstein, *Culture and Value*, 2d ed., ed. G. H. Von Wright with Heikki Nyman, trans. Peter Winch (Chicago: University of Chicago Press, 1980), pp. 11e, 11.
9. Ibid., pp. 24e, 24.

Philosophical Investigations thus instructs or moves us more by example or by call than by thesis or doctrine. Its poetic dramatizations of ongoing struggle show us the character of our humanity, reflect to us our standing problems of expressive freedom in culture. Against the full background of post-Kantian idealist and romantic thought and writing and philosophy of mind, it would require a particularly closed sensibility, committed no matter what to some form of dogmatism, to refuse the power of its enactments. As P. F. Strawson observes, "It would . . . be a very strong prejudice against this disregard [in *Philosophical Investigations*] of the ordinary [academic] conventions of expression, which could survive a careful reading of the whole book."[10] Sadly, but perhaps naturally enough, given our own wishes for doctrine and its authority and given the imperatives of professionalization, a number of forms of very strong prejudice have entirely overlooked the poetic and dramatic structure of *Philosophical Investigations*. Its most prominent philosophical readers have persistently found in it—projected into it—some metaphysical doctrine about the nature of human intentionality and self-conscious, conceptual experience, a doctrine that they have then taken it upon themselves conclusively to defend or conclusively to refute—in the very face of *Philosophical Investigations*' persistent doctrinal inconclusiveness. Five forms—not always sharply distinct—of metaphysical dogmatism in the reception, and refusal, of the text are particularly prominent and influential.

1. According to Michael Dummett, "Wittgenstein goes in for a full-blooded conventionalism; for him the logical necessity of any statement is always the *direct* expression of a linguistic convention. That a given statement is necessary consists always in our having expressly decided to treat that very statement as unassailable."[11] Accepting the traditional view, Dummett holds that necessary statements serve as the framework of all self-conscious, conceptual thought. In order to be counted as intentionally and conceptually conscious, one must accept necessary statements such as "Nothing is both red and green all over." Hence Dummett has projected commitment to a formulable and arguable doctrine of conceptual consciousness into Wittgenstein's texts. To be conceptually

10. P. F. Strawson, "Review of Wittgenstein's *Philosophical Investigations*, in *Wittgenstein: The Philosophical Investigations*, ed. George Pitcher (Garden City: Doubleday, 1966), p. 22. First published in *Mind* 63 (1954): 70–99.
11. Michael Dummett, "Wittgenstein's Philosophy of Mathematics," in *Wittgenstein: The Philosophical Investigations*, ed. Pitcher, pp. 425–26. First published in *Philosophical Review* 68 (1959): 324–38.

conscious is to conform in thought and speech to the conventions that make there to be logical necessity.

Dummett himself then goes on to criticize this full-blooded conventionalism that he has ascribed to Wittgenstein. "Wittgenstein's conception," he remarks, "is extremely hard to swallow"; it makes nonsense of the idea that proofs in mathematics are rationally persuasive—an idea that, according to Dummett, we cannot forego.[12] Here, in place of a drama of a continuing struggle to achieve expressive freedom, Dummett sees in *Philosophical Investigations* and *Remarks on the Foundations of Mathematics* a doctrine about the natures of necessary truth and conceptual consciousness, a doctrine he then finds it easy enough to dismiss, with considerable plausibility.

The full-blooded conventionalism that Dummett ascribes to Wittgenstein is further associated with a distinct moral ideal, a Schlegelian ideal of continuing iconoclasm, unchastened spontaneity, and "eternal agility," that Richard Rorty has taken pains to articulate as Wittgenstein's teaching. Since, according to this full-blooded conventionalist doctrine, each statement that we accept as necessary comes to us on its own, independently of any other commitments, as we lay down a new convention concerning it, there is then nothing—no fixed framework of conceptual consciousness, no ordering of things—to which we either are or should be responsible in our thinking. Unconstrained decisions create any order we accept; the more original and striking those decisions are (perhaps so long as they do not have cruel consequences, though it is unclear why there is this constraint, other than by authorial preference), the better. Once upon a time, philosophy sought to limn the structures of reality and of conceptual consciousness, therein establishing the nature and content of necessary truths. But now, according to Rorty, Wittgenstein in his conventionalism has taught us otherwise. He has shown us how to be agile, ironic, and satiric, and he has shown us that there is nothing else, in philosophy, to do.

> When Wittgenstein is at his best, he resolutely avoids . . . constructive criticism and sticks to pure satire. He just shows, by example, how hopeless the traditional problems are—how they are based on a terminology which is as if designed expressly for the purpose of making solution impossible, how the questions which generate the traditional problems cannot be posed except in this terminology, how pathetic it is to think that the old gaps will be closed

12. Ibid., p. 429.

by constructing new gimmicks. . . . [Wittgenstein] just makes fun of the whole idea that there is something here to be explained.[13]

Since, according to Rorty, Wittgenstein has shown us that there is no order of thought or being that makes necessary statements true and that we must acknowledge, the only task that is then left to philosophy, in concert with the iconoclastic arts, of which it is in any case one, is self-enlargement.

> One can use language to criticize and enlarge itself, as one can exercise one's body to develop and strengthen and enlarge it, but one cannot see language-as-a-whole in relation to something else to which it applies, or for which it is a means to an end. The arts and the sciences, and philosophy as their self-reflection and integration, constitute such a process of enlargement and strengthening. But Philosophy, the attempt to say "how language relates to the world" by saying what *makes* certain sentences true, or certain actions or attitudes good or rational is, on this view, impossible.[14]

Hence we should abandon Philosophy and embrace the arts, and we should see our lives not as a great quest for the real, not as a drama "in which a preexistent goal is triumphantly reached or tragically not reached" but instead as "a process of Nietzschean self-overcoming."[15]

It is easy enough to criticize full-blooded conventionalism—and indeed Dummett himself does so—as what Baker and Hacker call "a bizarre form of logical existentialism," an "absurdity,"[16] that is not to be ascribed to Wittgenstein. Yet, as Dummett says while criticizing it, "it is not clear what one wishes to oppose to it."[17] Wittgenstein is obviously not advocating a form of Platonic or Fregean logical realism. Moreover, Rorty's elaboration of Schlegelian iconoclasm as a moral ideal does catch a certain animus in Wittgenstein against the idea that a human life either is or can be a story "in which a preexistent goal is triumphantly reached," an animus against the idea that some metaphysical theory might transparently and rationally elaborate the nature of the good or the real in itself.

13. Richard Rorty, "Keeping Philosophy Pure: An Essay on Wittgenstein," in *Consequences of Pragmatism* (Minneapolis: University of Minnesota Press, 1982), p. 34.

14. Richard Rorty, "Introduction: Pragmatism and Philosophy," in *Consequences of Pragmatism*, p. xix.

15. Richard Rorty, *Contingency, Irony, and Solidarity* (Cambridge: Cambridge University Press, 1989), p. 29.

16. Baker and Hacker, *Rules, Grammar, and Necessity*, pp. 105, 302.

17. Dummett, "Wittgenstein's Philosophy of Mathematics," p. 429.

The difficulty that attaches to the reading of Wittgenstein as a full-blooded conventionalist, logical existentialist, and Schlegelian iconoclast is not so much that it ascribes the wrong doctrine to him, and an implausible one at that, but rather that it ascribes a doctrine to him at all. There is in *Philosophical Investigations* a continuing tragic not-reaching of a goal, and nonetheless a continuing aspiration to achieve expressive freedom, to bring *Willkür* to full information by *Wille*. The conditions and nature of intentional and conceptual consciousness are continually scrutinized, formulated, in the hope of reaching this end, yet the resulting formulae never yield it. It is this movement, this drama, of aspiration and its disappointment that the full-blooded conventionalist–logical existentialist–iconoclast reading misses, like any reading that ascribes a doctrine, theory, or thesis to the text. In this drama no description of either things or conventions finally *guides* consciousness, in the way that is sought by doctrines and isms.

2. Explicitly rejecting both conventionalism, whether full-blooded or moderate, and Platonic-Fregean realism, Barry Stroud has characterized Wittgenstein's views about logical necessity as naturalist. According to Stroud, Wittgenstein's view is that various abstract possibilities of accepting certain truths as necessary, and of thinking and following rules in certain ways, are ruled out by how we just happen to be. Our contingent nature makes us think as we do. "A contingent fact which is responsible for our calculating as we actually do is the fact that we take '1002, 1004 . . .' to be going on in the same way as putting down '996, 998, 1000, ...' It is a fact that we naturally go on in this way. . . . That we take just the step we do here is a contingent fact, but it is not the result of a decision; it is not a convention to which there are alternatives among which we could choose." Here our nature simply makes us conceive of things, follow rules, and accept certain truths as necessary in the ways that we do. There is no question either of decision or of getting Platonic-Fregean or categorial reality right; rather, given the way we happen to be, we simply "do not have any clear concept of the opposite in the case of logical necessity . . . ; there appear to be no alternatives open to us." When we try to imagine doing things otherwise, there is a "progressive decrease in intelligibility."[18] Other ways of conceiving of things, and of following rules, and of accepting certain truths as necessary just don't make sense for us; our

---

18. Barry Stroud, "Wittgenstein and Logical Necessity," in *Wittgenstein: The Philosophical Investigations,* ed. Pitcher, pp. 491, 486, 484, 488.

nature won't let us take them up. Stroud defends this naturalist view that he sees in Wittgenstein by noting the demerits of its Platonist and conventionalist competitors.

Like conventionalism, naturalism too articulates and supports a moral ideal. If it is simply a matter of natural fact that we conceive of objects and follow rules as we do, then the immediately suitable thing to do in order to grasp the nature of our intentional, conceptual consciousness is to describe and investigate natural facts. Descriptive psychology—perhaps cognitivist-functionalist, perhaps connectionist—supplemented and deepened by neuro-physiology and evolutionary theory appears to be the route through which our given biological nature takes itself as an object of study, without any prior epistemological-metaphysical first philosophy. There is a modest ideal of the continuing investigation of our conceptual capacities as they have been laid down in us by our biology and its evolutionary history. Wittgenstein is taken to have gotten rid of the idea that the introspective identification of qualia or sensibilia is the basis of conceptual consciousness, and he is taken to have pointed us in the right direction, to have freed us to look at how we are wired by our biology to think and act as we do. It is an advance to have reduced logical necessity to natural necessity. But the real work of grasping the contin-gent, biological nature of our conceptual consciousness is now being produc-tively carried on in the psychological, biological, and neurological sciences.

Here too it is easy to criticize this naturalist stance as both mistaken in itself and based on a misreading of Wittgenstein. As Baker and Hacker observe, for many of our rule-governed practices there *are* alternatives. Clocks and calendars, for example, have been constructed very differently at different times in the past. The length (in minutes, as we measure them) of (what seems closest to but is really incommensurable with) an hour varies in certain sys-tems. Nothing in our biological nature forces us to have one system of measur-ing time rather than another. In general, Wittgenstein's "concept of a form of life is not biological, but cultural." It is *not* that our biological nature forces us to play chess, or calculate, or prepare food, or dress as we do. In many places people do many of these things in very different ways. "Rather that we find it natural is what makes it reasonable *to make it correct.* What is natural to most of us is the *foundation* for a technique" that we have developed, are trained in, and continue or modify.[19]

19. Baker and Hacker, *Rules, Grammar, and Necessity*, pp. 323–25, 241, 328. Cf. p. 243.

But here again it is not clear what is to be opposed to naturalism. Cognitive psychology, linguistics, and neurobiology present certain apparent successes in describing and explaining some human capacities. Why should these successes not be extended through further investigation? Or if instead we should investigate anthropological, cultural, and historical phenomena of the possession of techniques and practices, then what is it to investigate that? Isn't that just the investigation of conventions (without convenings) in use?

Again the real mistake is that of ascribing to Wittgenstein a doctrine about the nature of conceptual consciousness, therein missing the dramatic movement of the text. It is in the dramatistics of *Willkür* and *Wille,* not through our victimization by either nature or convention, that we are what we are in the showing of *Philosophical Investigations.*

3. Seeking to find a way between full-blooded conventionalism and naturalism, Saul Kripke sees in *Philosophical Investigations* a kind of communitarian conventionalism. Meaningful utterance cannot be mere noise-making. Yet there is no "fact of meaning." No disposition, whether biological or cultural, no mental state, no grasp of a convention, no grasp of a concept or Platonic form— "no fact about an individual . . . could constitute his state of meaning" something in speaking.[20] Neither Platonic reality nor conventions adopted in individual will nor our biological-psychological nature makes us mean what we do in our sayings. None of these things determines that we must accept the truth of "Nothing is both red and green all over."

Yet it is not that we mean nothing by our words, and it is not that there are no necessary truths. Instead, Kripke claims, "Wittgenstein finds a useful role in our lives for a 'language game' that licenses, under certain conditions, assertions that someone 'means such-and-such' and that his present application of a word 'accords' with what he 'meant' in the past. It turns out that this role, and these conditions, involve reference to a community."[21] That is to say, how people manage to speak meaningfully, how they come to be committed to certain necessary truths, how they come to have a conceptual consciousness at all that they then evince in words—all these things are intelligible only by "reference to a community." The criteria for having a concept are determined, laid down, by the habits of a community. Someone possesses a concept and

20. Saul A. Kripke, *Wittgenstein on Rules and Private Language* (Cambridge: Harvard University Press, 1982), p. 39.
21. Ibid., p. 79.

evinces that possession in speech only insofar as that person uses a word (which will then come to express a concept) as the community does. Apart from that, there is no objectivity, no conceptual life, but only empty, unconstrained inclination.

> Any individual who claims to have mastered the concept of addition will be judged by the community to have done so if his particular responses [to addition problems] agree with those of the community in enough cases, especially the simple ones. . . . An individual who passes such tests is admitted into the community as an adder; an individual who passes such tests in enough other cases is admitted as a normal speaker of the language and a member of the community. Those who deviate are corrected and told (usually as children) that they have not grasped the concept of addition. One who is an incorrigible deviant in enough respects simply cannot participate in the life of the community, and in communication.[22]

Though there are permissible marginal deviations open to those who have already been accepted into the conceptual-linguistic community, leaving some room for the introduction of new concepts, there is no life of conceptual consciousness elsewhere. There is

> a restriction on the community's game of attributing to one of its members the grasping of a certain concept: if the individual in question no longer conforms to what the community would do in those circumstances, the community can no longer attribute the concept to him. Even though, when we play this game and attribute concepts to individuals, we depict no special "state" of their minds, we do something of importance. We take them provisionally into the community, as long as further deviant behavior does not exclude them. In practice, such deviant behavior rarely occurs.[23]

To see our conceptual consciousness arising and sustaining itself only through community habits of usage and of the acceptance and rejection of others does usefully hint at certain tensions in the life of conceptual consciousness. The issue of whether and how someone thinks is also an issue about whether and how we do or might get along with one another. But when it is taken as a theory or doctrine of conceptual consciousness, this communitarian

22. Ibid., pp. 91–92.
23. Ibid., p. 95.

view—if it is not itself reduced to a form of naturalism—yields a kind of sociological theory of consciousness.

Such a sociological theory of consciousness has been seen in Wittgenstein by such readers as Terry Eagleton, David Bloor, and David Rubinstein, working variously out of Marxist, Weberian, Durkheimian, and Mertonian stances in the sociology of knowledge and consciousness. According to Eagleton, "If Wittgenstein is right . . . , discourse is *internally* related to its social conditions."[24] The character and substance of both thought and language are determined by the social-material conditions of life, by how people labor under which social systems. This leads Eagleton to cast Wittgenstein's thought as a cogent critique of cognitive individualism, but as in the end only a prelude to a deeper, more explicitly social-material-historical form of theorizing about consciousness. Eagleton points to George Thomson and Antonio Gramsci as examples of this more advanced form of theory.

> Unlike . . . Wittgenstein . . . , however, Thomson is concerned to give an account of the historical conditions which brought metaphysical thought into existence in the first place. This is not only a question of the historical division of manual and intellectual labor, with thought's consequent illusory trust in its own autonomy; it is more particularly a question of the growth of commodity production. . . . Gramsci's historicist theory of thought rounds dialectically upon itself, in a way that Wittgenstein's philosophizing . . . dares not do: philosophy is itself a class-bound, historically determined activity, whatever the befuddled faith of ideas that they are the products of previous ideas.[25]

Here the Kripkean-communitarian view that people think and mean something by their words only insofar as they have adapted themselves to the ways of others has been accepted, but has given way to an effort to construct a historical theory of the characters of these adaptations and their causal determinants. If what sets up conceptual consciousness at all is a matter of the acceptance or shunning of people as normal or deviant, then this seems natural: Why not construct a historical theory of the normal and the deviant, including an account of the causes of these groupings?

---

24. Terry Eagleton, "Wittgenstein's Friends," *New Left Review* 135 (September–October 1982): 70.
25. Ibid., pp. 77, 78–79.

David Bloor similarly, but in more detail, offers Kripke-like slogans about the social character of thought, leading to a social-material theory of the rise and fall of forms of social life. According to Bloor, Wittgenstein "treated cognition as something that is social in its very essence. For him, our interactions with one another, and our participation in a social group, were no mere contingencies. They were not the accidental circumstances that attend our knowing; they were constitutive of all that we can ever claim by way of knowledge."[26] Yet we can and should go beyond Wittgenstein's critical insights to construct "a systematic theory of language games." Making use of Durkheim and Mary Douglas, Bloor then attempts to show in detail how logical intuitions are socially created. Which sentences people take to follow from other sentences depends, Bloor claims, on the positions of people within a social structure, what Bloor calls their *social interests*. "My claim is that a pursuit of the causes that makes us deploy our intuitions in one way rather than another, leads straight to social variables of this kind. . . . What Wittgenstein was referring to by 'needs' [underlying and motivating our customary practices] were the very things that sociologists refer to under the heading of social interests."[27] To have social interests is to be committed to trying to gain a greater social share of material resources and to becoming relatively more dominant, less subordinate, as an effective determiner of the allocation of resources. People naturally have such social interests; how they pursue them depends on the evolving character of the social systems under which they pursue them. These social interests and social systems are then, according to Bloor, the determinants of thought and consciousness, and hence the final proper object of theorizing, as the philosophy of mind is transmuted into historical-material social theory.

David Rubinstein suggests a similar move toward social theory. In his reading, Wittgenstein and Marx agree that, among other things, "human intelligence, i.e. a genuinely human being, necessarily emerges only in and through society."[28] Here too Marx is cast as going further, as having a deeper, more explanatory theory of the rise and fall of forms of social life.

26. David Bloor, *Wittgenstein: A Social Theory of Knowledge* (New York: Columbia University Press, 1983), p. 2.

27. Ibid., pp. 4, 136, 48.

28. David Rubinstein, *Marx and Wittgenstein: Social Praxis and Social Explanation* (London: Routledge and Kegan Paul, 1981), p. 2.

While both Marx and Wittgenstein imply the need for a theoretical understanding of an entire system of social praxis, Marx's thought has an important advantage on this count. Wittgenstein uses the term "form of life" to suggest the bearing of the larger system on the meaning of individual behaviors. But this is a vague term, that provides little guidance as to what sorts of features of the social context ought to be seen as decisive in its description. In contrast, Marx does specify what aspect of social organization ought to be considered decisive, and that, of course, is the mode of production.[29]

Here too our conceptual consciousness and cognitive practices are seen as functions of modes of social relationship, involving acceptance and rejection; these modes of social relationship themselves then become the object of an explanatory theory of forms of social life. Communitarianism in the philosophy of mind yields to some form of historical social theory.

Both as a reading of Wittgenstein and as a stance in the philosophy of mind, communitarianism (pointing toward social theory) has little to be said for it. Kripke's reading of the first sentence of the first paragraph of section 201 of *Philosophical Investigations* ("This was our paradox: no course of action could be determined by a rule, because every course of action can be made out to accord with the rule")—the basis of his initial elaboration of the "Wittgensteinian skepticism" about facts of mind and meaning that he later "solves" by a turn to communitarianism—is a travesty, as Baker and Hacker have shown.[30] In context, that sentence raises no specter of skepticism about meaning. The very next sentences undo the paradox by noting that there *are* facts of meaning in practice. "The answer was: if everything can be made out to accord with the rule, then it can also be made out to conflict with it. And so there would be neither accord nor conflict here" (§201). The point here is that rules in use don't need *interpretations* to settle what really accords with them; their accord-conditions are already laid down together with the use of the rule in practice. That fact and that fact alone makes both accord and conflict with a rule possible. The mistake—Kripke's mistake—is to think that there is a problem to be solved by introducing a new, correct interpretation. But nothing hangs in the air with rules in use. Only when rules are in use, with accord-conditions internally related to them, is there even any possibility

29. Ibid., p. 204.
30. G. P. Baker and P. M. S. Hacker, *Scepticism, Rules, and Language* (Oxford: Basil Blackwell, 1984), pp. 1–21.

of either accord or conflict with them. Kripke's "scepticism about what constitutes the correct application of a given rule," Baker and Hacker conclude, "is manifestly absurd,"[31] and so *eo ipso* is its communitarian solution. Whether someone thinks or has conceptual consciousness is a matter of the techniques—necessarily intelligible to others, but not necessarily in fact shared by others—that the person has for classifying objects and phenomena. Individual deviance in thought, the development of new techniques, is possible and sometimes fruitful. Our ability to think is not simply the causally engendered product of some buffeting social conditioning. It rather grows in us, like the ability to walk. Walking likewise has its socially shared styles and can be inhibited, but it does not arise only through social conditioning.

Yet here again it is not altogether clear what stance in the philosophy of mind Baker and Hacker wish to oppose to Kripke's. They hold that concepts and rules—together with their internally related accordants—are autonomous from external determination. Neither conventions rooted in individual will, nor human biological nature, nor patterned habits of community acceptance determine them. Concepts and rules, and our conceptual consciousness as it lives within them, are not fit objects of any form of explanatory theorizing, psychological, biological, or sociohistorical. But why not? And while cognitive deviance, the development of new concepts and techniques, is indeed possible and sometimes fruitful, is it so clear that the initial development of our ability to think, our conceptual consciousness, can occur in the absence of social relations? It is not even so clear that walking can. (Children abandoned in the wild typically die; if they survive, they may never quite have characteristically human, fully upright posture.)

Here again the real mistake is not to have ascribed the wrong doctrine about conceptual consciousness to Wittgenstein, but rather to have ascribed a doctrine at all, overlooking the entanglements—insisted on in the text—of the philosophy of mind with ethics. Adaptation to the ways of a community, in order to be counted as normal and as a conceptually conscious thinker, is not a smooth and certain route to the fit expression of our spontaneity and the full achievement of expressive freedom. But then neither is grasping fixed internal relations between concepts and their objects. Nothing is.

4. Seeking to avoid all of full-blooded or explicit conventionalism, naturalism, and communitarianism, Baker and Hacker see in Wittgenstein a kind of

31. Ibid., p. 100.

pragmatic conventionalism or conventionalism without convenings and without any single, philosophically specifiable determinants. Our commitments to necessary propositions are determined neither by explicit, locatable decisions (at least often they are not), nor by our biological-psychological nature, nor by the pressures of adaptation to a community. Necessary propositions are not held true in virtue either of their *forms* or their *meanings*. Rather, they are "constitutive of meanings."[32] Propositions such as "Nothing is both red and green all over" are frameworks for thought, akin to rules that we abide by in speaking and thinking at all. "Such propositions are used as norms of representation."[33] One who does not accept such a norm does not know what color words mean, does not know their grammar or conceptual structure. Nothing—not the nature of reality in itself, not their logical forms, not their meanings, not (usually) any explicit convenings, not our biological nature, not the habits of a community—makes us so use them. A thousand contextual reasons might incline us toward using any proposition as a norm. Our system of color terms has proven itself useful in manifold contexts: in food gathering and preparation, in designing flags and symbols, in painting, in fashion, in electrical wiring, among many others. But not all color systems are isomorphically equivalent in their divisions of the spectrum. Different terms might do similar jobs. Electrical resistors, for example, might be graded not by color but by the number of dashes inscribed on them. But then perhaps it is often quicker and easier to sort them by color. Yet nothing—not the nature of electrical resistors, not our biology, and so on—makes us use color terms here as we do. It is impossible philosophically to get behind or beneath these norms of representation to discover their basis in any fixed, philosophically scrutable something. "Grammatical rules are arbitrary, autonomous. There is no such thing as justifying grammar by reference to reality. For grammar determines the bounds of sense, what it makes sense to say." There are "natural limits to our symbolisms."[34] We cannot visually discriminate, and hence could not have visual color terms for, every distinct wavelength of light, but within these natural limits there is room for considerable variation. Particular histories and contextual needs will affect the adoption of various norms of representation. For example, uniform hour time measurement may be encouraged (though not mandated or determined) within a commodity production and wage econ-

---

32. Baker and Hacker, *Rules, Grammar, and Necessity,* p. 346.
33. Ibid., p. 343.
34. Ibid., pp. 332, 334.

omy. But nothing philosophical, nothing essential, determines our adoption of norms of representation in general. With regard to our norms of representation, "there is no behind, and rules are not answerable to reality in the currency of truth. Any deeper explanation [of our norms and rules] would simply be another rule of grammar standing in the same relation to the use of expressions as the rules it allegedly explains. Therefore philosophy must be flat. This insight shapes the whole of Wittgenstein's philosophy."[35] There are no philosophical discoveries of *the* basis of our norms and rules; all philosophy can do is survey these norms and rules and diagnose the conceptual confusions attaching to various attempts to ground, explain, or justify them essentially.

This is a considerable and powerful view. Put into practice, it yields trenchant criticisms of a great deal of work in linguistics, cognitive psychology, and the theory of perception that attempts, confusedly, to explain our norms of representation essentially. Affirmatively it yields careful, conceptual-historical studies of systems of norms in use: for example, studies of Egyptian time measurement or studies of the formal schemes of metaphysical poetry. Scrutiny of "the language of *X*" (of Egyptian time measurement, of railroad track route location, of seventeenth-century Dutch portraiture, of double-entry bookkeeping, or whatever) yields fascinating, textured, but not essentially philosophical results.

Yet, despite its powers and insights, this view is open to both textual and substantive objections. Textually, it too attributes to Wittgenstein a thesis— grammar is autonomous—in the face of Wittgenstein's rejection of theses. "If one tried to advance *theses* in philosophy, it would never be possible to debate them, because everyone would agree to them" (§128). Wittgenstein is said to have *held, insisted, thought, emphasized,* and so forth, various theses ("grammar is autonomous") that never quite appear with just that literalness and directness in the text. Substantively, insistence on the autonomy of grammar and on the internal relations between rules and their accordants misses the continuing, agonistic quality of our lives with rules and norms. To be sure, it is not that the interpretation of all or even very many rules hangs in the air. There could be no rules were that so. But what are the rules for applying the terms "mass" or "poem" or "fairness" or "health" or "love" or "cleverness" or "decency"? These terms, many of them humble and indispensable ones, can all be partially verbally elucidated; incontestable examples of their correct application can be

35. Ibid., p. 22.

given. These examples will often overlap helpfully, in multiple, crisscrossing ways. But neither these verbal elucidations nor these examples will settle all hard cases. The use of such terms is not everywhere circumscribed by rules internally related to their accordants, by a grammar that is everywhere transparent to us. Rules do not always and readily part literal from metaphorical, normal from deviant, successfully innovative from conceptually confused usages for us. The use of the word "game," for example, "is not everywhere circumscribed by rules; but no more are there any rules for how high one throws the ball in tennis, or how hard; yet tennis is a game for all that and has rules too" (§68).

To insist on the autonomy of grammar as itself a simple philosophical fact is then to underdescribe our lives with language and culture. This stance also severs the philosophy of mind too sharply from ethics, missing the agonies of the effort to bring *Willkür* to full information by *Wille,* to achieve full expressive freedom, that are woven into our lives as conceptually conscious beings living within antagonisms. Nothing—not anything external, but not our grammar either—determines everywhere how we are to go on in applying rules and concepts.

5. Overlapping to a considerable extent with the "grammar is autonomous" reading of *Philosophical Investigations* is a distinctively neo-Aristotelian reading, elaborated by both Anthony Kenny and Baker and Hacker. According to Kenny, Wittgenstein reverses Descartes' "substitution of privacy for rationality as the mark of the mental," therein reintroducing an Aristotelian-Thomist conception of mind as a power or capacity of reasoning.[36] "The mind is the capacity to acquire intellectual skills. . . . Human beings are living bodies of a certain kind, who have various abilities. The human mind is the capacity that human beings have to acquire intellectual abilities: a capacity that is itself an ability, but a second-order ability, the ability to acquire abilities." Capacities, abilities, and their exercises can be elucidated. We can say what the criteria are for having a certain ability. "Ready use of English," for example, "is a criterion of . . . knowledge of English." But criterial evidence is neither inductive nor deductive; it is, rather, conceptual or grammatical. And it cannot be supplanted by noting inductively correlated *symptoms* of an ability. Nothing about the brain—the vehicle of our rational abilities and capacities—will by itself

---

36. Anthony Kenny, "Cartesian Privacy," in *Wittgenstein: the Philosophical Investigations,* ed. Pitcher, p. 360.

show what our capacities are, will show what we do in having and exercising our capacities and abilities. To have a rational capacity or ability is to be able to do something. Doing that thing, or related things, is the decisive criterion for possession of a rational capacity or ability; facts of human biology will never supplant that decisive criterion. Kenny offers this example: "Suppose that Professor Chomsky were now to die, and on opening his skull we discovered that there was nothing inside it except sawdust. This is indeed an exotic suggestion: if it happened it would be an astonishing miracle. But if it happened it would not cast the slightest doubt on what we all now know, namely, that Chomsky knows English extremely well."[37]

To be rational, to have a mind, is then simply to have a certain set of abilities: to begin with, innate, second-order abilities to acquire more specific rational abilities (for example, the ability to speak English or to play chess or to sing a harmonic minor scale); later the first-order abilities actually to do these and other things. Conceptual consciousness is one of these rational abilities, partly second-order and partly first-order. Our commitments to necessary propositions arise out of the natures of these first- and second-order abilities. Just as one is committed to the proposition that the rook cannot move diagonally, insofar as one is able to play chess, one is committed to the proposition that nothing is both red and green all over, insofar as one can speak English. It may—or it may not—be causally necessary to have a human brain, or something very like it, in order to have any rational abilities, but what these rational abilities *are,* or what their character is, is a matter of the criteria for possessing them, a matter of their grammar.

Citing Kenny, Baker and Hacker develop a similar neo-Aristotelian metaphysics of abilities, extending the thesis of the irreducibility of abilities to states and structures to all abilities, not just to rational abilities.

> A power must be distinguished from both its exercise and from its vehicle, *a fortiori* from the structure of its vehicle. . . . Whisky can intoxicate. The vehicle of its ability is the alcohol it contains, but the alcohol is not identical with the intoxicating power. One can weigh the alcohol, but not the ability to intoxicate. . . . Science explains powers by discovering underlying structures, but it is a mistake to think that it *reduces* powers to the structure of

37. Kenny, "Language and the Mind, in *The Legacy of Wittgenstein* (Oxford: Basil Blackwell, 1984), pp. 138, 139, 145. Cf. Kenny, *The Metaphysics of Mind* (Oxford: Oxford University Press, 1992), pp. 66–67.

their vehicle. Hemlock possesses the power to poison; the vehicle of its power is conine; the molecular structure of that chemical, i.e. 2n-propylpiperidine, in conjunction with principles of physiology and biochemistry, explains how hemlock poisons. But its power to poison is categorially distinct from its chemical structure.[38]

Hence talk of powers and abilities, which are elucidated by giving the criteria for their possession and exercise, cannot be replaced by talk of states and structures. Our conceptual consciousness is one of our rational abilities. Nothing in our brain logically makes us have it. It too is something to be elucidated conceptually, grammatically.

But this neo-Aristotelian view of conceptual consciousness and of necessary propositions is itself a form of dogmatism. While this view does usefully challenge the Cartesian emphasis on privacy and interiority as the marks of the mental, it also ontologizes rationality excessively. It is unclear why powers and abilties cannot be reduced to states and structures. One *can,* in fact, measure the power or ability of alcohol to intoxicate by weighing it; how much alcohol there is determines, together with body weight, metabolic rate, and so forth, how much intoxication there will be. The power of conine to poison just *is* its chemical structure. Temperature—the ability of a substance to cool or heat various things with which it might come into contact—just *is* the mean kinetic energy of its molecules. It seems dogmatic either to deny these identities or just to say that it must be different with rational abilities, that they, unlike other abilities, are not reducible to states and structures.

More important, instead of seeing our lives with language and culture as involving continuing struggles to exercise and express rationality, sometimes in novel, iconoclastic ways, in departure or freedom from rules, the neo-Aristotelian view sees our rationality as a power that is wholly housed within the criteria and rules under which it comes to be. Like neopragmatist conventionalism, it fails to leave enough room for reasonable deviance. It fails to see how our spontaneities and our rational abilities can be, and are, opposed under cultural antagonisms and how those abilities can repudiate the prior conditions of their own exercise, can repudiate criteria. It is as though—despite the rejection of reductionism—our rationality were construed as the standing presence of a substance within us, something that by its nature simply does what it

38. G. P. Baker and P. M. S. Hacker, *Wittgenstein: Understanding and Meaning* (Oxford: Basil Blackwell, 1980), p. 611.

does, rather than as a power, sometimes of repudiation, that involves *Willkür* responding imperfectly to *Wille,* arbitrary choice responding to contestant reasonable norms. Rationality is construed as having univocal conditions of exercise, in various domains, as the criteria are met for being able to prove elementary logic theorems, or sing harmonic minor scales, or cook. Contestation within apprenticeship in practice and over the continuance of practice is overlooked.

✳

Against all five forms of dogmatic misreading of Wittgenstein on conceptual consciousness and necessary propositions—conventionalist, naturalist, communitarian, neopragmatist conventionalist, and neo-Aristotelian—there stands a distinctly post-Kantian reading, sensitive to the continuing play of *Willkür* and *Wille* in a human life within an antagonized culture. Under this reading, necessary propositions, criterial claims, are what Cavell has characterized as *claims of reason.* These are claims all at once to reason, to self-knowledge, and to community in the exercise of rational power.[39] Sometimes these are fairly trivial, are fairly fully determined by rules of our grammar. "Red is a color." "Five is a number." "All bachelors are unmarried." But sometimes they are not. Sometimes they call to a rational spontaneity within us, offering to that spontaneity contestable modes of articulation within which that spontaneity might, or might not, find itself at home. They call, sometimes, for a new exercise of a power of reason, a new awareness of oneself as a possessor of a rational power, and a new form of shared life under these claims. "Human beings must always be treated as ends and never as means only." "The Turing test is not a *test* of thinking: passing it perfectly, with all our human nuances of intonation and glance and touch, leaves no open question about whether we relate to the test passer as human; not passing it is not passing it."[40] "Human beings are bearers of rational power, imperfectly seeking its perfect expression."

To make such claims is to enter into a drama of negotiation and consent about the human. It is to play a role as oneself a bearer of rational power,

---

39. For an account of Cavell's notion of a claim of reason, see my "The Normal and the Normative: Wittgenstein's Legacy, Kripke, and Cavell," *Philosophy and Phenomenological Research* 46, no. 4 (June 1986): 570–71.

40. Cf. Stanley Cavell, "Perfecting an Automaton," in *The Claim of Reason* (New York: Oxford University Press, 1979), pp. 403–8.

within an antagonized culture, as one seeks to find or found a culture in which full rational expressiveness and full human self-conscious self-identity are possible. One makes such claims only out of one's embeddedness within an antagonized culture, taking up in part some of its contested terms of the articulation of the human, but also in an effort to go beyond, to refashion, one's antagonized culture as it stands. Criterial claims like these—contested efforts—are the framework of our lives in language and culture as conceptually conscious and self-conscious beings. They stand in the background of even our humble and domestic utterances as we take up and use a language. Our lives with language and culture are not simple matters of conventions, biology, community habits, many interests neatly pursued in many domains, or neo-Aristotelian capacities. They are the substance of our efforts to bring rational power to articulation and full expression in and through culture. "Meaning something is like going up to someone" (§457).

So there is for human beings, in their lives with language and culture, a continuing problem both of articulating one's own rational, self-conscious identity and routes of expression and of projecting new modes of rational human community, within which full, universal, expressive freedom and reciprocal acknowledgment are sustained. To say that we bear this as a continuing problem is, roughly, what Cavell means in pointing to the truth of skepticism, or in saying that we live our skepticism: "In saying that we live our skepticism, I mean to register . . . [that it is] as though we have, or have lost, some picture of what knowing another, or being known by another, would really come to—a harmony, a concord, a union, a transparence, a governance, a power—against which our actual successes at knowing, and being known, are poor things."[41] We experience ourselves as somehow bereft of, and in need of, a dim power of concord, external and internal. The achievement of self-conscious self-identity, the satisfaction of articulate desire, the full information of *Willkür* by *Wille,* the achievement of expressive freedom, all under the forms of expression afforded by a culture that reciprocally affords equally fulfilling forms of expression to all—these are the continuing burdens of human conceptual consciousness and rational life.

That Wittgenstein held such a view of the character of human life, and of the proper task of philosophy and of his writing, in responding to that problem—seeking more expressiveness, more justice, but never quite solving it—

41. Ibid., p. 440.

is evident in various remarks he makes about the nature of philosophy and its aims. The 1933 so-called "Big Typescript" explicitly connects the idea of work on oneself—on one's viewpoint and on one's will and its modes of expression—with the idea of the achievement of justice.

> DIFFICULTY OF PHILOSOPHY NOT THE INTELLECTUAL DIFFICULTY OF THE SCIENCES, BUT THE DIFFICULTY OF A CHANGE OF ATTITUDE. RESISTANCES OF THE WILL MUST BE OVERCOME.
>
> . . . Work on philosophy is—as work in architecture frequently is—actually more of // a kind of // work on oneself. On one's own conception. On the way one sees things. (And what one demands of them.)
>
> . . . THE METHOD OF PHILOSOPHY: THE PERSPICUOUS REPRESENTATION OF GRAMMATICAL // LINGUISTIC // FACTS. THE GOAL: THE TRANSPARENCY OF ARGUMENTS. JUSTICE.[42]

Carrying out this work on oneself, therein achieving expressive freedom and furthering justice, has two opposed sides or dimensions. Pride must be overcome. One must give up a belief that one can, as an isolate intellect or rational intelligence, go one's own way, cut through to the essence of things so as to find perfect orientation against or underneath the ways of culture. One must give up this pride, even when our spontaneity and our ability to criticize culture as it stands tempt us toward it. "The *edifice of your pride* has to be dismantled. And that is terribly hard work."[43] Vanity is a sin, a betrayal of our power and a refusal of others.[44] But at the same time the way of expressiveness is not the way of abasement. Culture is not to be accepted as it stands. A higher expressiveness, a more fit housing of power, is to be sought. "What is good is also divine. Queer as it sounds, that sums up my ethics. Only something supernatural can express the Supernatural."[45]

Satisfying these two demands—to overcome pride and to achieve a higher expressiveness—is a matter of the awakening of conscience or conscientiousness throughout one's life. "That too is why the greatness of what a man writes

---

42. Ludwig Wittgenstein, "Philosophy: Sections 86–93 of the So-Called 'Big Typescript' (Catalog Number 213)," in *Philosophical Occasions 1912–1951*, ed. James Klagge and Alfred Nordmann (Indianapolis: Hackett, 1993), pp. 161–63, 171.

43. Wittgenstein, *Culture and Value*, p. 26e.

44. Cf. Ludwig Wittgenstein, forward to *Philosophical Remarks*, ed. Rush Rhees, trans. Raymond Hargreaves and Roger White (Oxford: Basil Blackwell, 1975), p. 7.

45. Wittgenstein, *Culture and Value*, p. 3e.

depends on everything else he writes and does."[46] It is conscience or conscientiousness that holds together one's own individual spontaneity and power with a shared way of life in culture. The proper office of religion as Wittgenstein conceives it—if it could really come to be fulfilled—is to provide modes of shared, lived conscientiousness, within which our spontaneity and rational, critical powers are fully housed in cultural routines.

> It strikes me that a religious belief could only be something like a passionate commitment to a system of reference. Hence, although it's *belief,* it's really a way of living, or a way of assessing life. It's passionately seizing hold of *this* interpretation. Instruction in a religious faith, therefore, would have to take the form of a portrayal, a description, of that system of reference, while at the same time being an appeal to conscience. And this combination would have to result in the pupil himself, of his own accord, passionately taking hold of the system of reference. It would be as though someone were first to let me see the hopelessness of my situation and then show me the means of rescue until, of my own accord, or not at any rate led to it by my *instructor,* I ran to it and grasped it.[47]

Here passionately taking hold of a system of reference, out of conscience, so as to take up a way of living life and of assessing life, welds together *Willkür* and *Wille,* individuality and culture, spontaneity and shared rationality. Doing this will involve seeing objects not only as things to be used, but also as objects of reverence, bearers of meaning, part of a way of life. Rapaciousness must be supplanted by care in use and by responsiveness to things. It will involve seeing, and living with, other people as co-bearers of conscience and spontaneity housed in cultural routines, ways of life, rather than seeing them only as competitors for scarce resources. It will involve seeing lived time not as an arena only of consumptions, but rather as an arena for cultivation and for the expression of conscientiousness in practice.

Attaining to conscientiousness will involve above all—in a contrast Wittgenstein repeatedly draws—having together with others not a *civilization* but a *culture.*[48] "Perhaps one day this civilization will produce a culture." ("Einmal

46. Ibid., p. 65e.
47. Ibid., p. 64e.
48. The contrast between civilization and culture has a long history in German thought and letters. See Norbert Elias, *The Civilizing Process,* vol. 1, *The History of Manners,* trans. Edmund Jephcott (Oxford: Basil Blackwell, 1993).

wird vielleicht aus dieser Zivilisation eine Kultur entspringen.")[49] Yuval Lurie usefully characterizes the contrast between culture and civilization as it runs through Wittgenstein's work.

> Culture emerges . . . as a spiritual extension of natural life, [while] civilization can now be looked upon as a spiritual manifestation of *artificially* created life. The first is driven by powerful and basic forces residing in the heart of man, and its typical expression is to be found in past arts, rituals, and religion. The second is driven by the contrived and sophisticated force of intellect, and its typical expression is to be found in science, industry, and modern arts. The first constitutes the creation of a powerful spiritual bond among human beings, which aims to express the spirit of man in a lofty manner. The second consists in a host of disjointed and contrived efforts which no longer aim at anything lofty and eternal.[50]

Unlike civilization, culture, as Wittgenstein imagines it, is a housing for conscientiousness, affording expressive freedom to each of its members. It is a body of repertoires and practices under which *Willkür* is fully informed by *Wille*, under which we have self-conscious self-identities, under which we are at home, and under which our acts are coherent, their expressiveness and worth acknowledged.

> A culture is like a big organization which assigns each of its members a place where he can work in the spirit of whole; and it is perfectly fair for his power to be measured by the contribution he succeeds in making to the whole enterprise. In an age without culture on the other hand forces become fragmented and the power of an individual man is used up in overcoming opposed forces and frictional resistances; it does not show in the distance he travels but perhaps only in the heat he generates in overcoming friction. But energy is still energy and even if the spectacle which our age affords is not the formation of a great cultural work, with the best men contributing to the same great end, so much as the unimpressive spectacle of a crowd whose best members work for purely private ends, still we must not forget that the spectacle is not what matters.[51]

Yet, for all that Wittgenstein wishes for the emergence of a culture and sometimes presents it as a lost ideal, he is nonetheless pervasively aware of

49. Wittgenstein, *Culture and Value*, pp. 64e, 64.
50. Lurie, "Culture as a Form of Life," p. 203.
51. Wittgenstein, *Culture and Value*, p. 6e.

the antagonisms that trouble the present, aware that we bear the enduring burden of the task of moving toward full, reciprocal, universal, expressive freedom without ever arriving there. Unlike Spengler, for whom there were laws of history governing cycles of development and decay back and forth through civilization and culture, Wittgenstein regards culture as an "ideal," as a "principle determining the form of one's reflections."[52] Thought and philosophy are properly forms of responsiveness to this nonpresent ideal, involving awareness of both its commanding attractiveness and the antagonisms that stand in the way of its pursuit. In the formulation of Jacques Bouveresse, "In philosophy [Wittgenstein] gives the impression of behaving like someone who was working for a hypothetical distant future, the realization of which depends on factors over which neither he nor philosophy in general has any real hold, and who has renounced intervening directly in the present situation."[53]

✳

The pursuit of an ideal involving the reorientation of the will is already strongly in place as a human problem and possibility in the *Tractatus*. That ideal is described, however, in terms quite different from the achievement of culture, or free expressiveness, or *Willkür* fully informed by *Wille*. In the metaphysics of the *Tractatus*, there are fixed possibilities of combination possessed by sempiternal simple objects that are the substance of the world. "It is essential to things that they should be possible constituents of states of affairs. . . . If I know an object I also know all its possible occurrences in states of affairs. (Every one of these possibilities must be part of the nature of the object.) A new possibility cannot be discovered later."[54] That there must be such objects is inferred from the determinacy of sense as it shows itself in science (cf. 4.11) and in the objectivity of inference. Scientific truth and objective inference imply determinacy of sense, and that in turn implies that there must be simple signs. "The requirement that simple signs be possible is the requirement that

52. Ibid., p. 27e.
53. Jacques Bouveresse, " 'The Darkness of This Time': Wittgenstein and the Modern World," in *Wittgenstein: Centenary Essays*, ed. A. Phillips Griffith (Cambridge: Cambridge University Press, 1991), p. 23.
54. Ludwig Wittgenstein, *Tractatus Logico-philosophicus*, 2d ed., trans. D. F. Pears and B. F. McGuinness (London: Routledge and Kegan Paul, 1971), 2.011, 2.0123, pp. 7, 9. Subsequent references to this edition appear parenthetically in the text by remark number (e.g., 2.0123).

sense be determinate" (3.23). The existence of simple signs then implies the existence of simple objects, which have simple signs as their representatives. "The possibility of propositions [the bearers of truth and the constituents of inferences] is based on the principle that objects have signs as their representatives" (4.0132). These sempiternal simple objects with their fixed possibilities of combination—their logical forms—determine the limits of thought and language. Signs—verbal or written or mental—cannot be combined in speech or writing or thought in ways that are contrary to the possibilities of combination possessed by the simple objects that they represent. "Tuesday is to the left of the moon" is a nonsense string of marks, since the objects *Tuesday* and *the moon* just can't combine in that way (ignoring the fact that *Tuesday* and *the moon* are not simple, sempiternal objects). That sentence does not even so much as have an incoherent sense, but is an example of what Cora Diamond has dubbed *full-blooded nonsense,* a combination of marks without a use.[55] Philosophy, by noting that there are, that there must be, sempiternal, sense-determining, simple objects "sets limits to the much disputed sphere of the natural sciences. It must set limits to what can be thought; and, in doing so, to what cannot be thought" (4.113–14).

What is less important than the metaphysics of simple objects, which are in any case fairly conjectural and tendentious (there might be other ways of accounting for scientific truth and the objectivity of inference), is that the *Tractatus*'s sketch of this metaphysical system is intended to support an ideal of thought and speech and action. We are to respect the limits of thought and language, not try to say what cannot be said. To acknowledge and respect these limits is to experience the world as a whole differently, as a happy man, not a sad one. "The world of the happy man is a different world from the world of the unhappy man" (6.43). "In order to live happily I must be in agreement with the world. And that is what 'being happy' *means*."[56]

The dominant motif here is one of taking up the attitude of the acceptance of world as it is and of one's own inability to affect it. "The will is an attitude of the subject to the world" and to the limits that its sempiternal simple substances set for thought and language.[57] As James C. Edwards cogently notes,

---

55. See Cora Diamond, "Frege and Nonsense" and "What Nonsense Might Be," in *The Realistic Spirit: Wittgenstein, Philosophy, and the Mind* (Cambridge: MIT Press, 1991), pp. 73–114.
56. Ludwig Wittgenstein, *Notebooks 1914–1916*, trans. G. E. M. Anscombe (Oxford: Basil Blackwell, 1961), p. 75.
57. Ibid., p. 87.

here "will-as-attitude" comes to the fore. "Will becomes a way to view the world; it is an affective perspective toward whatever is there to be seen. It has nothing to do with altering the actual structure of what is viewed."[58] To have a rightly oriented will is to accept the limits of thought and sense. Simple objects can combine in the ways that they can combine; their possibilities are fixed. We can scrutinize these possibilities in science, and we can manipulate objects in engineering, but we cannot bring new metaphysical possibilities into being. We cannot make objects meaningful to and for us as free subjectivities. As Edwards observes, there are deep Stoic and Spinozistic motifs here. Acceptance and silence are the appropriate attitudes toward the objects of the world and to the limits of thought. "Once one has recognized one's inability to effect alteration in the natural flow of things [or in the possibilities of combination of things] . . . one resigns oneself to bear with equanimity whatever it is that fate puts in one's way."[59]

Despite the Stoic and Spinozistic themes, this is still, as Edwards notes, a hero story: "The heart of the *Tractatus* [is] its animating myth of salvation. Salvation is achieved through heroic ascent to a godlike self-consciousness. Only when the self has abandoned its traditional but degrading self-understanding [as causally effective in making meaning] . . . will it be possible for the self to achieve that permanent good willing which is the aim of ethics." But just in being a hero story, the *Tractatus* inadvertently reinstalls a picture of the will as effective in making meaning, inadvertently falls back into narcissism. "So the outcome of the *Tractatus* . . . is narcissistic: the self is the maker of meaning. We escape from the shadows of the Cave only to find, not some Reality which gives our lives meaning, but only ourselves: heroic will [in arriving at Stoic acceptance]." Edwards then suggests that the way out of or beyond this form of narcissism, the way taken by Wittgenstein in his later writings, is simply to accept "the *Pathos* of the world's existence," to adopt "a stance which treats the world as a *miracle,* as an object of love, not of will."[60]

But the problem with this suggestion is that it does not, in fact, differ very much from the narcissistic hero story of the *Tractatus*. It still urges on us the taking up of a stance, an attitude. And so it still sees the achievement of happiness as somehow, through a reorientation of will, under our control. Witt-

58. James C. Edwards, *Ethics without Philosophy: Wittgenstein and the Moral Life* (Tampa: University Presses of Florida, 1982), p. 42. Edwards introduces the term "will-as-attitude" on p. 41.
59. Ibid., p. 44.
60. Ibid. pp. 68, 71, 235, 236.

genstein's rejection of the narcissism of the *Tractatus* is in fact deeper and more consistent than the taking up of a religious, mystical attitude—or the taking up of any attitude at all. As Philip R. Shields notes, in criticizing Edwards's reading of Wittgenstein's development, what predominates in Wittgenstein's later writing is a sense of restlessness. There is no attitude that we can adopt that will bring peace; there is nothing we can do, given the antagonisms present in culture, through which alone we can attempt to lead our expressive lives, to achieve full expressive freedom and perfected, self-conscious self-identity. Edwards's picture of Wittgenstein's later religious mysticism is, as Shields puts it,

> an overly romantic and idealized description that does not do justice to the seriousness of sin. . . . Edwards paints a picture, as it were, of life in the garden of Eden before the Fall [into representational consciousness and a sense of oneself as possessed of interior subjectivity and spontaneity]. Wittgenstein expresses a strong sense that this natural order is corrupted, that the world is fraught with temptations, that our willful desires constantly lead us astray from the way shown by logical grammar. . . . It is in the light of a similar experience of aimlessness and despair that St. Augustine writes in the beginning of his *Confessions,* "Our hearts are restless until they can find peace in You." Wittgenstein is looking for an end to philosophical torments, for a resting place, for thoughts that are at peace. Edwards offers a description of what it would mean to be no longer restless, to know one's way about in an immediate and concrete way—like fish in the sea. Wittgenstein, like Augustine before him, never achieves this rest for himself. He remains troubled by the effects of our alienation, by the discrepancy between this religious vision and our own restless lives.[61]

Wittgenstein's dissatisfaction with the *Tractatus* is thus rooted in the fact that it attempts to tell a story of the full and final achievement of rational humanity in and through the reorientation of will. But the *Tractatus*'s particular story of redemption, like all such stories, is not concretely realizable, given the burdens of rational spontaneity's life within an antagonized culture. The other problems with the *Tractatus* that Wittgenstein later notes—the absence of any empirical psychology and linguistics to connect the signs of ordinary language with simple signs and simple signs in turn with simple objects of

61. Philip R. Shields, *Logic and Sin in the Writings of Ludwig Wittgenstein* (Chicago: University of Chicago Press, 1993), p. 106.

experience; the lack of any account of necessary truths such as those to be found in measurement systems ("Nothing is both red and green all over"); the failure to specify any examples of simple objects; the incoherence of the concept of an absolutely simple object—these are all problems that would have to be solved if the *Tractatus*'s doctrine of the reorientation of the will through the acceptance of the limits of language and thought were in fact to be received, taken up, and lived out by everyone or anyone. Some or all of these problems would have to be solved in order for its audiences to see from where they already are what exactly the limits of language and thought are and why and how those limits are forced upon us, in specific detail. That these problems cannot be solved means that the *Tractatus*'s doctrine is not receivable as a recipe for achieving rational peace.

The failure of the *Tractatus* to provide such a recipe, through a reorientation of will that is responsive to the metaphysical substance of the world, then signals, for Wittgenstein, the impossibility of any guiding doctrine, rooted in the nature of things, for the exercise of our powers and the achievement of rational peace and expressive freedom. Knowing something about some intentionality-determining substances will not, cannot, save us—will not, cannot, smoothly yield expressive freedom. Instead, "knowledge is in the end based on acknowledgement." ("Das Wissen gründet sich am Schluß auf der Anerkennung.")[62] Our knowings depend in the end always in part on our lives with others, with whom we share concepts and cultures. They are not on their own isolate, sempiternal-substance-determined achievements. Our lives with others no more assure smoothly expressive intentionality than do any substances, for our lives with others are, among other things, scenes of conflict and failures of acknowledgment. Nothing—no doctrine of physical substances or social life or the will of God or anything else—can guarantee the success of our efforts to achieve expressive freedom and sublime away our risks and responsibilities as bearers of intentionality within a divided culture. "When you are philosophizing you have to descend into primeval chaos and feel at home there."[63] Anything else would be dishonest to how we are.

Despite, however, the absence and impossibility of any guiding doctrine for the achievement of expressive freedom, our aspirations to expressive freedom, to self-conscious self-identity, and to the incarnation of perfected ratio-

62. Ludwig Wittgenstein, *On Certainty,* ed. G. E. M. Anscombe and G. H. von Wright, trans. Denis Paul and G. E. M. Anscombe (Oxford: Basil Blackwell, 1969), pp. 49e, 49.

63. Wittgenstein, *Culture and Value,* p. 65e.

nality do not lapse. The failure of the *Tractatus* to solve the problem of fully expressing rational self-consciousness in human life, but the sense of the persistence of that problem, then connect the later Wittgenstein to the immediately post-Kantian romantic writers who bore a sense of themselves as fitful bearers of a rational, expressive power whose conditions of full and perfect exercise are somehow blocked or mysterious, not in our power to command. (There is some justice in an aside of Edwards's that the later Wittgenstein stands to the earlier Wittgenstein as Kierkegaard stands to Hegel.[64] Kierkegaard himself has considerable affinities with the darker moments in Schiller and with certain passages in Schlegel.) What emerges from the ashes of the *Tractatus* is a sense of human beings as bearing a standing problem of finding their ways about, as self-conscious, rational beings possessed of an underlying spontaneity, in and through culture. A wish and an effort to know the absolute solution of this problem, to have a guiding doctrine of the fit expression of our intentionality and its underlying power, continually contend with the critical collapse of that wish and effort in either incoherence or in hopelessly abstract and practically useless dogmatism, just as the effort of the *Tractatus* collapsed. The solution is not achieved; the problem is not foresworn.

✳

To accept, but not to solve, the problem of expressive freedom, the problem of finding and articulating a doctrine to guide the exercise of spontaneity in and through culture, is to bring to the fore in one's writing not one's results but the dramatic struggles of a protagonist. *Philosophical Investigations* tracks the itinerary of such a protagonist, seeking doctrine, expressiveness, and rational peace, but finding any such effort crossed or undone by incoherence or by dogmatically abstract uselessness. It is these struggles, in their mix of aspiration and its frustration, that present us to ourselves, call us to a form of self-consciousness that is not doctrinal, in that no recipe for our power's expression and for the achievement of full self-identity is given. "By now it is becoming clear," Cavell writes, "that each of the voices, and silences, of the *Investigations* are the philosopher's, call him Wittgenstein, and they are meant as ours."[65] The voice of the philosopher, accepting our spontaneity and seeking a doctrine to guide its expression, and the voice of the philosopher's undoing, of the

---

64. Edwards, *Ethics without Philosophy*, p. 110.
65. Cavell, *Conditions Handsome and Unhandsome*, p. 83.

failure to arrive at a doctrine, are alike internal to our position as partly self-conscious, partly self-identical beings within a divided culture.

Philosophical Investigations lingers on conceptions of its own teaching that emphasize continuing critical activity within culture, as opposed to arriving at any final solution. "The work of the philosopher"—here one who has acknowledged the undoing of doctrinal ambition, one who has accepted that our lives as conceptually conscious and self-conscious beings are lived in and through a culture whose routes of expression we cannot command—"consists in assembling reminders for a particular purpose [ist ein Zusammentragen von Erinnerungen zu einem bestimmten Zweck]" (§127). There is no rational doctrine that controls and commands the full and fit expression of self-conscious, self-identical, fully expressive, rational humanity. "What *we* do is to bring words back from their metaphysical to their everyday use [*Wir* führen die Wörter—we lead words]" (§116). Leading words home is not the achievement of stillness and full rational peace. It is finding the life of words, and our lives as conceptually conscious beings, to lie within a complicated and divided culture, a culture of possibilities of expression to which we variously resonate, but also a culture of antagonisms. Something more, or different, or better, is wished for, and so a doctrine of the formation of a perfectly expressive and perfectly human culture is sought. As Novalis remarks, "Philosophy is actually homesickness *[Heimweh]—the drive to be home everywhere.*"[66] Philosophy—leading words back to their complex lives in culture—is this drive, this activity, not its rational completion under doctrine.

Implicit in this movement of longing and leading is the romantic motif, described by Geoffrey Hartman, of the philosopher-writer as a *halted traveler,* seeking home and rational peace.[67] The protagonist-traveler is stopped by wonder in a spot or *genius loci,* or by a liminal, exemplar figure who seems to promise a route toward expressive power. But this stopping, with its intimations of expressive power, occurs outside culture, on a journey or way, in a place of distance or alienation from culture as it stands. When the generalization of this intimated expressive power and its integration into and through the

---

66. Novalis [Friedrich von Hardenburg], *Schriften,* ed. Paul Kluckhohn and Richard Samuel (Stuttgart: Kohlhammer, 1960), 3:434; cited in Azade Seyhan, *Representation and Its Discontents: The Critical Legacy of German Romanticism* (Berkeley: University of California Press, 1992), p. 75.

67. Geoffrey Hartman, *Wordsworth's Poetry 1787–1814* (New Haven: Yale University Press, 1964), pp. 3–22.

ways of culture is then sought or imagined, there is only defeat or frustration. "Philosophy is actually homesickness."

Philosophical Investigations presents an open-ended series of such moments of halted travel, moments of aspiration and its undoing. This open-ended series forms a perspicuous representation of our humanity and its continuing burdens, of our lives as conceptually conscious and self-conscious beings in and through culture. "A perspicuous representation [Die übersichtliche Darstellung] produces just that understanding which consists in 'seeing connexions.' Hence the importance of finding and inventing *intermediate cases* [*Zwischengliedern*]" (§122). Through the series of moments of effort to articulate a doctrine of the achievement of expressive freedom, followed by the undoing of that effort, followed again by its resurgence, thence again its undoing, we become legible to ourselves in our humanity. The character of our lives as conceptually conscious and self-conscious beings is shown to us. The dramatic presentation of our struggles and their frustration shows us what we are. Schlegel: "The inner vision can become clearer to itself and quite alive only through external representation [Darstellung]."[68]

The protagonist figure of *Philosophical Investigations,* moving through successive moments of doctrinal aspiration and its undoing, becomes for us a figure of acknowledgment, someone in whom we might see ourselves. It is the movements of the thoughts—the "long and involved journeyings" ("langen und verwickelten [entangled] Fahrten"; Preface, ix)—that show us to ourselves. Expressive freedom and rational peace in and through cultural life are longed for and sought. Efforts are made to articulate their conditions of perfect achievement. But these efforts one and all founder. "Preaching morals is difficult, founding it impossible."[69] "And this is how it is: if only you do not try to utter what is unutterable then *nothing* gets lost. But the unutterable will be—unutterably—*contained* in what has been uttered."[70]

What is unutterably present in the protagonist's series of frustrated efforts in *Philosophical Investigations*—an aspiration to bring *Willkür* to full informa-

68. Schlegel, "Dialogue on Poetry," cited in Seyhan, *Representation and Its Discontents,* p. 7.

69. Wittgenstein, reported in *Ludwig Wittgenstein and the Vienna Circle: Conversations Recorded by Friedrich Waismann,* ed. B. F. McGuinness, trans. J. Schulte and B. F. McGuinness (Oxford: Basil Blackwell, 1979), p. 118.

70. Wittgenstein, "Letter to Paul Engelmann, 9 April 1917," in Paul Engelmann, *Letters from Ludwig Wittgenstein with a Memoir,* ed. B. F. McGuinness, (Oxford: Basil Blackwell, 1967), p. 7.

tion by *Wille,* to achieve perfect and assured expressive freedom and self-conscious self-identity, in and through a culture in which these achievements are reciprocally sustained by all, coupled with that aspiration's continual defeat—is present to us not as a doctrine or thesis or formula to guide our own efforts. Instead of being given a result, we overhear, as it were, the protagonist's internal struggles. Overhearing of this kind is, as John Stuart Mill noted, our characteristic relation to poetry: "Poetry and eloquence are both alike the expression or utterance of feeling. But if we may allow the antithesis, we should say that eloquence is *heard,* poetry is *overheard.* Eloquence supposes an audience; the peculiarity of poetry appears to us to lie in the poet's utter unconsciousness of a listener."[71] In enabling us to overhear these struggles, the text of *Philosophical Investigations* offers us, dramatically, what Bouveresse has called a "narrow path that passes between predication and nonsense"[72] in thinking all at once about human conceptual consciousness, self-conscious self-identity, spontaneity, expressive power, and value—the way of *poesis.*

71. John Stuart Mill, "What Is Poetry?" in *Autobiography and Other Writings,* ed. Jack Stillinger (Boston: Houghton Mifflin, 1969), p. 195. First published in *Monthly Review* (January 1833).
72. Bouveresse, " 'The Darkness of This Time': Wittgenstein and the Modern World," p. 39.

5

Augustine's Misbegotten Conversion: Proposal and Rebuke—§§1–38

Why does Wittgenstein care about Augustine? Why does *Philosophical Investigations* start with the citation and criticism of Augustine's remarks about language learning? The 1933 Big Typescript, the principal source for sections 1–188 of *Philosophical Investigations*, does not start in that way, but instead begins, as does *The Blue Book*, with a direct criticism of the thesis that understanding is a mental event that gives life to the sign.[1] If criticizing that mentalist thesis so as to arrive at a counterposition about understanding is the aim, then why Augustine? Does it matter that he held the view about language learning and understanding that Wittgenstein is concerned to engage? Is it just that Augustine's conception of language learning is, as Baker and Hacker suggest, an "Urbild," a "primitive picture," or a "proto-theory" that of itself is "an invisible force that moulds the theories of language of almost everyone"?[2] If that is true, then is *Philosophical Investigations* itself a work principally in the theory of language, offering us new theses about meaning and understanding, a book whose "critical preoccupation . . . is the nature of language and of linguistic meaning, together with the philosophical perplexities generated by reflection on meaning, language, and thought"?[3]

No doubt "one of the tasks of *Philosophical Investigations* is to show how [Augustine's picture of language] leads to error and confusion." *Philosophical Investigations* does seek to extirpate that picture of language, or at least to wean us so far as possible from "a paradigm that bedevils our reflections on

---

1. Baker and Hacker, *Wittgenstein: Understanding and Meaning,* p. 35.
2. Ibid., p. 36; P. M. S. Hacker, *Insight and Illusion: Themes in the Philosophy of Wittgenstein,* rev. ed. (Oxford: Clarendon Press, 1986), p. 130. Cf. Baker and Hacker, *Wittgenstein: Understanding and Meaning,* p. 46.
3. Baker and Hacker, *Wittgenstein: Understanding and Meaning,* p. 29.

meaning."[4] But just saying that does not make clear how our captivation by that amorphous picture of language, or various of its natural elaborations, is woven through our images of ourselves, our aspirations, and our ways of living. To say just that is to cast Wittgenstein as concerned simply to remedy an intellectual mistake, a mistake in "our reflections." This way of reading overlooks the moral urgencies of the text that arise in and through the engagement with Augustine.

Augustine's *Confessions* is one of the most authoritative conversion narratives in western literature, a story of the elevation of the person out of confusion, aimlessness, and self-dissipation and into full humanity, expressiveness, and love. Its only competitors for depth and range of influence as a conversion narrative are Plato's *Republic,* the conversions (especially Paul's) of the Gospels, Acts, and Letters, Descartes' *Meditations,* and Marx's narratives of the proletariat coming to see through its mystifications by political economy. Wittgenstein is said to have remarked that the *Confessions* is "possibly 'the most serious book ever written.' "[5] Norman Malcolm reports that Wittgenstein "told me he decided to begin his *Investigations* with a quotation from the *Confessions* not because he couldn't find the conception expressed in that quotation stated as well by other philosophers, but because the conception *must* be important if so great a mind held it."[6]

What then does Wittgenstein mean in noting the greatness of Augustine's mind? How is Augustine's greatness connected with his thoughts about language?

The *Confessions* depicts a person's conversion out of empty arbitrariness and the lustful consumption of experience and into coherence, self-unity, charity, continence, and faithfulness. Augustine dwells at length on his domination by pride, lustfulness, and perversity throughout his childhood and young adulthood, prior to his conversion at thirty-one. As an infant, the immediate demands of the body are entirely effective in bringing about bodily motions that are not self-conscious, that are more simple behaviors than human actions. "In those days," Augustine tells us, "all I knew was how to suck, and how to

---

4. Ibid., pp. 60, 97.
5. M. O'C. Drury, recalling a remark of Wittgenstein's, in Drury, "Conversations with Wittgenstein," *Recollections of Wittgenstein,* ed. Rush Rhees (Oxford: Oxford University Press, 1984), p. 90.
6. Norman Malcolm, *Ludwig Wittgenstein: A Memoir* (Oxford: Oxford University Press, 1958), p. 71.

lie still when my body sensed comfort or cry when it felt pain."[7] These bodily demands for comfort and satiety ramify as Augustine grows up. The pleasures that he pursues become wilder and more multifarious, but they remain equally effective in determining his behavior as the pursuit of completeness through the consumption of material things. "For as I grew to manhood I was inflamed with desire for a surfeit of hell's pleasures. Foolhardy as I was, I ran wild with lust that was manifold and rank" (II, 1, 43). Surfeit, completion, and satiety, not expressive freedom, not spontaneity housed within meaningful cultural routines, are the objects of his actions.

Augustine's submission to the imperatives of lust, consumption, and satiety then leads him to repress his capacity for acknowledging any higher realities, for discerning either an inner spontaneity or higher, nonmaterial objects, above all God, to which it might respond. "I was unable to conceive of any but material realities" (V, 11, 106). His routines of action stunt his capacities for understanding himself and his place in a divinely ordered world. Doing what he does, he is unable to see any way to do anything else, arriving at the condition that he will later call servitude, a form of bondage wrought by his own will upon itself. "I was held fast, not in fetters clamped upon me by another, but by my own will, which had the strength of iron chains. The enemy held my will in his power and from it he had made a chain and shackled me. For my will was perverse and lust had grown from it, and when I gave in to lust habit was born, and when I did not resist the habit it became a necessity. These were the links which together formed what I have called my chain, and it held me fast in the duress of servitude" (VIII, 5, 164).

Yet his life within this condition of servitude, wrought by the will distorting itself, nonetheless appears to Augustine to be the way of freedom. A life of lust and consumption gives unlimited scope to arbitrariness, to *Willkür* acting without responsiveness to any reasonable norms. Independence of any norms is prized for its own sake; unchastened spontaneity is enjoyed in itself. The will, as it were, senses and asserts its own spontaneous power to its own delight. "I loved my own way, not yours, but it was a truant's freedom that I loved" (III, 3, 58). Actions motivated by lust, by a desire for satiety, and by *Willkür*'s delight in itself are encouraged when others around one likewise reject the authority of norms and pursue the ways of consumption. "We are

7. Augustine, *Confessions,* trans. R. S. Pine-Coffin (Harmondsworth, England: Penguin Books, 1961), Book I, Section 6, p. 25. All subsequent references to this edition appear parenthetically in the text by book number, section number, and page number.

carried away by custom to our own undoing and it is hard to struggle against the stream" (I, 16, 36).

After his conversion it is, for Augustine, entirely different. The sways of lust, material realities, arbitrary desire, custom, and prideful delight in independence are overcome in the submission of the will to God's authority. Faith, charity, and continence are now effectively expressed in Augustine's actions, as he responds to nonmaterial, higher realities within and without, as he learns to recognize and act on his soul's longing for God. His actions and his understanding of himself come now to be shaped by a "new will which had come to life in me and made me wish to serve you freely and enjoy you, my God, who are our only certain joy" (VIII, 6, 164). Through grace, manifested in multiple friendships, books, conversations, and moments of the experience of beauty, all of which serve as calls to something better, God has changed Augustine's way of being. "You [God] converted me to yourself, so that I no longer desired a wife or placed any hope in this world but stood firmly upon the rule of faith" (VIII, 12, 178). Standing upon this rule of faith then enables genuine self-mastery and expressiveness rather than self-dissipation (cf. VII, 7, 143–44), and hence a unity of the self with itself, as it is coherently housed in cultural routines that are divinely ordained, above all in the routines of continence and charity. "Truly it is by continence that we are made as one and regain that unity of self which we lost by falling apart in the search for a variety of pleasures" (X, 29, 233).

The ability to undergo this conversion, this reorientation of the will, is attained not by the further pursuit of independence and not by further actions motivated by *Willkür* alone or by pride in its powers, but instead by a kind of active passiveness, an openness to the call of grace. "For Saint Paul teaches that he who sees ought not to boast as though what he sees, and even the power by which he sees, 'had not come to him by gift.' For, whatever powers he has, 'did they not come to him by gift?' By the gift of grace he is not only shown how to see you, who are always the same, but is also given the strength to hold you" (VII, 21, 155; citing 1 Cor. 4:7). This active-passive responsiveness to the call of grace, prepared by prior friendship, reading, and conversation, comes over Augustine fully all at once, in the moment of his conversion, and it brings him, at last, full peace and confidence.

> So I hurried back to the place where Alypius was sitting, for when I stood
> up to move away I had put down the book containing Paul's Epistles. I seized

it and opened it, and in silence I read the first passage on which my eyes
fell: "Not in revelling and drunkenness, not in lust and wantonness, not in
quarrels and rivalries. Rather, arm yourselves with the Lord Jesus Christ;
spend no more thought on nature and nature's appetites" [Rom. 13:13–14].
I had no wish to read more and no need to do so. For in an instant, as I
came to the end of the sentence, it was as though the light of confidence
flooded into my heart and all the darkness of doubt was dispelled.

(VIII, 12, 178)

This picture of conversion is enormously attractive to Wittgenstein. It offers
a way out of self-dissipation and into coherent self-unity. It offers escape from
the rivalries, uncertainties, and incoherences of a life dominated by *Willkür,*
by arbitrariness. Its account of an active-passive responsiveness to grace offers
an image of *Willkür,* spontaneity, and power all welded to *Wille,* orderly routines of action, and coherent expressiveness. It offers a model of the overcoming of the prideful self-assertiveness that is in fact arbitrary and hostage to
fortune ("The *edifice of your pride* has to be dismantled") without abasement.
One's actions and way of life will henceforth express who one is, as a being
coherently possessed of expressive power.

The language-learning scene in the *Confessions* is then of interest to Wittgenstein because it is there that the possibility of this later, compelling conversion is first dimly intimated, to both Augustine and the reader. The coherent
self-unity that comes after conversion is a mode of what Augustine will later
call *thoughtfulness.* It is thought as an active power that enables both conceptual
consciousness and self-consciousness. Mere sensory experience alone does not
produce them. In a stunning passage, Augustine ascribes to God's creation of
him both his ability to be conceptually conscious, which is a matter of certain
archetypes or recognition criteria that are "already in my memory, hidden
away in its deeper recesses," in "old lairs," and his ability actively to retrieve
and use these archetypes.

For I can run through all the organs of sense, which are the body's gate-
ways to the mind, but I cannot find any by which these facts [that certain
objects have certain qualities] could have entered. My eyes tell me "If they
have colour, we reported them." My ears say "If they have sound, it was we
who gave notice of them." My nose says "If they have smell, it was through
me that they passed into the mind." The sense of taste says "If they have no
taste, do not put your question to me." The sense of touch says "If it is not

a body, I did not touch it, and if I did not touch it, I had no message to transmit."

How, then, did these facts get into my memory? Where did they come from? I do not know. When I learned them, I did not believe them with another man's mind. It was my own mind which recognized them and admitted that they were true. I entrusted them to my own mind as though it were a place of storage from which I could produce them at will. Therefore they must have been in my mind even before I learned them, though not present to my memory. Then whereabouts in my mind were they? How was it that I recognized them when they were mentioned and agreed that they were true? It must have been that they were already in my memory, hidden away in its deeper recesses, in so remote a part of it that I might not have been able to think of them at all, if some other person had not brought them to the fore by teaching me about them.

. . . If for a short space of time, I cease to give [these facts] my attention, they sink back and recede again into the more remote cells of my memory, so that I have to think them out again, like a fresh set of facts, if I am to know them. I have to shepherd them out again from their old lairs, because there is no other place where they can have gone. In other words, once they have been dispersed, I have to collect them again, and this is the derivation of the word *cogitare,* which means *to think* or *to collect one's thoughts.* For in Latin the word *cogo,* meaning *I assemble* or *I collect,* is related to *cogito,* which means *I think,* in the same way as *ago* is related to *agito* or *facio* to *factito.*

(X, 10–11, 217–19)

That is, within the human person there are both archetypes and the powers to recall them and to use them to form propositions, to register facts. Both these archetypes and these powers are simply given, hence are gifts of God, not products of sensory processes. Thinking is the explicit recalling of these archetypes and the explicit exercise of these powers. This thinking is a kind of collection of the self and its contents, an achievement of coherent unity out of chaos. The ability to think is a power that is given. To exercise this power, therein collecting oneself, is already to bear possibilities of conversion and to be partly on the way toward them.

And it is thought which makes language learning possible. Hence to be capable of language learning as Augustine describes it is to bear the power or possibility of conversion. The thought that is exercised in language learning emerges here as a *scintilla animae,* a spark in the soul that is "a trace of the single unseen Being from whom it was derived" (I, 20, 40). To exercise this power, and to come to self-consciousness in exercising it, is already to respond, however fitfully and dimly, to a divinely given possibility of conversion, to God's gift. It is the presence within language learning of an active power of thinking that is itself latently an active power of conversion that attracts Wittgenstein's interest, and it is Augustine's sense of the presence of this power, and his account of its subsequent flowering into conversion, that makes his mind, to Wittgenstein, great.

A sense of language learning as accomplished by this active, conversion-enabling thinking runs insistently throughout the entire passage from Augustine that Wittgenstein takes up.

> I ceased to be a baby unable to talk, and was now a boy with the power of speech. I can remember that time, and later on realized how I had learnt to speak. It was not my elders who showed me the words by some set system of instruction, in the way that they taught me to read not long afterwards; but, instead, I taught myself by using the intelligence which you, my God, gave to me. For when I tried to express my meaning by crying out and making various sounds and movements, so that my wishes should be obeyed, I found that I could not convey all that I meant or make myself understood by everyone whom I wished to understand me. So my memory prompted me. I noticed that people would name some object and then turn towards whatever it was that they had named. I watched them and understood that the sound they made when they wanted to indicate that particular thing was the name which they gave to it, and their actions clearly showed me what they meant, for there is a kind of universal language, consisting of expressions of the face and eyes, gestures and tones of voice, which can show whether a person means to ask for something and get it, or refuse it and have nothing to do with it. So, by hearing words arranged in various phrases and constantly repeated, I gradually pieced together what they stood for, and when my tongue had mastered the pronunciation, I began to express my wishes by means of them. In this way I made my wants known to my family and they made theirs known to me, and I took a further step into the stormy life of human society, although I was still subject to the authority of my parents and the will of my elders.
>
> (I, 8, 29)

Here the learning of language is depicted as brought about by an individual power or ability, given by God ("I taught myself. . . ."; "It was not my elders who showed me. . . ."). Individual memory provides the archetypes or identity criteria under which objects are sorted prior to mastery of the public language in use. This memory is primitive and simply given ("which you, my God, gave to me"). There is a strong distinction between an active subject, possessed of memory, intelligence, and will, and the objects of experience, the things desired or refused. No particular theory of ideas is presupposed; ideas or images are *not* cast as the things immediately named, things that interpose between the subject and the object. Instead, words simply name the objects that are sought and avoided. Underlying this naming relation, there is less a system of ideas than there are various modes of mental activity: wishing, understanding, desiring, watching, and remembering. These modes involve the use of archetypes that are not themselves specified as images or ideas, but instead are simply presupposed as an unspecified ability to sort things into kinds. It is the mental activity of the subject, not the given archetypes, that is foregrounded in this account. Above all, this mental activity that brings about the learning of language is a step "into the stormy life of human society" that is to be followed by later steps through and beyond that society, steps toward God. To learn language through this mental activity is already to be part of the way along a path toward conversion into faithfulness. It is an enormously attractive picture, not only supported by the obvious fact of the species specificity of anything like human language, but also compelling in its presentation of a path toward a moral ideal of full and faithful humanity, within which one is free of anxieties of reception and competition, where one is instead received by God.

✳

But is Augustine's conversion, in preparation dimly, in ways not then evident to him, through the mental activity involved in the learning of language, in fact genuine and exemplary? Does Augustine succeed in describing a compelling route from infancy to boyhood to adolescence to early adulthood to conversion? There are a number of reasons to be suspicious of Augustine's account of his development. Augustine implicitly questions and qualifies his account, in ways that Wittgenstein may well be supposed to have noticed, and further grounds for suspicion of this account lie in the character of the antagonized culture that continues to resist it.

It is unpersuasive, both factually and normatively, that desire should disappear after conversion in the way that Augustine claims it has ("I no longer desired a wife or placed any hope in this world but stood firmly upon the rule of faith"). Augustine himself, after his conversion, provides a considerable catalogue of the continuing temptations of both the body and the mind.

> Day after day without ceasing these temptations put us to the test, O Lord. . . . Again I become a prey to my habits, which hold me fast. My tears flow, but still I am held fast. Such is the price we pay for the burden of custom! . . . Who can tell how often we give way? . . . What excuse can I make for myself when often, as I sit at home, I cannot turn my eyes from the sight of a lizard catching flies or a spider entangling them as they fly into her web?
>
> (X, 37, 245; X, 40, 249; X, 35, 243)

The charms of material realities for both the bodily senses and the mind's curiosity are not easily resisted. Faithfulness in orientation to higher realities is not easily maintained. There is even a faint suggestion, present in the images of the lizard and the spider catching flies, of persons as somehow trapped or entangled, unable after conversion to lead their lives by exercising powers that are genuinely their own. Factually, the natural attractions of sensory delights compete with what then appears to be a paler, less human commitment to faithfulness, continence, charity, and love.

Normatively, it is not clear that a full conversion to continence and charity is either possible or desirable. The very life of a person seems to disappear, once it is imagined as no longer inflected by temptation and unruly desire. This is reflected in the tendency of the protagonist of the *Confessions* to disappear as a presence after the conversion in Book VIII and a short denouement in Book IX recounting Augustine's return to Africa and the death of his mother. After Book IX Augustine as a human protagonist appears only fitfully, and then largely in the accounts of the recurrence of temptations in Book X. In Books XI to XIII, devoted to the interpretation of Genesis, the figure of Augustine as a central experiencing protagonist is generally absent, except for occasional interjections to God. Perhaps it is not possible to lead a human life in full faithfulness as Augustine conceives of it, and if it is not possible, then perhaps it is neither desirable nor necessary in order to achieve full humanity and live out one's ordained place in nature.

Wittgenstein noted in particular the arbitrariness and inhumanity of Augustine's account of continence as a necessity of faithfulness. In reaction to M. O'C. Drury's expression of surprise and shock that Egyptian religious sculptures should show a god with an erect phallus, Wittgenstein replied, "Why in the world shouldn't they have regarded with awe and reverence that act by which the human race is perpetuated? Not every religion has to have St. Augustine's attitude to sex. Why, even in our culture marriages are celebrated in a church; everyone present knows what is going to happen that night, but that doesn't prevent it being a religious ceremony."[8] Without the presence of desire that is in part unruly, and without the possibility of its expression, a human life may be distorted or flattened. It is certainly possible that Wittgenstein, despite his ascetic tendencies and self-image, may have been, as someone both generally attracted to men and of Jewish descent (hence an outsider with regard to surrounding social norms and subject to their unhappy suasions), particularly resistant to the official Augustinian theology of sexuality's redirection toward God. But whether or not Wittgenstein's suspicion of that theology can be explained in this way, that theology itself is not in any case entirely easy to believe. Temptations tend to linger, whatever joys in God's presence may be possible, and their lingering seems to have something to do both with what we are factually and with what we might be normatively.

There is even within Augustine's text a thread of persistent anxiety about his own claims to self-understanding and to have accomplished his conversion. Augustine wonders why he cares that other human beings should hear and accept his words, given that these words are addressed directly to God, and he goes on to hint that his self-understanding and claim to conversion are ratified fully only in their reception and repetition by other human beings. Yet his confessions can be received and repeated only by those who already are in the right spirit, who already can hear them with charity. So the reception and repetition of one's conversion and its confession seem to be necessary in order to certify its authenticity but at the same time impossible: those who are already in charity cannot now repeat that conversion; those who are not in charity cannot hear and receive that confession and take up its directions. Augustine worries about the truthfulness of his own confession, about his own truth to himself and to possibilities of human conversion, as he raises the question of his reception.

> Why, then, does it matter to me whether men should hear what I have to confess, as though it were they who were to cure all the evil that is in me? . . . And if a man recognizes his true self, can he possibly say "This is

---

8. Wittgenstein, cited in M. O'C. Drury, "Conversations with Wittgenstein," p. 148.

false," unless he is himself a liar? But charity believes all things—all things, that is, which are spoken by those who are joined as one in charity—and for this reason I, too, O Lord, make my confession aloud in the hearing of men. For although I cannot prove to them that my confessions are true, at least I shall be believed by those whose ears are opened to me by charity.

(X, 3, 208)

Augustine here confesses that his reception, his hearing by others, does matter to him. It would help to reassure one in one's confessions if those confessions were received by others and if the conversions they describe were repeated. Anyone who hears them with charity will see their truth. But who are these people? Where are they to be found, particularly in a divided, antagonized society, with multiple, conflicting cultural and material routines of life?

Wittgenstein was alert to the difficulties of establishing the truthfulness of a confession, particularly one that includes a claim to have accomplished a conversion in an antagonized society. "The criteria for the truth of the *confession* that I thought such-and-such are not the criteria for a true *description* of a process. And the importance of the true confession does not reside in its being a correct and certain report of a process. It resides rather in the special consequences which can be drawn from a confession whose truth is guaranteed by the special criteria of *truthfulness*" (II, xi, 222). These special criteria for the truthfulness of a confession include the possibility that this confession shall be taken up by others, who see themselves and their own possibilities of development reflected in it. Among the special consequences of a truthful confession are the facts not that it describes inner events, but rather that others do take it up, do live their lives out in its terms, seeing the modalities of lived value that the confessor pursues and avoids as their own. But how and when are such special criteria of truthfulness fulfilled, such special consequences of a truthful confession enacted? It is not at all clear that anxiety about truthfulness to oneself and to possibilities of the development of humanity can ever be overcome. A divided consciousness, uncertain about its housings within opposed routines of life in an antagonized society, is nearly inevitable.

✳

There are then good reasons—some of them partly noted by Wittgenstein, some of them making themselves felt in anxieties that persist in Augustine's text—for being suspicious of Augustine's claim to have accomplished an elevating conversion into full faithfulness, a conversion whose possibility is already prepared in the mental activity underlying the learning of language. The specific terms of Augustine's official conversion are too implausible and inhuman. The route toward that conversion, despite the importance to it of friends and conversations, is too intellectualistic in relying initially on the soul's divinely granted, isolate power to conceptualize the objects of its experience.

Yet a conversion like Augustine's, an elevation into higher possibilities of life, but one that is more humanly plausible, continues to attract Wittgenstein's interest. ("What is good is also divine. . . . Only something supernatural can express the Supernatural.") There is a wish for a wedding of spontaneity to the achievement of value. The possibility of conversion, as well as an aspiration toward it, must have something to do with the presence within the human being of a spontaneity and activity that make language learning possible, but less intellectualistically. The natural thing to do then is to investigate the nature of that mental activity that underlies language learning, to investigate the vehicle of a possible conversion of the person that is more humanly plausible, albeit less complete and perfect, than the conversion presented in Augustine's account of his development. The investigation of the nature of this mental activity or spontaneity, of the language learning that flows from it, and of the possibilities of conversion that it fitfully establishes is the opening move of *Philosophical Investigations*. Augustine's description of the learning of language attracts the interest of a protagonist in the text who wishes to scrutinize and refigure the possibilities of development and conversion that are latent within it. "These words, *it seems to me* [so scheint es mir], give us a particular picture of the essence of human language" (§1; emphasis added). But, implicitly, this picture seems to that protagonist not to be the only possible picture of linguistic development, and not even the right picture. Hence the possibilities of conversion to which that picture of linguistic development points are themselves not the only or the right possibilities for us either.

It is easy to see how Augustine's picture of the learning of language arises. In positing a primitive and divinely given mental activity underlying the learning of language, it upholds the species specificity of linguistic development. It captures, or seems to capture, the crucial aboutness of language—that words, or at least some words, can be used to sort and classify things. "If you describe the learning of language in this way you are, I believe, thinking primarily of nouns like 'table', 'chair', 'bread', and of people's names, and only secondarily of the names of certain actions and properties; and of the remaining kinds of word as something that will take care of itself" (§1).

Yet the picture is not the right one. It offers no account of "the remaining kinds of word." In failing to offer such an account, it represents our ability to classify objects under concepts and our ability to respond to our world conceptually, our bearing of conceptual consciousness, as a matter of archetypes within that await only triggers by experience, rather than as part of a course of development that involves entering into cultural repertoires through which moral aspirations are played out. It is as though our conceptual consciousness were simply guided by these archetypes within and by their matches with objects without, overlooking the growth of our conceptual consciousness in and through complicated and value-laden routines of culture.

So Augustine's picture of the learning of language is not the only or right picture, his account of conversion not the only or right account. We can point to a use of language for which Augustine's account is altogether unsuitable, a picture in which a word is significantly used within a routine, but not as the name of anything and not as the expression of any inner archetype.

> Now think of the following use of language: I send someone shopping. I give him a slip marked "five red apples." He takes the slip to the shopkeeper, who opens the drawer marked "apples"; then he looks up the word "red" in a table and finds a colour sample opposite it; then he says the series of cardinal numbers—I assume that he knows them by heart [er weiss sie auswendig: outwardly, by rote]—up to the word "five" and for each number he takes an apple of the same colour as the sample out of the drawer.—It is in this and similar ways that one operates with words.
>
> (§1)

"Five" is not the name of any object, not the name of a class of classes or of a Platonically subsistent number that the mind somehow grasps or recognizes. It is, instead, an expression that is used here within a primitive cultural routine. Augustine's account of the essence of language will not do. Hence his account of what it is to learn language cannot be right, and it is unclear whether the possibilities of development toward conversion that he presents can be taken up.

Crucially, however, the wish for a route from an inner spontaneity and toward conversion does not lapse. It is not enough just to say that we have this word "five" and certain routines of using it. Something in us wishes to know how we have that word and those routines and, further, what possibilities of development are therein open to us. A voice—one of the voices of the protagonist, a voice occurring within the protagonist's consciousness, not without—intrudes, interrupting the criticism of Augustine's picture in order to demand some picture in its place, some account of our spontaneity. Augustine's picture has been rejected. But something—some account of the roots of conceptual consciousness, of our ability to learn language, and of the courses of development that are open to us—must be put in its place. "But how does he know where and how he is to look up the word 'red' and what he is to do with the word 'five'?" (§1). The thought that there just are routines of cultural activity is not one that it is easy to rest with, without an account of them.

Yet the demand for a new account of how one knows how to use the word "five" is itself immediately rejected. "I assume that he *acts* as I have described. Explanations come to an end somewhere" (§1). To give an account of how mastery of "five" is rooted in knowledge of some Platonic object or in the presence of some archetype within would be to fall back into the sort of intellectualistic account of the learning of language that is present in Augustine, and it would likewise be to fall back into a conversion narrative—the story of the perfected unleashing of this given intellectual power—that would overlook the antagonisms of cultural routines and their resistance to perfect rational expressiveness.

But again the demand for an account is entered. The appeal to the sheer existence of routines of practice cannot stand on its own, or is not allowed to stand on its own by one side, one voice, of the protagonist's consciousness. "But what is the meaning of the word 'five'?" (§1). Some account of our powers, of the nature of our ability to use language, is still wanted. Yet this want too is rebuked in turn: "No such thing was in question here, only how the word 'five' is used" (§6). As a corrective to an Augustinian, intellectualistic picture of the learning of language, this is compelling; as an account of the nature of our power to use language and of our possibilities of development, it is empty and unsatisfying.

Hence there arises in the text an internal dialectic, an unending critical conversation within the protagonist, between two voices that are equally its own. One voice demands a ground for, an account of, "the way one operates with words," of how one is so much as able to do this at all, and of the possibilities of development and conversion of and within culture that are open to such a being, possessed of that power. A second voice of rebuke or repudiation rejects any account of our power that is offered as intellectualistic and as insensitive to the torturous entanglements of conceptual consciousness with opposed cultural routines that it can never master. This voice seeks not mastery but silent charity and peace, without philosophizing ("Explanations come to an end somewhere" [§1]). In this seeking of peace, this voice exercises the very power for which the first voice demands an account. Hence it is a voice that cannot, in the energies of its repudiations, uphold the view that cultural routines are mere natural happenstances that we do not actively make. It is a voice that thus acknowledges the existence of an inner spontaneity despite itself, the very spontaneity that the first voice then seeks to grasp and release, perfectly. "*I struggle again and again* [Ich kämpfe immer wieder]—*whether successfully I do not know*—against the tendency in my own mind [die Tendenz in meinem eigenen Geiste] to set up (construct) rules in philosophy, to make suppositions (hypotheses) instead of just seeing what is there."[9] "I must plunge into the water of doubt again and again."[10]

Thus even so apparently simple an utterance as "Five red apples" raises—within the protagonist's internal reflections—questions about the nature of intentionality and about the possibilities of conversion into full expressive humanity that intentionality may bear within it. The sentence "Five red apples" is syntactically complex. It is introduced into the internal conversation in order to block the question "Of what is five the name?" and therein to undo the Fregean-Platonic picture of meaning as always involving a route to a referent. Instead of pursuing such answers to a question that is misbegotten, we are instead to see that the word "five" is a tool, something that we use to do certain things. "It is in this and similar ways that one operates with words [operiert man mit Worten]." Yet this claim does not settle—it rather invites—the question how we manage thus to operate with words. Pursuing answers to that question leads only to rebukes directed against the effort to get beneath the surface of our practice, but these rebukes in turn rest only on reminders of what we do—reminders that themselves invite further questioning of their bases. Questioning our practices and seeking to explain them are figures of

9. Wittgenstein, cited in Baker and Hacker, *Wittgenstein: Understanding and Meaning,* p. 74 n. 11; emphases added.
10. Wittgenstein, "Remarks on Frazer's *Golden Bough,*" trans. John Beversluis, in *Philosophical Occasions,* ed. Klagge and Nordmann, p. 119.

a wish for control, mastery, and immunity from criticism in the release of intentionality into perfect expressiveness; rebukes to these efforts and reminders of what we do are figures of reattachment to the complex and divided ways of our common practices, where the complexities and liabilities of our conceptual lives within those common practices sustain a wish to be free of them, thus in turn motivating questioning and efforts at explanation.

Perhaps it could be different. Both internal voices join in this suggestion—the explanation-seeking voice wishing to find the basis of intentionality; the rebuking voice seeking to show us that nothing is hidden, that everything is on the surface in what we do. In pursuing this suggestion, the criticism and correction of these voices by one another are continued and deepened, not brought to closure. The conception of meaning as a route to a referent, as involving naming at its core, and the conceptions of intentionality and language learning and possibilities of conversion that attend that conception of meaning, involve "a primitive idea of the way language functions" (§2). That—in a primitive idea ("in einer primitiven Vorstellung")—is where that conception of meaning is at home ("zu Hause") (§2). "But one can also say that it is the idea of a language more primitive than ours" (§2). We might hope to grasp the nature of intentionality by looking at such a primitive language. Perhaps an explanation of how a human being comes to speak such a primitive language will leap into view. Or perhaps everything will be on the surface, so that the wish for explanation lapses. "Let us imagine [Denken wir uns] a language for which the description given by Augustine is right"—the "block, pillar, slab, beam" language (§2). "Conceive this [Fasse dies . . . auf] as a complete primitive language" (§2). Does this help? Does it bring the internal conversation, the play of explanation-seeking and rebuke, to an end?

The thought is that the "block, pillar, slab, beam" language might be both paradigmatic of language at its core and yet so simple that everything is evident in the acts of using it, nothing is hidden and nothing is to be explained. It is to be a language for which Augustine's account of the nature of language as consisting of names for objects is right, but where no inner understanding can readily be supposed to be involved, where no *scintilla animae* or spark of intentionality seems to underlie linguistic action. Everything—understanding, responsiveness, and intentionality—is to be evident in what is done. But the command to conceive the "block, pillar, slab, beam" language as "a complete primitive language [als vollständige primitive Sprache]" (§2) turns out to be one that it is not easy to carry out. As Cavell has noted, "That there are more things to be said in language than there are words to say them is analytic of 'language.'" The words of a language by their nature as tools in use admit of being turned and twisted rather than being tied as though by steel to particular referents. We learn words by using varieties of their uses ("a block of stone," "to block a rushing lineman," "to block a hat," "block voting," "block party"). This is why we are not sure, Cavell notes, "that the 'four word/sentence' language game of §2 . . . is really a language."[11] When we try to conceive the "block, pillar, slab, beam" language as a complete primitive language, then what happens is mostly one or both of two things. *Either* we fail to imagine a language-game that is enough like our language to make the emergence of our language out of it readily intelligible. Therein the players of the "block, pillar, slab, beam" language-game become unintelligible to us, become primitive, or Neanderthal, or other; it isn't ourselves that we're imagining in imagining them.[12] *Or* we do succeed in imagining a complete language, but then feel that there must be some inner understanding lying behind the mastery of the language, behind the ability of that language's masters to use any one of its words to refer to evidently numerically and discernibly different things. Therein the speakers of the language become for us like us, but therein also the wish arises to explain how they have this ability and to know how they will express their inner understandings in dealing with objects—as we do or not? How far, and how deeply, and on what basis are they like us in their lives with language? We imagine somehow sharing a world with these speakers, moving blocks and pillars about ourselves, and wondering too whether we will move and respond in concert with them.

The anxiety and uncertainty that arise when we imagine these primitive speakers to be problematically like us—masters of a language and able to use it, not its passive and mechanical instruments, yet masters in ways we know not how—resemble the anxieties and uncertainties that attach to relations with children. Will they take to the ways of language and culture in detail as we do, as time goes on? So much seems unpredictable apart from actual performance with the language. It would be reassuring to discover some module of prelinguistic thought or intentionality, or some brain state, that will determine future performances and potentially still our anxieties and uncertainties, reas-

---

11. Cavell, *The Claim of Reason,* p. 78.
12. See Cavell, *This New Yet Unapproachable America,* pp. 62–64, for a sketch of the varieties of our responses to the command to conceive the "block, pillar, slab, beam" game as a complete primitive language.

suring to know what makes another, especially a child, like (or unlike) oneself in the child's life with language and culture. How does a child move from knowing only "how to suck, and how to lie still when [its] body sense[s] comfort or cry when it [feels] pain" to an active life in culture and to participation in thought? How did one do this oneself? Is the path of this achievement shared with others? In what ways, at what depth, and in what directions? These questions attach to any effort to conceive a complete language, as the effort to bring everything about the mastery of language into the open founders. Either we do not imagine a language and its mastery, when we find everything open and mechanical, or we do imagine a language and its mastery, but the nature of that mastery remains hidden, an object of anxieties and uncertainties that in turn motivate the wish for a theory or explanation of the essence of that mastery.

These problems are then interwoven with one another, in the protagonist's effort to imagine a complete language that will make clear how the learning of language takes place. How do we learn language? What is the nature of our ability to enter into language and culture? What is the nature of our understanding and mastery of the language we do use and of our ability to carry out cultural routines? How are children brought into language and culture at all? How, and how far, have we achieved identity and coherence of personality in mastering linguistic and cultural routines? How, and how far, are these achievements shared with others? Might full coherence and expressiveness of rational personality be arrived at along with others in following out one's life in culture in a certain new way—might *Willkür* come to be fully informed by *Wille?*—and, if so, how? Or are the risks of responsibility and isolation in one's life with language permanent and enduring?

After indulging in the failed effort to bring the mastery of language fully into the open, the dramatic protagonist immediately falls back into a consciousness of the continuing presence of these questions, into an awareness that the appeal to the "block, pillar, slab, beam" language has failed. "Not everything that we call language is this system" (§3). The essence of language and of our mastery of it eludes us. "One has to say this ['not everything that we call language is this system'] in many cases" (§3). "Is this an appropriate description or not?" (§3). ("Ist diese Darstellung [this presentation of language] brauchbar, oder unbrauchbar [useful or unuseful—i.e., does it fulfill our needs, answer to our wish to uncover the essence of language]?") "The answer is, 'Yes, it is appropriate [brauchbar], but only for this narrowly circumscribed region, not for the whole of what you were claiming to describe' [nicht für das Ganze, das du darzustellen vorgabst—not for the whole that you pretended to present]" (§3). The essence of language and of our mastery of it, and therein the essence of our reflective lives in culture, elude the protagonist's, and our, conceptual efforts to specify it. The rebuke here criticizes not only Augustine's picture of language, but also the protagonist's own efforts to supplant that picture with an alternative one, to specify in section 2 a language that will make clear everything about our life with language, to conceive a language in which nothing is hidden. "Augustine's conception of language is like such an over-simple conception of script [of letters as corresponding only to sounds, one by one, not as bearing meanings, serving as instruments of communication, enabling ordering, questioning, commanding, joking, wishing, and so on]" (§4). So too is the "block, pillar, slab, beam" language an oversimple conception of the essence of language, a conception that overlooks varieties of usage, fails to elucidate our mastery, fails to answer, but in fact reinforces, our wish to overcome the risks of our lives with language and culture, under a theory of the nature of perfect, rational mastery.

Perhaps then there is no "general notion of the meaning of a word." Perhaps that notion "surrounds the working of language with a haze which makes clear vision impossible" (§5). Perhaps we would be better off to abandon any such notion and to cease theorizing about the essence of language altogether. Against the Augustinian vision, it at least "disperses the fog to study the phenomena of language in primitive kinds of application in which one can command a clear view of the aim and functioning of words" (§5). Here—even if mastery is not elucidated—the temptations to intellectualist theorizing about prelinguistic intentionality, or *scintilla animae,* or a language acquisition device, or neural modules, are at least diminished. In primitive cases, such as the "block, pillar, slab, beam" language, the connections between learning and mastery and action are not severed. "Here the teaching of language is not explanation, but training [kein Erklären, sondern ein Abrichten]" (§5). "The children are brought up [Die Kinder werden dazu erzogen] to perform *these* actions, to use *these* words as they do, and to react in *this* way to the words of others" (§6). There are many "primitive forms of language" (§5) that children learn to use through training, are brought up to use. "This ostensive teaching of words [Dieses hinweisende Lehren der Wörter] can be said to establish an association between the word and the thing" (§6).

Against Augustinianism, against various scientistic or intellectualistic or behavioristic or neuroscientific programs for the explanation of the essence of language and of our mastery of it, these reminders of the multiplicity of primitive forms, of the importance of example and repetition in language learning, and of the connections between understanding and action, are useful. But this vague talk of "establishing an association through training" does not itself capture the essence of language or of our mastery of it, for us or for the protagonist. It does not answer to the sense that mastery of language is a problematic human achievement, that for us something about that mastery is hidden, something that we wish or fantasize might be explained or laid clear, even if such a wish or fantasy comes again and again to naught. Something in the protagonist—a wish or fantasy or voice—does not let reflection rest in the thought that language is simply learned through training that lays down "an association between the word and the thing" ("eine assoziative Verbindung [an associative connection] zwischen dem Wort und dem Ding"; §6). "But what does this mean?" ("Aber was heißt das?"; §6). What is the nature of that associative connection, and of the intentionality that brings it about? The question recurs. The wish for knowledge of the essence of the mastery of language, and of the power that underlies the ability to live a life in language and culture, does not disappear. It is invited, again, by talk of training and an associative connection. Just what do these terms mean? The effort to quell the impulse toward theorizing by offering reminders of multiplicity and of the importance of example and action in the learning of language keeps the topic of the natures of mastery and of the power to lead a life in culture before us, keeps a wish for knowledge and theory alive.

A play of query and rebuke, of wish and its refusal, ensues in the consciousness of the protagonist. A reminder is entered that talk of training setting up an association is *not* itself a theory of language or understanding. This talk "can mean various things; but one very likely thinks first of all that a picture of the object comes before the child's mind when it hears the word" (§6). A theory of understanding is still sought. "But now, if this does happen—is it the purpose of the word" (§6), unlike the purpose of a blow, which might also get someone to do something? Is understanding having a picture in mind? Well, words can be used to evoke pictures, but they are not used that way in the "block, pillar, slab, beam" language; no theory of the essence of understanding is intended in the talk of training setting up an association between the word and the thing; nor is any theory intended in talk of a picture coming before the mind; nor is any theory intended in noting that the understanding of language is bound up with action, as in the "block, pillar, slab, beam" language. But what then is the understanding? If training causes someone to act correctly when given a command, then can we say that the essence of understanding is whatever power it is that is thus set up by training? "But if ostensive teaching has this effect,—am I to say that it effects an understanding of the word" (§6), that understanding *is* whatever is thus set up? The wish for theory makes itself felt, forces itself on the protagonist. And it goes nowhere. "With different training [Mit einem anderen Unterricht] the same ostensive teaching of these words would have effected a quite different understanding" (§6). Something about understanding—"the whole rest of the mechanism" (§6) that lies beneath teaching—remains hidden, unelucidated by talk of training. The physical behavior of acting in response to a word by itself does very little; it must be surrounded by both training in techniques and a power in the pupil if it is to have any effect in bringing about understanding. Awareness of the need, always, for techniques that surround sample behavior and for powers in the pupil to take to techniques, if understanding is to be achieved, is both the defeat of a theory of understanding and a provocation to it. Techniques and powers are always presupposed, taken for granted. No understanding that is prior to them, and that construes techniques as bits of information, can be specified. All one can do is talk vaguely of a power to take to language. But what is the nature of this power that lies at the heart of our understanding of language?

Here is one possibility, entered again in the (fruitless) hope to defeat finally the impulse to theorize. ("I struggle again and again—whether successfully I do not know—against the tendency in my own mind to set up [construct] rules in philosophy, to make suppositions [hypotheses] instead of just seeing what is there.") We might say just this: that language is a matter of practice. "In the practice of the use of language (2) one party calls out words, the other acts on them" (§7). We might hope now that nothing is hidden, that we have conceived of the understanding of language in such a way that the masteries achieved by others, and the alignments or misalignments of those masteries with one's own, no longer provoke anxiety. "We can also think of the whole process of using words in (2) as one of those games by means of which children learn their native language. I will call these games 'language-games' and will sometimes speak of a primitive language as a language-game" (§7). Is anything hidden in the games that children play? Is their mastery of what they do a cause of anxiety and uncertainty? "Think of much of the use of words in games

like ring-a-ring-a-roses [Reigenspielen—a round dance or roundelay, suggesting archaic, primitive, pastoral, and innocent action at the roots of language learning]" (§7). Ritualistic repetition in play may be cast as the diffuse
origin of active understanding and the mastery of language. We may hope
here to grasp the nature of understanding without having to talk about obscure
powers or faculties, about intellects or brain-states or a *scintilla animae*. We
may here grasp our conceptual life with language as a matter of the existence
of practices, routines of doing things repetitively and immediately, without
reflection, rather than thinking of ourselves as disengaged intellects or subjectivities or loci of understanding prior to our engagements in practices. "In
instruction in the language the following process will occur: the learner *names*
the objects; that is, he utters the word when the teacher points to the stone.—
And there will be this still simpler exercise: the pupil repeats the words [der
Schüler spricht die Worte nach] after the teacher—both of these processes
resembling language [beides sprachähnlich Vorgänge]" (§7). Given the resemblances of these processes to language, as we know it and use it, and given
their apparent transparency, and given the apparent fact that we come to them
through repetition, without forethought, perhaps we can conceive the rest of
language as "an expansion [eine Erweiterung—a broadening] of language (2)"
(§8). Again the hope is that nothing is hidden, that there is nothing about the
mastery of language, in oneself or in others, that provokes a wish for theories
and explanations of our powers. Does this conceptualization of language and
of the nature of our understanding of it settle the topic and solve the problem—for the protagonist or for us? Does it allow us to rest, in confidence in
our lives with languages and our alignments with others in what we say and
do?

No. Again the voice, within oneself: "Now what do the words of this language *signify* [*bezeichnen*]?" (§10). Unless the power of words to sort things
into kinds and to refer to individuals is somehow explained, and unless the
nature of our abilities to grasp that power of words is further elucidated, then
again it will not be language and its understanding that have been brought
into view. "Will this training [in language (2) and its extension into language
(8) through addition of 'there', 'this', and the series of letters of the alphabet
used as numerals] include ostensive teaching of the words?" (§9). Ostensive
teaching seems not so readily to reach to numbers and demonstratives. And
even more pressingly, so far as it is to be used (nothing else is to bring about
understanding in these games), the use of ostensive teaching points again to

the fact that how we grasp *it* has not yet been elucidated. Through what powers and in what directions is ostensive teaching received? What are the mechanisms, the powers, that lie behind it? The appeal to the autonomy and sufficiency of practice as a ground of any actions that we can recognize as evincing mastery of language founders, in the consciousness of the protagonist and for us. "Now what do the words of this language *signify?*" (§10).

"—What is supposed to shew what they signify, if not the kind of use they have? And we have already described that" (§10). The demand or wish for a theory of understanding, a theory of our powers to take to language and culture and of their perfected exercise, is again rebuked. A considerable catalogue of differences in the uses of words runs throughout sections 11–19, interwoven with hortatory remarks about the importance of remembering these varieties of use and about the emptiness of the demand for a general theory of signification. Different words ("hot," "not") may appear similar but be altogether different in their functions, as different from one another as are "a hammer, pliers, a saw, a screw-driver, a rule, a glue-pot, glue, nails, and screws.—The functions of words are as diverse as the functions of these objects. (And in both cases there are similarities.)" (§11). The claim that all words signify something is empty, useless, except perhaps as a contrast to strings of nonsense syllables (§13). The problem of how we can connect words to things should not call for a general theory of our mastery of language. It is a mistake to think that there are words on the one side, the world on the other. Instead, we should remember that we do things in the world with words. We are trained in their use. Is the jack of spades a thing in the world or is it a marker in a game? The contrast is misbegotten. No theory of how we connect words with a world that is apart from them and us is called for. "It is most natural, and causes least confusion, to reckon the samples among the instruments of the language" (§16). Different words resemble different chessmen, objects that we learn to use in the course of learning to play chess, where our classifications of them as like and unlike depend on our aims and on the structure of the game. (Bishops and knights have roughly the same value for mounting an attack; bishops and rooks both move in straight lines.) There is nothing further that we must grasp or understand in order to grasp language. We simply find our ways about within it. "Our language can be seen as an ancient city: a maze of little streets and squares, of old and new houses, and of houses with additions from various periods; and this surrounded by a multitude of new boroughs with straight regular streets and uniform houses" (§18). But there is no plan or grid that governs the development of the whole of language, nothing that we need to know or could know first in order to find our way about in it. Different regions of language are different regions of life and human activity (§19). There seems then to be no possibility of following out the wish to know *the* nature of *the* power that enables us to take to language and culture, no way to grasp a something that enforces or might enforce our alignments with others. And also no need. Understanding language involves multitudinous powers to do many different things. Signification is not the essence of language, for language has no essence. There is no one thing that we must understand in order to understand language. The use of language is an array of activities in the world in which we may be trained—like cooking and playing tennis and building and whistling.

But is this right? At any rate, does the protagonist's consciousness here rest in these thoughts about the multitudinous character of linguistic activities in the world? Even if all these things about the many ways in which language is used in the world are true, does awareness of them stop the protagonist, or stop us, from wishing to know how we achieve conceptual consciousness and knowledge of language and wishing further to know how those achievements might be perfected and aligned with those of others? Again the voice of these wishes returns: "But what about this: is the call 'Slab' in example (2) a sentence or a word?" (§19). To ask this is to ask again how our words, and underneath or via them our concepts, connect with the world. It is to ask for an account of these connections. A reply to that question, and a reasonable rebuke, would be to say that it is neither a sentence nor a word; rather "it is a call" (§19), part of an activity in the world and not primarily a vehicle of representation. But the reasonableness of that rebuke does not stop the presence or the power of the wish to know how conceptual consciousness and knowledge of language are achieved. The fact that "Slab" in language (2) is a call, not a report, does not clearly illuminate what goes in our activities of reporting, classifying, asserting, describing, informing, ordering, or inquiring. We can say, "Bring *two* slabs," "*Hand* me a slab," and "Bring *him* a slab." Unlike language (2), "*our language* contains the possibility of those other sentences" (§20). But then there is no smooth path of merely accumulative growth from the simplicity of the call of language (2) to the complexities of our language. To say that our concepts and our lives with language begin with calls in languages such as (2) is to rebuke and suppress, not to answer, the question of how we arrive at conceptual consciousness and how we might perfect it. Such rebukes and suppressions may be reasonable, particularly when directed against a program for the analysis of our linguistic abilities and conceptual consciousness that takes language to be entirely representational and that overlooks the pervasiveness and variety of our linguistic actions in the world. But they neither explain the nature of conceptual-representational consciousness nor make the wish for such an explanation disappear.

Insistently, the text acknowledges this. The voice that seeks an explanation of the nature of conceptual consciousness reasserts itself. It asks what sets up the differences noted in our language between such things as bringing a slab and handing a slab: "Is there not something different going on in him [who uses the word 'Slab' as a call, but uses it in contrast with 'Bring me a slab' or 'Hand me a slab'] when he pronounces it,—something corresponding to the fact that he conceives the sentence as a *single* word?" (§20). What in us makes us aware of a difference between bringing and handing? What gives us those concepts?

These queries have their counters. We are not generally conscious of anything going on in us when we use language. "Are you conscious of ['Bring me a slab'] consisting of four words *while* you are uttering it?" (§20). Any differences in us that determine whether we are using one word or four, or whether we are calling or commanding, or whether we are asking someone to bring a slab or hand it, will themselves have to show themselves in our linguistic actions if they are to be relevant to our linguistic actions. No inner accompaniments, and certainly not conscious ones, necessarily determine these differences. What matters is that "you have a *mastery* of this language [du *beherrschst diese Sprache*]" (§20). What matters, particularly for our relations with others, is what we do, how we act linguistically, not whatever might or might not be mysteriously and unconsciously inside.

But these counters again do not answer the question, do not respond to or quiet a wish to know the nature of our conceptual consciousness and knowledge of language. The question resurfaces, in a calmer tone, as though to acknowledge its naturalness, to acknowledge that it has not been settled by these counters. "Now what is the difference between the report or statement 'Five slabs' and the order 'Five slabs!'?" (§21). The counter comes that the difference is not an inner event. Rather it is simply that our language makes available these different roles—reporting and ordering—for words to play. "Well, it is the part which uttering these words plays in the language-game" (§21). Contrary to Frege (§22), it is not the case that all moves or actions within our language arise through combining a propositional content ("that the number of slabs is five") with an indicator that the speaker is reporting or ordering or wishing ("I report that . . . "; "I command that . . . "; "I wish that . . . "). What matters is that we act with certain linguistic forms. Often quite varied ones may do the same job. We need not accept the thought that there is a propositional or representational core to our uses of language, or even to our conceptual consciousness at all.

These reminders of the multiplicities of linguistic activities and of the forms available to carry them out culminate in a general thought. "There are *countless* [unzählige] kinds [of sentences]: countless different kinds of use of what we call 'symbols', 'words', 'sentences'. And this multiplicity is not something fixed, given once for all; but new types of language, new-language games, as we may say, come into existence, and others become obsolete and get forgotten" (§23). To say this, as Baker and Hacker have noted, is to say not that there is an infinite number of language games or actions we can perform with language, but that there are uncountably many.[13] There is no way to order or classify the things we do with language so as to begin a count. There is not simply asserting, questioning, and commanding. There is a vast array of multiply overlapping, unsortable activities. This fact undoes the hope of analyzing the complex nature of language and our knowledge of it by appeal to a central function or activity of reporting, for there is no single, central function or activity of using language. "It is interesting to compare the multiplicity of the tools in language and of the ways they are used, the multiplicity of kinds of word and sentence, with what logicians have said about the structure of language [über den Bau der Sprache]. (Including the author of the *Tractatus Logico-Philosophicus*)" (§23). "We do the most various things with our sentences" (§27). Exclaiming, for example, is altogether different from naming or referring (§27).

This open-ended, unorderable multiplicity in what we do with language blocks any effort to grasp the essence of language or conceptual consciousness. But it also blocks, therefore, the effort to elucidate our uses of language on the models of calls or of the uses of tools. Seeing that we do things with language like "Singing catches [Reigen singen]" (§23) will not by itself explain or elucidate how we use language to report or inform or order. The explanation-rebuking emphasis on the multiplicity of our activities in using language turns on itself. It blocks any depiction of language in general as arising in any

13. Baker and Hacker, *Wittgenstein: Understanding and Meaning*, p. 157.

intelligible way out of actions or practices such as calling. The very multiplicity of linguistic activities that is emphasized in an effort to rebuke the philosophical activity of constructing explanations of language's essence leaves room for a mysterious autonomy of reporting and representing from calling. So how do we manage to represent the world to ourselves and to others in ways that other creatures apparently do not?

It is natural then—the question has been neither answered nor dismissed—that the issue of the difference between ordinary human conceptual consciousness and animal consciousness should arise. "It is sometimes said that animals do not talk because they lack the mental capacity. And this means: 'they do not think, and that is why they do not talk.' But—they simply do not talk" (§25). What differences in mental events between us and other animals could be more obvious, deeper, and more important than the simple fact that we talk and they do not? Yet the obviousness, depth, and importance of that fact does not yield an explanation of it. More important, the topic of the difference between animal and human consciousness, together with the larger topic of the nature of conceptual consciousness in general, is a figure for the yet larger topic of how we might grasp and transfigure our exercise of our powers, so as to live in perfect human solidarity, self-consciousness, and expressive freedom. Simply noting that we are different from animals does not either block or still our interest in and anxieties about expressive freedom. Even if various intellectualist stances for explaining the nature of conceptual consciousness have been rebuked, incompletely, the interests and anxieties that motivate those stances have not been met. There is no closure of self-consciousness with itself in the remark that we are different from animals; there is no achievement of full human identity and expressive freedom in the remark that we do many things with language.

Thus, unstopped, the wish and its questions arise again: "But how can two be defined like that [saying 'two' when pointing to two nuts]?" (§28). That is, just how do we have language and conceptual consciousness? What enables us or determines us, unlike other animals, to form and take to language? Surely it must be something. And what are its prospects for full expression? The central mystery of human being and its possibilities of worldly expression remains unelucidated. How is the abandonment of intellectualist programs and their misleading hypostatizations supposed, in itself, to lead us toward full humanity, charity, peace, and expressiveness?

Nothing in us will guarantee that conceptual consciousness and dimensions of expressiveness will be shared. Any definition can be misunderstood. "An ostensive definition can be variously interpreted in *every* case" (§28). Instead of trying to ground or explain our words, their definitions, and our uses of them in the deliverances of some interior faculty of understanding, we should note that we have many techniques for using words. These techniques are routines of action and application. A technique of application is, we might say, "the post at which we station the word" (§29). It is where we send it for use. "Misunderstandings are sometimes averted" (§29) by saying explicitly that magenta is a color or an angstrom is a unit of length. But there is no general way to guarantee that any definition, ostensive or verbal, will be understood. There is no general scheme of the prelinguistic categorial classification of the world into which the terms of our language need to be mapped. There are, instead, many things we do with language. "How he 'takes' the definition [wie er die Erklärung 'auffaßt'] is seen in the use that he makes of the word defined" (§29), not anywhere else, not within the mind or brain.

But then it follows that there is a phenomenon of taking or grasping a word. What is it that we see when we see how someone takes a definition? "One already has to know (or be able to do) something in order to be capable of asking a thing's name. But what does one have to know?" (§30). How do we fit into the world as possessors of conceptual consciousness? How might that consciousness be expressed and sustained? How and how far might it be shared? The questions do not go away.

In confronting them, a nonsense answer—that conceptual consciousness and the ability to take to language flow from a prelinguistic and practice-governing intentionality, an answer that is nonsense in hypostatizing our abilities and in abstracting from our techniques and practices, wherein alone language has life—plays off against a disappointing answer that does not respond to our wishes and to the obvious mystery of human conceptual intelligence— the answer that there are only the facts that we use language to do many things. Can we find our way to an answer that is neither nonsensical nor disappointing? The chess analogy (§31) is no help; it simply notes the same facts that raise the problem. Just as the shape of a chessman is fit to the rules for its use, so a linguistic pattern or form—a word or phrase or sentence— is fit to its uses. There is no accord between form and use that is fixed anywhere else, apart from the game or linguistic practice. It is nonsense to look to the nature of reality to determine whether the shape of the rook rightly fits the rules for its movement. Likewise it is nonsense to look to the world to see whether apart from linguistic practice the word "mica" rightly fits its object. The criteria of rightness in application are set up within the practice, not anywhere else. Yet at the same time human beings, not chimpanzees or zebras or dolphins, have invented chess and language and teach these activities to one another. How? "Only someone who already knows how to do something with it can significantly ask a name" (§31), and one learns what to do with a name from within, by entering into the practice of naming. But how does one learn how to do *that?* Just what are we capable of and why?

The protagonist here arrives at a summary thought that our capabilities are not determined by some prelinguistic act or phenomenon of intellection, itself determined by some hypostatized thing, a mind-brain, in us. To think that is to intellectualize our lives with words, abstracting from our routines and techniques of doing things with them. This is Augustine's mistake. "Augustine describes the learning of human language as if the child came into a strange country and did not understand the language of the country; that is, as if it already had a language, only not this one. Or again: as if the child could already *think,* only not yet speak. And 'think' would here mean something like 'talk to itself' " (§32). It is not like that. Instead it is "circumstances [Umständen]" (§33), actions, practices, the language-game, that fit a linguistic form to its many uses. A life within these circumstances—a life of risks and responsibilities and possible deviations from others—cannot be transcended by grasping the operations of a hypothetical perfect language-generating machine within.

Yet the wish does not go away. The questions again recur. "Suppose, however, someone were to object: 'It is not true that you must already be master of a language in order to understand an ostensive definition: all you need— of course!—is to know or guess what the person giving the explanation is pointing to' " (§33). Perhaps it is a matter of concentrating one's attention on the right thing. You have conceded that we must know something, be able to do something, in order to learn the name of a thing. Why isn't it that— concentrating one's attention? Perhaps our conceptual consciousness is rooted in the fact that we can do *that.*

No. The picture of the activity that underlies our ability to take to language is altogether unclear. "Point to a piece of paper.—And now point to its shape—now to its colour—now to its number (that sounds queer).—How did you do it?" (§33). What matters, always, is what the teacher of language is overtly doing (teaching colors or teaching shapes) and what the pupil then does. Certain mistakes will be corrected in certain ways, other mistakes in others. Learning to attend to something is just as much an achievement of linguistic ability and conceptual consciousness as applying a word. Conceptual attending is not a prelinguistic foundation of our mastery of language. We have no picture of what conceptual attending would be (dwelling on the identity of something, not merely being absorbed by the visual sensations it produces) apart from a life with language. What matters is what we do. "For neither the expression 'to intend the definition in such-and-such a way' nor the expression 'to interpret the definition in such-and-such a way' stands for a process which accompanies the giving and hearing of the definition" (§34). When we "imagine various different cases" of intending a definition in a certain way or of interpreting a definition, then what we find is that we imagine someone doing something in overt linguistic practice, playing a certain game wherein form is fit to usage; we do not imagine a process taking place in the mind or brain.

And yet the obvious fact that human beings do these things—play these games and take to words, in ways in which other beings do not—is not met or accounted for. Why doesn't the phrase "to interpret a word" stand for an inner process, perhaps an unconscious one? As Jerry Fodor famously and cogently remarks, there are several senses to questions like "What makes the linguistic form 'red' apply to red objects?"[14] One of these senses is a causal one. While it is true and perhaps important to say that the linguistic form "red" applies to red objects only within a practice of language using, it is also apparently licit to ask how and why that practice has arisen and how and why it is taught and learned. What causes this continuing connection between a linguistic form and its extension? It seems to be only a matter of insistence, and of an unscientific refusal to investigate what is going on in us materially or mentally when we learn and apply a word, to say that this causal question is settled only by the practice, by the rules of the game. What exactly are the circumstances in which we do what we do with the linguistic form "red"? When we want to know what learning and being able to apply a word *are,* then why is "what we should say"—for example, "whether we would call *that* red"—the crucial issue? What does our grasping "the post at which we station the word" (§29)—something we do—*consist in?* How do we do it? How does one become "master of a game" (§31)?

The text itself raises these questions. They are not external to the drama of the protagonist's self-interrogation but are its very substance. They not only arise in the voice or mood that explicitly seeks an explanation of the nature of our linguistic and conceptual abilities; they also are worked into the summary remarks that insist on the importance of practice, as that insistence itself notes that we *take* a word in a certain way (§29), that "one has already to be know (or be able to do) something in order to be capable of asking a thing's name" (§30) and that one must be "already master of a game [schon ein Spiel beherrscht]" (§31) in order to understand an explanation of a rule. "But what does one have to know?" (§30). A wish to know *how* we have our practices and how we might perfectly live within them, free from risks and responsibilities as perfect masters, pushes us toward explanations—but explanations that never answer to that wish. Either the processes and states that are appealed to as the source and essence of a mastery of language and concepts are unconscious, so knowledge of them fails to confer perfect mastery on us, but remains as much an achievement within a correctable public practice as any other form of knowledge. Or they are conscious but are false intellectualizations, hypostatizations, of an overt ability that alone gives these hypostatizations sense. Only public practice, circumstances of play, gives life to our signs, even if that life is also always mysteriously begun in us. But this view leaves unappeased our standing wish to become perfect masters within our practice.

In the face of such a persistent but unappeasable wish, all one can do is fall back on diagnosis of the roots of the wish and on its rebuke or repudiation—strategies that are not likely wholly to succeed. How and why we *wish* to explain our abilities in a certain way becomes a topic of investigation. "Because we cannot specify any *one* bodily action which we call pointing to the shape (as opposed, for example, to the colour), we say that a *spiritual* activity [eine *geistige Tätigkeit*] corresponds to these words. Where our language suggests a body [Wo unsere Sprache uns einen Körper vermuten läßt] and there is none: there, we should like to say, is a *spirit* [dort, möchten wir sagen, sei ein *Geist*]" (§36). Our language *lets us suspect* ("uns . . . vermuten läßt") that there is a body—the meaning—behind a linguistic form, a body that we somehow grasp or take, either intellectually or bodily, either consciously or unconsciously. We do things with linguistic forms—take to them and use them. No linguistic form by itself, in virtue only of its structure and apart from practices of its use, means anything. So its meaning must apparently be a thing that lies elsewhere, something in us, we who use that form.

It is natural then to seek to know what that meaning-thing is and how it is connected by us with a linguistic form. And underlying this natural curiosity there is a deep wish to be oneself a perfect master of linguistic and conceptual practice, to have one's ways of conceiving and speaking of things be fully and transparently expressive of rational freedom, rather than contestable, accidental, or imposed by nature. It is a wish to have one's thoughts and actions flow from *Willkür* fully informed by *Wille,* a wish for perfect, rational, expressive freedom in and through the ways of culture.

Thus it is natural to ask, "What is the relation between the name and the thing named?" and to ask what "sort of thing this relation *consists in* [*worin diese Beziehung etwa besteht*]" (§37; emphasis added). This question embodies a wish to know what lies underneath our practices of conceptual consciousness and the use of words, so that one might become a perfect master within them. The effort to find what our practices metaphysically *consist in* "springs from a tendency to sublime the logic of our language—as one might put it [*rührt von einer Tendenz her, die Logik unserer Sprache zu sublimieren—wie man es nennen könnte*]" (§38). Succumbing to this tendency is a particular habit of the philosopher.

> For philosophical problems arise when language *goes on holiday* [*wenn die Sprache feiert*]. And *here* we may indeed fancy naming to be some remarkable act of mind [*ein merkwürdiger seelischer Akt*], as it were a baptism of an object. And we can also say the word 'this' *to* the object, as it were *address* the object as 'this'—a queer use of this word, which doubtless only occurs in doing philosophy [*der wohl nur beim Philosophieren vorkommt*].
>
> (§38)

Here the tendency to sublime the logic of our language, the tendency to do philosophy, is not external to the protagonist or to us. It is built into our lives with language, with all their risks and responsibilities, as our uses of language can idle—fail to be received by others as free expressions of a recognizable conceptual consciousness. The wish to defeat this risk is the wish that issues in philosophy and its efforts to grasp *how* words apply to things, a wish that is unappeasable, but present in the life of the protagonist.

When that wish and the efforts of philosophy are rebuked, then the protagonist is seeking to root out of himself the moral ideal of perfect mastery or control, possessed by a detached or disengaged self, in conceptual and linguistic practice. The protagonist is tempted to conceive of himself in the manner of the self of Augustine's *Confessions*—as possessing a *scintilla animae,* a spark or point or locus of power to accept, reject, or transform conventions of conceptualization in accordance with its wishes and discoveries. This *scintilla animae* is conceived of as hidden, yet causally effective in thought, language learning, and linguistic behavior. The self is conceived of as a locus of beliefs that are to be assessed as well founded or not, thence accepted or rejected. It possesses, or may come to possess through its discoveries, fully authenticated standards of conceptualization and interest. By hewing to these standards, once uncovered, one may hope to lead a life that is perfectly expressive of freedom and rationality, themselves in harmony with the order of things. Or so, at least, one may wish when one thus conceives of oneself.

When that conception of the self and its *scintilla animae* is rebuked or repudiated, then the moral ideals of control and of perfect rational freedom are also repudiated. Or the protagonist is seeking to root out of himself his attachment to that ideal. He is asking himself to accept the thought that criteria of correctness in thought and in linguistic performance are laid down, multiply and waywardly, only in linguistic practices as they stand. Standards of performance are at best immanent in practices, with all the risks and responsibilities that attach to the multiple and overlapping uses that practices accord to linguistic forms. The order of things is received by us as conceptually conscious beings only in and through our acceptance of frameworks of language and culture ("Nothing is both red and green all over") that we are unable either to criticize or to justify against more self-authenticating, perfectly rational standards. How anyone takes to these frameworks, to linguistic practices, and to conceptual consciousness is a standing mystery: it flows from an inscrutable power. The manner of that taking can be elucidated, as one can point to one manner or way rather than another in which one in a certain context "takes" the word "stand" (as a command, as a noun referring to a device for holding music, as a description of a position in a battle, as a verb meaning "to tolerate," and so on). But the nature of the process that everywhere underlies any takings to language and that might somehow itself be mastered and controlled cannot be elucidated or explained. Hence a life of risks and responsibilities in thought and language is inevitable, insofar as one always confronts in various contexts the multiple and overlapping ways in which language might be used and insofar as one therein confronts the standing otherness of others.

Is one of these pictures of the self *correct?* Is it just *true* that we are capable of perfect rational freedom in our acts, through a philosophical discovery of self-authenticating standards of conceptualization and linguistic performance? Or is it, on the contrary, just *true* that we are *not* thus capable and that the wish for this capability can be repudiated, put behind us, and our antagonized lives with others simply accepted? What proof, argument, or consideration could decide these issues—for the protagonist or for us? The demand for proof to decide these issues is a demand that is associated with the picture of a belief-holding self, possessed or potentially possessed of rational standards for the adjudication of belief. This demand goes unmet, as standards and criteria that we can apply to assess performances appear only within public practices, contestably. But the claim that human beings, as conceptually conscious beings, are cultural beings, capable of thought and linguistic performance only insofar as they are acculturated, is itself a second dogmatic picture. Subscription to this picture embodies a hope of moving beyond intellectualism and into a region of perfect humility and solidarity. But this hope too is disappointed. No such region is available: our practices are multiple, disordered, and in antagonism with one another. A sense of ourselves as having, dimly and inscrutably, powers that give life to language and that enable its transfiguration tempts us too to ask how we take to language and to ask what the foundation is of this picture of human beings as (merely, it then seems) cultural beings. A demand for a metaphysical explanation of our capacities, an explanation that will thence enable their perfect cultivation and exercise, is entered. And it comes to nothing.

In the cycle of metaphysical proposal and its rebuke, what shows itself then is a picture of human beings as having a standing "tendency to sublime the logic of language." This claim itself admits of no proof. No deeper or prior reasons are entered in its favor. Rather, the endless itinerary of proposal and rebuke within the consciousness of the protagonist shows that it is so, shows that we remain caught between an aspiration to rational expressive freedom, power, and conversion and our implication in the tangled and opposed ways of common practice. Or it fails to show itself, if we make metaphysical and epistemological demands on the text, asking for arguments in favor of conclusions, proofs in favor of truths. No thesis about the nature of conceptual consciousness is proven in this itinerary. Yet we are enabled, through tracing its progress, to acknowledge what we perhaps ineluctably are.

6
Simples and Samples:
Realism versus the Ordinary—§§39–65

Throughout sections 1–38, the protagonist moves through a cycle of pro-posal and rebuke. Conceptions of how to set about explaining intentional-conceptual consciousness and our ability to learn language are put forward, only to be rebuked as leading nowhere. Either these explanations both hypos-tatize our powers to take to linguistic and conceptual practice and distort the multitudinous ways in which those powers are actually exercised, or they ap-peal to mysterious unconscious processes in ways that fail to engage with what we do in practice at all. Despite these criticisms, however, the efforts at expla-nation do not lapse; new routes of explanation are repeatedly proposed. Peace within practice, wherein the modes of exercise of one's conceptual powers are securely shared, is not achieved. Yet the release of these powers into assured expressiveness remains an ideal that motivates both renewed efforts to grasp the nature of these powers and rebukes of these efforts.

Section 39 then opens a new direction within the effort to grasp and perfect the expression of the powers that both make for conceptual consciousness and themselves enjoin the project of seeking a life of expressive freedom. Instead of only continuing in the movement of proposal and its rebuke, there is now a turn toward the investigation of the nature of the desire to grasp and to release, perfectly and securely, the powers that make for intentional-conceptual con-sciousness. There is a dim echo, albeit unacknowledged and almost surely unintended, of Hegel's great turning point at the beginning of chapter 4 of the *Phenomenology,* where consciousness, in investigating itself, "leaves behind it the colourful show of the sensuous here-and-now and the nightlike void of the supersensible beyond, and steps out into the spiritual daylight of the pres-ent."[1] Here, in Hegel, consciousness in reflecting on itself no longer asks only

---

1. Hegel, *Phenomenology,* paragraph 177, pp. 110–11.

"what is the nature of conceptual awareness of an object?" but also "what is it to lead a life as a being who actively desires to know the nature of consciousness?" Section 39 of *Philosophical Investigations* repeats this turn within the protagonist toward the acknowledgment and diagnosis of desire: "But why does it occur to one [Aber warum kommt man auf die Idee—why, in what way, does one come to the idea] *to want to make* precisely this word into a name [gerade dieses Wort zum Namen *machen wollen;* emphasis added], when it evidently is *not* a name?" (§39). What makes one so much as want to do this—carry out this transformation so as to make words like "this" or "not" into names, so as to characterize the essence of language in terms of naming? How and why does one come to the idea to do this? Who are we in having this desire?

The answer is that construing *all* things as inert objects of our active naming is precisely what we wish to do. "That is just the reason. For one is tempted to make an objection against what is ordinarily called a name. It can be put like this: *a name ought really to signify a simple [daß der Name eigentlich Einfaches bezeichnen soll]*" (§39). This is what we think and wish: that a name—something we make, in an act of laying down a convention—should attach perfectly, timelessly, as though by adamantine bonds, to something indestructible, simple. In this way, words and world might never come apart. Hence our acts of using words, against the background of conventions secured by these adamantine bonds, might be immune from criticism, reappropriation, or refiguration. We would no longer have to worry about whether *that* is gold, or *that* is a half-cadence in C-sharp minor, or *that* is love. Our tests, our criteria, for these things—for anything—would be reliable and would be shared by others who likewise would engage with the simple substances of reality under the same perfect names. Our expressive powers would be exercised under conventions that guaranteed their reception. We wish for names to signify, absolutely, such simple and indestructible objects.

With ordinary names, it is not like that. Ordinary names are not tethered to reality absolutely, and their connections to their referents can fail or be queried, criticized, or refigured. As a result, anxieties about one's expressiveness and its reception can continue to attach to using ordinary names. To overcome that anxiety, "one is tempted to make an objection against" *them,* "against what is ordinarily called a name" (§39). The world can fail to answer to ordinary names, can defeat our powers to speak about it by using those names.

The word "Excalibur" [Nothung], say, is a proper name in the ordinary sense. The sword Excalibur consists of parts combined in a particular way. If they are combined differently Excalibur does not exist. But it is clear that the sentence "Excalibur has a sharp blade" makes *sense* whether Excalibur is still whole or is broken up. But if "Excalibur" is the name of an object, this object no longer exists when Excalibur is broken in pieces; and as no object would then correspond to the name it would have no meaning. But then the sentence "Excalibur has a sharp blade" would contain a word that had no meaning, and hence the sentence would be nonsense. But it does make sense; so there must always be something corresponding to the words of which [the sentence] consists.

(§39)

The underlying assumption in this argument is that the sense of any meaningful expression must itself ultimately be guaranteed by the indestructible simple substances of the world that then serve as the referents of the simplest expressions. Instead of having the senses and uses of expression be contestable, as our powers are redeployed within stable yet shifting linguistic practices, the very stuff of the world is to guarantee the sense, and hence also the reception, of our words. "There must always be something corresponding to the words of which [a meaningful sentence] is composed. So the word 'Excalibur' must disappear when the sense is analysed and its place be taken by words which name simples [die Einfaches]. It will be reasonable to call these words the real names [die eigentlichen Namen]" (§39). This is our wish: that our words, or the simplest words, the real names that are to serve as the bases for the construction of further expressions, should be wedded absolutely to the world, to its simple, indestructible substances, so that our powers to take to language and conceptual consciousness shall have absolute rails along which to run, therein freeing them from play. That is why it occurs to one to make the word "this," which is evidently not a name, into a simple name, an absolute name. That maneuver is a way of pursuing that wish. There must, we think, always be something corresponding to our words, something in the world that itself tells us how or what to say at the simplest, most absolute level. "Naming appears as a *queer* connexion [eine *seltsame* Verbindung—a peculiar, singular binding or joining] of a word with an object" (38). The world is to be there over and against our active subjectivity in naming it, but also there for us, telling us what to say and how to exercise our conceptual powers. Conventionalization is to enter into our practices only at the level of the choice of an arbitrary signifier for one of the simple substances that reality presents. Once chosen, that signifier will then stay tethered to its referent, and our expressive powers will be unproblematically exercised in an uncriticizable and obvious responsiveness to the stuff of the world—to indestructible stuffs that are there *for us* to name and to arrange and control, once we have grasped their natures and possibilities of combination.

We wish then to grasp indestructible simple substances of reality absolutely, under names that pick them out unproblematically, without any play. Is this wish coherent or intelligible? That is, can we genuinely and fully imagine metaphysically simple objects that would satisfy this wish? Are we able to articulate our own wish in a way that would enable us to recognize its satisfaction?

No. In ordinary language, names are not absolutely tethered to indestructible, metaphysically simple objects.

> It is important to note that the word "meaning" [Bedeutung] is being used illicitly if it is used to signify the thing that "corresponds" to the word [das dem Wort "entspricht"]. That is to confound the meaning of the name with the *bearer* of the name. When Mr. N. N. dies, one says that the bearer of the name dies, not that the meaning dies. And it would be nonsensical to say that, for if the name ceased to have meaning it would make no sense to say "Mr. N. N. is dead."
>
> (§40)

Since it does make sense, the idea that ordinary names are absolutely tethered to indestructible objects must be given up.

Yet that was not really the route through which the wish to grasp the simple substances of reality articulated itself. Both "Excalibur" and "Mr. N. N." are clearly and evidently not names that are attached to indestructible substances. Rather, these ordinary names are used to talk about things that are not sempiternal. "For a *large* class of cases—though not for all—in which we employ the word 'meaning' [Bedeutung] it can be defined thus [kann so erklären—can be explained, elucidated, made clear]: the meaning of a word is its use in the language" (§43).

Here the ordinary use of a word is just what our wish seeks to overcome or defeat. Ordinary uses of ordinary names do not put us in contact with the simple and indestructible stuffs of a self-subsistent reality that we might grasp. Rather they refer to things that exist or have existed only contingently, things that might be broken up or might die or that might have already been broken or died. This is what leads us to reproach these ordinary names or be disappointed by them and to seek to construct or discover "absolute names" in their places.

If ordinary names do not articulate our wish, perhaps "names" on the model of demonstratives will do. "But we can imagine a language-game with names (that is, with signs which we should certainly include among the names) in which they are used only in the presence of the bearer; and so could *always* be replaced by a demonstrative pronoun and the gesture of pointing" (§44). These special, quasi names would then be conventional abbreviations for acts of attending to, demonstrating, or pointing to a present something. In these acts, reality would then be absolutely present to us as conceptually conscious beings, we might think. "The demonstrative 'this' can never be without a bearer. It might be said: 'so long as there is a *this,* the word "this" has a meaning too, whether *this* is simple or complex'" (§45). At least the word "this" seems to be always attached to *something,* just as something or some collection of things seems always to be already over against us, passively ready to be grasped and named by us actively. Perhaps then "this" is the point of contact between our active subjectivities, as users of names, and the stuffs of the world. Perhaps in saying "this" to *this,* we are necessarily, undeniably, in contact somehow with what there is.

But this effort to articulate our wish now in turn also collapses. "This" so used is not a name. It points us to everything and anything, not to any sempiternal substance of reality. The fact that "this" is always attached to something or other "does not make the word into a name. On the contrary: for a name is not used with, but only explained by means of, the gesture of pointing" (§45). Demonstratives as we use them cannot be combined solely with one another as the constituents of thoughts or propositions. They are used only with a gesture of pointing, or anaphorically, so that they do not on their own, via conventions of language alone, refer to anything. Hence they offer no illumination of how we actively engage with a standing reality. With only demonstratives, and without concepts and general terms whose applications are open to play within practice, there is only stuttering, not conceptual consciousness of reality. As Hegel remarks,

> those who put forward such an assertion [e.g., that a sensuous *this* is the stuff of reality that is grasped in applying the word "this"] also say to themselves the direct opposite of what they mean . . . . They speak of the existence of *external* objects, which can be more precisely defined as *actual,* absolutely *singular, wholly personal, individual* things, each of them absolutely unlike any-

thing else; this existence, they say, has absolute certainty and truth. . . . In
the actual attempt to say [this particular identifiable thing—e.g., a bit of
paper], it [both description and object] would therefore crumble away [inso-
far as they would be confined to the use of only the word "this"]; those who
started to describe it would not be able to complete the description. . . .
Consequently what is called the unutterable is nothing else than the untrue,
the irrational, what is merely meant [gemeint—barely quasi-intended, not
grasped conceptually].[2]

Far from being the point of contact between conceptual consciousness and
absolute reality, acts of using the word "this"—a word that always has a referent but never carries a conceptual content on its own—point only to an unutterable otherness. Uses of "this" express not a self-founding conceptual grasp
of reality, not a cognitive achievement, but rather presuppose gestures, the
contents of which come from concepts and contexts of practice that are already
laid down. Our wish to grasp reality absolutely, therein uncovering the nature
of our conceptual consciousness and affording it conditions of perfect release,
again founders. Our conceptual consciousness and the objects to which it
responds remain unilluminated, unfounded, their natures unelucidated. Pointing and demonstrating presuppose conceptual consciousness rather than
founding it.

What, then, inclines us to think that there must be a point of absolute
contact between our conceptual consciousness and an order of indestructible,
simple substances? "What lies behind the idea that names really signify simples?" (§46). What is the content of our wish or desire? What are its possibilities of fulfillment? It is a wish for things that simply and enduringly are, a
wish for unchanging substances of the world. "Socrates says in the Theaetetus:
'If I make no mistake, I have heard some people say this: there is no definition
of the primary elements—so to speak—out of which we and everything else
are composed; for everything that exists in its own right [alles, was an und
für sich ist—everything which in and for itself is] can only be *named*, no other
determination is possible, neither that it *is* nor that it *is not*'" (§46). Prior to
us, we think, and independently of any coming into being or passing away,
there must be things that simply are, things toward which our conceptual
consciousness is somehow mysteriously directed. Our thoughts are somehow
about things, ultimately about things that really, enduringly, indestructibly are;

2. Ibid., paragraph 110, pp. 65–66.

otherwise they are not really *about* anything, are not fully object-directed. If only we could grasp this order of the ultimate, sempiternal, simple substances of the world, then we could put our thoughts in an order that incontrovertibly mirrors it. Therein our conceptual consciousness would perfect itself into absolute knowledge of what there absolutely is, and therein would we achieve perfect expressiveness of both what there is and our own conceptual consciousness. What we do and say would be then no longer accidental, but would be determined by our grasp of what there absolutely is. The wish or thought of grasping a reality composed of sempiternal simples is a fantasy of perfection in conceptual expression, of immunity from criticism in thought and speech. "We look," as Cavell puts it, "for 'absolute simples' (and, I will add, absolute anythings: responsibilities, actions, meanings, certainties, see-ables) when we try (or have, or come) to speak absolutely, that is, outside language-games" with all their ordinary risks and responsibilities.[3]

But our wish again comes to nothing. There is no way to articulate it. Each articulation is undone by the ordinary terms in which it is formulated. "But what are the simple constituent parts of which reality is composed?" (§47). That is, what do we mean when we say to ourselves that reality has, or must have, absolutely simple parts? "What are the simple constituent parts of a chair?—The bits of wood of which it is made? Or the molecules, or the atoms?—'Simple' means: not composite. And here the point is: in what sense 'composite'? It makes no sense at all to speak of the 'absolutely simple parts of a chair' [von den 'einfachen Bestandteilen des Sessels schlechtweg' zu reden]" (§47). The word "simple" is—for us, in ordinary practice—a contrastive term. Its various applications are fixed by our interests in drawing particular contrasts in contexts with what is composite or complex. "Absolutely simple" is a kind of oxymoron, an expression we are unable to apply. To try to conceive of what is absolutely simple, apart from any context of comparison that is set by our interests, as though we could just gaze on reality in itself—free of any but pure cognitive interests, free as well of our entanglements in our ordinary language games—is to do nothing, to break down in thought, when in the grip of a fantasy. "Asking 'Is this object composite?' *outside* a particular language-game is like what a boy once did, who had to say whether the verbs in certain sentences were in the active or passive voice, and who racked his brains over the question whether the verb 'to sleep' meant something active

3. Cavell, *The Claim of Reason*, p. 226.

or passive" (§47). The question "Is this—an electron, a hadron, a boson, a quark, a taste, a color patch, a touch, a pitch—an absolutely simple element of reality?" makes no sense; it asks nothing that we could conceivably answer. "Simple compared to what?" It may be natural or immediate for us, in most cases, when presented with an array of colored squares, to call a single square a simple element of the array—natural and immediate, but not mandated by reality, apart from our interests and contexts of comparison. "I do not know what else you would have me call 'the simples', what would be more natural in this language-game. But under other circumstances I should call a monochrome square 'composite' consisting perhaps of two rectangles, or of the elements colour and shape" (§48). It may be natural and immediate, and there may be good reasons in contexts when certain comparisons are held in mind, to call some things simple and others composite. But these judgments, however reasonable, are not dictated to us by reality as it is in itself. "Does it matter which we say, so long as we avoid misunderstandings in any particular case?" (§48) There is no way to make absolute contact with a simple thing in itself. A thing "has not even *got* a name except in the language-game [Es *hat* auch keinen Namen, außer im Spiel—it doesn't even have a name, outside of the game, the play]" (§49).

But is this a necessary truth? Or does it only reflect how things are for us now? Nothing has any identity for us—there are no criteria of identity—outside of our language games. That is what we find whenever we attempt to describe what is absolutely simple. In this attempt, we run up against the fact that the word "simple" has application only in a specific context of comparison with the application of "complex"; it fails to have absolute application conditions determined by reality itself. But must that be true? Does the wish to grasp and talk of the sempiternal substances of reality collapse, once these facts about our present abilities to apply the word "simple" are remembered? As though to acknowledge that the fantasy is still in place, section 50 opens with the question "What does it mean to say that we can attribute neither being nor non-being to elements?" (§50). Seeking the perfect information and release of *Willkür*, a voice proposes, apparently, that there *must* be something that neither comes into existence nor passes away—some standing substance of the world that awaits our grasp of it. It is an idea that it is difficult to repudiate: surely our thoughts and concepts and words are somehow *about* something that *is there,* that exists, without being brought into being by our thoughts or concepts or words. No matter how much our attempts to characterize the simple founder, it is still true that "one would, however, like to say: existence cannot be attributed to an element, for if it did not *exist* [denn *wäre es nicht*], one could not even name it and so one could say nothing of it at all" (§50).

Can this idea be repudiated, this fantasy overcome? "Let us consider an analogous case [einen analogen Fall!]. There is *one* thing of which one can say neither that is one metre long, nor that it is not one metre long, and that is the standard metre in Paris.—But this is, of course, not to ascribe any extraordinary property to it, but only to mark its peculiar role in the language-game of measuring with a metre-rule" (§50). The standard meter-bar is a *sample,* something that has been set up as a standard of comparison for other lengths. It has no special extraordinary property that we have discovered. Rather it is we who have made it into a standard. "What looks as if it *had* to exist, is part of the language. [Was es, scheinbar, geben *muß*, gehort zur Sprache.] It is a paradigm [ein Paradigma] in our language-game; something with which comparison is made" (§50). Thus the case of the standard meterstick fails to provide a good model for what it is for a thing to have a property metaphysically or absolutely or necessarily. This thought can be rejected. One might, after Kripke, in a realist spirit, pursuing the fantasy, begin to think about necessary truths and necessary properties—for example, properties of gold or of bosons. One might even nonsensically extend the concept of necessary truth about the world to the claim that the standard meterstick is one meter long. That this maneuver is sometimes made shows how powerful the realist wish and fantasy are.

More important, however, the text acknowledges that the case of the standard meterstick is in any case *only an analogy* to the case of putative simple, sempiternal substances. The necessary length of the standard meterstick is not an ultimate and given metaphysical property of it, but instead only the nonmysterious result of our setting it up as a standard of comparison. But what does this show about the putative necessary existence of metaphysical simples? How far does the analogy take us in undoing the wish to grasp the substance of the world that our language is about, thence to come to perfect expressiveness?

Section 52 acknowledges the continuing presence of this wish, even while challenging its sense. "If I am inclined to suppose that a mouse has come into being by spontaneous generation out of grey rags and dust, I shall do well to examine those rags very closely to see how a mouse may have hidden in them, how it may have got there and so on. But if I am convinced that a mouse cannot come into being from these things, then this investigation will perhaps be superfluous" (§52). Here the analogy lies between being convinced that a mouse cannot come into existence out of rags and being convinced that reality must be composed of simple, sempiternal substances toward which our thought and language are somehow directed. We would be better off to look at the details of how a mouse might have hidden itself in the rags and dust, hence by analogy better off to look at the details of the workings of our language as it is, to see how *aboutness* is set up there, without interaction with anything absolute or ultimate. But even while this analogy criticizes the belief in absolute simples and urges us to examine the details of our uses of language as they stand, it also acknowledges the primitiveness and the force of our belief or wish. We can be *convinced*—primitively, in a way that resists all arguments and analogies—that there *must* be simples. When this happens, "if I am convinced [Bin ich . . . überzeugt]" (§52), then looking at the details of our language games as they are now will be, for me, beside the point, "superfluous [überflüssig]" (§52). In the grip of this fantasy, belief, or conviction—that reality must be composed of simple substances, awaiting our perfect grasp of them—one will hold our language games themselves up against an ideal of exactness and absoluteness. One will continue to pursue perfect correspondence between the things that there are and our concepts and words. What "we must learn to understand" is "what it is that opposes such an examination of details in philosophy [das sich in der Philosophie einer solchen Betrachtung der Einzelheiten entgegensetzt—sets itself against]" (§52): the nature and force of our desire to move beyond the ordinary into a grasp of reality in itself and into perfect expressiveness. Learning to understand this is a task not of knowledge of how that desire can be satisfied, but instead is the task of acknowledging its continuing presence and force, as something that is ineliminably woven through our conceptual consciousness.

Sections 53–55 further insist on the presence and ineliminability of a desire for perfect rational expressiveness, as a new proposal and counter are entered. Perhaps our uses of language either are or might be controlled by a table connecting a word with its referents, by a sort of rule. In considering this possibility, the suggestion is that our language games are surely not arbitrary. We can't do just anything with language. Surely our uses of words are somehow rule-governed. Why should we not then attempt to uncover the rules for describing reality that reality itself has written into it? The fantasy of perfect expressiveness migrates into a new route of articulation under the concept of rules rather than under the concept of metaphysical simples. Sections 53 and 54 emphasize that there is a multiplicity of rules that lie behind our uses of language and that rules themselves play a variety of roles as criteria of correct usage. "Let us recall the kinds of case where we say that a game is played according to a definite rule" (§54). There are rules that are used in teaching: practical bits of advice such as "Castle early" or "Keep the ball deep" or "Use a fluid motion in bowing, with full arm extension." There are rules that set the framework of a game, that define what game is being played: "the game ends when the king cannot escape capture," "a game is won when one player has accumulated four points, with a margin of at least two; in the event that the score is either 4-3 or 4-4, play continues until a margin of two is reached"; "the player is to play the notes that are indicated in the score." While there are many different kinds of rules that are used in many different ways—sometimes as bits of advice, sometimes as defining the game being played, sometimes as standards of criticism—to note this fact is to note also that our uses of words and concepts are somehow controlled under them. Nothing that we call a rule answers to the fantasy of grasping and conforming to an absolute rule, one laid down or dictated to us by reality itself. Rules are our multiple creations, within the multiple sorts of things we do. But nonetheless in controlling our practice—in functioning as definitions and standards of criticism—they keep alive the image of a practice that is wholly transparent and adequate to reality itself. Awareness of the multi-rule-governed character of our practices keeps alive the thought that, at least sometimes, in some ways, there is something that one *must do,* if one is to be playing the game aright, or something such that if one does it, then one *is* playing the game aright (trying to checkmate one's opponent, trying to get four points with a margin of two, following the score).

It is unclear, therefore, how the appeal to the multiplicity of rules might serve to still a desire for perfect expressiveness. That appeal keeps alive the image of the control of performance by something else, something deeper, and hence it nurtures that desire. Section 55 introduces the reminder "I must not saw off the branch on which I am sitting" (§55), suggesting that we should not derogate the quite ordinary and variable descriptions, words, and rules that we use and appeal to in ordinary practice. Only they make it possible to say anything at all. But in employing these ordinary descriptions and rules, there still arises a fantasy of perfect conformity to rules, of perfect rational expressiveness. And in any case, no matter how much the variety of our rules and practices is emphasized, there remains too the primitive conviction that our language is directed to something that *simply is,* not of our own volition. "I must not saw off the branch on which I am sitting," must not deny that there is an indestructible substance of reality. The sense of the phrase "the branch on which I am sitting" in this context alternates unstably but undecomposably between "our conventional, ordinary uses of language" and "the simple substances of reality," depending on whether the sentence in which it appears is taken as a criticism or as an elaboration of the brief argument for the existence of simples that is given in the two preceding sentences that appear in quotation marks. In this alternation of senses, no thesis is definitely urged— not the thesis that our ordinary uses are self-founding; not the thesis that the simple substances of reality are the targets of our uses of language, which have aboutness only by being directed at them. Instead, what is here enacted is a play of temptations and efforts to find a foundation for our uses of language and our conceptual consciousness. Are we to find our conceptual consciousness to be founded in and enabled by ordinary uses of language or in and by the substances of reality? It is both and neither; there is no settling of the thoughts. We can give no example of an ultimately simple substance that we somehow name, in thought, apart from all uses of ordinary language. To name something is to use an expression from ordinary practice. Yet we cannot give up the thought that our uses of language and our thoughts are somehow, mysteriously, directed to an order of substances that is independent of our speaking, thinking, and willing, and we cannot give up further wishing to know how this is so.

Nor will mental simples help to resolve our wishes. One might think or hope that simple substances, or some perduring features of them, are immediately present to us there, within our mental lives, in a way that is deeper than, prior to, and enabling for our engagements with ordinary linguistic practices. Surely, it may seem, sensible qualities—colors and textures and sounds—are present to us in consciousness, in ways that we recognize, and it may seem that these recognitions lie beneath our lives with ordinary language. "But what if no such sample [no 'paradigm used in connection with the language'—i.e., no criteria of identity that are laid down in ordinary practice] is part of the language, and we *bear in mind* [*merken*—note, mark] the colour (for instance) that a word stands for?—'And if we bear it in mind then it comes before our mind's eye when we utter the word. So, if it is always supposed to be possible for us to remember it, it must be in itself indestructible'" (§56). Perhaps aspects of reality are primitively present to us here, as immediate and preconventional objects of conceptual consciousness, within consciousness itself. Perhaps there are simples in mind that are more fixed, more given, than the samples associated with ordinary names for public objects.

Yet this thought, however tempting or natural, fares no better than the argument that reality must be composed of simple substances that are the objects of our thought and talk. No objects, whether mental or physical, of themselves provide criteria for the use of an expression or the application of a concept. Those criteria are laid down only within linguistic practice, not given in an order of things. "But what do we regard as the criterion for remembering it [the indestructible mental 'simple' that is nonconventionally tied to an expression or concept] right? . . . we do not always resort to what memory tells us as the verdict of the highest court of appeal" (§56) in the application of an expression or a concept. Physical samples that are analogues of these putative simple mental samples—chips of color, say—can fade or darken. We do not rely on any single physical sample to determine the application of "magenta." Rather, the identity-criteria for magenta are laid down within our ordinary language. We sometimes reject corrupted or altered physical samples, and we sometimes correct applications of "magenta" that are based on such samples, checking not against some other authoritative physical sample, but instead against many applications of "magenta" to various things in various lights.

Just so, the mental sample that is brought explicitly into consciousness may alter. The expression "ultramarine" may evoke an image that is now brighter or now less intensely blue. The application of "ultramarine" is checked and controlled not by appeal to an invariant mental sample; instead a present application is compared with numbers of past and present ones. "Hold this cloth patch next to that color chip, and you'll see that it's not quite ultramarine— it's too green. —But only in that light, if you hold it over here, or compare it with these other chips, then you'll see . . . . And so on." Samples or paradigms, whether mental or physical, can alter or be lost or forgotten. We can forget the uses of expressions, can forget which samples go with expressions such as "picaresque" or "flat" (applied to paintings). What blocks such forgetting—should it fail to occur—is not any order or substance of reality in itself, either mental or physical. It is only that a certain game continues to be played, that certain expressions are applied and accepted. "When we forget which colour this is the name of, it loses its meaning for us; that is, we are no longer able to play a particular language-game with it. And the situation is comparable with that in which we have lost a paradigm which was an instrument of our language" (§57).

The primordial presence of things to us as objects of conceptual consciousness, prior to, independent of, and enabling for our engagements in linguistic practice, is thus not elucidated in the suggestion that we might associate "indestructible" mental simples with an expression or a concept. The expressions of ordinary language and the concepts of ordinary life have their criteria of application laid down differently, multiply, elsewhere, within ordinary practice. The wish to grasp how reality is present to us, so as to perfect our conceptions of it and our expression of those conceptions to ourselves and others, founders.

There is disappointment in this thought. Noting how applications of "magenta" or "ultramarine" or "flat" are controlled within ordinary language, by its criteria, quite evidently has not brought the mouse out of the rags. It has not shown *how* conceptual consciousness arises or what its perfect expression might be. The examination of the details of ordinary usage—of how we use words like "simple" and "red"—has not answered to our wish. When reflecting, when doing philosophy, something in us sets itself against, opposes, such an examination of details (§52), finds it to be inadequate or disappointing. The aspiration toward perfect rational expressiveness that lies behind this disappointment is not stilled. The examination of the details of ordinary usage blocks the efforts to map a route toward perfect expressiveness but does not stop the wish.

Hence new proposals arise in pursuit of this wish. One may try to contort language so as to point toward an elucidation of the metaphysical nature of conceptual consciousness. " 'I want to restrict the term *"name"* to what cannot occur in the combination "X exists."—Thus one cannot say "Red exists," because if there were no red it could not be spoken of at all' " (§58). In this way, one might hope to grasp the nature of a necessary existent over against which our consciousness must stand and toward which it must be directed. One might hope to point to something whose existence is so necessary that it cannot even be predicated of the thing; it simply is. But again the effort founders. "Red exists" is a quite ordinary expression with a quite ordinary use. To say "Red exists" is "as much as to say that something exists that has that color"

(§58), and there is no metaphysical news, no elucidation or perfection of our conceptual powers, in that thought.

Or again we may say, " 'A *name* signifies only what is an *element* of reality. What cannot be destroyed; what remains the same in all changes' " (§59). We may wish to know what is perdurably there for us to think and speak about. But the words "element" and "part" do not help us in this effort. Ordinarily when we talk about an object, we do *not* assume that it is composed of metaphysically simple elements or parts. "Suppose that, instead of saying 'Bring me the broom,' you said 'Bring me the broomstick and the brush which is fitted on to it.'!—Isn't the answer: 'Do you want the broom? Why do you put it so oddly?' " (§60).

It is possible to say that "Bring me the broomstick and the brush which is fitted on to it" and "Bring me the broom" mean the same.

> Certainly I too should say that an order in (a) [the game of naming "composite" objects such as brooms, chairs, tables, etc., as though they were wholes] had the same meaning as one in (b) [the game in which "only the parts are given names and the wholes are described by means of them"; §60]; or, as I expressed it earlier, they achieve the same. . . . But that is not to say that we have come to a *general* agreement [Aber damit ist nicht gesagt, daß wir uns . . . im *Allgemeinen* verständigt haben—that is not to say that we have understood generally, universally] about the use of the expression "to have the same meaning" or "to achieve the same."
>
> (§61)

Neither sentence is directly attached to reality as it is, prior to our uses of it within ordinary practice. Neither sentence grasps the given and fixed elements of reality. If the words "element" and "part" have uses, they are always humble ones, where what counts as a composite or a whole is specified contrastively in context. No absolute translation scheme takes us from a sentence that is "directly connected" with reality, such as the sentence about parts in game (b) to the "ordinary sentence" that stands in need of an analysis, such as the sentence about whole brooms in game (a). What matters, always, both for speaking about objects and for taking different sentences in use to mean the same, is what game is being played.

> In what sense do the symbols of this language game [the game of giving names to color rectangles composed of two squares; a rectangle "which is

half red half green (may) be called 'U'; a half green half white one, 'V'; and
so on" §64] stand in need of analysis? How far is it even *possible* to replace
this language-game by (48) [in which each square has a name: "red," "green,"
and so on]?—It is just *another* language-game; even though it is related to
(48).

(§64)

"It is just *another* language-game [Es ist eben ein *anderes* Sprachspiel]"
(§64). It is *this* remark—unavoidable in its power to defeat efforts to grasp
the simple substances of reality or otherwise to perfect our conceptions and
expressions, yet disappointing in thus defeating efforts we cannot disown—
that leads directly to the great outburst of section 65 that asks for a specification of the essence of language.

> Here we come up against the great question that lies behind all these
> considerations.—For someone might object against me: "You take the easy
> way out! You talk about all sorts of language-games, but have nowhere said
> what the essence of a language-game, and hence of language, is: what is com-
> mon to all these activities, and what makes them into language or parts of
> language. So you let yourself off the very part of the investigation that once
> gave you the most headache [Kopfzerbrechen—headbreaking, pondering],
> the part about the *general form of propositions* and of language."
>   And this is true.—Instead of producing something common to all that
> we call language, I am saying that these phenomena have no one thing in
> common which makes us use the same word for all,—but that they are *related*
> to one another in many different ways. And it is because of this relationship,
> or these relationships, that we call them all "language." I will try to explain
> this [Ich will versuchen, dies zu erklären—I want to try to clarify, to explain
> this].

(§65)

The protagonist here evidently identifies with the voice that repudiates the
effort to specify the essence of language, therein providing an account of the
nature of conceptual consciousness and its perfection. "For someone might
object against *me* [Denn man könnte *mir* nun einwenden]" (§65) is the phrase
that introduces the demand for an explanation. The protagonist is prepared
here to try to persist in the repudiation of the effort to analyze the essence of
language, and instead to arrive at a sort of peace in the use of ordinary language
that is free of the hubris of an aspiration to perfect rational expressiveness, in
the perfect information of *Willkür* by *Wille*. The protagonist will go on to elabo-

rate how it is that language need not have an essence, how we are capable of using the word "language" with perfect right and accuracy without having grasped any essence or nature. And yet the phrase "I want to try to explain this" itself acknowledges the persistence of a desire that remains unstilled even after the repudiations of philosophical efforts and their hubris.

What would it be to want to try to explain or clarify why and how language has no essence? How might one go about explaining this? A clarification here *could not* take the form of insistence on a dogma of the autonomy of language games from the world, or a dogma of linguistic idealism, or a dogma of the creation of language games *ex nihilo* through sheer and arbitrary will. Each of these dogmatic stances would indeed deny the idea that the essence of language is somehow determined by the given nature of either conceptual consciousness or the world. But in doing so, each of these stances would in turn introduce a new specification of the essence of language as consisting in free-floating convention, or self-proliferating, subjectless creativeness, or arbitrary volition. Not only would these claims fail to carry conviction, in betraying a primordial sense of language and thought as intentional, as about an independent reality, however difficult it might be to articulate and sustain the content of such a conviction; they would also, and more important, repeat the metaphysical game of specifying the essence of language. Any of these quasi-conventionalist, quasi-idealist, quasi-voluntarist stances would misdescribe the character of our ongoing lives with language. If the claims of these stances were installed, we would be left only with the choices of being arbitrarily conservative in hewing to conventions groundlessly in place or arbitrarily willful and iconoclastic in pursuing a wayward and inauthentic creativity. Our abilities as possessors of conceptual consciousness both to hew to and to transform standing uses of expressions to talk about things, where these uses are for us both stable and shifting, would be misdescribed and potentially undone, were any of these forms of dogma to be lived out.

To explain or clarify, or to want to explain or clarify, how and why language has no essence cannot then be to assert conventionalist or Heraclitean or voluntarist theses about the sources and applications of concepts and expressions. But it also and equally cannot be to revert to how the nature of language is fixed as a function either of the nature of the simple substances of reality or an autonomous and prior life of consciousness in relation to reality. What then could an explanation or clarification be? How might one bear the desire to explain or clarify language's lack of an essence? What would it be to want to try to explain this? What is it to be a protagonist, an I, in possession of such a wish?

Instead of articulating and defending any version of either realism or idealism, one would have to track our endless alternations between our satisfactions in our criteria and our language games as they stand and our disappointments in and frustrations by these criteria and language games. One would have to follow out how it is that our criteria and language games as they stand enable us to grasp things and to express our grasps, and therein to be received as possessors of a spontaneity that has been brought into conceptual articulation. But one would also have to follow out how it is that our criteria and language games as they stand disappoint and frustrate us, leaving us inexpressive, dumb, or opaque to one another, and to ourselves, in failing to enable a grasp of things or in failing to articulate, in ways that might be acknowledged, sometime dim half-grasps of how things are or might be. A life with language that lacks an essence will be a life, always, of such satisfactions and disappointments, a life in which our spontaneity seeks and always partially, but only partially, finds rational routes of conceptual articulation and acknowledgment, a life in which *Willkür* is always partially, but only partially, informed by *Wille*.

There will be then no plot of human life culminating in the achievement of perfect rational expressiveness, as we think and speak in the terms and concepts that are written into reality itself, but likewise no plot of the abandonment and dismissal of efforts toward perfect expressiveness, in acceptance of the claim that all thought and speech are groundlessly conventional, or in unconstrained flux, or arbitrarily willful. In failing to present either a plot of the final discovery of the basis and conditions of perfect development of our powers or a plot of the ecstatic abandonment of efforts to grasp and develop our powers, self-interrogative philosophical writing will come to look literary and endless. It will be impossible to distinguish exhaustively between serious science, epistemology, and metaphysics, on the one hand, and merely entertaining or provocative or amusing belles-lettres, on the other hand. A certain antinomianism will predominate, as routes of the development of rational powers are traced, where these routes lie between the mirror dogmas of materialism and conventionalism-idealism-skepticism. Recognizing things, and articulating and expressing recognitions in ways that are open to acknowledgment from and with others and within one's own life in time, will be no more and no less possible and delicate than acknowledging another person as a bearer of rational power under certain routes of articulation, alike but different.

Grasping and living with the world, in and through thought and language, will run strand by strand with grasping and living with others, in ways that philosophical doctrines of our power will be unable to control or foreclose. Sensing always both the power and the limits of our criteria in enabling our rational commerce with the world, with one another, and with ourselves, we will find ourselves always in what Cavell has called

> the circumstances that it is I, some I or other, who counts, who is able to do the thing of counting, of conceiving a world, that is I who, taking others into account, establish criteria for what is worth saying, hence for the intelligible. But this is only on the condition that I count, that I matter, that it matters that I count in my agreement or attunement with those with whom I maintain my language, from whom this inheritance—language as the condition of counting—comes, so that it matters not only what some I or other says but that it is some particular I who desires in some specific place to say it. If my counting fails to matter, I am mad. It is being uncounted—being left out, as if my story were untellable—that makes what I say (seem) perverse, that makes me odd. The surmise that we have become unable to count one another, to count for one another, is philosophically a surmise that we have lost the capacity to think, that we are stupefied. I call this condition living our skepticism.[4]

To want to try to explain why and how language has no essence is to confront living our skepticism as a standing possibility not to be foreclosed by philosophical theses, but not necessarily to be embraced (in glumness or apocalyptic ecstasy) either, insofar as articulations and acknowledgments of our conceptual powers remain, fitfully, possible.

4. Cavell, "Being Odd, Getting Even," in *In Quest of the Ordinary*, p. 127.

7

Perspicuous Representations and Anxieties of the Normal—§§66-142

"I want to try to explain this" (§65). Sections 66–142 take up this effort. They represent a break in the interior dialogue of proposal and rebuke. The persona in the text and the historical writer here come close to being merged under direct characterizations of the persona-writer's activities of thinking: "*I* can think of no better expression to characterize these similarities than 'family resemblances'" (§67, emphasis added). The occurrences of an interrupting, explanation-seeking voice, a voice that seeks necessities to govern thought and expression, diminish markedly in favor of more magisterial pronouncements, as, for example, "A picture held us captive" (§115). The wish to have an explanation of conceptual consciousness, so as to enable the release of that consciousness into perfect expressiveness, held us in thrall. Now, apparently, we are beyond that. When the interruptive, explanation-seeking voice occurs, it comes now often within quotation marks, or otherwise explicitly represented as other to the voice of the protagonist, as in "But if someone wished to say: [Wenn aber Einer sagen wollte:]" (§67); or as in the references to "your scruples [deine Skrupel]" and "your questions [deine Fragen]" (§120). Or the explanation-seeking voice is explicitly identified with Frege, someone with whom the protagonist disagrees, as in section 71.

In light of this great shift in tone, it is then no accident that these sections have often been read as offering the most accurate compressed summary of what might be received—in abstraction from the dramatic structure of the text—as *Wittgenstein's views*. It is fairly clear, moreover, what sorts of views about the natures of understanding, meaning, and conceptual consciousness are here apparently asserted. These views involve, above all, the rejection of seeking to explain the nature of conceptual consciousness, meaning, and understanding by appeal to sempiternal objects, standing inner archetypes, Platonic forms, or anything else. Instead, the determinacy of sense is reconstrued as something that is established *within* language games and nowhere outside of them. Meaningful explanations then, as opposed to grandiose and misbegotten philosophical ones, are always humble accounts that are formulated within language games. "Bow in an inverted U shape to get a less scratchy and more resonant sound." "A tropical storm is classified as a hurricane when its maximum winds reach 75 miles per hour." But there is no explanation of how and why there are such things as explanation and understanding and meaning at all. The autonomy of language games from explanation is not to be sublimed away in favor of some pseudogrounding in the brain or forms or simple objects.

This account of the establishment of determinate sense in and by language games, and only in and by language games, in turn motivates a radical reconceptualization of the task of philosophy, or of some successor discipline that might replace philosophy, avoiding its errors and better meeting our needs where they can be met. We are no longer to attempt to give an absolute account of the metaphysical facts that create sense and conceptual consciousness *überhaupt*. Instead, the task of philosophy, or of its successor, is more simply to *describe* the varieties of meaningful utterance that are available to us within our language games as we have them, with no further moves toward any deeper grounding of them. "In philosophy one is constantly tempted to invent a mythology of symbolism or of psychology, instead of simply saying what we know."[1] This temptation is now to be foregone. The idea that there *must* be some metaphysical ground, outer or inner as may be, that explains the nature of conceptual consciousness and the determinacy of sense is now to be given up. As Baker and Hacker put it, "The demand for determinacy of sense is a striking example of philosophical dogmatism. It is not a description of how language actually works based on simple observation. It is imposed as part of a misguided attempt to demonstrate that language and communication are really possible."[2]

Now we are to do better. We are to accept the fact that it is *always possible* (albeit rarely actual) for irresolvable disagreements about the application of a term to arise.[3] Nothing fixed in any order of nature or mind forecloses this possibility and makes determinate sense absolute. No realist metaphysical

---

1. Ludwig Wittgenstein, *Philosophical Grammar,* ed. Rush Rhees, trans. Anthony Kenny (Oxford: Basil Blackwell, 1974), p. 56.
2. Baker and Hacker, *Wittgenstein: Understanding and Meaning,* p. 367.
3. See ibid, p. 376.

scheme—no scheme, that is, that seeks to characterize an order of reality that is conceptually external to and capable of governing our conceptual conscious-ness and our linguistic practice—can vouchsafe an absolute impossibility of disagreement in the use of terms, ensuring that thought and linguistic practice are transparently informed by an absolute understanding of ultimate things.

What *we want,* as we take up this new stance, in which we see determinacy of sense established only relatively and within practice, is now described di-rectly. "We want to establish an order in our knowledge of the use of language: an order with a particular end in view; one out of many possible orders, not *the* order" (§132). We are to achieve a view of the varieties of determinate sense that are available to us within our conceptual and linguistic practices, foregoing the realist dream of ultimate explanations that might sublime away our risks of deviance and repudiation within them. Achieving this view, and in doing so weaning ourselves from the realist temptation, is to bring us peace within our shifting practices as they are.

Doing this is described explicitly as a *new* task for philosophy (or for its heir) in a variety of ways. We "want . . . to get a clear view of [übersehen wollen] our entanglement in rules [Vergangen in unsern Regeln]" (§125). We set up language games as "*objects of comparison [Vergleichsobjekte]*" (§130), not as "a preconceived idea to which reality *must* correspond" (§131). We do the work of "assembling reminders for a particular purpose" (§127), not for the general purpose of understanding the natures of thought and language *über-haupt.* We note that we do this, and this, and this with words. "We must do away with all *explanation,* and description alone must take its place [Alle Erk-lärung muß fort, und nur Beschreibung an ihre Stelle treten]" (§109). We are now to "*command a clear view [übersehen]* of the use of our words" through generating a "perspicuous representation [übersichtliche Darstellung]" (§122). The term "Darstellung" here emphasizes the materiality and figurality of lan-guage as we use it that we are now to acknowledge and accept. In contrast with "Vorstellung," which suggests something inner, mental, and potentially practice-independent, "Darstellung" conveys the sense of a material *presenta-tion* in the public world of discourse and practice, such as the *Darstellung* of a play.[4] In section 122 its use suggests a presentation put forward by the (post-)philosopher after surveying our uses. It promises not the representation

---

4. See the brief discussion of the history of *Darstellung* in romantic criticism in Seyhan, *Repre-sentation and Its Discontents,* p. 7.

of some inner, intellectual grasp of ultimate realities, but a public and material offering of a public reality: our various uses of words and the multiple determinacies of sense that are to be found within our language games and nowhere else.

Historically, as M. W. Rowe and Joachim Schulte have shown, the major influence on the sense of the importance of commanding a clear view of what is already before us that surfaces in these sections of *Philosophical Investigations* is Goethe. Goethe recommends that one look to a neighboring case in order to become clearer about what one is seeing, or would say, in a present, more doubtful one. "We hope that the genius of the analogy may stand by us, as a guardian angel, so that we may not fail to recognize in a single doubtful case a truth which has stood the test in many other instances."[5] If we are uncertain whether *that* is a *goldcrest* or a *resolution in C-sharp minor* or a *cry of pain*, so that skepticism threatens and our grip on the world seems to waver, then we are to return ourselves to confidence in our awareness of our world, not through a general intellectual argument about ultimate realities that guide consciousness and speech, but instead by surveying other, related, more familiar cases of things we already know. Confidence in one's conceptual consciousness comes not out of an ultimate ground, but out of comparisons, surveys, and reminders that are fit to the occasion of anxiety. The Goethean stance comes to Wittgenstein not only from Goethe himself—Goethe is the figure most often mentioned in Wittgenstein's *Remarks on Colour*—but also by way of an entire Goethean tradition in German and Austrian science. As Baker and Hacker note, "Almost all the thinkers to whom Wittgenstein explicitly acknowledged an intellectual debt display precisely this hankering for surveyability, a profound belief that the deepest problems are resolved or grasped or laid to rest, not by scientific hypotheses or research, but by seeing connections, arranging what is known, looking at what is there in the right way. This is typical of Hertz, Boltzmann, Ernst, Kraus, and . . . Spengler."[6]

Not only does this apparently guiding theme of *Philosophical Investigations* trace back to Goethe; the structure of *Philosophical Investigations* is likewise an analogue of the structure of Goethe's *Theory of Colours*, his *Farbenlehre*. As Rowe describes the *Farbenlehre*, its main body "contains 920 numbered sec-

5. J. W. von Goethe, *Die Schriften zur Naturwissenschaft* (Weimar, 1947), quoted in H. B. Nisbet, *Goethe and the Scientific Tradition* (London: Institute of Germanic Studies, 1972), p. 54; in turn quoted in M. W. Rowe, "Goethe and Wittgenstein," *Philosophy*, 66 (1991): 291.

6. Baker and Hacker, *Wittgenstein: Understanding and Meaning*, p. 547.

tions and a short conclusion, roughly grouped according to subject matter; some are several pages in length, others consist of no more than a short sentence. It is often quite difficult to know how each remark relates to those around it: some seem like short interjections, others form part of a large argument, some offer summaries, others methodological aphorisms."[7]

Associated with both the emphasis on the importance of analogy and the deliberately open structure of the texts is a resistance to dualism that is common to both Goethe and Wittgenstein. Just as it is a mistake to try to ground conceptualizations in their reference to some ultimate reality (either mental-archetypal or Platonic or quasi-physical–quasi-atomistic), so too it is a mistake to separate the mind as an conceptually isolate container of ideas from the world that our ideas are about.

> Writing to Schiller after reading one of Schelling's early works, [Goethe] remarked that he saw no more possibility of transcendental idealists being able to get from mind to bodies than of materialists getting from bodies to mind. Until the philosophers should decide the matter, he continued, he preferred to remain "in dem philosophischen Naturstande" (in the philosophical state of nature) and to make the best possible use of his "undivided existence."[8]

One's life as a thinking being is here, for Goethe, led within both nature and one's ordinary conceptual and linguistic practices (which are not themselves to be reduced to mere reflexes of nature). Mindedness in relation to nature comes to be what it is only in and through practices. It is not to be explained by reference to either a purely nonnatural, mental ground or a purely biophysical, natural ground. In Goethe, the *Urpflanze*—the schema of the primal plant that organizes our perceptions of all particular, individual plants—is to be found *both* in us and in things. It is partly our creation and partly something that is there to be seen in individual plants.[9] These two sides of the organizing schema cannot be pulled apart from one another, cannot be decomposed into abstract pattern and material particular. And it is just this conception of mindedness achieved in practice in nature that likewise lies behind the rejections of dualism, behaviorism, and physicalism that figure in *Philosophical Investigations.*

Both the rejection of dualism and the positive conception of understanding

7. Rowe, "Goethe and Wittgenstein," p. 296.
8. Ibid., p. 284, citing Goethe, Letter to Schiller, January 6, 1798; quoted in E. M. Wilkinson, "The Poet as Thinker," in *Goethe: Poet and Thinker* (London, Edward Arnold, 1962), p. 138.
9. See Rowe, "Goethe and Wittgenstein," p. 289.

within linguistic and conceptual practices, themselves autonomous from ultimate explanation, are further associated, in both Goethe and *Philosophical Investigations,* with a specific hostility to scientistic metaphysics and to any effort to privilege experimentation and mathematical-physical description over perception in showing us some of the ways of the world.

> Goethe wished to discredit . . . theoretical distortions and artificialities, by placing the phenomenon back in the real world where it belonged, and establishing a much broader base for investigation. In particular, he wished to draw attention to the colour effects everyone experiences (or could experience) in everyday life, and the reader of the *Farbenlehre* is bombarded with a thousand quotidian observations: the sun goes red as it sets, smoke from your neighbor's chimney grows light as it rises, distant mountains look blue, tobacco smoke turns roses green. Experienced *en masse,* such phenomena have the effect of making us see just how limited the kind of phenomena investigated in laboratories actually are, and draw attention to the quite extraordinary range and complexity of the phenomena we have experienced— but frequently overlooked—in daily life.[10]

And in *Philosophical Investigations:* "The aspects of things that are most important for us are hidden because of their simplicity and familiarity. (One is unable to notice something—because it is always before one's eyes.) The real foundations of his enquiry do not strike a man at all" (§129). A primitive and autonomous *ability* to notice things—unbacked by archetypes, forms, or atoms— stands at the center of our lives as conceptually conscious beings.

About the nature of this ability, nothing is hidden. It is a mistake to try to go deeper than the acceptance of this ability as we exercise it, in an effort to explain its genesis and control its exercise. Goethe: "Don't look for anything behind the phenomena; they themselves are the theory."[11] *Philosophical Investigations:* "Don't think, but look!" (§66). For each figure, acceptance of one's life within ordinary conceptual, perceptual, and linguistic practices is to be the fruit of simply noticing what we already do. As Joachim Schulte puts it, "For both [Goethe and Wittgenstein] it is not a matter of pushing into a new domain in order to uncover there what has never before been seen; rather

---

10. Ibid., p. 287.
11. Goethe, *Maximen und Reflexionen,* ed. Max Hacker (Weimar, 1907), quoted in Wittgenstein, *Remarks on the Philosophy of Psychology,* vol. 1 (Oxford: Basil Blackwell, 1980), §889; quoted in turn in Rowe, "Goethe and Wittgenstein," p. 295.

they seek to make perceptible what already lies under our eyes."[12] "It is . . . of the essence of our investigation that we do not seek to learn anything *new* by it. We want to *understand* something that is already in plain view. For *this* is what we seem in some sense not to understand" (§89). Accommodation to and within our lives as possessors of conceptual consciousness is to be found where we are. If there is a guiding doctrine of *Philosophical Investigations,* it is this Goethean stance that dominates sections 66–142 and that has so often controlled the reception of the text.

✳

But there are also important differences between Goethe's strategies of attention in constructing perspicuous representations of phenomena and those that figure in *Philosophical Investigations.* These differences have to do both with the *objects* of attention and, consequently, with *what is uncovered* and with *how peace is attained* through attention to those objects. For Goethe, the objects of attention are phenomena in physical and biological nature: the looks of colors, the drift of smoke, the structures of plants. Goethe seeks not an inner, hypothetical-theoretical representation of an outer reality, but nonetheless a kind of observational-perceptual understanding of *things.*

In *Philosophical Investigations,* in contrast, the primary objects of attention are not natural phenomena, but uses of language, or language games. These can be invented as well as observed. As Schulte remarks, after cataloguing similarities between them, "Nonetheless the philosopher Wittgenstein pursued 'not natural science; nor yet natural history—since we can also invent fictitious natural history for our purposes' [II, xii]—a possibility that to Goethe the investigator of nature was altogether closed off."[13] In *Philosophical Investigations,* the attention to language games, some of them invented, is designed not primarily to enable us to notice some natural phenomenon that is there for us, but instead to free us up to do a variety of things with language, to bring us to awareness of how little our uses of language are controlled by anything fixed. Norman Malcolm reports that Wittgenstein made this remark in a lecture:

> What I give is the morphology of the use of an expression. I show that it has kinds of uses of which you had not dreamed. In philosophy one feels

12. Joachim Schulte, "Chor und Gesetz: Zur 'Morphologischen Methode' bei Goethe und Wittgenstein," *Grazer Philosophischer Studien* 21 (1984): 30; my translation.
13. Ibid., p. 31; my translation.

forced to look at a concept in a certain way. What I do is to suggest, or even invent, other ways of looking at it. I suggest possibilities of which you had not previously thought. You thought that there was one possibility, or only two at most. But I made you think of others. Furthermore, I made you see that it was absurd to expect the concept to conform to those narrow possibilities. Thus your mental cramp is relieved, and you are free to look around the field of use of the expression and to describe the different kinds of uses of it.[14]

Unlike looking at natural phenomena that are there for us to notice, looking at language games leads us not to something that is there, but instead to an awareness of the permanent possibility of multiple uses that attaches to terms. When we look and see what we do—or could do—with language, we find that there is room for anxiety about our relations to language and to others. Words might be used differently than they are now. There is a spontaneity to the human use of language that can issue in innovative usages. What an aptly innovative use will be is something that is never determined in advance by reality or mind apart from uses.

In thinking about our relations with language, sometimes we feel ourselves to be, as Baker and Hacker put it, "at the mercy of samples."[15] If *that* is a sample of red, then I *must,* I may feel, call *that* red as well. But the nature of this "must" remains obscure to us. Do others feel it in the same way that I do? Do I know how and why I feel it? I can seem, as I use language, opaque to myself and to others.

If we then say, but "our fate is in our hands," since *we make* the samples, and "it depends on how we do use samples,"[16] then our feelings of anxiety, opacity, and potential repudiation are not stilled. How do *I* know what *we* do? I may find that what I thought was our practice is a joke on me. ("I thought we were going back to the house because you had forgotten to turn off the coffee maker, and our friends leap out from behind the sofa.") In looking at our uses of language, and especially at surprising, invented, apt usages—themselves nowhere controlled by forms, inner archetypes, or atoms—we can find ourselves having strange experiences simultaneously of familiarity and unfamiliarity: experiences of the uncanny.

14. Wittgenstein, cited in Malcolm, *Ludwig Wittgenstein: A Memoir,* p. 50.
15. Baker and Hacker, *Wittgenstein: Understanding and Meaning,* p. 289.
16. Ibid., pp. 289, 290.

In attending to various uses of language, *Philosophical Investigations* is not so much a representation of the way our language use is always and obviously controlled on the surface as it is both a representation and an enactment of the anxieties that are bound up in our lives with language: of the wish to bring *Willkür* to perfect information by *Wille* so as to achieve perfect, irrepudiable expressiveness and self-unity. Through showing that we wish to *know how* forms or mental processes or conceptual archetypes or the simple substances of reality somehow control apt language use—a wish that continues in some way or other—*Philosophical Investigations* is itself a perspicuous representation, a survey of cases, of our various temptations to sublime our ability to use language into *theoretical knowledge of something,* in such a way that our anxieties might be stilled. It tracks how these temptations arise, mutate, and come to exhaustion rather than satisfaction.

The structure of sections 66–142 within this complicated survey and enactment of our temptations and their exhaustion is then something like this. These sections begin from thoughts about meaning-facts or the basis of usage of general terms such as "game." That basis of usage lies not in some essence, form, or set of necessary and sufficient conditions that are attached or "contracted" to term-types. Instead it lies only in piecemeal resemblances that are themselves sanctioned within practice, not behind it, as relevant to the applications of words. This thought about the basis of usage of general terms then motivates thoughts about the impossibility of metaphysical philosophy, which would seek to uncover a permanent, practice-independent, fixed and given basis of linguistic usage and conceptual thought. Thoughts are entered about the form of attention to the use of words that might replace the efforts of metaphysical philosophers, a new form of attention that will acknowledge that only piecemeal resemblances lie at the basis of our usages. But the text does not stop there. Instead it in effect turns on itself to ask: Do these admonitions not to do metaphysical philosophy, but instead to stay on the surface, to accept our simultaneously stable and shifting uses of language as they are, satisfy us? Do *they* quiet our anxieties? Do they satisfy our wish to overcome via knowledge the possibility of repudiation by others of our thought and speech? Do they satisfy our longing for self-unity? Do they wean us from the fantasy of the achievement of the perfect information of *Willkür* by *Wille*?

And the answer to these questions is "No." When we look and see what we do in thinking and speaking, then we find that our lives with language, with others, and with ourselves are uncanny. Anxiety about this fact is natural, ineliminable. That this is so is evident in a number of ways in these crucial sections about the nature of philosophy and about the possibility of a successor discipline of surveying our uses of language. First, the naturalness of anxiety is registered in these sections in the insistent noting of the fact that nothing everywhere controls our apt linguistic performances. Second, it is registered in the litany of remarks about what we wish for from logic or philosophy: the discovery of something permanent that lies at the basis of thought and language. Third, it is registered in the images of being blocked or at a loss, and of walking or moving forward as something we need still to learn how to do. "A philosophical problem has the form: I don't know my way about [Ich kenne mich nicht aus]" (§123). Walking, or knowing one's way about, is an image of the possession of a power or ability within a practice, an image of the achievement of a sense of unity with oneself that can be displayed in movement, as one's body responds to one's will. And it is presented here as something that we still need or wish to learn how to do. Finally, and most important, the naturalness of anxiety is registered in the reversion, in sections 134–142, to the topic of *how* we understand words. The topic of *how* we are able to do this, *how* we can follow a rule, has neither disappeared nor received an answer that would ground us in our possession of this ability, free from anxiety. The very turn to attending to what we do, or could do, with language—a turn that was to replace the metaphysical philosopher's obsession with discovering the fixed bases of thought and meaning—itself brings us back to this topic: How do we go on with language, with others, in our thoughts? What is it to have this ability? The announcement of a mode of attention to the use of language that will replace metaphysical theorizing itself induces a recurrence of anxiety, associated with uncertainties about its own reception. (Such swerves between confidence recovered and announced, on the one hand, and recurrent anxiety about the reception of any such announcement, by others and by oneself, on the other, constitute a major structure of romantic writing.)[17]

The whole development of sections 66–142, in leading from thoughts about a new, postmetaphysical mode of attention to uses of language to the recurrence of the question of how one is able to think and use language at all, goes roughly as follows. "Behind" or, better, "woven within" our uses of some general terms such as "game," there is nothing more or less than "a complicated network of similarities overlapping and criss-crossing: sometimes

17. See Eldridge, "Internal Transcendentalism," esp. pp. 68–69.

overall similarities, sometimes similarities of detail" (§66). Some affinities (*Verwandtschaften*) between things rightly called by the same name are direct; some are indirect (§67). Particularly in relying on indirect affinities in using a general term, "we extend our concept [wir dehnen unseren Begriff . . . aus—spread it out], . . . as in spinning a thread we twist fibre on fibre" (§67). That is, we make something—general-term meanings and class memberships simultaneously—out of something that is already there: direct and indirect similarities. This view is inconsistent with all of rationalist realism, empiricist realism, idealism, and skepticism as traditionally conceived. What we do in applying a term, against a background of settled applications and potential extensions, is partly rooted in the real, but partly open, up to us, in ways that can never be disentangled finally and according to principle from one another. No absolute essences stand behind what we do. "I can use [the word 'number'] so that the extension of the concept [der Umfang des Begriffes—the circumference or circuit, the line drawn around the members of a class to which a concept applies] is *not* closed by a frontier [nicht durch eine Grenze abgeschlossen ist—is not locked up or sealed off by a limit, edge, or boundary]. And this is how we do use the word 'game'. . . . Can you give the boundary? No." (§68). As Cavell comments on this passage, the vision is that "universals are neither necessary nor even useful in explaining how words apply to different things."[18] The use of a word "is not everywhere circumscribed by rules [ist nicht überall von Regeln begrenzt]," any more than there are rules for "how high one throws the ball in tennis, or how hard" (§68).

This is a negative thought, a thought about our inability to know any fixed basis for usages. "No universal or definition would, as it were, represent my knowledge," in the sense of my ability to apply a word.[19] "Isn't my knowledge, my concept of a game, completely expressed in the explanations I could give? That is, in my describing examples of various kinds of game; shewing how all sorts of other games can be constructed on the analogy of these; saying that I should scarcely include this or this among games; and so on" (§75). This is *not* to say that we are either ignorant or arbitrary in our applications of words. It is to say that there is no possibility of theoretical knowledge of our knowledge of language, of our ability to apply a term. There is too much room left, at least in principle, for extensions and innovations in the applica-

18. Cavell, *The Claim of Reason,* p. 188.
19. Ibid.

tions of terms. "How would we explain to someone what a game is? I imagine that we would describe *games* to him, and we might add: 'This *and similar things* are called "games".' And do we know any more about it ourselves? Is it only other people whom we cannot tell exactly what a game is?—But this is not ignorance. We do not know the boundaries because none have been drawn" (§69).

For a considerable range of cases there is nothing we can say about *how* we know what we know. Consider "how a clarinet sounds" (§78). No third entity, and no set of necessary and sufficient conditions, mediates between us and our experience of the sound of the clarinet, such that we can recognize that sound again. The description "it's a reedy, woodwind sound, deeper than a flute, fuller or rounder than a oboe in its upper register, somewhat thinner than a bassoon" is neither necessary nor useful. One could not understand the description if one did not already know many of the instruments of an orchestra. Knowing the sound of a clarinet rests on nothing more than human attentiveness exercised within a world in which there are clarinets. The content of our awareness of the sound of a clarinet is not determined by any rule or pattern laid down elsewhere.

This negative view about our inability to say what we know in knowing the applications of many general terms extends to proper names as well. "I use the name 'N' without a *fixed* meaning [ohne *feste* Bedeuting]" (§79). If one is queried as to whom one means by a name, then there is "a whole series of props in readiness" (§79). One can say that one means the first cellist in the community orchestra, or the coach of the soccer team, or the person who's cooking dinner over there. Each of these explanations of what one means might clear up a particular misunderstanding. "But where are the bounds of the incidental? [Wo aber ist die Grenze des Nebensächlichen?]" (§79). Where is it laid down what one *must* know in order to be able to use a name and in order to explain its application *in every case*? Not that there are not individuals and classes in the world. But nothing tells us the identity conditions for an individual or the conditions for class membership apart from our ways in practice of determining these things. (Neither metaphysical realism nor metaphysical idealism is true.)

Beyond general terms and proper names, this negative view—this sense of our inability to say what it is that we know when we know how to apply a term—extends to our operations with language in general. We "cannot say that someone who is using language *must* be playing such a game," *must* be operating "according to fixed rules [nach festen Regeln]" (§81). Perhaps that is true sometimes. Sometimes we have a definite prop ready to hand to clear up a particular misunderstanding: "In conjugating regular verbs in English, one forms the past tense by adding *-ed* to the stem." But this is true only of a range of cases, to which there are acknowledged exceptions: irregular verbs. And what are the rules for recognizing *them*? Simply, inter alia, that one doesn't form their past tenses by adding *-ed.* There is nothing that *makes us* in common have this rule ready to hand. There is nothing that marks off cases such as this as central to our linguistic practices generally. Our linguistic performances are not "everywhere circumscribed by rules" (§69). Shifts in sense and application, the emergence of an irregular case, and the need for a new, ad hoc explanation of what one is doing in thinking and speaking are *always possible.* No rules guide us by themselves, in all circumstances, against all contingencies. Any rule that guides us at all does so only against a background of training in the technique of *its* application. "One learns to look [a] picture up in a table by receiving a training [durch Abrichtung], and part of this training consists perhaps in the pupil's learning to pass with his finger horizontally from left to right; and so, as it were, to draw a series of horizontal lines on the table" (§86). But nothing that is simply given in mind or reality makes this the training in technique that alone could tie a rule formulation to acts that comply with it. Nothing marks out the cases in which we have even the most definite rules ready to hand, together with the background training in techniques that the compliant use of them presupposes, as central to our lives with language generally. "And is there not also the case where we play and—make up the rules as we go along? And there is even one where we alter them—as we go along" (§83). This happens, often and ineliminably, in our lives with language, with one another, and with ourselves. (And this happens likewise in this text, which is not guided by a *theory* of the nature of fixed meaning-facts that everywhere control linguistic practice: there are none; and this text, knowing that, hence cannot purvey a doctrine about their nature.)

In one way, this is a negative, antifoundationalist *result.* Language is not absolutely tethered to reality by means of proper names for individuals; there are no games that we must play that control our apt uses of general terms; there are no rules that guide us in using language independently of training in techniques, where training can be taken in different directions as interests shift. All this is part of our ordinary life with language; it is *not* a ground for skeptical anxiety about the existence or the possibility of understanding.

"But then how does an explanation help me to understand, if after all it is not the final one? In that case the explanation is never completed; so I still don't understand what he means, and never shall!"—As though an explanation as it were hung in the air unless supported by another one. Whereas an explanation may indeed rest on another one that has been given, but none stands in need of another—unless *we* require it to prevent a misunderstanding. One might say: an explanation serves to remove or to avert a misunderstanding—one, that is, that would occur but for the explanation; not every one that I can imagine. (§87)

"No single ideal of exactness has been laid down" (§88), and none is needed.

But in another way, and at the same time, these recordings of what we see when we look at our uses of language—and what we do when we give explanations, avert misunderstandings, and work things out in particular cases—acknowledge the existence of a continuing desire or *eros*, a wish for absoluteness in our control of language. "You will find it difficult to hit upon such a convention; at least any that satisfies you [Aber es wird dir schwer werden, so eine Festsetzung zu treffen; eine, die dich befriedigt—it will be hard for you to run up against such an establishment, an arrangement, a holding fast, an appointment, at least against one that satisfies you]" (§88). Any route we can imagine to the satisfaction of our *eros* or desire or wish goes nowhere. We meet no satisfaction. This is as true of our attentions to our ordinary uses of language as of attempts to revert to forms or atoms or adamantine rules. What we see when we look at our uses of language does not satisfy us. Those uses are, even where shared and stable, also open to refigurations, uncontrolled by anything absolute. Types of marks do not wear their uses on their sleeves.

It was logic that we looked to in order to find something sublime, an absolute constraint on licit performances in thought and speech. "Logic lay, it seemed, at the bottom of all the sciences.—For logical investigation explores the nature of all things. It seeks to see to the bottom of things and is not meant to concern itself whether what actually happens is this or that" (§89). Logic, we think, should say to us, articulate for us, what we *must* do in speaking or thinking genuinely, rather than emptily or only apparently. Conformity to its dictates would enable the perfect information of *Willkür* by *Wille*, at least up to a point. Its articulations would free us, we think, from anxiety about how to go on in thought and speech. One *must*, we think, accept *for all p, not both p and ~p* or *5 is a number*. One *cannot* say "some spaniels are felines," where "spaniel" is understood as having "canine" as part of its content and "canine" is understood as having "not feline" as part of *its* content. If one tries to say any such thing, one says, does, or thinks nothing. One arrives only at making empty sounds. "Logic lay, it seemed, at the bottom of all the sciences." It reposes on and expresses, and so "takes its rise from, . . . an urge to understand the basis of everything empirical [Sie entspringt . . . einem Streben, das Fundament, oder Wesen, alles Erfahrungsmäßigen zu verstehen]" (§89). This urge, or striving, lies behind "the subliming of our whole account of logic" through our giving vent to "the tendency to assume a pure intermediary between the propositional *signs* and the facts [Die Tendenz, ein reines Mittelwesen anzunehmen zwischen dem Satzzeiche und den Tatsachen]" (§94). It is a wish, or urge, or striving, or tendency to give some explanation of how we do this queer thing of speaking or thinking *about* things at all.

When we give vent to this tendency, we then find that "nothing out of the ordinary is involved [es mit gewöhnlichen Dingen zugeht—it has to do with ordinary things]" (§94). We can clear away ordinary misunderstandings in practice. "Some spaniels are felines" is inadmissible in biology. If someone were to utter such a sentence, we would go back over the concepts of *spaniel* and *feline* to try to discover and clear up a specific misunderstanding that lies behind this misbegotten noisemaking. But "look at that spaniel's narrow face; see how feline it is" stands in order. Nothing prevents the mark-type "feline" from being predicated of some referent of the mark-type "spaniel." Yet wishing to have some way of sorting out which particular predications, in thought or in speech, are licit and which are illicit, we also have "a tendency to assume a pure intermediary" (§94). This tendency too shows itself in our life with language. "The idea now absorbs us [Wir leben nun in der Idee—we live now in the idea]: that the ideal '*must*' be found in reality" (§101). After all, our intentional, assertational thoughts and utterances are somehow, it seems, controlled; they are not mere avowals or subjective expressions. Our ordinary conceptual and linguistic performances invite us to try to grasp the nature or roots of this control.

Yet when we do this, we find that we can only clear up particular misunderstandings. We never meet or run up against necessities that control thought or language use in general. All words have only "a humble use [eine niedrige . . . Verwendung]" (§97), not an absolute one.

Perhaps then we should simply give up this striving for absoluteness, should root out this tendency and wish to see our thoughts and uses of language as somehow responsive to something ideal and unchangeable. "It is like a pair of glasses on our nose through which we see whatever we look at. It never occurs to us to take them off" (§103). Instead of seeking to uncover the nature of the ideal that lies behind our thoughts and uses of language, we should instead "rotate . . . the axis of reference of our examination . . . about the fixed point of our real need" (§108). We can be clear about particular uses of words, about what it makes sense to say when, in *this* circumstance (but by no means in all). And so we can attain to clarity about what is possible for us in using language. We can "command a clear view of the use of our words" (§122).

The trouble—the one that invites anxiety and a reversion to metaphysical thinking—is that when one does command a clear view of humble uses of language, then one "can bring forward only externalities about language [nur Äußerliches über die Sprache vorbringen kann]" (§120). One tracks related, stable, yet shifting *variations* in usage (and in thought), rather than finding something that controls thought and usage absolutely. Even after or in our surveys of what we do and can do in using language, we remain, ineluctably, "entangled in our own rules" (§125). Whether we look to Platonic forms, atoms, the propositions of logic, or even what we do in our ordinary uses of language, what happens is that "we lay down rules, a technique, for a game, and . . . when we follow the rules, things do not turn out as we had assumed" (§125). The *possibilities* of misunderstanding and repudiation are not fore-closed. *Willkür* does not become transparently informed by *Wille*. This is "the fundamental fact [die fundamentale Tatsache]" (§125) of our lives in thought and language.

In approaching language and thought—no matter whether metaphysically, in the hope of finding some fixed entities or rules or necessities that control apt thought and speech, or, as it were, innocently, in simply surveying what we do, "arranging what we have always known" (§109)—this is what we find: language both invites and defeats our wish for the perfect information of *Willkür* by *Wille*. Language solicits the aspiration to uncover and articulate control-ling necessities and at the same time, in its open-endedness, its tolerance of variation, fails to satisfy it. Hence "philosophy is a battle against the be-witchment of our intelligence by means of language [Die Philosophie ist ein Kampf gegen die Verhexung unsres Verstandes durch die Mittel unserer Sprache]" (§109). The prepositional phrase and embedded genitive construc-tion "by means of [durch die Mittel unserer Sprache]" is ambiguous in a considered way. Language is here both the cause of our bewitchment and the instrument of resistance to it. Language bewitches us in inviting us to seek a metaphysical ground for our linguistic and conceptual practices. It is about the world—assertational and directed at things, not merely subjectively expressive. But it is semantically open: what people notice and talk about is subject to gradual variation. Hence we are both anxious in our linguistic and conceptual performances, since repudiation resulting from variations in which we find ourselves to have no share is always possible, and bewitched, enchanted with the thought of overcoming this anxiety by finding a ground for any apt linguistic and conceptual practice. The only resistance to this bewitchment by metaphysical philosophy consists then in noting what we do in using language. Our linguistic and conceptual performances remain simultaneously, on the one hand, directed to the world, partially controlled by it, and shared and, on the other hand, open, variable products of a spontaneity that may in oneself take a wayward turn. In Cavell's formulation, metaphysical thinking about language, motivated by anxieties of repudiation,

> has become an inescapable fate for us, apparently accompanying the fate of having human language. It is a kind of fascination exercised by the promise of philosophy. But philosophy itself can also call for itself, come to itself. The aim of philosophy's battle, being a dispelling—of bewitchment, of fascination—is, we could say, freedom of consciousness, the beginning of freedom. The aim may be said to be a freedom of language, having the run of it, as if successfully claimed from it, as of a birthright.[20]

When we survey our lives with language, what we find—unlike the passage out of Plato's cave—is the persistence in that life of the aspiration to freedom of consciousness and language, unsatisfied by the discovery of any fixed objects, rules, or necessities.

Hence there is no final end to the battle against the bewitchment of our intelligence by means of language. The problems are deep—bound up with efforts to achieve expressive freedom in thought and speech and to overcome the risk of repudiation. "The problems arising through a misinterpretation of our forms of language have the character of *depth* [den Charakter der *Tiefe*—the character of the deep]. They are deep disquietudes [Beunruhigungen]; their roots are as deep in us as the forms of our language and their significance is

---

20. Cavell, *This New Yet Unapproachable America*, pp. 54–55.

as great as the importance of our language" (§111). There is no method for solving these problems, no technique for the permanent stilling of these disquietudes. "There is not *a* philosophical method [including, presumably, the method of surveying language games; it cannot still all our anxieties and disquietudes], though there are indeed methods, like different therapies" (§133), or perhaps like different works of music, painting, and poetry that can seem, in some moments of their reception by some audiences, to exemplify and sum up possibilities of expressiveness.[21]

In simultaneously soliciting and undermining efforts to find a fixed ground to our thinking and speaking, language is for us—we may see if we survey our uses, and our reactions to our uses—something uncanny. It is both our home, something which we accept, in which we live, and something strange, unfamiliar, alien. We wish for more from language—or for more control within it, for more assured routes of expressiveness and of the overcoming of the possibility of repudiation—than it affords. Again in Cavell's phrasing,

> the uncanniness of the ordinary is epitomized by the possibility or threat of what philosophy has called skepticism, understood . . . as the capacity, even desire, of ordinary language to repudiate itself, specifically to repudiate its power to word the world, to apply to the things we have in common, or to pass them by. (By "the desire of ordinary language to repudiate itself" I mean—doesn't it go without saying?—a desire on the part of speakers of a native or mastered tongue who desire to assert themselves, and despair of it.)[22]

We hoped that logic might enable the full satisfaction of this desire to assert oneself, to achieve perfect expressiveness, by uncovering necessities that control all apt thought and speech. But we found only the humble uses of words such as "sentence," "proposition," and "true," not objects or rules that control all apt thinking and speaking. Then we hoped likewise that simple attention to what we do in our ordinary thinking and speaking might bring satisfaction. But we found there only a mixture of stability and openness to change, and hence also only continuing anxiety and desire within our ordinary lives with language.

21. This remark about "summing up" I owe to Cavell's tracing of the grammar of the aphorism in offering "completeness, pleasure, and breaking off" in his lecture "The *Philosophical Investigations*' Everyday Aesthetics of Itself," University of Pennsylvania, October 23, 1995.
22. Cavell, *In Quest of the Ordinary*, p. 154.

The central image of our life with ordinary language that then emerges is that of *walking* as something yet to be achieved, but only imperfectly achievable, through continuing engagement with and acknowledgement of the ordinary's enabling of imperfect expressive freedom.

> The more narrowly we examine actual language, the sharper becomes the conflict between it and our requirement. (For the crystalline purity of logic was, of course, not a *result of investigation:* it was a requirement [eine Forderung—a demand].) The conflict becomes intolerable; the requirement is now in danger of becoming empty.—We have got on to slippery ice where there is no friction and so in a certain sense the conditions are ideal, but also, just because of that, we are unable to walk. We want to walk, so we need friction. Back to the rough ground.
>
> (§107)

Actual language ("tatsächliche Sprache") does *not* satisfy our requirement, our demand, that our thinking and speaking should come to be controlled by perfect necessities. It rather conflicts, intolerably, with our demand that this should be so. We need to move away from idealizations—away from logic and its necessities, away from forms or atoms or rules—in order to *move,* to get on with our thinking and speaking and relations with others. But we do have that desire, did make that demand, so that this movement is something that remains to be achieved. Walking is here an image of natural gracefulness in our commerce with ordinary language as it stands, and with one another, freed of the enervating sting of misbegotten metaphysical pursuits of desire. But it is here an image of something we still need to learn or relearn to do. "A philosophical problem has the form: 'I don't know my way about' ['Ich kenne mich nicht aus']" (§123). And this, it seems, is something that we do not always and assuredly know within our ordinary lives with language, wherein our desire for more control, for a perfected expressiveness, is solicited.

As a result, we continue to want to *know where or how* we are in language. Surely we (speakers of English) know, for example, that "the casserole is in the oven" indicates (correctly or incorrectly, as may be) a state of affairs in a way that is independent of individual will. We know how to use such a sentence to convey a piece of information. Or we might use it to make clear to a child the meaning of the word "casserole" ("Go and see what's in the oven and you'll see what a *casserole* is"). But *how* can we do these things? *How* do we know these things?

In section 134 we begin to see that these questions are not foreclosed or consigned to the region of dispensable nonsense, even if we have and can have no answers to them, and even if we confine ourselves to the surveying of our ordinary lives with language. Sections 134–142 describe the reawakening of a desire for perfect expressiveness grounded in knowledge of necessities that control thought and language, a reawakening that becomes explicit in the great question that is inaugurated in section 143: "How do I know how to go on to continue a series?" In section 134 we are invited, again, to think about yet another proposal for describing the relation of language in general to the world. "Let us examine the proposition: 'This is how things are.'—How can I say that this is the general form of propositions?—It is first and foremost *itself* a proposition, an English sentence, for it has a subject and a predicate. But how is this sentence applied—that is, in our everyday language? For I got it from there and nowhere else" (§134).

Here again the result is negative. The *nature* of a proposition, *how it is about things,* is *not* illuminated by observing that a proposition says *how things are* or indicates *what is the case.* It is true that one can prefix any indicative mood sentence with "Such and such is the case" or "This is the situation" or "This is how things are [es verhält sich so und so]." Contrary to Frege, however, none of these formulae or schemata makes clear the kind of thing that is a thought or proposition or sentence. None of these formulae shows how thoughts or propositions or sentences are or can be representations. Rather, we play a game in which sentences and thoughts *fit* such formulae. For example, we can say, "A proposition is what is true or false." This seems to show something about the natures of the proposition and of reality. But in fact it rests on nothing deeper than the fact that we have these formulae and have indicative mood sentences. The fact that we can say "A proposition is what is true or false" is no more illuminative of the real relations of thought and reality than the sentence "The king in chess is *the* piece that one can check" is illuminative of the *real,* game-independent nature of the king. This sentence "can mean no more than that in our game of chess we only check the king" (§136). Its truth and its usefulness in explaining the game of chess to someone rest on no deeper necessities than that that is how we do things in that game. Likewise, then, with "A proposition is what is true or false." That sentence fails to satisfy our desire for illumination of the natures and interrelations of thought, language, and reality. There is nothing here that is deeper than "L" *fitting* "K" as we recite the letters of the alphabet (§137).

Yet for all that the result here is negative—a new proposal for illuminating thought, language, and reality has come to nothing in the face of what we ordinarily say and do with words—it is equally important here that the voice of temptation has reinserted itself within the consciousness of the protagonist. No peace has come from the reminders of the importance of surveying what we ordinarily say and do with words. The structure of question and reply, proposal and rebuke, reinsinuates itself within the text and within the consciousness of its protagonist. Questions come tumbling out. "But haven't we got a concept of what a proposition is, of what we take 'proposition' to mean?" (§135). "Must I *know* whether I understand a word?" (p. 53 n). "But can't the meaning of a word that I understand fit the sense of a sentence that I understand? Or the meaning of one word fit the meaning of another?" (§138). For example, the meaning of "spaniel" somehow, it seems, "fits inside" the meaning of "canine," so the sentence "Spaniels are canines" is, it seems, true in virtue of meaning alone. Anyone who denied the truth of this sentence would thereby, it seems, be discredited as a competent speaker of (this region of) English. The competent speaker somehow *knows,* it seems, some *facts* about the meanings of words. What sorts of facts, and how are they known? There's something that we do. We do "*understand* the meaning of a word when we hear or say it" (§138). Just what then do we do, and how do we do it?

The proposals, the expressions of temptation and of the wish for the perfect information of *Willkür* by *Wille,* now force themselves forward, into the consciousness of the protagonist who had thought to put them all aside, in favor of reminders of what we do. But no: "What really comes before our mind when we *understand* a word? [Was ist es den eigentlich, was uns vorschwebt, wenn wir ein Wort *verstehen?*—what hovers, floats, or swims before us?]—Isn't it something like a picture? Can't it *be* a picture?" (§139).

In reply to this question, or proposal, two contending answers are suggested: (a) it's a picture or rule and (b) it's *some* sample uses, which we could always elaborate, extend, or modify as any particular occasion demands. The first answer is then criticized. It cannot be that our grasping ("erfassen") or understanding ("verstehen") the meaning of a word *consists in* having a picture or rule before the mind, for all rules and pictures admit of multiple projections (§139). And yet we know, in most circumstances, what counts as a correct usage of a term, as a licit projection of a rule. Hence what we know cannot be a matter only of having a picture or rule in mind. Finding an appropriate word on an occasion is more like discovering or finding (or both discovering and finding) which among a number of possible tools works best on this occasion, and this is something that one does not do or know how to do simply by having the tools on hand (p. 54 n).

So it seems then that (b) is the correct answer. In grasping the meaning of a word we imagine some sample uses, which we could always elaborate, extend, or modify to suit an occasion. But does this settle matters? *How do we do that?* Nonhuman animals don't do it. Not all of us do it alike on all occasions. What anxieties about waywardness, and what wishes for perfect expressiveness, haunt our doing what we do? "What," the protagonist asks, "was the effect of my argument? [Was tat denn mein Argument?—what did my argument *do*?]" (§140; emphasis added). What does the criticism of answer (a) amount to? Does it make everything clear and on the surface? Does it quiet one's anxieties about how to go on in using language normally and acceptably? Does it satisfy one's wish for perfect expressiveness?

No picture or rule need come before the mind when we understand a word. Instead an application, a use ("eine Anwendung"), can itself directly come before the mind (§141). We can think of a case. We can just see that *this* is how we can use "chair" or "gracefully." But does this make things so clear? Sometimes pictures do occur, and they can suggest different, and conflicting, usages. You imagine Oksana Baiul skating for "gracefully"; I imagine Samson François playing Ravel's *Mother Goose Suite*. Does this show that there is nothing, or something, between us? Here anxieties about how to go on in using language, and a wish for perfect expressiveness to defeat this anxiety, are explicitly connected up with the presence of *others*.

> Can there be a collision between picture and application? There can, inasmuch as the picture makes us expect a different use, because people in general apply *this* picture like *this*.
> I want to say: we have here a *normal* case and abnormal cases [einen *normalen* Fall und abnormale Fälle].
>
> (§141)

There are abnormal cases and abnormal applications (sometimes associated with different pictures or images, sometimes just abnormal). How then is the normal to be separated from the abnormal? Statistical preponderances can change. The law is rife with contentions about applications. Is that "fraud" or "self-defense" or "negligence" or "sexual harassment"? So is education. Is that "science" or "mathematics" or "psychology" or "literature"? So is family life.

Is that "love" or "fairness to your sister" or "rejection"? How am I then to get on with others in using language? Do I know whether I am myself normal? No survey of what we ordinarily do in using language settles this. How, and how far, are *my* envisionings or projections of usages *ours*?

A natural anxiety about how far one is normal thus attends the thought that one's knowledge of language consists solely in envisioning sample usages and being able to go on to elaborate, extend, or modify those samples in various ways. There is no knowledge of usage-dispositive facts of meaning. And so it seems that one might lose one's grip on one's language games, might fall out of relationship with others in going on as one does.

> It is only in normal cases that the use of a word is clearly prescribed; we know, are in no doubt, what to say in this or that case. The more abnormal the case, the more doubtful it becomes what we are to say. And if things were quite different from what they actually are—if there were for instance no characteristic expression of pain, of fear, of joy; if rule became exception and exception rule; or if both became phenomena of roughly equal frequency—this would make our normal language-games lose their point.
>
> (§142)

So there must be normal cases, normal uses. They are the only stays there are against pointlessness in thought and speech, against the vaporization of intentionality. The fact that we do have intentional thought and speech shows then that there are normal cases, that they are functioning as these stays. But then just how firmly fixed are *they*? For *us*? Nothing stands behind *them*. The turn toward a survey of what we do in our ordinary uses of language—a turn that was to lead us away from agonized metaphysical theorizing and into peace—has itself returned us to the very anxieties of possible inexpressiveness and repudiation from which we began, now redoubled by awareness of the fact that the turn to the ordinary has failed to eliminate them.

In Book I of the *Prelude,* the poet-protagonist sets out, escaped from the city, a gentle breeze on his cheek, to consecrate his liberty by writing the great poem, by undertaking to "pour forth that day my soul in measured strains / that would not be forgotten." In this way, the poet seeks to achieve perfect expressiveness, thus overcoming anxieties of repudiation, standing as "A renovated spirit singled out, such hope was mine, for holy services."[23] Yet these

23. Wordsworth, *The Prelude,* Book I, ll. 48–49, 53–54, p. 194.

hopes are dashed. No theme capable of supporting the poet's holy services and achievement of perfect expressiveness announces itself. Each theme seems partial, seems too ordinary and seems to lead to other themes, endlessly, without any fixed resting point. No route toward perfect expressiveness presents itself.

> Thus my days are past
> In contradiction; with no skill to part
> Vague longing, haply bred by want of power,
> From paramount impulse not to be withstood,
> A timorous capacity from prudence,
> From circumspection, infinite delay.[24]

The poet's awareness of thus existing in contradiction intensifies. A sense of partial spontaneity and power in thinking and using language, and in leading one's life, coupled with anxiety about its reception, motivates a wish for perfect expressiveness—for the perfect expression of this spontaneity—whose realization is blocked by its being housed always within our ordinary life and language and history. The possibility of perfect expressiveness—and perhaps then of human expressiveness at all—seems almost foreclosed. Silence may be all,

> . . . for either still I find
> Some imperfection in the chosen theme,
> Or see of absolute accomplishment
> Much wanting, so much wanting, in myself,
> That I recoil and droop, and seek repose
> In listlessness from vain perplexity,
> Unprofitably travelling toward the grave,
> Like a false steward who hath much received
> And renders nothing back.[25]

Silence may be all, the human may not admit of realization, until the poet, in this plight of mind housed in the ordinary, asks, "Was it for this . . . " that I was raised where and how I was,[26] in possession of whatever perceptual, conceptual, and expressive talents I have? Must my stewardship always be

24. Ibid., ll. 237–42, p. 198.
25. Ibid., ll. 261–69, pp. 198–99.
26. Ibid. l. 269, p. 199.

false, come to nothing? Is our human life with language and with others always only a camel ride to the tomb?

Then in the asking of these last questions, narrative energy and a sense of a humbler destiny are recovered, and the poet goes on. His past ordinary, at least not yet prophetically poetic, life now enables something, some pursuit of expressiveness. To ask "Was it for this . . . ?" is to find one's routes toward human expressiveness within the routines of one's common human life. Reflection on the ordinary past supports a new exercise of reflective spontaneity, a new enactment of the human, but then also one still freighted with anxieties of the normal.

After surveying the ordinary, and then finding myself bereft of a master theme to part the normal from the abnormal, and to settle my relations with others, do I then do nothing? How do I ordinarily know how to go on to use a word, to generate the next term in a series? Was it for this—the repudiation of the human, in the acceptance of conventionality and biological nature everywhere, and human spontaneity and expressiveness nowhere—that I am able to speak and think at all? "A philosophical problem has the form: I don't know my way out" (§123). How do I go on?

8

Following a Rule: Conceptual Consciousness and the Wish for Absolute Assurance—§§143–242

What the Discussion of Following a Rule Is About

It is or should be readily apparent, first, that the dramatized conversation in *Philosophical Investigations* about how anyone knows how to follow a rule, or is able to go on to generate the next term in a series, is a conversation about what it is to possess a concept, *eo ipso* what it is to possess conceptual consciousness or discursive understanding. It is or should be readily apparent, second, that this conversation somehow resists both *intellectualism* and *naturalism*, as Charles Taylor has described them.

Intellectualism, as Taylor construes it, involves a demand for "securely founded knowledge" of how to follow a rule, a knowledge that "is assumed to reside somewhere within us" when we are competent and that is assumed to determine out of all possible alternatives, and against all possible misunderstandings, what it is to follow a given rule correctly.[1] Intellectualism thus reduces an ability exercised in linguistic and cognitive practice to a state of having something in mind—a pattern, archetype, form, concept, or whatever—as itself an object of immediate and certain knowledge.

Naturalism, in contrast, involves taking our ability to go on, our grasp of a concept, to consist in "a series of de facto links." When certain phenomena are present—a series of numbers followed by a query, or certain irradiations of our retinas—then these de facto links make us say or think "27" or "rabbit." No question of justification arises about what we do. It is all a matter of "brute connections" that may be either "somehow 'wired-in' " or "imposed by society" or both, as the mind-brain's natural propensities of response are causally shaped by society's conditionings.[2] (Such a "social naturalism" makes evident

---

1. Charles Taylor, "To Follow a Rule," in *Rules and Conventions: Literature, Philosophy, Social Theory,* ed. Mette Hjort (Baltimore: Johns Hopkins University Press, 1992), pp. 169, 168.
2. Ibid., p. 170.

the lack of distance between Kripke's view that the community lays down criteria for calling anything a chair, say, and a more purely biological naturalism. According to Kripke, no question can be raised about whether what the community does is correct; it simply does what it does, and an individual will either adapt to that or be counted deviant. In both Kripke's so-called Wittgensteinian communitarianism and more direct, individualist naturalisms, such as those of Chomsky and Fodor, what lies behind concept possession is what de facto happens in the course of nature, whether on the level of the individual and its biological evolution, on the level of the community's habits, or on both levels at the same time. In positing a level of social material fact that controls our conceptualizations, Kripke, as Cavell puts it, "evades Wittgenstein's preoccupation with philosophy's drastic desire to underestimate or to evade the ordinary."[3] Against Kripke's social naturalism, the progress of the protagonist of *Philosophical Investigations* shows, one might say, how we live that preoccupation as we seek for ourselves the perfect information of *Willkür* by *Wille,* or perfect expressiveness.)

In their joint demand that our ability to apply a concept be grounded in something factual "behind" our thought and speech—a state of individual archetype-knowing, or a causally effective neural state, or a state of social fact—both intellectualism and naturalism *reify* a practical ability. They offer a theory of how certain *entities,* minds or mind-brains or social collectivities, naturally and necessarily express their given nature. Either the individual mind possesses some knowledge of concepts innately, or the mind-brain, whether individual or social, does what it does when presented with stimuli.

According to these conceptualizations, we are to recognize ourselves through tracing the roots of our conceptual consciousness, as it arises out of the necessary motions of ultimate entities, acting as their natures in interaction require them to act. Intellectualism and naturalism are alike metaphysical pictures, forms of dogmatism that attempt to get beneath our practices to a determining reality, conceived of as a system of entities that through their natures determine what we do. In Pierre Bourdieu's formulation, "to slip from *regularity,* i.e. from what recurs with a certain statistically measurable frequency and from the formula which describes it, to a consciously laid down and consciously respected *ruling* [*règlement*], or to unconscious *regulating* by a mysteri-

3. Cavell, *Conditions Handsome and Unhandsome,* p. 68.

ous cerebral or social mechanism, are the two commonest ways of sliding from the model of reality to the reality of the model."[4] We sublime away our responsibilities for our engagements within our linguistic and cognitive practices by casting our performances as events within the natural histories of things—a God-given intellect and its given grasps of things, or material objects, as may be. "We predicate of the thing what lies in the method of representation [*Darstellungsweise*—manner of presentation]" (§104). We think that whether anyone can really reasonably say, or think, "The bear and the piglet are friends" is determined by the natures of bears and piglets, rather than by our having or not having found a use for that sentence. But no: "What looks as if it had to exist is part of the language" (§50).

According to Taylor, following *Philosophical Investigations* as he reads it, such reificationist metaphysical moves rest on a mistake. They are not faithful to the fact that we can give reasons for what we have said and thought, or can say that these are among the criteria we have for applying the terms "rabbit" or "the sum of 57 and 68." Significantly, these criteria are not simply present in consciousness, in the mind-brain, or as a matter of social fact, prior to our thinking and acting. Nor do our subsequent recountings of our criteria prevent all possible misunderstandings, for they too may be misunderstood or may simply fail to engage with the attentions of someone not on one's own immediate path in thinking or speaking. In resting on criteria that can be stated up to a point and that can clear up some misunderstandings, our thought and speech evince understanding. They are not brute natural happenstances. But it is "a mode of understanding" that involves "a kind of unarticulated sense of things."[5] To say what one's criteria are is not to specify an intellectual archetype that determines all one's performances in applying a term, and it does not point to natural processes that are deeper than our mindedness (even if they are, perhaps, naturally necessary in order for our mindedness to exist). Recountings of criteria are instead the articulation of one's commitments in linguistic and cognitive practice against some possible modes of misunderstanding, makings-manifest of a shape of a technique of conceptualization that one has mastered. To say "Here is how I add 57 and 68; this is what I do to find a sum" is to articulate the manner of one's mindedness.

4. Pierre Bourdieu, *Le sens pratique* (Paris: Minuit, 1980), p. 67; cited in Taylor, "To Follow a Rule," p. 180; Taylor's translation.
5. Taylor, "To Follow a Rule," p. 170.

But what then is the nature of the conceptual and linguistic consciousness that is exercised in practice and can be made articulate in recountings of criteria? That consciousness is neither a matter of a clairvoyant presence in mind of a perfect archetype nor a matter of wiring in the mind-brain of either individuals or the species or society. But what is it?

We are able to apply the word "rabbit" and to add numbers. These abilities are elaborations of natural capacities that are rooted in the brain. Other animals do not speak of rabbits or do addition. But as articulations of what is natural, they reflect a history of interests in focusing attention, actualizing it, in one way rather than another. There is no getting beneath the mix of natural capacity and history of interest to find only the pure natural capacity itself. When we get beneath our practices, we find only brain states and evolutionary histories of the species, not articulated but somehow natural linguistic-cognitive abilities. Instead, all we can say is: "This is what we do." We have only partial criteria for ascribing a linguistic or conceptual capacity to any creature that has not yet entered into a history of patterns of focusing attention in certain ways (Werner Herzog's *Kaspar Hauser*). This is part of the anxiety of child rearing: a fear of autism, of their possible unbridgeable difference from us, despite significant phenotypic likeness. The look of children leads us to expect and to hope for them to enter into our histories of interest, our modes of conceptual consciousness, our elaborations of natural abilities. But the relief and gratitude that come when this happens are not to be sidestepped by the favorable-sounding report of an EEG or a CAT scan. Natural capacities both underlie the explicit abilities within practice that articulate them, and yet are themselves not fully ascribable in the absence of their flowering through training into some such articulations. (Once one has learned, say, English, however, there is good reason to say that learning Hindustani is at least possible in principle; an English speaker will have the natural capacity for it, even if other conceptual and practical commitments stand in the way and make one unable in fact to do it.)

The anxiety of child rearing is a species of a general anxiety that is present in human relationships. Will others exercise abilities as I do, bring their natural capacities to articulation along my routes of interest? (Part of the interest and appeal of successful jokes lies in their power to show that unexpectedly, out of routine, we *are* alike.) Will we share modes of *Wille*? Even if, especially if, there is no private self-certainty about how one is to go on in following a rule, there are still natural anxieties of attunement and the difficult tasks of the acknowledgment of (some) differences as embodying rationality and freedom. Here lie the sources of unease between parents and children, or husbands and wives, or colleagues, or neighboring cultures, over the courses of lifetimes.

In involving the elaboration of a natural capacity into an explicit, articulated ability, conceptual consciousness is inherently social, but in a quite special sense little considered in the philosophical literature.[6] It is not that linguistic solitaries are impossible. Robinson Crusoe, marooned on his island, having left all interlocutors behind, might well develop a system of terms and criteria to suit his perhaps quite novel surroundings. Why should he not take note of the varieties of breadfruit he finds? It is not true that all language is necessarily social in the sense that it must be spoken by more than one person in order to be language. Yet no one passes unaided from mere possession of a natural capacity to having articulated conceptual and linguistic abilities. Wolf children do not speak. Capacities must be shaped and focused through training and interaction in order to flower into actual abilities. The articulation of natural capacity into conceptual ability involves entering via the direction, correction, and reciprocation of one's gaze into a history of interests and patterns of attention that can have as their subject or bearer only a collectivity of some extent, temporal and transpersonal. In this sense—they require social interaction for their explicit, articulate life—conceptual consciousness and linguistic con-

---

6. For example, Baker and Hacker hold that language is not necessarily social, either in fact or in Wittgenstein's thinking. The reason they give is that, as Wittgenstein recognizes, Crusoe-like linguistic solitaries are possible (*Rules, Grammar, and Necessity,* p. 171). Norman Malcolm holds that any language is necessarily shared among a number of persons, just as there can only be trade between two persons, and that Wittgenstein is clearly committed to this ("Wittgenstein on Language and Rules," *Philosophy,* 64, no. 247 [January 1989], pp. 5–28). David Pears is the most subtle of the commentators on this point, in suggesting that Wittgenstein's late view is "enigmatic" (*The False Prison* [Oxford: Clarendon Press, 1988], 2:334). Wittgenstein, according to Pears, presents no "theory of a single decisive loss" that bears on linguistic ability, when others are not present (p. 364). In the 1930s Wittgenstein did hold that linguistic solitaries are possible, but *Philosophical Investigations* is more cautious on this point (pp. 373–75); it "smothers the question" of the social (p. 381). In general we can say that Wittgenstein perhaps came to wonder whether the origin of a capacity might be relevant to its nature (p. 367). But since solipsism is Wittgenstein's main enemy, and it is sufficient to defeat *it* to establish that language learning requires public objects, Wittgenstein does not really present any developmental psychology of consciousness or language learning (p. 365). Pears's line here is subtle and interesting, although it perhaps overlooks, first, the extensive discussion of *training* in a practice in *Philosophical Investigations* and, second, interconnections between the investigation of solipsism and its diagnosis as one mode of (hysterical and misbegotten but all too intelligible) response to (natural) anxieties of the normal.

sciousness *are* inherently social, even if once launched they may then chart their own ways. There is indeed a sense in which, as Taylor puts it, *Philosophical Investigations* "departs radically from the old monological outlook that has been dominant in the epistemological tradition."[7]

Rules and Their Accordants: The Baker and Hacker Reading and Some Difficulties with It

What is involved in this departure? What is the conception of the nature of understanding that is worked into the conversation about following a rule in *Philosophical Investigations*?

Baker and Hacker have presented the most careful and fully elaborated account of a position about the natures of rules and of understanding that seems to them to be worked out in *Philosophical Investigations*. According to them, *Philosophical Investigations* announces that rules have certain features. That is, our calling anything a rule is governed by certain criteria for anything's being a rule—criteria that are part of our linguistic practice, part of the grammar of "rule." These criteria include at least the following:

1. Rules are *normative*. They are "standards of correctness and guides to action. For an activity to be rule-governed at all is for rules to have a role in justifying or criticizing performances, in teaching or explaining."[8]

2. Rules have objective accord-conditions; it is always possible to fail to follow a rule that one has undertaken to follow. "It is always possible to distinguish someone's trying to follow a rule from his actually following it; the first issue turns primarily on his intentions but the second depends primarily on what he actually does. Somebody's sincerely believing that he is following a rule never logically guarantees that he is following the rule; whether he really follows the rule requires that his action conforms with it, and this is settled not by his believing himself to have followed it."[9]

3. Rules are *transparent*; a rule is *expressible* by those whose practice the rule describes, and such that expressions of the rule are *recognizable* by those whose practice it describes. "There is no such thing as a rule which cannot be expressed, or a rule every expression of which transcends the understanding of the persons who are following it. For what is inexpressible

---

7. Taylor, "To Follow a Rule," p. 171.
8. Baker and Hacker, *Rules, Grammar, and Necessity*, p. 63.
9. Ibid., p. 156. See also p. 62.

cannot be consulted for guidance, cited in justification or criticism, used as a standard of evaluation, etc. . . . . One can no more follow completely opaque, unknown rules than one can see completely invisible objects." Whether someone has followed a particular rule "depends on what he would have done if he had been challenged or called upon to make his behaviour intelligible."[10]

4. Rules must be complied with *regularly*, as part of a pattern of conformity. Rule-following requires *a plurality of performances*, with no single, clear first performance. What matters is that rule-following performances should fall into *a regular pattern*. There is no such thing as following a rule on a single occasion only.

> We can speak of a technique and its exemplification in practice only where an established pattern of behaviour is discernible. . . . Regular behaviour of the right kind is the criterion for the acquisition and persistence of mastery of a technique. . . . What is crucial about a regularity exemplifying a technique of applying a rule is that the agent not only acts in a regular fashion (a bee or bird does *that*), but also that he sees a certain pattern *as* a regularity and that he intends his actions to conform to this pattern.[11]

Once these criterial features of rules are noted, it is then possible to clear up various misunderstandings about what it is to follow a rule and what it is to possess a concept. There is no gap between understanding a rule and knowing to what things the rule applies. The relations between a rule and accordant performances, between a concept and its instances, are *internal*, not *external*. "This rule would not be the rule that it is, nor would this act be the act that it is, if this act were not in accord with this rule. . . . [T]he relation is internal . . . . Nothing can be inserted between a rule and its application as mortar is inserted between two bricks."[12]

Rules exist if and only if there are techniques in practice for following them. Once there are techniques, there is neither any need nor any possibility for appealing to any third entities to explain what makes an act accord with a rule or an instance with a concept. *Images* or *ideas, mental processes, machine states and processes, interpretations, instincts* or *dispositions, community consensus* or *agreement, decisions, intuitions,* and *relations of identity*—these are one and

10. Ibid., pp. 62, 63, 159.
11. Ibid., p. 162.
12. Ibid., p. 91. See also pp. 82–83 and 85–94 generally.

all otiose as mediators between rules and their accordants, concepts and their instances. It is neither necessary nor possible for any of them to do the job of connecting rules with accordants; that is rather done by rules themselves in conjunction with techniques for their application and patterns of regular practice.

Where then do rules and internal relations between rules and their accordants come from? Not from agreements. Explicit conventions for the use of a term are rare, not at the heart of either language use generally or conceptual consciousness; and general agreement among people about what sorts of things exemplify which patterns is a *background* condition for the existence of rule-following at all, not something that holds together any particular rule with its particular accordants.[13] Not from biology. Other rules are both possible and imaginably natural and easy for us. "Facts of psychology do not force our concepts upon us."[14]

Instead, "grammatical rules are arbitrary, autonomous. There is no such thing as justifying grammar by reference to reality." Rules are "creatures of the will. . . . human creations, made not found. They are not true or false, and they are not answerable to reality; in this sense they are *arbitrary*." Grammar—a set of rules, criteria, techniques, and practices—"is antecedent to all theories, and presupposed by them." But rules are not arbitrary in the sense that they are either contextually unmotivated (even where alternatives are possible) or emergent ex nihilo. Custom and agreement, and nature and instinct, together conspire against a background of already existent practice to introduce innovations and modifications in rule-following and in conceptualization. "It is noteworthy that what belongs to *physis* and what to *nomos* is inextricably intermingled even at the highest flights of the intellect."[15]

The reading presented by Baker and Hacker is philosophically intriguing in uncovering putative errors in intellectualist-Cartesian, cognitivist-computationalist, and naturalist conceptions of understanding. The picture of the nature of rules that they present has considerable support in manifold bits of text; remark after remark seems to say that this is the view that must be accepted, after working through the confusions that attach to all rival views. But is it quite right, either philosophically or textually? Does this reading fully capture what is involved in moving, as Taylor puts it, beyond the monological

13. Cf. ibid., pp. 236, 248.
14. Ibid., p. 237.
15. Ibid., pp. 332, 63, 53, 236 n. 4.

epistemological tradition? (Can we make any sense of the claim that the text so moves?) There are a number of difficulties—some philosophical, and some textual—that trouble the position that Baker and Hacker articulate and ascribe to the text.

1. Children typically produce certain sorts of regular, patterned performances that seem reasonably to be called rule-followings and yet do not involve rules that are either transparent or normative. As Chomsky has observed, "At a certain stage in language growth, children characteristically overgeneralize: They say *sleeped* instead of *slept, brang* (on the analogy of *sang*) instead of *brought,* and so forth. We have no difficulty in attributing to them rules for formation of past tense, rules that we recognize to be different from our own. . . . We may, then, say that the child is following a rule of his or her language at the time, one of the possible human languages, but not exactly ours."[16] Children who overgeneralize past-tense formations are in one sense "correct": they are doing something regular. They are producing patterned linguistic behavior. But they cannot cite or express the rule that describes that patterned behavior, nor would they typically recognize and accept a rule formulation that describes their behavior ("add *-ed* to form the past tense," say), since they may lack any articulate or conscious concept of a past-tense verb form. So their patterned behavior seems to grow out of a simply given tendency to produce patterned behavior under certain stimulus conditions. These tendencies may well be multiple, adaptable, open-ended in what they include, and so forth, so that there is a considerable departure from behaviorism here. Yet, crucially, neither the tendencies nor the rules that describe what children who overgeneralize past-tense formations early in their linguistic lives tend to do are either transparent to the children themselves or normative. The rule formulation cannot be cited by them in justification of their behavior, and it is not clear that it can even be recognized by them. Why should we not then see patterned linguistic and cognitive behavior within a population of adults who can recognize, formulate, and cite rules as simply growing out of convergences between the dispositions of different speakers as they adapt to one another's linguistic and cognitive behavior? Perhaps *rule* does not have the grammar or criterial features that Baker and Hacker take it to have.

There are a number of counters to Chomskyan cognitivist dispositionalism that can be made on behalf of Baker and Hacker. Young children might very

16. Noam Chomsky, *Knowledge of Language* (New York: Praeger, 1986), p. 227.

well someday recognize rule formulations that describe their early linguistic behavior. Perhaps the fact that they can and will do this someday is part, even a central part, of what makes us able to extend the concept of *rule-following behavior* to this somewhat marginal case of past-tense overgeneralization. Perhaps, that is, it is intelligible to call young children rule followers only insofar as they will someday typically be able to formulate rules, cite rules in justification of their behavior, and so forth. Moreover, it *is* a somewhat marginal case; in certain respects it is analogous to more central cases of rule-following (it is linguistic behavior), and in certain respects it is quite different from other, more central cases (e.g., carrying tens when adding; scoring a game in tennis), both linguistic and nonlinguistic.

Yet the point that Chomsky's criticism highlights is that Baker and Hacker present no account of *how* patterned linguistic and cognitive behavior arises. Fodor has been complaining for some years that Wittgensteinians lack any theory of language learning.[17] One need not accept Fodor's own computationalist account of language learning in order to find Baker and Hacker's account of our development of linguistic competence to be thin and unconvincing. Just how are we imagined to catch on to internal relations between terms and their accordants? What is involved in having a life in, or with, language in time?

At first, children don't understand language. Then, after a time and with training, they do. What is going on here? What tensions, resistances, and accommodations inhabit this development? For Baker and Hacker, it is only a matter of whether one has gotten the explicit ability, grasped the internal relation, or not (though it may take many performances for anyone to discern this). But compare the development of linguistic competence with the development of other abilities. When does someone know how to play tennis? Is there one correct way to play tennis? Compare Sampras's forehand, or way of developing a point, to Agassi's. Or when does someone know how to play the piano? After one lesson and "Twinkle, Twinkle, Little Star"? After Mozart's "Ah, je vous dire Maman"? Compare Arrau's phrasing with Brendel's.

In each case there are various criteria for success: playing well, winning (some) points, returning the ball regularly enough; or maintaining an even tempo (allowing for appropriate rubato), hitting the right notes, and phrasing appropriately. But what it is to satisfy these criteria is not specified sharply in

17. See Fodor, *The Language of Thought*, chap. 2.

any rules that describe conformity with them in exact, extensional terms. Instead, one who is attempting to develop these abilities is given multiple, often inconsistent, bits of advice, or told rules of thumb that must be adapted to circumstances, together with lots of examples, practice, and corrections. One must catch on to the aims of the enterprise and develop one's own repertoire of techniques, somewhat improvisatorily, against a background of techniques that have been found useful in the past. Isn't learning a language something like that—always a matter of ongoing adaptation and improvisation, something that is never quite wholly settled—rather than a matter only of grasping (temporary?) internal relations?

2. Baker and Hacker hold that there are internal relations between rules and accordant performances. Once internal relations are in place, then everything is settled (skeptical questions cannot arise), and without internal relations there are no rules. But is this quite right? Consider the rule "Grade this paper in the way that you graded the others." Do I know what this means? Yes. Is what I will do then wholly determined by the rule? No. Grading a paper involves weighing various values and degrees of exemplification of them. There can be reasonable disagreement, especially over marginal differences. But the rule or instruction or command is not empty either. It is not just a matter of decision, within limits, to go one way rather than another. There can sometimes be argument, and right and wrong, and genuine disagreement, and disagreements can sometimes be resolved based on the emergence of something that was not in place previously: a shared reasonable understanding of the rule and a history of patterns of values and weightings to which the rule directs our attention. And likewise for a host of other rules: "Play it *dolce*"; "Castle early"; "Play closer to the bridge in higher positions"; "Use more arm weight on the downbeat"; and so on. Are all rules of language so different from these? ("Don't use pronouns too far in discourse from their antecedents." "Maintain an interesting cadence or rhythm." "Don't digress.")

3. Baker and Hacker note that developments of rules and concepts are neither simply natural and instinctive nor brutely conventional. Neither nature nor historically discernible convention directly explains or justifies grammar. ("It is noteworthy that what belongs to *physis* and what to *nomos* is inextricably intermingled even at the highest flights of the intellect.") But one of the ways in which they express this point is to say that grammar, a repertoire of concepts and techniques for their application, is *arbitrary*. Is this right? It is right to reject cruder forms of both naturalism and conventionalism. But can there not

sometimes be reasonableness without rules in the development of new concepts, techniques, and practices? (Plato in the *Republic* thought it much more important to describe the education of the guardians than to specify an ideally just constitution: he saw that in political life reasonableness that is not sharply rule-circumscribed will inevitably be necessary. Similarly, for Kant, what it is to have a good will, acting out of respect for the self-legislated law of practical reason, cannot itself be altogether specified for all circumstances but requires reasonableness—and perhaps something like grace—in specific contexts.)

According to Baker and Hacker, "The accord of an act with a rule is one of a range of concepts that preoccupied Wittgenstein in the early 1930s. . . . He thought this matter to be a focal point of philosophical confusions, and during this period he wrote about it extensively. In his view he resolved these problems and did not return to them. In particular, the *Investigations* does not examine *in detail,* the concept of the accord of an act with a rule."[18] That matter is settled. Where there are rules, there are techniques for their application and internal relations between rules and accordant performances. Skepticism cannot arise. All is settled in practice.

But this view overlooks the possibility of non-rule-legislated reasonableness in going on with and modifying rules to suit new occasions. As Cavell notes, in criticizing David Pole's similarly "Manichean" conception of rules and Carnapian distinction between "internal" and "external" questions, "That everyday language does not, in fact or in essence, depend upon such a structure and conception of rules, and yet that the absence of such a structure in no way impairs its functioning, is what the picture of language drawn in the later philosophy is about."[19] And this thought about the limits of rules, and about the possibility of reasonableness beyond rules, albeit drawing upon them, surfaces repeatedly in Wittgenstein's writing after the early 1930s. "Here *seeing* matters essentially: as long as you do not see the new system, you have not got it."[20] "Do you think I have a theory? Do you think I'm saying what deterioration is? What I do is describe different things called deterioration."[21] "Tradi-

18. Baker and Hacker, *Rules, Grammar, and Necessity,* pp. 236 n. 4, 85.
19. Stanley Cavell, "The Availability of Wittgenstein's Later Philosophy," in *Must We Mean What We Say?* p. 48.
20. Wittgenstein, *Ludwig Wittgenstein and the Vienna Circle,* ed. B. F. McGuinness, p. 123.
21. Ludwig Wittgenstein, *Lectures and Conversations on Aesthetics, Psychology, and Religious Belief,* ed. Cyril Barrett (Berkeley: University of California Press, 1967), p. 10.

tion is not something a man can learn."[22] Increasingly, there is a sense of what Monk has called "the fluidity of the grammatical/material distinction" in the later writing,[23] a fluidity that requires acknowledgment of the possibility of reasonableness emerging out of a background of rule-following, but going beyond present rule-following and transforming it. Rules that are always open to such transformations do not leave room for rule skepticism, but do not have their relations to their accordants always settled within arbitrarily fixed internal relations either.

4. Understanding an expression and grasping a rule are not only akin to being able to generate the next term in a series, they are also akin to understanding a musical theme, understanding a joke, and understanding a person. In these latter cases, it is not clear that a definite performance or definite range of definite performances counts as exhibiting understanding. There is nothing definite, but many indefinite things, that one can do to evince understanding. The situation is unlike that of a rule with fixed and definite accordant performances. Understanding language has affinities with these forms of understanding, as well as with understanding an arithmetical series.

5. The emphasis that Baker and Hacker place on internal relations between rules and their accordants suppresses the odd respect in which rule-following and understanding language are inherently social phenomena. While there can be linguistic solitaries, in the event, say, that all other speakers of a language die out or that someone who has already mastered English creates an entirely new language, it seems also to be the case that the explicit development of linguistic ability out of a brute natural capacity requires social interaction, and even social interaction at crucial stages of maturation. If a creature possessing a biologically afforded linguistic capacity (a second-order ability to acquire first-order linguistic ability) is *not* exposed to language, through social interactions, at certain crucial stages in life, then linguistic ability does not develop, and the very capacity for language becomes attenuated. Hence there cannot be internal relations between rules and accordants in the absence of social interaction. What then goes on in social interaction—all the phenomena of tension, accommodation, and resistance—thus forces one to wonder what goes on in rule-following generally as well.

22. Wittgenstein, *Culture and Value,* p. 76.
23. Ray Monk, *Ludwig Wittgenstein: The Duty of Genius* (New York: Macmillan, 1990), p. 468.

6. It is not clear that rule-following is transparent to the rule follower. Rule followers cannot always cite the rule that justifies their behavior, nor can they always recognize formulations of the rule when they are offered. At least, many experiences of *following, Philosophical Investigations* suggests, seem to have nothing to do with anything that is present to consciousness, actually or potentially. "We can also imagine the case where nothing at all occurred in B's mind except that he suddenly said 'Now I know how to go on'—perhaps with a feeling of relief; and that he did in fact go on working out the series without using the formula" (§179). "Or: you are guided by a partner in a dance; you make yourself as receptive as possible, in order to guess his intention and obey the slightest pressure. Or: someone takes you for a walk; you are having a conversation; you go wherever he does. Or: you walk along a field-track, simply following it" (§172).

7. Lastly, if Wittgenstein wished to assert what Baker and Hacker claim he did assert (that rules are transparent, normative, and, in a certain sense, arbitrary), then why does the text of *Philosophical Investigations* have that peculiar form? Why is there a recurring voice of temptation? Is it just a matter of the continual resprouting of hydra-headed confusions, as Baker and Hacker claim? But then what makes the confusions hydra-headed? Why don't they just go away? Is it just a peculiar psychological compulsion on Wittgenstein's part that he crisscrosses again and again over the same ground? And why does the discussion of rule-following occur after sections 66–142, after the discussions of general terms, the nature of philosophy, and truth, and before section 243, the beginning of the discussion of sensations? Would it not be better to read sections 143–242 in connection with the cycles of proposal and rebuke that occur before section 143 and in connection with the continually foundering effort to reach conclusiveness about both the nature of understanding and the nature of philosophy? Reading in this way would require a vigilant refusal to draw any distinction between the treatment of understanding and the treatment of philosophy, between philosophy and metaphilosophy, between the teaching of the text and its form. Instead, trying to figure out what understanding is must be seen as internally related to trying to figure out what philosophy is and trying to arrive at the perfect information of *Willkür* by *Wille,* at perfect expressiveness. The text's saying and thinking things—or, better, its ways of entertaining ways of saying and thinking things—would have not to be parted from its form, and the conceptions it encodes of *how* things can honestly be thought and said, of when and in connection with

which projects such sayings and thinkings can arise, leading to what forms of closure or dissipation or exhaustion in thinking. Emphasizing the (sometime) existence of internal relations between rules and accordant performances seems not to catch much or any of all that.

Saying "These Are My Criteria"

We can, then, sometimes reshape our conceptual and linguistic abilities; we can sometimes successfully refigure what counts as an appropriate exercise of those abilities against a background of stable yet tolerant techniques. What counts as following a rule in practice, or applying a concept or understanding, is not always and necessarily something that is fixed according to the nature of things, or brains, or even internal relations laid down in practice between rules and accordants (even if there must be a stable background). How we understand, how we go on to articulate and exercise our conceptual abilities further, can sometimes differ. You take for an insult what I meant as a joke. *Must* one of us be right? *Must* the language, or its rules, or our mind-brains, make it either an insult or a joke? Embedded in stable yet flexible practices and techniques as they are, rule-followings, as Taylor puts it, may be "experienced as [freighted with] suspense and uncertainty in practice." Action does not simply "flow from [the rule] but actually transforms it," as practices are spun out in time. The concrete actuality of rule-followings as they occur in stable yet flexible practices over time and the "as it were . . . 'phronetic gap' between the formula and its enactment . . . together yield the uncertainty, the suspense, and the possibility of irreversible change that accompan[y] all significant activity."[24] Not all action: often, ordinarily, how we conceive of things, what criteria we have, will be agreed on in practices, without gaps. "But where are the bounds of the incidental? [die Grenze des Nebensächlichen]?" (§79). "It is only in normal cases that the use of a word is clearly prescribed; we know, are in no doubt, what to say in this or that case. The more abnormal the case, the more doubtful it becomes what we are to say" (§142). "The use of the word . . . is not everywhere circumscribed by rules" (§68).

That rule-followings, conceptualizations, are sometimes subject to contestation and uncertainty and controlled by nothing more deeply or naturally factual than how we have, in pursuing our interests, articulated our capacities

24. Taylor, "To Follow a Rule," pp. 182, 181.

into abilities as well as how we might do so now—this is what Cavell has characterized as *the argument of the ordinary*,[25] taking it that "the ordinary is subject at once to autopsy and to augury, facing at once its end and its anticipation."[26] How we have thus far articulated our capacities in practices—whoever we are—is the vehicle of the life or lives of our understandings, but also that which we may wish to transfigure out of present interest. When we say, "Here are my criteria of intelligence, of philosophical ability, of sympathetic tact, of culpable negligence, of coherent argumentation, of justice or of respect," and then we wait, or when we say, "This is what I do," then "what kind of crossroads" in our conceptual histories and in our lives with language and with others are we stopped at?[27] In what manner have we halted along the path of the history of our conceptual articulations?

To say "These are my criteria" is first of all to stake and test oneself as an envisioner of routes of coherent continuation or alteration of conceptual practice. Things have not gone smoothly. Perhaps someone needs instruction or clarification where a technique of conceptualization is not yet shared; perhaps the case is hard, and one is oneself unsure about how to go on. In either case, techniques of conceptualization as they stand have failed to show themselves to bear on this case, either for us or for me, in the absence of bringing them to words. They need articulation, either to attach or reattach us to one another or oneself to them. Such articulations function as reminders of something ordinary that suits our histories, interests, and powers, or they direct our powers toward new interests and possibilities of expression. To focus on the dramas of reattachment and redirection that are played out in the making of claims about one's criteria, as these dramas are rehearsed in the conversations of *Philosophical Investigations,* is to note what Cavell describes as "the irreconcilability in Wittgenstein between our dissatisfaction with the ordinary and our satisfaction in it, between speaking outside and inside language games, which is to say, the irreconcilability of the two voices (at least two) in the *Investigations,* the writer with his other, the interlocutor, the fact that poses a great task, the continuous task, of Wittgenstein's prose, oscillating between vanity and humility."[28]

In staking and testing oneself as an articulator of criteria, one is at the same

25. Cavell, *Conditions Handsome and Unhandsome,* p. 64.
26. Cavell, *In Quest of the Ordinary,* p. 9.
27. Cavell, *The Claim of Reason,* p. 19.
28. Cavell, *Conditions Handsome and Unhandsome,* p. 83.

time staking and testing one's relationships with others. We say: "This is what I do"; "Here is how I add two-digit numbers"; "It was a beautiful performance"; "That is not what I call treating someone with respect"; and we wait. "We know," says Cavell, that "[the other] is not completely unintelligible to us," is biologically human, with (one trusts or hopes) certain natural capacities, and, perhaps further, has shared so much of a history of thought and language with us. "We feel he *must* be able to follow our directions," take to what I do. "And we know we are impotent in this moment," as he doesn't go on, or goes on differently, "to get him to. The cause of our anxiety is that *we cannot make ourselves intelligible* (to him). But why does this create anxiety? Is it that we read our unintelligibility to him as our unintelligibility as such? What gives him this power over us? Why have we given it?"[29] Perhaps this gift marks the fact that our own entry into the possession of conceptual abilities at all occurs through our interactions with other conceptual ability exercisers, that our own conceptual abilities—and our identities—have no life that sidesteps dependence on those interactions. And if we are thus dependent on others in our possessions of conceptual abilities, it is then human enough to wish that some superfact about clairvoyant ideas or mind-brains might somehow, once discovered by me, secure me in my conceptual abilities against such dependence, might sublimely immunize me against repudiation and madness. "I might wish there to be such a fact, as some assurance that I will not become deviant, go out of control, an assurance against a certain fear of going mad, or being defenseless against the charge of madness. It may seem a fear for the human race."[30]

But all I can do is speak, say "These are my criteria," and wait. No superfact presents itself, no matter where I look. The drama of the staking of oneself and one's relations to certain ways of going on is not foreclosed, either in the purity of the essential, the purity of the supersensible, or the purity of the transparent ordinary. To attempt to foreclose it is the madness of our aspiration to philosophical explanations, an aspiration that haunts us. "See how philosophical explanations will seek to distract you from your interests (ordinary, scientific, aesthetic); how they counterfeit necessity. That the advice is all but impossible to take is Wittgenstein's subject," what moves his writing. "We do seek, and therewith we demand a finding, and therein comes the skeptical

29. Cavell, *The Claim of Reason*, p. 115.
30. Cavell, *Conditions Handsome and Unhandsome*, p. 86.

conclusion, or solution: the demand for a solution is the skepticism."[31] We long for our choices, our acts of thinking and speaking, generated out of *Willkür*, our natural arbitrariness taking up its background, to be fully informed by *Wille*, by norms of rational, free willing. And we are disappointed, therein returned to the ordinary, our conceptual abilities as elaborated, as simultaneously the occasioning scene of, and the balm for, our disappointments. There is, in our life with the ordinary, with our conceptual abilities as they stand, "a continuous effort at balance, or longing for it, as to leave a tightrope."[32] We are, it seems, in a kind of argument with the ordinary, both in dependence as thinkers on its criteria, which we must take as ours in order to think at all, and yet capable of transforming them and of wishing to escape their shifting sways.

> It is exactly as important to Wittgenstein to trace the disappointment with and repudiation of criteria (which is how *The Claim of Reason* interprets the possibility or threat of or the temptation to skepticism) as to trace our attunements in them (to which Austin confined himself). We understandably do not like our concepts to be based on what matters to us . . . ; it makes our language seem unstable and the instability seems to mean what I have expressed as my being responsible for whatever stability our criteria may have, and I do not want this responsibility; it mars my wish for sublimity. The human capacity—and the drive—both to affirm and to deny our criteria constitute the argument of the ordinary. And to trace the disappointment with criteria is to trace the aspiration to the sublime—the image of the skeptic's progress.[33]

> We are trying to get hold of the mental process of understanding [den seelischen Vorgang des Verstehens], which seems to be hidden behind those coarser and therefore more readily visible accompaniments. But we do not succeed; or, rather, it does not at all amount to a real effort [es kommt garnicht zu einem wirklichen Versuch]. . . . And how can the process of understanding have been hidden, when I said "Now I understand" *because* I understood?! And if I say it is hidden—then how do I know what I have to look for? I am in a muddle [Ich bin in einem Wirrwarr].

> (§153)

---

31. Ibid., p. 97.
32. Cavell, *The Claim of Reason*, p. 44.
33. Cavell, *Conditions Handsome and Unhandsome*, p. 92.

A Demand and Its Disappointment

How, then, is this muddle enacted, and so brought to consciousness as our condition, in *Philosophical Investigations,* particularly in the sections on following a rule? A demand for an account of what understanding consists in ("worin dies Wissen besteht"; §148) is continually entered and played off against its disappointment, as various specific routes toward its satisfaction are successively seen to collapse into incoherence. Imagining these routes toward an account "does not at all amount to a real effort" (§153). Crucially, section 143's "Let us now examine the following kind of language-game [Betrachten wir nun diese Art von Sprachspiel]" is already a *repetition* of section 2's "Let us imagine a language for which . . . [Denken wir uns eine Sprache, für die . . .]." Despite the intervening sections on the nature of philosophical understanding that aim at quieting the impulse toward philosophical explanation, the wish for an explanation of the nature of our linguistic and conceptual capacities resurfaces. The effort is again to survey a language game in which the nature and basis of our ability to understand is clear, unfreighted with the temptations of interiority and possible madness set against the ways of community. And yet again this new effort at a survey arises within an overall dramatistic structure within which temptations and reaccommodations are played out. "The same or almost the same points were always being approached afresh from different directions, and new sketches made" (p. ixe).

Section 143 makes again the main point that understanding is *articulated out of* a natural capacity via training. The pupil brings something, a natural capacity, to the scene of instruction in generating the next term in an arithmetical series "independently [selbstständig]." At the same time, samples of arithmetical series must be put before the pupil, in order that the pupil shall have something to catch on to, in order to give the pupil's natural capacity some articulated patterns with which to engage. Without *both* a natural capacity *and* sample series, there is, it seems, no hope of any pupil's coming to be able to go on independently to generate arithmetical series.

These points do not, however, quiet the wish for explanation of what is really going on—what sort of mental or neural processes are occurring—in the scene of instruction, but rather invite the pursuit of that wish. "*How* does he get to understand this notation [the series of natural numbers in decimal notation; *Wie* lernt er dieses System verstehen?]" (§143, emphasis added). This much alone is a mystery that invites the construction of explanations. How does anyone so much as manage to master the generation of the series of natural numbers? Various kinds of mistaken performance are possible, some "random" and some "systematic," though there is "no sharp distinction" between the two kinds of mistakes (§143). Hence we do not know exactly *what* to do or say *when* a certain *type* of mistake has appeared: we lack the relevant systematic understanding of types of mistake and their cures; we lack the relevant understanding of the *nature* of the capacity that is manifested in compliant and noncompliant performance. Somewhat improvisatorily, we can try out various strategies for correcting mistakes. "Perhaps it is possible to wean [the pupil] from the systematic mistake (as from a bad habit). Or perhaps one accepts his way of copying and tries to teach him ours as an offshoot, a variant of his" (§143). But there is no strategy available for knowing *which* strategy will or must work. One may even be able to do nothing. "And here too our pupil's capacity [die Lernfähigkeit unseres Schülers—the learning ability, the second-order ability to develop articulate, first-order abilities in practice] may come to an end [abbrechen—break off, stop short]" (§143).

What is the point of saying that? "What do I mean when I say 'the pupil's capacity to learn *may* come to an end here'?" (§144). Is this a *mere* empirical observation? "Do I say this from my own experience? Of course not. (Even if I have had such experience.)" (§144). No, the point is partly the grammatical one that even when success in bringing about understanding is typical or normal, it is nonetheless always *possible* for misunderstanding to occur. Nothing—in particular, no grasp of states or structures or processes that somehow underlie and mandate compliant performance—rules out the possibility of misunderstanding and removes the teacher and pupil from the drama of (possible) resistance and accommodation. To say that the pupil's capacity ("die Lernfähigkeit des Schülers") may come to an end here is *both* (a) to emphasize the importance of *capacities,* in particular to try to wean us away from philosophical analyses and explanations of capacities in terms of states or structures or processes, *and* (b) to remind us of the natural anxieties about community and intelligibility—of us to one another and of us to ourselves—that are built into us as possessors of conceptual consciousness and language as outgrowths of natural capacities within practices.

Together (a) and (b)—the importance of capacities that do not admit of reductive explanations and the anxieties that attend that fact—change our "*way of looking at things*" (§144). What it is to possess an articulate ability within a going practice *as* an outgrowth of a natural capacity is different from what we had thought it to be. It is freighted with more anxieties, more a matter of *Willkür* open to information by *Wille* and yet resistant to its perfection, than we had thought. One can compare understanding and being able to speak a language "with *this* rather than *that* set of pictures" (§144)—with, say, the ability to perform a piece of music, or the ability to tell a joke, or the ability to respond sympathetically to another, and not only to, say, the output of a machine after certain inputs. Teaching anyone to understand then emerges as a matter of "drawing [the pupil's] attention [lenke seine Aufmerksamkeit]" (§145) to certain things, guiding or steering ("lenken") the pupil by emphasizing this or that, and then waiting. It is not possible to prescind from the drama of (possible) resistance and accommodation.

"But why do you say that? *so* much is obvious [*das* ist selbstverständlich]?" (§145). The protagonist does not rest with the thought that guiding or steering, and so coming to be able to apply a concept—to think and to understand— are caught up in dramas of resistance and accommodation. Again the demand comes: What do one's capacity to respond to guiding and one's present ability to go on *consist in*? Only this knowledge would quiet anxieties of repudiation and still the internal tension of consciousness, caught in its effort to bring *Willkür* to full information by *Wille*. And yet the answer does not come. "Now, however, let us suppose that after some efforts on the teacher's part he continues the series correctly, that is, as we do it. So now we can say he has mastered the system.—But how far need he continue the series for us to have a right to say that? Clearly you cannot state a limit here" (§145). No matter how many accepted, rule-accordant performances have been generated, it remains possible that something will come between teacher and pupil, between oneself and others, or between oneself and oneself. The fact that there *must be* backgrounds of *both* natural capacities to extend rules in certain ways *and* a plurality of occasions of rule-accordant performance *in order for there to be* rule-following and understanding at all does *not* show, here and now, that there is either rule-following or understanding between us or transparent, rationally informed conformity to a norm within oneself. Nothing else than further performances and the playing out of dramas of accommodation and resistance (with others and within oneself) will provide any reassurance and any sense of identity in the possession of one's articulated abilities. Yet that seems not to be enough. It seems not to be what we want, or, at any rate, not to be what the protagonist wants.

And so the efforts at explanation recur. "Perhaps you will say here: to have got the system (or, again, to understand it) can't consist in [kann nicht darin bestehen] continuing the series up to *this* or *that* number: *that* is only applying one's understanding. The understanding itself is a state [ein Zustand] which is the *source* of the correct use [*woraus* die richtige Verwendung entspringt]" (§146). Perhaps one will say this. But it does not help. The thought cannot be worked out; the state of understanding cannot be investigated in such a way as to sublime away our need for criteria and performances in open conformity with them in order to establish the existence of understanding. "But this is where we were before. . . . The application is still a criterion of understanding" (§146). Both our need for and our disappointment with criteria are still in place.

It *seems* that conformity to criteria for understanding that are articulated within practice *cannot* be the whole story. Other animals do not generate the sorts of practices that we do. Something in us brings us to these practices. We *want* conformity to criteria articulated within practice *not* to be the whole story. We want to overcome our dependence on conformity to criteria that seem to be merely articulated in practice, and thus potentially shifting, unreliable sources of difference between us, or within oneself. (There is such a thing as not knowing one's own identity as a possessor of rational powers.) And so one says: "But how can it be? When *I* say I understand the rule of a series, I am surely not saying so on the basis of the *experience* that up until now I have applied the algebraic formula in such-and-such a way! In my own case at all events I surely know [Ich weiß doch von mir selbst jedenfalls] that I mean such-and-such a series; it doesn't matter how far I have actually developed it" (§147). One wants to know, thinks one can or might know, *from oneself* what it is to understand, to be able to go on to generate the next term in a series, prescinding from any roles, past or present or future, actual or potential, in dramas of resistance and accommodation.

"But what does this knowledge consist in?" (§148). Can we imagine the *nature* of this knowledge of how to go on, of this state of understanding, in such a way that we can investigate it further and determine whether it exists in a given case, independently of criteria-compliant performances, which seem all too dependent, secondary, and unreliable? Even if the answer is "No; the fantasized *state* of understanding *consists in nothing,* is not real, is only the object of a fantasy" so that this answer stands as an overall rebuke to the project of providing an explanation of the nature of our capacities and abilities, it is also true that this very remark continues to play the "consists in" game. It offers its own characterization, oriented toward conformity in performance to criteria that are articulated in practice, of the nature of understanding, of being able to go on. Hence this remark is not beyond or to one side of interrogations of our powers. It is not apart from the dramas of the effort to bring *Willkür* to full information by *Wille,* so as to achieve perfect expressiveness, but is itself caught up within them. It has an accommodationist ring to it that requires, and finds, the criteria-rejecting, explanation-seeking voice as its counterpoise.

What, then, does this putative *state of understanding* or knowledge of how to go on *consist in?* Can the thought that there is, or must be, such a state that stands as the source of criteria-compliant performances be filled in, in such a way that our ongoing dependence on criteria-compliant performances as tests of our understanding is sublimed away? Various ways of going on in this effort—of characterizing the nature of the fantasized state of understanding— collapse. They turn out *not* to provide us with what we want. They turn out *not* to release us from our dependence on criteria and performances in conformity with them. Four possibilities are considered.

1. Could the putative state of understanding be a *"disposition,"* a "state of a mental apparatus (perhaps of the brain) [den Zustand eines Seelenapparats (etwa unsres Gehirns)], by means of which we explain the *manifestations* of that knowledge [*Aüßerungen* dieses Wissen]" (§149)? No; the thought that understanding *consists* in a mental or neural disposition collapses. If it were true, then "there ought to be two different criteria for such a state: a knowledge of the construction of the apparatus, quite apart from what it does" (§149). That is, one should be able say that A understands that p *either* by reviewing A's criterion-compliant performances that manifest that understanding *or* by examining directly, say by a brain-scope, the mental or neural structure in which the disposition is instanced, "quite apart from what it does." Moreover, the two *different* criteria would have to be such that conformity to one of them is always accompanied by conformity to the other, and necessarily so. If the disposition is that in which the understanding (as displayed in performance) *consists,* then it *must* be present every time the understanding is or could be manifested, and vice versa. But in fact it is not like this. There is "a grammatical difference" between understanding as it is expressible in performance and being in a dispositional state; they have different criteria. What a soul does, when understanding is displayed or displayable, is *not* definitely circumscribable. It does *not* start sharply at a particular moment, and it admits of various routes or man-

ners of expression in many cases. It is not, for example, possible to say definitely *when* one has begun to understand Bach's cello suites or Pynchon's sentences, or another person, and not possible definitely to say how such understanding *must* be displayed in one and only one way. In contrast, a disposition that is *instanced in a structure* is either present or not. A physical or "mental structural" system (on the model of a physical system) either definitely has various causal powers or lacks them, *ceterus paribus.* The grammar of ascribing a disposition is different from the grammar of ascribing an ability, which typically involves "'mastery' of a technique [Eine Technik 'beherrschen'],'" where the emphasized or hesitant "mastery" or "beherrschen" suggests something that can be partial or tentative or variable within limits, as one might "catch on" at various levels and in differing ways to fly-fishing or string quartet playing or parenthood.

2. Or could the putative state of understanding *consist in* the occurrence of a formula (or pattern or image or archetype) within consciousness? Perhaps, for example, "A has written down the numbers 1, 5, 11, 19, 29; at this point B says he knows how to go on" (§151). Perhaps "After A had written the number 19 B tried the formula $a_n = n^2 + n - 1$; and the next number confirmed his hypothesis" (§151). But this is only one of the "things [that] may have happened here" (§151). The occurrence of a formula or other pattern within consciousness is not necessary for understanding. Perhaps instead A "says nothing at all and simply continues the series" (§151). One can sometimes "just see" how to go on, just as, for example, one continues the series of natural numbers without thought. Nor is the occurrence of a formula in consciousness sufficient for understanding. "For it is perfectly imaginable that the formula should occur to him and that he should nevertheless not understand" (§152). Again the grammar of "understands" does not fit the grammar of the description of that in which understanding putatively consists.

3. Or could the putative state of understanding *consist in* having "a new insight—intuition [eine neue Einsicht—Intuition]" (§186)? No; in order for this insight or intuition to have any content, it would have to be formulable. It would require that the insight take the form of grasping in consciousness a formula, pattern, or rule. Hence this suggestion is no different from, and no better than, the suggestion that understanding consists in having a formula in consciousness.

4. Or could the putative state of understanding *consist in* being in a ma-

chine state? Here again the grammars come apart. Partly when one understands there is something, or some range of things, that it is correct to do. Understanding is normative. In contrast, any machine might physically misfire, might in fact break down in completely unpredictable and untoward ways. "Do we forget the possibility of [the parts of a machine] bending, breaking off, melting, and so on?" (§193). So we might instead say that it is only the operations of a machine *ceterus paribus,* under normal conditions and as the machine is designed to work, that provide a model of what understanding consists in. "We use a machine, or the drawing of a machine, to symbolize a particular action of the machine" (§193). But then either this case reduces to that of the disposition, insofar as a definite output determined *ceterus paribus* by a physical structure is envisioned; in that case again the types and degrees of required and permissible variation in manifestations of understanding will not match the types and degrees of output that are possible, and the definite presence or absence of the physical structure will not match the indefiniteness and permissible variability of the articulation of a capacity into an ability. Or one instead uses the symbol of the machine to determine exactly the performances that one will accept as manifestations of understanding. One says, for example, that accepting *that* as a *dog* or as a *joke* or as a *tort* is *not* what was "built into" the machine symbolized, conceived as operating ideally: rather, accepting *that* is. So the movements of the "machine-as-symbol" can be made to match the performances that one will accept as manifestations of understanding, whatever these should turn out to be. But in this case one is not really any longer investigating actual machines and their physically determined possibilities of movement under normal conditions. The language of machine states has been used to give expression to a fantasy about a fixed basis for expressions of understanding. "The waves subside as soon as we ask ourselves: how do we use the phrase 'possibility of movement' when we are talking about a given machine?" (§194). When we use this phrase otherwise than in the grip of philosophical fantasy, we are then again thrown back into the inept dispositional model.

Each of these attempts—the models of the disposition, the formula in consciousness, the intuition, and the machine state—"does not amount to a real effort" (§153). When we try to fill them in, they come to nothing. The criteria for each of these states either *do not match* the criteria for the existence of understanding (they pick out different conditions or acts), or they are *engi-*

neered to match in imagination, so they are not ability-independent characterizations of physical or mental states or structures. The ability to understand
a concept, a rule, a formula, an expression, a joke, a piece of music, or a
person may seem to be something secondary, the derivative of a state of the
person that one may attempt to characterize independently. But it is not like
this. "If there has to be anything 'behind the utterance of the formula' it is
particular circumstances, which justify me in saying I can go on—when the
formula occurs to me" (§154). These particular circumstances include having
a natural *capacity* (itself not discernible independently of its articulations into
actual, first-order abilities) to "take to" rule-following practices and the ways of
culture, the actual *existence* of rule-following practices and the ways of culture,
together with *training* in them, and having an *interest* (though not necessarily
an articulate or even quite articulable one) in wedding capacity or power to
the ways of culture, in taking up *this* way of doing things, *this* technique.

Yet how can these circumstances—capacities, practices and techniques,
training, and interest—be all there is to understanding? It seems all so exterior.
Mustn't there be something more, something inner, something hidden? "I am
in a muddle" (§153). There is something apparently species-specific about the
sorts of language and thought at which human beings arrive. Some sort of
natural power is necessary for the emergence of conceptual consciousness and
understanding. But training in the ways of an existing practice is also necessary
for bringing this natural power into explicit articulation. Interest mediates between natural power and its training, inflecting the ways in which practices,
rules, and techniques are taken up or repudiated. There seems to be no way
to pull these various circumstances and requirements apart, no way to part
and identify natural capacity independently of its training in pursuit of its
interests within a practice. Efforts to identify the relevant natural capacity and
the states of the acquisition of understanding that it supports founder, either
by failing to match our ascriptions of understanding or by tautologically drawing on those ascriptions. There are then no criteria for the ascription of understanding that prescind entirely from actual performances within a practice.
There are no states of understanding, dispositional or otherwise, that are identifiable and characterizable in conceptual independence of what we do to manifest understanding, in various ways, within practices, and in extending them.

These facts motivate a natural anxiety about one's own powers, and hence
about one's own identity and relations with others. The coherence of the person as a possessor of intentional consciousness and an explicit ability to go

on within and in extending a practice is not fixed by any substance, pattern, or state that is identifiable independently of dramas of resistance and accommodation—though no more is coherent possession of understanding, the ability to go on in a practice, either a fiction or an arbitrary construct. What it is to understand, and to render the world aright, in one way rather than another, is something that is never settled perfectly by any science of the mind, intellect, or mind-brain. It is instead something that is worked out between us, as the real, and our coherences (such as they are) with ourselves and with one another appear within our practices.

The natural power or spontaneity—the openness both to training and to reasons—that makes language and thought possible is not isolable as an independently identifiable mental or physical state. It is rather describable and ascribable only in the dimmest and most figurative (or tautological) terms as a power that is evident in its expressive effects in practice. Words and thoughts have a life. They do not proceed as marks generated according to the sorts of laws of nature that describe physical motion. Nor are they mere conventional significations of ideation independent of training, practices, and performances within practice. And yet we continue to wish to grasp and fix what it is that gives life to our words and thoughts, to substantialize our power for language and for understanding in a *thing* that we can grasp and control, so as to secure our expressiveness (to ourselves and to one another), thus bringing *Willkür* into perfect information by *Wille*. "Where our language suggests a body and there is none: there, we should like to say, is a *spirit*" (§36). Wanting to say this—and not any actual or possible discovery—is what lies behind the attempts that do not amount to a real effort to specify the state in which understanding consists.

> When we do philosophy, we should like to hypostatize feelings where there are none. They serve to explain our thoughts to us.
> "*Here* explanation of our thinking demands a feeling!" It is as if our conviction were simply consequent upon this requirement.
>
> (§598)

It is this requirement for explanation—rooted in the anxieties over and wishes for self-coherence, attunement with others, and possession of the world as in principle fully comprehensible—that lies behind the misbegotten efforts to say in what understanding consists, to say how we can so much as follow a rule.

For us, of course, these forms of expression [these attempts to specify the
nature of understanding in terms that are independent of performance and
practice] are like pontificals which we may put on, but cannot do much with
[mit dem wir aber nicht viel anfangen können: with which we cannot even
begin very much], since we lack the effective power [the ability to prescind
in our thinking about thinking from all practices and temporality: the ability
of a god] that would give these vestments meaning and purpose.

(§426)

Were it not itself too metaphysical or too substantializing a formula, one
might try to characterize the natural powers of taking to training, and of resig-
nification—of going on in one way rather than another, intelligibly, and yet
always possibly in some novel and perhaps repudiatable way—as powers of
Imagination or Spirit. Coleridge theorizes about our lives with language in this
way: "Life may be *inferred,* even as intelligence is from black marks on white
paper—but the black marks themselves *are truly 'the dead letter'* . . . [that is
backed by] the worth and dignity of poetic Imagination, of the fusing power,
that fixing unfixes & while it melts & bedims the Image, still leaves in the
Soul its living meaning."[34]

Similarly, Kant describes imagination (*Einbildungskraft*), as the power which
"allows a concept to be supplemented in thought by much that is indefinable
in words, *whose* feeling quickens the cognitive faculties [*dessen* Gefühl die Er-
kenntnisvermögen belebt] and binds up language, which otherwise would be
mere letters, with Spirit [mit der Sprache, als bloßem Buchstaben, Geist ver-
bindet]."[35] One may even wish to go further, and to characterize the Imaginative Power that enables us to take to training and to move within, and transform, practice—the power that gives life to language and to thought—as itself
the vehicle and sign of God's presence in us. Coleridge does not shrink from
this. "My nature requires another nature for its support, and reposes only in
another from the necessary indigence of its being. Intensely similar yet not
the same (must that other be); or, may I venture to say, the same indeed, but
dissimilar, as the same breath sent with the same force, the same pauses, and

34. Samuel Taylor Coleridge, *The Notebooks of Samuel Taylor Coleridge,* ed. Kathleen Coburn
(Princeton: Princeton University Press, 1989), 3:4066; cited in Laurence S. Lockridge, *The Ethics
of Romanticism* (Cambridge: Cambridge University Press, 1989), p. 85.

35. Kant, *The Critique of Judgment,* p. 179; translation modified; *Kritik der Urteilskraft* (Frankfurt: Suhrkamp, 1974), §49, p. 253.

the same melody pre-imaged in the mind, into the flute and the clarion shall be the same *soul diversely incarnate.*"[36]

The resistance in *Philosophical Investigations* to pseudoscientific, putatively explanatory, but misbegotten explanations of our present abilities to think and use language in terms of states and structures is akin to this line of romantic thinking. Something informulable—not a definite mental or physical state or disposition, but something more like a power—lies behind our lives with thought and language and our possession of conceptual consciousness. It alone makes it possible for us to take to training and pursue interests in relation to practices as they are offered to us. But then this informulable something is not really nameable, not even within a Metaphysics of Imagination. Coleridge's Metaphysics of Imagination, like the scientisms that it opposes, also substantializes a power and leads us nowhere--except back into certain regions of comparison, as understanding a language and thinking are seen to be akin to discerning beauty or following the development of a musical theme. "Thus what I wanted to say was: when he suddenly knew how to go on, when he understood the principle, then possibly he had a special experience—and if he is asked: 'What was it? What took place when you suddenly grasped the principle?' perhaps he will describe it much as we described it above—but for us it is *the circumstances* under which he had such an experience that justify him in saying in such a case that he understands, that he knows how to go on" (§155). Nowhere else—not in any discernible fact or condition or state within the person—is one's life with thinking and language either discernible or existent.

✳

But how can this be? Is this thought now transparent, and such that one can rest in it, in possession of an account of one's nature as a possessor of conceptual consciousness? Has the temptation to explain "external" performance by reference to some independently characterizable "internal" states and processes been quite dissolved or undone? Again the protagonist undertakes to go back over the ground, showing that what one can do when one accepts something like these thoughts about one's life with thinking and language is not so much

36. Coleridge, *Anima Poetae,* in *The Portable Coleridge,* ed. I. A. Richards (Harmondsworth, England: Viking Penguin, 1978), p. 308.

or so plausibly to enunciate a (Coleridgean) thesis about the nature of that life as it is to work through cases. The protagonist's attention turns to another case of expressive performance, related to but different from the manifestation of understanding.

> This [the impossibility of developing conceptually independent character-izations of "inner" states and processes that bring about performances] will become clearer if we interpolate the consideration of another word, namely "reading." First I need to remark that I am not counting the understanding of what is read as part of "reading" for purposes of this investigation: reading is here the activity of rendering out loud what is written or printed; and also of writing from dictation, writing out something printed, playing from a score, and so on.
>
> (§156)

What do these remarks about reading show about expressive perfor-mances? What thoughts is the protagonist again working through here?

1. Reading is normative. It evinces an ability, and the underlying power (of life or imagination, one might say) to develop an ability, rather than be-ing the outcome of a mere natural process. Even when one is functioning "as a mere reading-machine: I mean read[ing] aloud and correctly without attending to what [one] is reading," one is nonetheless producing a norma-tively acceptable performance: one is reading "correctly" (§156). "But in the case of the living reading-machine [der lebenden Lesemaschine] 'reading' *meant* reacting to written signs in such-and-such ways. This concept was therefore quite independent of that of a mental or other mechanism" (§157, emphasis added). No description of a mechanism characterizes this reaction (unless that description is itself tautologically derived from a prior descrip-tion of the performance). Unlike the definite presence or absence of a mech-anism, reading develops as a natural capacity is articulated into an explicit ability, as one takes to the techniques of a practice. "The change when the pupil began to read was a change in his *behaviour* [seines *Verhaltens*-behavior, but also attitude or approach]; and it makes no sense here to speak of 'a first word in his new state' " (§157).

2. When one learns to read, something uncanny—and problematically related to the order of material nature—happens, something that we are tempted to explain. The protagonist wonders: "But isn't that only because of our too slight acquaintance with what goes on in the brain and the ner-

vous system? If we had a more accurate knowledge of these things we should see what connexions were established by the training, and then we should be able to say when we looked into his brain: 'Now he has read this word, now the reading connexion has been set up'" (§158).

3. But each of these attempts at explanation founders, "does not amount to a real effort." "The part the word plays in our life [Die Rolle aber, die das Wort in unserm Leben spielt—the role of the word 'reading' but also *the word* in general, taking the conversation about reading as a stand-in for a conversation about our life with words, about our natural powers and possibilities of development in relation to and with *logos*], and therewith the language-game in which we employ it, would be difficult to describe, even in rough outline" (§156). No definite process presents itself as that in which reading consists. It is difficult to separate the contributions to the ability to read that are made respectively by natural power and ongoing practice. When we look at cases of people learning to read, we find only "a continuous series of transitional cases" between the repetition of a memorized text and fluent performance with a new text (§161). The "dividing line" between a scrutable procedure—one we can recognize and follow as a performance from a text—and "a random one" (§163) is not clear. Nothing presents itself as the essence of rule-following. "We use the word 'to read' for a family of cases. And in different circumstances we apply different criteria for a person's reading" (§164). When we survey all these phenomena, "Can we say anything but that after a while this sound comes automatically when we look at the mark?" (§166), without any further explanation in terms of inner states and processes?

4. And yet ascriptions of reading, and of rule-following competence generally in ordinary life, are "extremely familiar to us" (§156). The mixture of something mysterious, hidden, in need of explanation, with something familiar, everyday, woven throughout our lives as human beings in culture, amounts to an instance of *the uncanny*. We are haunted by the simultaneous familiarity and strangeness of words and of our life with language and thought. "The mere look of a printed line is itself extremely characteristic"; "the look of a word is familiar to us [uns in ähnlichem Grade vertraut ist—is trustworthy for us to a similar degree] in the same kind of way as its sound" (§167). And yet words—printed or sounded—can be strange, unfamiliar. *How* do they exercise their strange influence over us? "I should like to say: when I read I feel a kind of *influence* of the letters working on me"

(§169). Or again: "I might say that the written word *intimates* [*eingebe*] the sound to me.—Or again, that when one reads, letter and sound form a *unity* [eine *Einheit* bilden]—as it were an alloy" (§171). But it is all quite mysterious. We do not find a common process in all cases of reading. Most often we find nothing: we simply read. We don't even know what sort of a thing we are supposed to look for, in order to understand this mysterious process.

> But now read just a few sentences in print as you usually do when you are not thinking about the concept of reading; and ask yourself whether you had such experiences of unity, of being influenced and the rest, as you read.—Don't say you had them unconsciously! Nor should we be misled by the picture which suggests that these phenomena came in sight "on closer inspection." If I am supposed to describe how an object looks from far off, I don't make the description more accurate by saying what can be noticed about the object on closer inspection.
>
> (§171)

That is, we don't know what sort of a thing we are to look for when we are to undertake to describe the process in which reading consists. Descriptions of actual "inner" processes either pick out conscious states of various intensity and duration that have little to do with the exercise of the ability to read (they are neither normally nor necessarily present when that ability is exercised) or they pick out neurochemically characterized brain states that succeed one another. Nowhere do material vehicle, state of felt consciousness, and exercise of ability join together to form something transparent and scrutable. "I am in a muddle." We desperately wish to grasp the essential: to *know* that in us which is such that knowing it would enable perfect expressiveness. "Here I should like to say: 'No, it isn't that; it is something more inward, more essential.'—It is as if at first all these more or less inessential processes were shrouded in a particular atmosphere, which dissipates when I look closely at them" (§173). But nothing comes. "No description satisfies me" (§175). The uncanniness—the mixture of familiarity and unfamiliarity, of at-homeness and estrangement, in our lives with words, with language and thought, with one another, and with ourselves, in our linguistic and conceptual performances, does not dissipate.

> Make some arbitrary doodle on a bit of paper.—And now make a copy next to it, let yourself be guided by it.—I should like to say: "Sure enough,

I was guided here. But as for what was characteristic in what happened—if
I say what happened, I no longer find it characteristic."

But now notice this: *while* I am being guided everything is quite simple,
I notice nothing *special;* but afterwards, when I ask myself what it was that
happened, it seems to have been something indescribable. *Afterwards* no description satisfies me. (§175)

It is like this, in general, in our lives with language and as possessors of
conceptual consciousness. These lives—our words, thinkings, speakings, in-
tendings, and actings—are familiar, everyday, and yet strange. In leading them
we live with and within an unsatisfiable desire for mastery, wholeness, completion, transparency (with oneself and with others), and for perfect expressiveness. We want to get beneath everything that seems exterior, derivative, secondary, and imperfect to what is essential: what makes anyone able at all to
think, speak, intend, and will, thence to perfect our own performances by
giving them a perfect derivation, commanded by *Wille.* But what we wish for
does not come. (Were it to come, it would make our lives within time, as
possessors of conceptual consciousness within practices, in relation to others,
unrecognizable to us; it would make us other to ourselves, possessors of wish
and desire as we are.) "Here we must be on guard against our thinking that
there is some *totality* of conditions [eine Gesamtheit aller Bedingungen] (e.g.
for a person's walking) so that, as it were, he *could not but* walk if they were
all fulfilled" (§183).

No condition or state of a thing (*Be-ding-ung*) or totality of conditions or
states of things brings about normative performance without the intervention
of *Willkür,* and so of possibilities of difference, and desire, and dramas of
resistance and accommodation. Hence the *possibility* of divergences in the exercise of an ability (with oneself, with others) cannot be foreclosed by knowledge
of any thing and its states and processes.

> Now we get the pupil to continue a series (say +2) beyond 1000—and
> he writes: 1000, 1004, 1008, 1012.
> We say to him: "Look what you've done!"—He doesn't understand.
> (§185)

That this can happen in a scene of instruction shows *not* that only a (normal)
biological nature rules this out (Stroud), *not* that an existential decision is
necessary in order to continue a series or apply a concept (Dummett), *not* that
only the verdicts of a community constitute criteria of correctness (Kripke),

and *not* that the pupil doesn't understand a transparent internal relation between rule and accordant performance (Baker and Hacker). Rather, it shows that no knowledge of any thing that is simply given—in or to mind, in or to the order of nature, in the ways of a community, or anywhere—can provide immunity against all divergences, control the ways of one's own rule-following or that of a community, or secure perfect expressiveness. Dramas of resistance and accommodation in rule-following cannot be prescinded from through the acquisition of knowledge of things. There is no legislative directive written into the ordering of the intellect, of nature, or of community habits that secures the perfect information of *Willkür* by *Wille*.

But that knowledge, the satisfaction of our desire for perfect expressiveness guaranteed by one's grasp of some fixed order, was what we wanted. "Your idea was that that act of meaning the order had in its own way already traversed all those steps: that when you meant it your mind as it were flew ahead and took all the steps before you physically arrived at this or that one" (§188), and we wanted to know how a mind might do that, what might guide it in its flights.

But really, when in the grip of this desire, or fantasy, "You have no model of this superlative fact, but you are seduced into using a super-expression" (§192). True: one can sometimes say that the rule determines the use of an expression, determines what accords with it, when (but only when) there are in fact prevailing and stable habits of use, prevailing and stable techniques and practices.

> We use the expression: "The steps are determined by the formula . . . ."
> *How* is it used?—We may perhaps refer to the fact that people are brought by their education (training) so to use the formula $y = x^2$, that they all work out the same value for y when they substitute the same number for x. Or we may say: "These people are so trained that they all take the same step at the same point when they receive the order 'add 3.'" We might express this by saying: for these people the order "add 3" completely determines every step from one number to the next.
>
> (§189)

But it is not always and necessarily like this. These facts about normal rule-following practice are not themselves mandated or secured by any deeper order of necessities, nor are they left free as arbitrary contingencies up for decision. Normally, within a stable and prevailing practice (one's own or shared with others), what it is to follow a rule does not come into doubt. But this is "in contrast with other people who do not know what they are to do on receiving this order, or who react to it with perfect certainty, but each one in a different way" (§189).

It is entirely acceptable to say, against a background of stable and prevailing practice, that the formula determines its accordants, that a concept determines its use. "The sentence only seems queer when one imagines a different language-game for it from the one in which we actually use it" (§195)—that is, when we attempt to do philosophy: to prescind from dramas of resistance and accommodation (internal and external), and to explain our rule-following abilities, in such a way as to secure perfect expressiveness. The idea that a formula determines its accordants seems queer—does not amount to a real effort to explain our abilities—when it is introduced as a philosophical super-expression about *the* nature of rules. When it is thus introduced, then it comes to nothing—does not still our anxieties or fulfill our wishes, does not satisfy us.

Then "what sort of a connexion is there here" (§198) between a rule and its accordants, a sign and its uses? One cannot get beneath practice—in its mixtures of stability and openness that structure aspiration and internal tension—so that one can say only this: "Well, perhaps this one: I have been trained to react to this sign in a particular way, and now I do so react to it" (§198). This seems not be a *consists-in* answer, not to yield the sort of explanation of what enables us to be rule-followers at all, such that knowing this we might achieve perfect expressiveness. And so one's reactions to this answer are divided. It seems, on the one hand, to be merely an external answer. "But that is only to give a causal connection; to tell how it has come about that we now go by the sign-post; not what this going-by-the-sign really consists in" (§198). And yet it is not merely an external answer. One cannot give a better one—and this naturally occasions dissatisfaction, disappointment, the leaving open of desire—about what rule-following consists in. "On the contrary; I have further indicated that a person goes by a sign-post only in so far as there exists a regular use of sign-posts, a custom" (§198). So the connection between rule-following and training, custom, and practice is a logical or grammatical one. It is not possible for there to be rule-following, or uses of signs and concepts, or conceptual consciousness, or understanding, in the absence of a regular use, a custom. Only within a practice is a rule connected with its accordants, a sign with its use.

Is what we call "obeying a rule" something that it would be possible for only *one* man to do, and to do only *once* in his life?—This is of course a note on the grammar of the expression "to obey a rule."

It is not possible that there should have been only one occasion on which someone obeyed a rule. It is not possible that there should have been only one occasion on which a report was made, an order given or understood; and so on.—To obey a rule, to make a report, to give an order, to play a game of chess, are *customs* (uses, institutions).

To understand a sentence means to understand a language. To understand a language means to be a master of a technique [Eine Sprache verstehen, heißt eine Technik beherrschen].

(§199)

Natural power, capacity, or spontaneity is articulated into an explicit ability only through taking to (and sometimes departing from) the ways of a shared practice, through interactions with others. *Willkür* cannot be sublimed into perfect information by *Wille* independently of articulation by the ways of a human community. When *Willkür* takes up those ways so as to find substance—when one weds one's spontaneity to particular social routines and routes of identity, inflected by a personal style and sensibility, but always a personal style and sensibility that are not expressible independent of such connections—then divergence and repudiation are always possible, and a sense of remainder or reserve of oneself is normal (or repressed through violence, internal or external). One can come to feel somehow hidden, or unexpressed, by and in social routine. One can fear the reception of one's expressiveness, imperfect as it is—fear both its misconstrual and its accurate construal as imperfect.

And this is, again, not what we wanted. It is not what the protagonist wanted, or what he continues to be aware of himself as wanting. The only way to connect a rule with its accordant, a sign with its uses, a concept with its instances, mind and identity with world, is through practice, wherein "there is a way of grasping a rule which is *not* an *interpretation,* but which is exhibited in what we call 'obeying the rule' and 'going against it' in actual cases" (§201). That is what there is: the home or habitation of understanding, conceptual consciousness, mindedness, intentionality. "*What we call* 'obeying the rule' *and* 'going against it' *in actual cases* [von Fall zu Fall der Anwendung—from case to case of use, a range of varying cases, with the resonance in *case* of accident, ruin, decline; emphasis added]": we experience *this* condition ("diesen Fall") of conceptual consciousness as a condition of decline, or imperfection, or belatedness—something one wishes to overcome, or fantasizes about overcoming. Because of this experience, there is the desire for perfect expressiveness that gives birth to attempts (which then do not amount to real efforts) to explain the nature of mind, of understanding, of intentionality. This wish or fantasy or desire *comes from* the experience of rule-following and understanding as possible only from case to case in practice, in connection with dramas of accommodation and resistance. *"Hence there is an inclination [Darum besteht eine Neigung]* to say: every action according to the rule is an interpretation" (§201, emphasis added). That is, there is an inclination (a tendency, a leaning, an orientation) toward regarding *every* instance of rule-following and understanding, as they actually exist in practice, as belated, secondary, exterior, as "merely an interpretation," as something with which a philosophically enabled grasp of the essence of rule-following, itself enabling perfect expressiveness, is somehow to contrast. But this inclination comes to nothing. Pursuing it, for all that it grips us, does not lead us out of what we experience as the exteriority of ordinary rule-following in practice and into perfect expressiveness.

> But we ought to restrict the term "interpretation" ["Deuten" aber sollte man nur nennen] to the substitution of one expression for another.
>   And hence also "obeying a rule" is a practice. And to *think* one is obeying a rule is not to obey a rule. Hence it is not possible to obey a rule "privately": otherwise thinking one was obeying a rule would be the same thing as obeying it.
>
> (§201–2)

The fantasy of self-sufficient authority in conceptualization and its performance, of isolate and perfect expressiveness, is not filled in by anything that any efforts at explanation can uncover.

There is here (an acknowledgment and a performance of) a certain structure of conceptual consciousness and intentionality—a *sollen* structure in which we must always regulate our conceptual performances and enact a balance between the contributions to them of our spontaneity and the contributions of practice. "One ought [man sollte]" really to accept, accommodate oneself to, the ways of practice and the impossibility of the philosophical discovery of an essence of thinking for which one longs. But one will find it difficult to do this. It will require self-regulation and reminders of what is possible and impossible. And in any case ("in jedem Fall") the desire will persist. Our life with language—and in our thinking—is an experience of familiarity, motion, empowerment, and authority, played off against unfamiliarity, stasis, weakness, and uncertainty. "Language is a labyrinth of paths. You approach from one side and know your way about; you approach the same place from another side and no longer know your way about" (§203).

And it is just this structure of self-regulation and of risks of divergence and repudiation that we wish to overcome. Resistance to acceptance of this structure reasserts itself as an objection, as the proposal that we *can* think about intention (and understanding and conceptual consciousness) taking place independently of any connections with customs and practices. " 'But it is just the queer thing about *intention,* about the mental process, that the existence of a custom, of a technique, is not necessary to it. That, for example, it is imaginable that two people should play chess in a world in which otherwise no games existed; and even that they should begin a game of chess—and then be interrupted' " (§205). Mustn't our language, and thought, and rule-governed practice somehow *grow out of what we are?* Can we not hope to grasp how this happens and to express purely and perfectly whatever that is? But no: "Isn't chess defined by its rules? And how are these rules present in the mind of the person who is intending to play chess? . . . The common behaviour of mankind is the system of reference by means of which we interpret an unknown language" (§205, §206), including any language we can come to know.

This thought, or moral, naturally raises the charge of philosophical conventionalism, of either scanting our power to grasp, cite, and refashion our norms, concepts, and rules or scanting how our norms, concepts, and rules are responsive to some ordering of things. Are these all only a matter of otherwise ungrounded statistical preponderances? "Then am I defining 'order' and 'rule' by means of 'regularity'?—How do I explain the meaning of 'regular', 'uniform', 'same' to anyone?' " (§208). Mustn't I be either just at liberty to count whatever I like as *the same* (and to explain that to someone else) or bound in my thinking by some ordering in which some things are really, essentially, the same as others (in such a way that I can either get that right or not)? Mustn't either philosophical conventionalism or philosophical realism be true? How can there be a space between them?

But no: this is what happens.

I shall explain these words to someone who say only speaks French by means
of the corresponding French words. But if a person has not yet got the *concepts,* I shall teach him to use the words by means of *examples* and by *practice.*—And when I do this I do not communicate less to him than I know
myself. . . .

I do it, he does it after me; and I influence him by expressions of agreement, rejection, expectation, encouragement. I let him go his way, or hold
him back; and so on.

(§208)

And in doing this, "I do not communicate less to him than I know myself."
That is, I *influence myself* in coming to know, and in applying, a word, a concept by "expressions of agreement, rejection, expectation, encouragement."
Self-influence (in relation to practice) and self-regulation are part of the structure of conceptual consciousness, which is not given otherwise, and is not
governed by arbitrary conventions, or by absolute samples or archetypes laid
down in an ordering of things, or by transparent internal relations between
concepts and instances. An evolving orientation, involving possibilities of motion and resistance, toward things, toward others, and toward oneself, is bound
up with the structure of conceptual consciousness and its animation in relation
to practice. This is not a matter of a given *archetype* (either in mind or nature)
and not a matter of an arbitrary convention and not a matter of something
simply and transparently fixed in 'what we do,' but instead a part of a process, a
life with and in language and conceptual consciousness. Something—a natural
power—is brought into effective articulation and life, within this process of
accommodation and resistance, within oneself, with others in practice. We are
not bound in our thinking and speaking by anything that is simply and unal-
terably given, but yet are not able to articulate and exercise that natural power
on our own, isolate, either. "Teaching which is not meant to apply to anything
but the examples given is different from that which '*points beyond*' them"
(§208)—the normal form of the teaching and learning of a word, a rule, a
concept.

It is not easy to rest with this thought. The wish somehow to liberate the
natural power that is animated in this process and that in turn animates it—
the power to go beyond particular examples—reasserts itself, within the consciousness of the protagonist, together with its rebuke. " 'But then doesn't our
understanding reach beyond all the examples?'—A very queer expression, and
a quite natural one!" (§209). Proposal and rebuke then together inhabit the

consciousness of the protagonist, issuing in a sense of felt uncertainty about how one inhabits the practices that animate and are animated by one's thought, a sense of a lack of any guaranteed orientation. " 'But is that *all*? Isn't there a deeper explanation; or mustn't at least the *understanding* of the explanation be deeper?'—Well, have I myself a deeper understanding? Have I *got* more than I give in the explanation?—But then, whence the feeling that I have got more?" (§209).

Perhaps teaching a word or concept or rule to another person is simply a matter of getting the other to catch on to what is already present within oneself—a pattern that guides one's (correct) responses to all the particulars one might encounter. So perhaps there is something somehow "inner" that is legislative for our thinking and speaking and conceptual performances. " 'But do you really explain to the other person what you yourself understand? Don't you get him to *guess* the essential thing? You give him examples,—but he has to guess their drift, to guess your intention' " (§210). That is, isn't there something there in one who understands—the essence of the intention—that controls conceptual performance? Can we not still seek to grasp that essence? "Every explanation which I can give myself I give to him too" (§210). There is nothing there *in me* which enables me in my conceptual performances to prescind from dramas of accommodation and resistance in relation to practice, nothing that controls my own performances absolutely (though they are not arbitrary and uncontrolled either).

The case of what one is able to say to another so as to guide the other's acquisition and application of a concept and the case of what one knows oneself in acquiring and applying a concept are not different. "How can he *know* how he is to continue a pattern by himself—whatever instruction you give him?—Well, how do I know?—If that means, 'Have I reasons?' the answer is: my reasons will soon give out. And then I shall act, without reasons" (§211).

When I acquire and apply a concept, it is, then, like this. I have reasons. My conceptual performances take up and are responsive to already existent patterns of usage that I am able to cite in order to make clear what I do. But these patterns of usage are not absolute samples, but instead open-ended patterns that it is up to me to continue, against the background of their nonabsolute guidance. Hence thinking and understanding and applying a concept are all modes of action; they occur only in and through exercises of *Willkür* that remain unperfected. I am not immunized by existent patterns of usage against divergences, the collapse of assurance, and the diminution of self-identity as a possessor of rational power. "A doubt was possible in certain circumstances. But that is not to say that I did doubt, or even could doubt" (§213).

Nothing masters and controls the play of circumstances that ordinarily is enough to guide me, to make my conceptual performances less than wholly arbitrary, apart from the play of circumstances, apart from natural power imperfectly wedded via training to existent norms. No one of my performances in applying a concept is necessarily immune to doubt or challenge. No appeal to the idea that one must apply the same words or concepts to things that are identical will help to achieve perfected necessity in conceptual performances, no matter how much one may wish or fantasize this. " 'A thing is identical with itself.'—There is no finer example of a useless proposition, which yet is connected with a certain play of the imagination [mit einem Spiel der Vorstellung verbunden ist]. It is as if in imagination we put a thing into its own shape and saw that it fitted" (§216).

And yet for us the questions of how we apply words and concepts and how we have conceptual consciousness, themselves the expression of the wish to uncover the conditions of the full exercise of our obscure natural powers, persist. "How am I able to obey a rule?" (§217). Sometimes, under the force of our wish, we grope to say something simply in order to have the appearance of an explanation, when in fact no explanation does any work to ground us in our possession of our conceptual abilities. "Remember that we sometimes demand explanations not on account of their content, but of their form. Our demand [Unsere Forderung] is an architectonic one; the explanation is a kind of sham-ledge [eine Art Scheingesims] that supports nothing" (§217; translation modified). Hence self-transparency and self-assurance in conceptual performance, self-certainty brought to assured truth in perfect expressiveness, is not achieved or achievable through any explanation-giving. We are brought to an image of the partial improvisatoriness and lack of full clairvoyance of all action, including the conceptual performances of thinking and understanding. "When I obey a rule, I do not choose. I obey the rule *blindly*" (§219). No absolute sample that would control all my actions and conceptual performances would do me any good in coming to terms with myself in relation to others in practices as they are. "If something of this sort were really the case [if there really were an 'absolute rule'], what help would it be to me? [was hülfe es mir?]" (§219).

In one sense, the rule as we use it, together with our techniques laid down in practice, determines its application. There, in ordinary conceptual practice, when there are no divergences and challenges, rule and accordant do not come apart. There is, moreover, no possibility of thinking or understanding or conceptual performance apart from some form of engagement with some such practices. Only in relation to ordinary conceptual practice can utter arbitrariness and immersion in the course of inert nature be defeated; only in relation to ordinary practice are mindedness and agreement with oneself in what one does possible. "The word 'agreement' [Übereinstimmung—being overall of one pitch, mood, or humor] and the word 'rule' are *related* to one another, they are cousins. If I teach anyone the use of the one word, he learns the use of the other with it" (§224).

And yet the picture of our absolute commandment, potential or actual, within practice by an absolute sample is a mistake; it fails to engage with how we are minded.

> We only look up to the mouth of the rule and *do something* without appealing to any further guidance [wir nur auf den Mund der Regel schauen und *tun,* und an keine weitere Anleitung appellieren]. . . .
>
> "The line intimates to me how I am to go [Die Linie gibt's mir ein, wie ich gehen soll]."—But that is of course only a picture. And were I to judge that it intimated this or that to me as it were irresponsibly [verantwortungslos], then I would not say that I followed it as a rule. . . .
>
> "The line intimates to me how I am to go on": that only paraphrases: it is my *last* resort for how I should go on ["Die Linie gibt's mir ein, wie ich gehen soll": das paraphrasiert nur: sie sei meine *letzte* Instanz dafür, wie ich gehen soll].
>
> (§§228, 222, 230)

The rule as it is laid down and followed in practice is my last resort for how I am to go on. There is no inspiration that I can await that will tell me in the face of practice as it is—if its circumstances are not here, for me, enough—exactly what I am to do (cf. §232). A wish for inspiration—something to which one might hearken—is already a sign that the circumstances are here, this time, not enough. But couldn't it be otherwise (the protagonist again asks himself)? Could it not be as though together we were transparent to ourselves and one another in being guided absolutely in what we do, as though our lives were holy? "Would it not be possible for us, however, to calculate as we actually do (all agreeing, and so on), and still at every step to have a feeling of being guided by the rules as by a spell [wie von einem Zauber], feeling astonishment at the fact that we agreed? (perhaps thanking the godhead for this agreement) [Der Gottheit etwa für diese Übereinstimmung—this attunement—dankend]" (§234).

But the wish for this possibility goes nowhere. We have no way ourselves to pursue it. Our attempts to construct explanations do not amount to real efforts. And if there is then no assurance of one's rational identity and powers as a grasper of norms, and if one is not immunized against repudiation and secured in expressiveness, then it feels, or can feel, as though one's thoughts and actions were merely conventional in not being backed by adamantine necessity. "So you are saying that human agreement [die Übereinstimmung der Menschen] decides what is correct [richtig] and what is false?" (§242). No; the absence of adamantine necessities is not a conventionalism of identifiable decisions (though not a mere naturalism of biological imperatives free of *Willkür* either). "It is what human beings *say* that is correct [richtig] and false; and they agree in the *language* they use [in der *Sprache* stimmen die Menschen überein]. That is not agreement in opinions but in form of life" (§241).

Agreement in form of life, attunement in *Lebensform,* is not anything absolute. Logical necessities ("nothing is red and green all over") are created within frameworks we must share in order to think at all. But departures from them in life are possible. And these frameworks do not legislate for all cases that may arise. "A certain constancy in results of measurement . . . also determines . . . what we call 'measuring'" (§242). Our thinking and understanding, our speaking and our conceptual performances, are *partly determined* by a background of ordinary practice. Apart from this partial determination, there is no thinking and understanding, no mindedness. But "It is only in normal cases that the use of a word is clearly prescribed; we know, are in no doubt, what to say in this or that case. The more abnormal the case, the more doubtful it becomes what we are to say" (§142). But where are the bounds of the normal? What are the limits—and tolerances—of *a certain constancy?*

In preoccupation with these questions—ranging from the implicit and practical to the articulate and self-absorbed—the protagonist enacts and brings to consciousness his, our, form of life, with ourselves, and with others. Proposal and rebuke, temptation and its disappointment, the effort to bring *Willkür* to perfect information by *Wille,* less than full coherence with oneself in the possession of rational abilities, a wish to know how to go on—these are elements of the grammar of the human form of life as this protagonist moves within it.

9

"Inner Experience," the Exhaustion of Temptation, Remembrance, Gratitude—§§243–308

Why the Topic of "Inner Experience" Arises

In section 243 the reflections of the protagonist turn away from rule-following competence in general and toward the particular topic of the relations between understanding and "inner experiences." Why? If the point that characterizations of rule-following competence cannot prescind from dramas of resistance and accommodation (internal and external) has been established, then why investigate the role of inner experience in conceptual consciousness now? If we cannot explain how our natural capacity for language and understanding (itself characterized independently of its display in performances) gives birth to conceptual consciousness, understanding, and linguistic performance, then why (does the protagonist) think about inner experience now?

The answer is that the characterizations, articulated in sections 143–242, of how we *cannot* characterize our natural capacity for conceptual consciousness independently of its subsequent elaboration into an explicit ability are in fact not yet quite established. The protagonist is unable yet quite to rest with those characterizations, and this is because the fantasy of having perfect control of one's expressiveness—even if only to oneself—has not yet been fully articulated, worked through, and exhausted. Partly this is because "inner experience" has not yet been fully investigated and criticized as a candidate for the inner states and processes that independently lie behind and explain public conceptual and linguistic performances. This is partly too because the connection between having an account of what controls public conceptual performance and being oneself free from risks and responsibilities in practice—through arriving at perfect expressiveness and the perfect information of *Willkür* by *Wille*—has not been fully accepted and criticized as a fantasy. That is, the temptation to explain how one is in general able to think and speak has not yet been fully diagnosed, first as a fantasy (rather than a research problem) and second as a fantasy that cannot be foregone in that it is essential to the structure of consciousness. To say this is to say that what must still be shown—or, better, accepted—are one's ineliminable dependencies in thinking and speaking on others and on a background of going practice. The protagonist's investigation of the role of inner experience in public conceptual and linguistic performance is the story of the final exhaustion of routes toward the satisfaction of temptation, hence the story of the acceptance of the persistence of temptation and desire and of a structure of resistances and accommodations (internal and external) as essential to conceptual consciousness. What must be tracked is how the protagonist arrives at this acknowledgment of the condition of conceptual consciousness, unable to achieve perfect mastery and immunization against risks and repudiations, and yet not impotent, and not ungrateful in having conceptual consciousness either. How are such acknowledgment and gratitude arrived at? How are possibilities of such acknowledgment and gratitude, as well as possibilities of their repudiation, part of the structure of consciousness, as this protagonist inhabits it and enacts it?

One of the first things to be recognized about the fantasy of having knowledge of inner experiences and how they lie behind, explain, and justify one's public performances is that it *is* a fantasy about the acquisition of authority. When one holds (perhaps because of some version of an argument from error or illusion: "When I see a tomato there is much that I can doubt") that at least one can recognize absolutely, without any possibility of error, the phenomenal stuff—say, a certain quality of wetness, or a certain quality of sound—that is before one's consciousness, and when one holds further that *some* of these "inner recognitions" provide one with absolutely known premises, from which *some* claims about public objects—*some* of the sort of claims that are issued in public performances—can be validly deduced using only reliable epistemic rules and pure logic, then one is fantasizing about coming to acquire a certain perfect mastery in one's public practice of claiming.

This is especially clear in seventeenth- and eighteenth-century developments of the theory of ideas. Descartes explicitly describes his intellectual discovery that all the members of a class of privately recognizable "inner objects"—the clear and distinct perceptions—are veridical as a discovery that immunizes him from error. "Whenever I restrain my will in making judgments, so that it extends only to those matters that are clearly and distinctly shown

to it by the intellect, it can never happen that I err."[1] In this way, by basing
one's judgments only on clear and distinct perceptions, *Willkür*, or choice,
may come to be perfectly informed by *Wille*, or irrepudiable rational authority.

Likewise Locke describes the mind as having first an innate ability to recognize its own contents. The mind abstracts certain *ideas* out of its stream of
inner experiences, and it uses these ideas, so abstracted, to recognize elements
of the stream of inner experience.

> The mind makes the particular ideas received from particular objects to become general; which is done by *considering them as they are in the mind such appearances,—separate from all other existences, and the circumstances of real existence, as time, place, or any other concomitant ideas.* This is called ABSTRACTION, whereby ideas taken from particular beings become general representatives of all the same kind; and their names general names, applicable to whatever exists conformable to such abstract ideas. Such *precise, naked appearances in the mind,* without considering how, whence, or with what others they came there, the understanding lays up (with names commonly annexed to them) as the standards to rank real existences into sorts, as they agree with these patterns, and to denominate them accordingly.[2]

Once the mind has thus established via abstraction its own standards for sorting and recognizing its contents, it can then go on to use certain of its ideas—
the simple ideas—as the basis for irrepudiably reliable judgments about the
reality of things apart from the mind.

> Our knowledge . . . is real only so far as there is a *conformity* between our ideas and the reality of things. But what shall be here the criterion? How shall the mind, when it perceives nothing but its own ideas, know that they agree with things themselves? This, though it seems not to want difficulty, yet, I think, there be two sorts of ideas that we may be assured agree with things.
>
> *First,* the first are simple ideas, which since the mind, as has been showed, can by no means make to itself, must necessarily be the product of things operating on the mind in a natural way, and producing therein those perceptions which by the Wisdom and Will of our Maker they are ordained and adapted to. From whence it follows, that simple ideas are not fictions of our

---

1. Descartes, *Meditations on First Philosophy,* in *Discourse on Method and Meditations on First Philosophy,* trans. Donald Cress (Indianapolis: Hackett, 1980), Meditation IV, p. 84.

2. John Locke, *Essay Concerning Human Understanding,* ed. Alexander Campbell Fraser (New York: Dover, 1959), Book II, chap. XI, sec. 9, pp. 206–7; emphasis added.

fancies, but the natural and regular productions of things without us, really operating on us; and so carry with them all the conformity which is intended; or which our state requires: for they represent to us things under those appearances which they are fitted to produce in us: whereby we are enabled to distinguish the sorts of particular substances, to discern the states they are in, and so to take them for our necessities, and apply them to our uses. Thus the idea of whiteness, or bitterness, as it is in the mind, exactly answering that power which is in any body to produce it there, has all the real conformity it can or ought to have, with things without us. And this conformity between our simple ideas and the existence of things, is sufficient for real knowledge.[3]

Thus one may, by constructing a sound theory of human understanding and thence acting in one's judgments in accordance with it, avoid constructing empty, merely definitional "castles in the air" and instead arrive at a genuine, rationally irrepudiable knowledge of things.[4] At least by basing one's public performances in judgment only on one's simple ideas, which "represent to us things under those appearances which they are fitted to produce in us," one may have perfect authority in judgment, may never make a mistake.

No matter what one makes either of the senses of phrases like "clear and distinct perceptions" and "simple ideas" or of the reliability of what they are supposed to denominate, it is true that in each case the program put forward—the fantasy—is of the acquisition of perfect authority in public performance, of *Willkür* fully informed by *Wille*, within a certain sphere. Not only, however, is this true in seventeenth- and eighteenth-century articulations of the theory of ideas, it is also the case that a fantasy of perfect authority in conceptual performance is in the forefront of the consciousness of the protagonist in his investigation of the possibility of language, constructed entirely "within," for inner experiences. "But could we also imagine a language in which a person could write down or give vocal expression to his inner experiences—his feelings, moods, and the rest—for his private use?—Well, can't we do so in our ordinary language?—But that is not what I mean. The individual words of this language are to refer to what can only be known to the person speaking; to his immediate, private sensations" (§243). Where another person cannot understand, and where the words refer only to what is inner, there is no possibility of correction or repudiation, no possibility of failing to conform to pat-

3. Ibid., Book IV, chap. IV, secs. 3–4, pp. 228–30.
4. Ibid., Book IV, chap. IV, sec. 1, p. 227.

terns of use, or their extensions, that are laid down in public practice. The fantasy is that of "subjective justification" (§265), of being justified before and to oneself independently of any possibility of correction. Here, within oneself, "the assumption of an error is a mere show" (§270); things cannot go wrong.

It is clear that the idea of being able to describe to oneself the content of one's inner experiences, in a transparent language intelligible only to oneself, *can* be articulated as a fantasy. The protagonist articulates it (and in doing so takes up the self-understanding of the modern epistemological tradition). The issue is whether this fantasy can be lived as anything other than a fantasy. Can any program of achieving perfected self-understanding and perfect expressiveness be based on it? Does the fantasy lead to anything that we can do, in the hope of subliming our possession of conceptual abilities into something perfect, irrepudiable?

This issue—can an articulable fantasy be lived as anything other than a fantasy?—is clearly not settled by any considerations about rule-following and the need for training in order to have public conceptual consciousness that are entered prior to section 243. Up to this point, the protagonist has come to the thought that no inner process can explain or justify one's efforts to display conceptual consciousness and produce criteria-compliant performances in public practice. The criteria—our criteria, in practice—for understanding and having conceptual consciousness include at least regular linguistic performance in conformity with patterns of the application of a word that are laid down in public practice.

But could there be *another form of understanding*? Could there be a realm of inner experience in which conceptual performances were somehow transparent to oneself and never mistaken? Could such inner experience *somehow*, in some as yet uncharacterizable way, have *something* to do with the very nature of conceptual consciousness? Whether one's "understanding" of inner experience is—potentially—connected with public performance normatively, say by providing transparent and irrepudiable justifications based on self-stipulated "synonymy statements" between a private and public language, might be left to one side for the moment. Surely the first thing to find out is whether a perfected "inner understanding" of "inner experiences" is possible.

This issue is not foreclosed by any considerations about either verbal or ostensive definitions. Having a verbal definition for the use of a term is *not* sufficient to establish competence in ordinary applications of a term in public practice; one must in addition have mastered a technique of rule-following, in such a way that one's performances are regularly criteria-compliant. Similarly, having ostensive definitions of terms or being presented with samples (such as "This is red") is not sufficient to establish competence. One must know what aspect of a thing is referred to (by, say, "red"), and one must again have mastered a technique.

But these points about what is required for competence in public practice do not touch what might be required and sufficient for some form of inner understanding that is *not* immediately connected with public practice. As Anthony Kenny observes, perhaps there is some "private analogue" of training in the ways of a public language that is itself sufficient for inner understanding.

> [According to a defender of private languages,] private language [or the capacity for "inner understanding"] might be learnt from private sensations not by bare ostension [which one must be trained to "take to"] but by some private analogue of training in the use of words. This suggestion shows that the critique of the primacy of ostensive definition [as implanting a state of grasping the meaning of a word in a public language] does not render superfluous the later explicit discussion of private languages. What that later discussion does, in effect, is to show that there *cannot* be any analogue of the background which is necessary if the public ostensive definition is to convey meaning.[5]

Fodor's Cognitivist Story

But what is the nature of this *cannot*? *Mustn't* it be like this? *Mustn't* understanding *in some sense* be *inner* or *subjective*? (Other animals don't do what we do; something "in" us makes a difference to what we do in thinking and speaking.) Jerry Fodor has persuasively developed a relevant and powerful view of "subjective understanding" for some years.

According to Fodor, what is fundamental to human conceptual consciousness and linguistic performance is the storing of sentences in a language of thought. First of all, there *are* sentences—types or structures of specific physical marks that are tokens or instances of them. Second, human subjects *store* both sentences and attitudes toward them. They believe, or doubt, or hope, or fear, or wish that the *content* that is presented in these stored structures is true. These stored structures are physical, and they are processed according

---

5. Anthony Kenny, *Wittgenstein* (Cambridge, Mass.: Harvard University Press, 1973), pp. 180–81.

to physical laws. But they also have intentional or world-directed content. Only this view, according to Fodor, makes it possible to understand human action both in ordinary psychological terms, as we all do every day, and in physical terms, as our best current science requires us to do.

That is, ordinarily human action is explained *psychologically*, by appeal to the subject's beliefs and desires. For example: Jonathan believes that here is a cookie; he desires to eat a cookie; and *therefore* he eats a cookie. The outer performance—eating a cookie—is explained by reference to the inner events of believing and desiring. Similar patterns explain linguistic performances. Jonathan believes that the dog is in the study; he desires to inform Joan that the dog is in the study; and *therefore* he says, "The dog is in the study."

Outer performances are, however, in addition physical events, and all physical events are explicable according to laws that describe necessary successions of types of physical events. Hence the bodily motions of grasping and then chewing a cookie and the bodily motions of issuing the pattern of sounds "The dog is in the study" must also be the outcomes of chains of physical events, characterizable as necessary series under some descriptive physical law.

It is a natural puzzle, then, to try to figure out the nature of the relation between these two varieties of explanation: intentional and physical-causal. Fodor offers the following story. Genuine, exceptionless, and necessary physical laws describe successions of types of physical events. Though perhaps our best science so far has only *ceterus paribus* laws, we are continually approaching the ideal of complete physical explanation. Believing and desiring are physically stored attitudes toward physically stored sentences. Intentional explanations describe genuine (but not exceptionless) regularities that are implemented by physical states and processes that are exceptionless, but that match up only imperfectly—more or less well—with the regular associations between subjective states and public performances. It is, Fodor claims, like the relation between the exception-admitting regularity that tall parents have tall children and the genetic, physical properties that roughly implement that regularity. "It's a law, more or less, that tall parents have tall children. And there's a pretty neat story about the mechanisms that implement that law. But the property of *being tall* doesn't figure in the story about the implementation; all that figures in that story is *genetic* properties."[6] Similarly, then, beliefs and

6. Fodor, "Appendix: Why There Still Has to Be a Language of Thought," in *Psychosemantics: The Problem of Meaning in the Philosophy of Mind* (Cambridge: MIT Press, 1987), p. 140.

desires are *implemented in* complex physical states: the storing of a sentence S plus the storing of attitudes toward S. All genuine causal relations are physical, or in principle capturable under exceptionless physical laws. There is no independent intentional causation. Nonetheless, belief-desire talk and intentional explanation are genuinely reliable and useful. In daily life it is hard to do without them, and in science such talk and explanations can guide research into the physical states and structures that implement the intentional states to which they refer.

According to Fodor, a picture like this follows from three central hypotheses about persons and about causality that everybody accepts, or should accept if they were serious and thought clearly. First, "There are beliefs and desires and . . . there is a matter of fact about their intentional contents." Second, the physical sciences that refer ultimately only to physical states and structures, linked in patterns of necessary succession under physical laws, provide so far the best schemes for explaining events that we have, and it is wise to accept the working ontological commitments of one's most successful scheme of explanations. In short, it is reasonable to accept "the coherence of physicalism." Third, "Beliefs and desires have causal roles and . . . overt behavior is typically the effect of complex interactions among these mental causes."[7] If these three central hypotheses are true, then, according to Fodor, one must accept his picture of the nature of inner understanding; one must accept the real-enough-to-be-useful-and-physically-implemented status of beliefs and desires, as they are referred to in our present intentional cognitive psychology and ordinary talk, while also acknowledging genuine and in principle exceptionless causal laws implemented only at the level of physical events, independently of any intentional descriptions.

It seems clear that arguments are presented and stances taken in *Philosophical Investigations* that reject this picture. In particular, against the second hypothesis—the coherence of physicalism—the protagonist of *Philosophical Investigations* urges us to reject all pictures of "ultimate entities" or metaphysical simples. What is simple and what is composite always depends on the occasions on which questions about the constituents of things arise and on the interests that are brought into play on such occasions. "The correct answer [to a question about 'component parts'] is: 'That depends on what you understand by "composite"'" (§47). That will vary with occasions and interests.

7. Ibid., p. 135.

What is a *simple,* what is an *ultimate component,* is not something fixed absolutely by reality itself. (This, for Fodor, is an untenable idealism that rejects the successes of working physical science.)

Against the third hypothesis—the idea that beliefs and desires are "real enough" but not "qua themselves" inner causes of outer events— *Philosophical Investigations* counterposes a picture of understanding and criteria-compliant performance as *normative,* not physically caused. What simply happens physically—for example, machines break down—does not match up with what it is correct to do (cf. §193). In general, when one produces a performance that manifests understanding, "nothing is hidden" (§435). There is no need to *explain* or justify outer performance by reference to some hidden inner process. "How do I know that this colour is red?—It would be an answer to say: 'I have learnt English'" (§381). No system of inner states and events stands behind, explains, and justifies public performance. What happens is rather something public. "You learned the *concept* 'pain' when you learned language" (§384). (For Fodor, this stance involves an unthinking and unmotivated rejection of all efforts at explanation—a hopelessly superficial and inadequate quasi-behaviorism.)

Against the first hypothesis—the idea that there is a "matter of fact" about the intentional contents of beliefs and desires—again the emphasis of *Philosophical Investigations* seems to fall on the idea that nothing is hidden, nothing is behind the public performance.

> But didn't I already intend the whole construction of the sentence (for example) at its beginning? So surely it already existed in my mind before I said it out loud!— . . . But here we are constructing a misleading picture of "intending," that is, of the use of this word. An intention is embedded in its situation, in human customs and institutions. If the technique of the game of chess did not exist, I could not intend to play a game of chess. In so far as I do intend the construction of a sentence in advance, that is made possible by the fact that I can speak the language in question.
>
> (§337)

> When I think in language, there aren't "meanings" going through my mind in addition to the verbal expressions: the language is itself the vehicle of thought.
>
> (§329)

The whole picture put forward by Fodor of believing and desiring as intentional states that are implemented in physical states that then themselves causally lie behind public performances seems here to be rejected as somehow out of order.

Here Fodor replies that the emphasis on conformity to what is laid down in public practices, techniques, and customs as criterial for understanding amounts to nothing more, and nothing more reputable, than a misbegotten and explanatorily impotent behaviorism. It is true, Fodor concedes, that there are conceptual questions about what *counts* as a manifestation of understanding within our ordinary linguistic practice, and such conceptual questions are indeed answered by recounting our *criteria*. There is a *conceptual story* about what makes calling *that* a barn door (in certain appropriate circumstances) a manifestation of understanding, but such conceptual stories are independent of *causal stories* about how anyone comes to be able to generate such a performance. "Answers that belong to the conceptual story typically do not belong to the causal story and vice versa. . . . What *is* essential is that some causal story or other must be true."[8] Public performances do not spring into being ex nihilo; something—and, given our best current science, something physically causal—must be said about where they come from (while preserving our customary but not ultimate reliance on intentional explanations as well). To hold otherwise and exclusively to emphasize the importance of conceptual stories about what counts as a manifestation of understanding is simply to have no theory at all about how understanding is either acquired or physically implemented.

> While an eighteenth-century Empiricist—Hume, say—took it for granted that a theory of cognitive *processes* (specifically, Associationism) would have to be the cornerstone of psychology; modern philosophers—like Wittgenstein and Ryle and Gibson and [eliminative materialist connectionists] *have* no theory of thought to speak of. I do think this is appalling; how can you seriously hope for a good account of belief if you have no account of belief *fixation?* But I don't think it's entirely surprising. Modern philosophers who haven't been overt behaviorists have quite generally been covert behaviorists. And while a behaviorist can recognize mental states—which he identifies with behavioral dispositions—he has literally no use for cognitive processes such as causal trains of thought. The last thing a behaviorist wants is mental causes ontologically distinct from their behavioral effects.

8. Fodor, *The Language of Thought,* pp. 7, 6.

... it's painfully obvious that Wittgenstein, Ryle, and Gibson never [out-grew] . . . the behaviorist legacy.[9]

Something must be said about where *believing, desiring, thinking,* and *understanding* come from, and about how they are physically implemented.

Both behaviorism and conceptual stories about the criteria for the possession of a concept are manifestly inadequate to meet this demand. There are no such things as dispositions (describable in terms of occasions or stimuli) to say "The cheese is in the cupboard." Our linguistic performances are plastic. Anyone might say nearly anything in any situation. "Pay me enough and I will stand on my head iff you say 'chair'."[10]

Someone might develop a sophisticated form of neobehaviorism according to which people develop large numbers of "*independent* mental dispositions" as a result of training and experience, without our having to bring into the causal story any talk of physically implemented intentional states.[11] But while such a story might in some slender—not really explanatory—sense account for the plasticity of our linguistic performances, it would not account for the systematic interrelatedness of our linguistic capacities. Thus Fodor argues that "You don't, for example, find native speakers who know how to say in English that John loves Mary but don't know how to say in English that Mary loves John,"[12] and this implies that a normal speaker grasps (the sense of or rules determining the extension of) a two-place predicate "———— loves ————." It is hard to see how grasping this could be the result of training and experience in public practice, without bringing talk of underlying intentional states into the causal story.

Happily, according to Fodor, we do have available a model of the kind of causal story that would explain how we come to have the productive and systematic linguistic capacities that we have. Wittgensteinians may be right to think that conceptual elucidations of the public criteria for the public manifestation of understanding are in order and sometimes useful, though wrong to think that these conceptual elucidations render causal stories either otiose or misbegotten. Wittgensteinians may be right to attack sense-data theory and phenomenalism—that is, to attack the ideas that thinking, believing, and understanding are *introspectible* mental processes.

9. Fodor, "Appendix," p. 147.
10. Fodor, *The Language of Thought,* p. 63.
11. Fodor, "Appendix," p. 148.
12. Ibid., p. 149.

But work in contemporary cognitive psychology and artificial intelligence theory avoids these mistaken assumptions and provides us with just the sort of causal story that we need. Beliefs, desires, and other intentional states exist as physically implemented mediators of inputs and outputs just as *machine states in a computer* are the physical mediators of inputs and outputs in an appropriate software language. Very roughly, what happens as we enter commands into a computer is something like this.[13] One types in something like "DELETE FILE 1" in an appropriate software language. A compiler then associates that typed-in formula with a certain configuration of electrical impulses according to a biconditional: something like "DELETE FILE 1 if and only if 10011010," where "10011010" describes a certain pattern of electrical impulses setting certain switches on or off. That pattern of electrical impulses and switch settings in turn *causes* further patterns of impulses and switch settings, according to the physical design of the machine. At a certain point a new pattern of impulses and switch settings results: say "11110." The compiler then associates this with a formula in the software language according to a biconditional—say "FILE 1 DELETED if and only if 11110"—so that it then displays on its screen the message "FILE 1 DELETED."

Here there are genuine causal regularities. Typing in "DELETE FILE 1" as input generally causes "FILE 1 DELETED" to be displayed, *ceterus paribus*. But these causal regularities are implemented not at the level of the software language, but instead at the level of the machine language—its patterns of electrical impulses and switch settings, interacting according to the laws of physics— and the operations of its translator or compiler. None of the processes—either of the compiler in translating formulae or of the machine in moving through a series of physical states—that implement this causal regularity are either *conscious* or *volitional*. But there is a productive and systematic relation between inputs and outputs, *ceterus paribus*. Problems about *qualia,* or the felt quality to us of our mental states and processes, might either for the time being be pushed to one side or construed as themselves problems not of characterizing a phenomenal feel so much as of predicting and explaining when and how "Ouch!" is uttered. Problems about the transparency of thought or about our own awareness of our thoughts might be treated similarly.

The research program is then to try to *model* the competence of human beings in using language—say, their systematic production of outputs on the

---

13. The account here paraphrases Fodor's in *The Language of Thought,* pp. 65–66.

basis of inputs—by writing programs in a software language to run on some appropriate piece of hardware. Perhaps some day we will be able to compare the hardware's architecture directly with that of the brain. For the time being, however, we will at least, by writing appropriate programs, have a *model* of the nature of our competence.

Notice again that the computer neither volitionally controls its own internal states nor is it aware of them nor does it assess them as correct or incorrect. But it does not follow, Fodor observes, that there cannot *be* correct and incorrect performance on the part of the machine. Wittgenstein has shown, according to Fodor, that it must be possible to *make* a mistake in applying a term—a term must have objective accord-conditions that are in principle public—in order for the generation of a token of a term to be a genuine use of language (as opposed to a random noise-making). "A term ungoverned by a convention is a term that may be used at random. And a term that may be used at random is no term at all. And a language without terms is no language at all."[14]

But the requirement that there *be* criteria of correctness in order for there to be genuine uses of language is fully satisfied in the computer's manipulations of software-language symbols. A computer does what it is correct to do, according to some appropriate criteria, just in case its outputs-on-the-basis-of-inputs are precisely the outputs that it was designed to produce—just in case, that is, its outputs are *normal* and not distorted by power surges or random shakings. "The use of a language for computation does not require that one should be able to *determine* that its terms are consistently employed; it requires only that they should in fact *be* consistently employed."[15] To hold otherwise is to lapse back into some version of a misbegotten verificationism, associated with an equally misbegotten picture of the transparency of understanding to itself.

In this way, then, consistent employment or regularity in the generation of output on the basis of input (however productive and systematic and uncontrolled by stimulus conditions alone) constitutes all we need in the way of objective accord-conditions for the use of a term. Behind our uses of terms lies, on the model of the computer, not a stimulus-definable *disposition,* and not a transparent state of consciousness, but instead a set of wired-in, complex, productive tendencies normally to produce certain outputs systematically on

14. Ibid., p. 69.
15. Ibid., p. 70.

the basis of inputs. Learning a language, coming to be able to employ a term in a public language with understanding, is *not* a matter of Wittgensteinian training or apprenticeship: these notions are empty of any power to explain our systematic productive capacity. Rather it is a matter of translating English, say, into some sort of internal machine code, itself given biologically, through some mix of evolutionary inheritance and sensory experience. It is developing a compiler.[16]

Only some story of this kind, Fodor argues, has any possibility of explaining *how* (unlike dogs or chimps) we come to do what we are able to do. As Fodor sums up his view,

> Either it is false that learning L is learning its truth definition, or it is false that learning a truth definition for L involves projecting and confirming hypotheses about the truth conditions upon the predicates of L, or no one learns L unless he already knows some language different from L *but rich enough to express the extensions of the predicates of L.* I take it that, in the current state of theorizing about language and learning (and barring the caveats discussed in the first part of this chapter) only the third disjunct is tolerable.[17]

Hence we arrive at a kind of representationalist antidualism and anti-introspectionism—an "extreme nativism" in which certain tendencies to class experienced objects together in certain ways, and hence also certain tendencies to produce compilers in certain ways, are simply given biologically.[18]

In response to Fodor's tripartite disjunction, some Wittgensteinians may well claim that both the first two disjuncts are more tolerable than the third. It may be insisted that learning language is *not* centrally a matter of learning "truth definitions": to hold *that* is to hold mistakenly that *the* central and defining offices of language are to describe and inform. Instead learning language is akin also to learning to walk or learning to whistle. Or it may be insisted that learning language is *not* centrally a matter of projecting and confirming hypotheses: to hold *that* is to indulge in an extreme and misbegotten intellectualism. Instead learning language is a matter of training or apprenticeship, again like learning to walk or learning to whistle or, say, learning to sustain a friendship.

16. See ibid., p. 64.
17. Ibid., p. 82.
18. Ibid., p. 96.

But here Fodor can reply that talk of training or apprenticeship collapses into behaviorism and doesn't give *any* causal account of our acquisition of systematic and productive linguistic capacities, and moreover that such things as sustaining friendships and joking are possible only on the basis of *believing* and *understanding.* (Walking and whistling are perhaps different modular capacities with different biological-psychological explanations.) Given our natural wonder at our having linguistic and conceptual capacities, and a natural wish—arising partly out of a further wish for control and perfect expressiveness, but partly also out of natural curiosity—to know *how* we come to be able to do these things that other species do not, something like Fodor's story seems the normal order of the day. Wittgensteinians just can't be serious. There's only one way to begin pursuing our natural curiosity about our linguistic and conceptual capacities.

> No doubt it's puzzling how a rock (or the state of having a rock in your intention box) could have a propositional object; but then, it's no less puzzling how a formula (or the state of having a formula in your intention box) could have a propositional object. It is, in fact, approximately equally puzzling how *anything* could have a propositional object, which is to say it's puzzling how Intentional Realism could be true. . . . [But] everybody thinks that mental states have intentional objects; everybody thinks that the intentional objects of mental states are characteristically complex—in effect, that propositions have parts; *everybody thinks that mental states have causal roles;* and, for present purposes at least, everybody is a functionalist, which is to say that *we all hold that mental states are individuated, at least in part, by reference to their causal powers.* . . . To be—metaphorically speaking—in the state of having such and such a rock in your intention box is just to be—literally speaking—in *a state that is the normal cause of certain sorts of effects and/or the normal effect of certain sorts of causes.*[19]

Typical Replies to Fodor: A Standard Version of the "Private Language Argument"

Against this powerful and persuasive picture that Fodor articulates, what arguments have any force? According to one strain of Wittgensteinianism, most powerfully articulated by Peter Hacker, the considerations advanced in *Philosophical Investigations* about private languages "diagnose a disease of thought"

19. Fodor, "Appendix," pp. 137–38; emphasis added.

from which seventeenth- and eighteenth-century theorists of ideas suffer and which is also

> rife in the arguments of those who purport to engage in empirical studies of, or simulations of, the mind and the capacities of creatures with minds. It is important to note that the most adamant anti-Cartesians such as central-state materialists or computational functionalists harbour this infection in subtle and not easily detectable forms. . . . Wittgenstein's private language argument offers a cure for this illness—for those who wish to be cured.[20]

What then is this cure? Is it sufficient for a reasonable person to break an attachment to a Fodorian picture, or its cousins? And where is this cure presented in the text?

The crucial point is that no act or event—no matter whether volitional and transparent to consciousness (as in the seventeenth- and eighteenth-century theory of ideas) or unconscious and simply caused by one's biological and psychological wiring (as in contemporary functionalism and its cousins)—of establishing a "private sample" for the use of a term, and no other "inner," "mental" analogue of public training, can be sufficient to provide a criterion of correctness for the use of a term and so to found rule-following behavior. Remembering that *this is S,* where *S* is a private sensation, cannot be something that one *just does,* let alone does in such a way that public rule-following behavior may later be founded on this act or event. As Hacker puts the point, explicating section 258,

> A genuine definition has the role of establishing the meaning of a sign by laying down a rule for its use, but concentrating one's attention on a sensation and saying "*S*" does not do this at all. . . . The point does not concern the fallibility of memory, but is rather that the putative mental ostensive definition was intended to provide a rule for the correct use of "*S*" and now it transpires that in order to do so it presupposes the concept "*S*." For to remember *correctly* can only be to remember that a certain sensation or mental image is an image of *S.*[21]

In contrast, when the objects to which terms are to apply are public, and the techniques of application can in principle be taught by giving examples and correcting performances (whether or not in fact there are others who have

20. Hacker, *Insight and Illusion,* pp. 246–47.
21. Ibid., p. 267.

these techniques), then—and only then—can there be rule-following behavior. Then and only then can there be *assertion* and *recognition* and *conceptual consciousness* and *uses of language*—all of which involve rule-following.

Similarly, Anthony Kenny argues that "the kernel of the private language argument" is that it is "futile" to "attempt to start from pseudo-pain [i.e., 'incommunicable pain' recognized 'privately,' not by reference to some publicly laid down concept of pain] and add to it a linguistic correlate" in order to explain how rule-following behavior and uses of language occur.[22] Again, there can be no "inner act" that founds rule-following behavior, assertational ability, recognition competence, conceptual consciousness, and the ability to use language. Explicating sections 258 and 265, Kenny observes:

> Even to think *falsely* [as opposed to making a mere noise] that something is S I must know the meaning of "S"; and this is what Wittgenstein argues is impossible in the private language. . . . If the private-language speaker says "By 'S' I mean *this*," gesturing, as it were, to his current sensation, then it is clear that "This is S" is not a genuine proposition capable of being true or false [but is rather a mere noise-making; it is an avowal, not an assertion]; for what gives it its content is the very same thing as gives it its truth: the significance of the predicate is supposed to be settled by the reference of the subject. "Whatever is going to seem right to me is right" therefore, and "That only means that here we can't talk about 'right.' "[23]

No act of identifying a sensation, or any other inner experience, without drawing on a concept or rule already established together with its objective accord-conditions, can found rule-following behavior and its normativity in general—nor can any merely caused events, no matter whether mental or physical. The crucial point is that correctness and incorrectness—the possibility of making a mistake—can arise only when rules and their accordants are already laid down objectively, in publicly checkable (even if not shared) practices and techniques. This is, in this reading, the great moral of sections 258 (the S-diary game), 265 (the mental image of a timetable provides no justification by itself), 270 (the manometer's confirmation of a rise in blood pressure), and 202: " 'Obeying a rule' is a practice. And to *think* one is obeying a rule is not to obey a rule. Hence it is not possible to obey a rule 'privately': otherwise thinking one was obeying a rule would be the same thing as obeying it." With

22. Kenny, *Wittgenstein*, p. 190.
23. Ibid., pp. 192, 193.

"subjective meaning" alone, all normativity, any possibility of a mistake, would disappear.

Explicitly separating and distinguishing the several assumptions, the argument would run something like this:

1. There must be rules for the uses of expressions in order for there to be behavior properly described as *using* language (as opposed to mere noise-making or some other merely caused events). (Likewise, one understands something, or recognizes something, or can apply a concept to an object—hence one has conceptual consciousness—*only if* one's understanding or recognition or act of predication is achieved in accordance with a rule.)

2. All rules are such that it is possible to make a mistake in applying them. There is no normativity, and no rule-following, if it is not possible to remember a rule or concept correctly, and then to misapply it, if there are no objective accordants of rules, beyond either whim or a simple succession of caused events.

3. But it is not possible to make a mistake in applying a rule for the use of an expression that applies only to one's private experiences (themselves supposed *not* to be recognized in accordance with any public rules and techniques), for in that case whatever one takes to be a correct application of the expression will be correct: talk of correctness would make no sense.

4. Therefore (from 2 and 3), there can be no rules for the use of expressions that apply only to one's private experiences (themselves supposed *not* to be recognized in accordance with any public rules and techniques).

5. Therefore (from 1 and 4), there can be no behavior properly describable as using a private language, in which expressions apply only to one's private experiences (themselves supposed *not* to be recognized in accordance with any public rules and techniques). (Likewise, one *cannot* understand anything or recognize anything solely through undertaking to sort and classify "private experiences," themselves supposed *not* to be recognized in accordance with any public rules and techniques.) The notion of a "private recognition" competence or ability to understand that is simply given within a person is incoherent.

Without *acts* of rule-following, or predication, or understanding, there can be no normativity at all, no rule-following or understanding at all, but only causality. "Rules guide or direct action; or better, *we* guide or direct our actions *by reference to* rules. . . . The normative guidance of a rule is not a form of causality."²⁴ But the acts that are required *cannot* be purely inner, *cannot* be independent of *public* practices and techniques. "For here [with regard to 'inner experiences alone' independent of any public rules and techniques] there are and can be no rules, *a fortiori* no ostensive definitions, no samples and no techniques of application, no distinction between correctly and incorrectly following a rule, but only a *Schein-praxis*—an illusion of meaning."²⁵ This result about rule-following and about genuine uses of language applies equally to all the other abilities that presuppose rule-following and the having of a genuinely conceptual consciousness, including the abilities to *understand* and *recognize* conceptually. "In the absence of a capacity to formulate a rule or recognize a rule-formulation, a creature lacks other capacities distinctive of rule-following."²⁶ The ability to follow a rule, and hence the abilities to understand and to have conceptual consciousness, cannot be founded on "inner acts" alone, and they cannot be cobbled together out of otherwise merely caused, normatively empty events. Only within a practice that is *public* (even if not in fact shared) are rule-following, understanding, and conceptual consciousness possible. "A rule for the use of an expression and the acts that accord with it are not independent of each other, but two sides of the same coin, two aspects of a *practice* (which may or may not be a social practice), an *activity* of using symbols."²⁷

Some Difficulties in the Standard Version
"Private Language Argument"

Is this argument *clearly sound*? Is it a *proof* that understanding is necessarily a public phenomenon, a proof sufficient to wean any reasonable person from fantasies of private, perfect authority and fantasies of the grounding of normativity in some order of nature? These considerations *are* present in the text: sections 258, 265, 270, and 202 advance them. But how are they advanced? Do they constitute a proof about the nature of understanding, and does the protagonist regard these considerations as constituting a proof?

There are, to begin with, considerations within the text of *Philosophical Investigations* that make each of the premises of this argument less than trans-

---

24. G. P. Baker and P. M. S. Hacker, *Language, Sense, and Nonsense* (Oxford, Basil Blackwell, 1984), p. 251.

25. P. M. S. Hacker, *Wittgenstein: Meaning and Mind* (Oxford: Basil Blackwell, 1990), p. 21.

26. Baker and Hacker, *Language, Sense and Nonsense*, p. 255.

27. Hacker, *Insight and Illusion*, p. 250.

parently evident, and so make the argument less than transparently a proof. With regard to premise 1—the claim that there must be rules in order for there to be either genuine uses of language or genuine understanding—one might observe that both *language* and *understanding* are family-resemblance concepts that lack sharp and decisive necessary and sufficient conditions. It is not obvious *exactly* what concepts of *language* and *understanding* we ought to use in thinking about our capacities and abilities. As Chomsky notes, "The scientific approaches [to language], I believe without exception, depart from the commonsense notion [of language] in several ways; these departures also affect the concepts of knowledge or understanding of language, use of language, rule of language, rule-guided linguistic behavior, and others."[28] Is it so clear then—does premise 1 make it clear?—that there *cannot* be a scientific study of language, of understanding, of rule-following?

With regard to premise 2, one might wonder why there *cannot* be rules or concepts that force themselves on us, with the objects to which they apply so present to us that we cannot make a mistake in applying them: perhaps a concept like "my thinking" would do. As A. J. Ayer observes in criticizing the private language argument, "Verification must stop somewhere,"[29] so why not in some (perhaps quite special) experience of the transparent and unmistakable presence to consciousness of an object (if not the sensation of *red,* then perhaps the voice of God). To this objection there is the counter that no putative act of transparent understanding, with no possibility of a mistake, can serve as a genuine *act* of understanding or recognition; it would be a mere event or avowal, a subjective saying of how things seem, but not a genuine predication. "It can't be said of me at all (except perhaps as a joke) that I *know* I am in pain" (§246). But that counter—taken as a decisive step in an intellectual argument, apart from dramas of wish and accommodation—simply repeats the premise. And *why* should it be so? *Why* isn't the capacity to make even *avowals* (does my dog do that?) rooted in a kind of capacity for receptive attention that is simply given and that somehow has to do with the nature of conceptual consciousness and understanding?

With regard to premise 3, one might wonder whether it is so clear that one *cannot* make a mistake in judging the objects or qualities that present themselves in inner experience, even independently of any ability to judge

28. Chomsky, *Knowledge of Language*, p. 15.
29. A. J. Ayer, "Can There Be a Private Language?" in *Wittgenstein: The Philosophical Investigations,* ed. George Pitcher (Garden City: Doubleday, 1966), p. 260.

public objects. There are two distinct ways in which we might be able independently of any public abilities to judge objects and qualities that are present in inner experience.

First, it may be that there is simply a distinct *kind* of objectivity that may attach to judgments of phenomenal qualities. Thomas Nagel has argued for a this view, coming close to suggesting not only that this kind of objectivity is distinct from the objectivity of judgments about public objects, but also—though he does not quite say this—that the ability to make judgments about phenomenal qualities is possessable independently of the ability to make judgments about public objects. John Searle has put forward a similar view.[30] "There must," as Nagel puts the point,

> be a notion of objectivity which applies to the self, to phenomenal qualities, and to other mental categories, for it is clear that the idea of a mistake with regard to my own personal identity, or with regard to the phenomenological quality of an experience, makes sense. . . . I may think falsely that the way something tastes to me now is the same as it tasted to me yesterday. . . . There is a distinction between appearance and reality in this domain as elsewhere. Only the objectivity underlying this distinction must be understood as objectivity with regard to something subjective—mental rather than physical objectivity.[31]

Mental objectivity is distinct from and irreducible to physical objectivity, and the kinds of qualities that are present to us in our mental lives are distinct from and irreducible to physical objects and qualities. "Mental concepts . . . refer to subjective points of view and their modifications," and these are real things. "Perceptions and specific viewpoints . . . were left behind as irrelevant to physics but . . . seem to exist nonetheless. . . . The physical is not [the] only possible interpretation [of objectivity]. . . . Some things can only be understood from the inside . . . , [such as] raw feels [and] how scrambled eggs taste." Perhaps there is only a kind of weak or deviant, specifically nonphysical and imaginative objectivity or way of making a mistake in applying a mental concept to a mental reality. But there *is* a reality here, according to Nagel. "The subjectivity of consciousness is an irreducible feature of reality"—real enough to offer objects and qualities as objects of objective judgments. Nagel

---

30. John Searle, *The Rediscovery of the Mind* (Cambridge: MIT Press, 1992), pp. 54–55, 116–18.

31. Thomas Nagel, *The View from Nowhere* (Oxford: Oxford University Press, 1986), p. 36.

concedes that Wittgenstein (on a standard reading, along the lines of Kenny and Hacker) held "that psychological concepts meet the condition of being governed by objective rules, *in virtue of* the connection between first-person and third-person ascription."[32] So it is at least possible to hold Nagel's view without regarding the *ability* to apply mental concepts as *logically independent* (let alone as the foundation) of the *ability* to apply physical concepts. But Nagel remarks that that "positive account" is troubled by "its famous obscurity and reticence." "Mental concepts," Nagel holds, "are sui generis."[33] And if this is true, is it so clear that one *cannot* make a mistake in using a term that applies only to one's inner experiences, independently of any ability to apply terms to public objects? Will it help as part of an intellectual argument simply to *assert* that one cannot? Does an argument containing such an asserted premise have the power conclusively to wean us from fantasies of reconstruing the nature of our rule-following capacities and abilities?

Second, the ability to follow rules and to make genuine judgments about *both* mental and physical objects might be regarded as *emergent* out of the causal histories of the individual and the species, without any need to introduce the notion of a public *practice*. It might be that coming to make objective judgments and to follow rules is something that certain creatures just *come to do* in light of certain experiences. Thus Chomsky argues that theorizing about a person's rule-following behavior is the same sort of enterprise as theorizing about fruit flies, sheepdogs, cockroaches, and spiders and the behaviors that they produce under various circumstances.[34] We amass all the evidence we can, and we try to describe and explain what happens when; we theorize about "the kind of 'machine' [a person] is, if one likes." To say that someone follows a rule is simply to describe a certain pattern of regular behavior that is *typically* unconscious. We can *describe* the regular linguistic habits of a child, of speakers of a dialect, and of someone who has deviant semantic rules. "The rule R is a constituent element of [a speaker's] language (I-language [idiolect, or personal pattern of regular performance]) if the best theory we can construct dealing with all the relevant evidence assigns R as a constituent element of the language abstracted from [the speaker's] attained state of knowledge."[35] If *this* is how objectivity or normativity is initially established—in patterns of

32. Ibid., pp. 37, 15, 17, 18, 25, 7; emphasis added.
33. Ibid., p. 37.
34. Chomsky, *Knowledge of Language*, pp. 236–39.
35. Ibid., pp. 237, 227–28, 244.

regular behavior rather than in transparent public practices—then there is no clear reason to think there *cannot* be a form of objectivity or normativity that attaches to "judgments" about inner experiences. It might be that we simply begin, independently of any public training or correction, to express to our-selves dawning *recognitions of pain or hunger,* say, just as spiders instinctively spin their webs. Against this sort of account of the natural emergence of nor-mativity out of regular behavior, will it help simply to insist on premise 3? Is it clear that natural processes *merely happen,* without any emergence of norma-tivity, and that normativity *must* instead flow *only from acts* (not events) within *public practice?* How is the will supposed to be present in such acts, so as to lift them out of the mere succession of events in nature, if *not* from the self-sufficient volitions of isolate individuals? *Couldn't* natural tendencies be enough to found rule-following behavior?

Beyond Proof: Leading a Human Life

Taken as a proof or demonstrative argument then, the considerations about private languages that are advanced in *Philosophical Investigations* are impotent to undo commitments to either phenomenological-Cartesian research pro-grams (Nagel, Ayer) or explanatory naturalist research programs (Chomsky, Fodor, connectionism). Simply asserted as transparently true, the premises of the so-called private language argument beg crucial questions. The views about the nature of our conceptual capacities that it forwards amount to a kind of unorthodox conventionalism (a conventionalism without convenings). As it-self a kind of view about the nature of our capacities that is in contention with others, this unorthodox conventionalism fails to explain either how normative practices arise or what the nature of the presence of the will is in anyone's mastery of normative practices—even though the view everywhere presup-poses the presence of the will in normative practices in order to distinguish them from mere sequences of caused events in nature. Hence this unorthodox conventionalism leaves room for a wish to explain the nature and conditions of emergence of our normative practices reasonably to assert itself. One can still reasonably, in light of the considerations about private language taken as a demonstrative argument, wish to know how we have the normative practices we have and how the will is present in them. Since this wish remains reason-able—there is something that seems in need of an explanation—the consider-ations about private language considered as a demonstrative argument are likewise impotent to represent either phenomenological or naturalist schemes of explanation as products of confusion and fantasy.

Why should we not try—perhaps in some not yet fully articulated way, involving a reconstrual of concepts such as "understanding" and "rule"—to explain the nature of our capacities and abilities in relation to normative practices? There is something here that we distinctively do, something that has to do with us. This point is acknowledged in the text.

> Only of a living human being and what resembles (behaves like) a living human being can one say: it has sensations; it sees; is blind; hears; is deaf; is conscious or unconscious.
>
> (§281)

> We only say of a human being and what is like one that it thinks.
>
> (§360)

Why then cannot we wish reasonably to know, or to explain, what in us, or in nature or intellect in us, makes this the case, makes us able to think, and understand, and bear conceptual consciousness, and have normative practices? Can we help wishing to know this, how mindedness either sustains itself or is grounded in the operations of nature, and wishing to know further how *Willkür* might be fully informed by *Wille,* how conceptual performances might become irrepudiable, in expressing only the essence of a minded being, and not anything accidental, arbitrarily willful, and repudiable? Considerations about the normativity and transparency of rule-following behavior in ordinary practice as we currently describe it are impotent to defeat this wish, or even to capture the connection between a wish to explain the nature of mindedness and fantasies about the perfection of one's conceptual abilities.

What might be *persuasive,* though not amounting to a proof, is instead a different, richer *description* of what is involved in understanding, in using language, and in following a rule. Such a description would have to focus *not* on the transparency of rule-following behavior, *not* on the natural emergence of rule-following out of biologically given dispositions, and *not* on the transparency to themselves of certain autonomous, inner, intellectual acts of judgment, but instead on how wishes, anxieties, and efforts at expressiveness and self-coherence (to and for oneself and others) attach to ordinary conceptual performances. Such a description would have to focus on the fitful, shifting presence of voluntariness, of *Willkür* always only partially informed by *Wille* and never quite transparent, in what we do. And such a description would have to take the form not of a *theory* of how some object independent of the description—scrutable conventions, the ordering of physical nature, or a God-given intellect—controls conceptual performances, but instead of an acknowledgment. It would have to acknowledge itself as a conceptual performance that enacts and expresses these very wishes, anxieties, and efforts at expressiveness and self-coherence. Who and what one is oneself, as a being capable of conceptual performances, would be something that is being tested and worked out, continually, within the generation of the description of conceptual performances. Only such a description of conceptual performance that is indistinguishable from a narrative of a protagonist's enactment of unstilled temptations attaching to conceptual performance might make it clear, persuasively (to whom? subsequent to the occurrence of what sorts of transformative self-recognitions?), how the mind, in Cavell's phrase, is *not* "a medium of somethings,"[36] but rather how we, with all our wishes and anxieties, are present in our conceptual performances.

When, but only when, our (one's) conceptual performances are described (displayed in the self-interrogative itinerary of a protagonist) as thus structured by *Willkür* always only partially informed by *Wille,* then conventionalism, naturalism, and phenomenological intellectualism (each of various stripes) may become legible as misbegotten fantasies of perfect expressiveness. Conventionalism sublimes the anxieties of conceptual performance into smooth accommodations to current practices, underplaying the possibilities of resistance and risk that are sometimes involved in shifts in orderings of concepts. Phenomenological intellectualism sublimes these anxieties into a perfect, but initially and predominantly inner, self-transparency, urging withdrawal from these practices so as to achieve perfect assurance, and therein overemphasizing our powers of resistance to the conventional. Naturalism sublimes away the anxieties of conceptual performance into merely caused happenstances, denigrating voluntariness and reducing notions of action and performance to mere behavior.

But then—or at least so the protagonist's itinerary of self-interrogations may persuasively enact and show—these anxieties, wishes, temptations, and

36. Cavell, *Conditions Handsome and Unhandsome,* p. 95.

fantasies persist. They are not something we grow out of, or can grow out of, in the course of simply accepting the role of current practices in enabling the articulation of natural capacity into an explicit ability, in the course of doing normal science or in the course of intellectual self-reflection. Rather there is in the protagonist's itinerary—in ours—a pattern of oscillations between the migration of a desire for perfect expressiveness into the fantasy of uncovering a phenomenal realm of fully transparent, fully authoritative concept application and a return from that migration into the acceptance our lives as possessors of conceptual consciousness in relation both to nature and to conceptual practices. This is the dramatic movement of sections 243–308, the continuing but always broken effort to bring *Willkür* to perfect information by *Wille*, the movement of what Cavell calls *living our skepticism* or "the truth of skepticism . . . —an argument of the self with itself (over its finitude)." "The threat, or the truth, of skepticism [is] that it names our wish (and the possibility of our wishing) to strip ourselves of the responsibility we have in meaning (or in failing to mean) one thing, or one way, rather than another."[37]

Understanding conceptual performances (which is itself a conceptual performance) then involves seeing them as always freighted with this wish or possibility of wishing, together with the impossibility of satisfying it. It involves *reading* them so as to uncover their expressions, or expressions through (often reasonable) suppressions, of such wishes, of a desire for perfect authority and irrepudiable expressiveness.

What do we find when we read sections 243–308 in this way? It is important to begin with the fact that, as Cavell remarks, "Wittgenstein does not say that there can be no private language."[38] This is not an asserted impossibility, grounded in a demonstrative argument. Rather, the protagonist

> introduces his sequential discussion of the topic, at §243, by *asking:* "Could we also imagine a language . . . in which a person could write down or give vocal expression to his inner experiences—his feelings, moods, and the rest—for his private use," where "private" is to mean "another person cannot understand." The upshot of this question turns out to be that we cannot really imagine this, or rather that there is nothing of the sort to imagine, or rather that when we as it were try to imagine this we are imagining something other than we think. . . . Its point is to release the fantasy expressed in the

37. Cavell, *In Quest of the Ordinary*, pp. 5, 46, 135.
38. Cavell, *The Claim of Reason*, p. 344.

denial that language is something essentially shared. The tone of the sections dealing explicitly with the idea of a private language [is] peculiarly colored by the tone of someone allowing a fantasy to be voiced.[39]

The fantasy, or wish, or temptation that the protagonist here queries solves a problem—if it is coherently pursuable. To be able to recognize and sort "private samples" in inner experience, independently of any training in public languages and of dramas of accommodation and resistance, is to have a kind of perfect authority. It is to be immune from the possibility of criticism or repudiation in one's conceptual performances. ("Whenever I restrain my will in making judgments so that it extends only to those matters that are clearly and distinctly shown to it by the intellect, it can never happen that I err." "Simple ideas are not fictions of our fancies.") It is to arrive in one's conceptual performances at *Willkür* perfectly informed by *Wille,* at perfect expressiveness and self-coherence in the exercise of power, at least in one region of one's conceptual life. One's applications of concepts become absolute and transparent to oneself. One sustains—if it is possible—a conceptual life apart from accommodations to any public practice. One can wish for this sort of private authority.

> A fantasy of necessary inexpressiveness would solve a simultaneous set of metaphysical problems: it would relieve me of the responsibility for making myself known to others—as though if I were expressive that would mean continually betraying my experiences, incessantly giving myself away; it would suggest that my responsibility for self-knowledge takes care of itself— as though the fact that others cannot know my (inner) life means that I cannot fail to. . . . The wish underlying this fantasy covers a wish . . . for the connection between my claims of knowledge and the objects upon which the claims are to fall to occur without my intervention, apart from my agreements.[40]

But this fantasy goes nowhere. "As the wish stands," Cavell observes, "it is unappeasable." Whenever the protagonist tries to imagine what it would be to manage perfected conceptual performances, actually to achieve *Willkür* perfectly informed by *Wille* in one's inner life, then the protagonist finds that this imagining has no content. At best, when concept application in an inner life is successfully imagined, it then turns out to be the application of concepts

39. Ibid.
40. Ibid., pp. 351–52.

that anyone *could* understand and apply, hence concepts that have no absolute inner foundation, apart from the vicissitudes of public practice. "He has asked *himself* whether we can imagine something. He, as it were, looks up at himself and replies that of course we can use ordinary language to note our inner experiences for some private purposes (e.g. people often develop shorthand devices for their diary entries in order to keep their thoughts to themselves. . . .) Then he feels that this is not what he means; it has not hit off the fantasy of privacy which he wants to give voice to."[41]

What one wishes for, in trying to imagine a private language, is a means to overcome one's ordinary expressiveness—one's ordinary legibilities and liabilities in relation to a public practice—in favor of an absolute achievement, something deeper and more secure than anything done in a public practice. "In each of [the] attempts to realize the fantasy of a private language, a moment arises in which, to get on with the fantasy, the idea, or fact, of the *expressiveness* of voicing or writing down my experiences has to be overcome." That is, what must be overcome, when one is in the grip of the fantasy, is that one's conceptual performances are expressive of, or are legible as, acts that proceed from the *imperfect* information of *Willkür* by *Wille*. Yet whenever one tries to imagine a perfected, absolute, irrepudiable conceptual performance, rather than an empty noise-making, then one finds oneself imagining only something that is or might be done within ordinary practice, by anybody. In one's inner life, "However far you have gone with it, you will find that what is common is there before you are. . . . The soul is impersonal."[42]

What is impersonally there is *not* a system of wired-in conformity to rules, not only a set of natural tendencies, and not transparent conformity to public rules, but the imperfect presence of *Willkür* in action, connected with the possibility of a fantasy, a possibility that one can, and perhaps should, foreswear, but a possibility that is not forecloseable through intellectual argumentation.

If this, then, is what we are like—bearers of *Willkür* imperfectly present in actions and conceptual performances, subjects caught up in the possibility of fantasy and its emptiness—then we are to be understood by having our conceptual performances and our indulgences in and disappointments in this fantasy *read* (not by "modeling our conceptual behavior under a system of rules"; not by "tracing our natural tendencies"; not by discovering the opera-

41. Ibid., pp. 352, 345.
42. Ibid., pp. 348, 361.

tions of a self-sufficient intellect in oneself; not by restating the ways of ordinary rule applications). Our wish for *Willkür* perfectly informed by *Wille,* arising out of the imperfect presence of *Willkür* in our actions and conceptual performances, is standing, unappeasable, constitutive of who we are. The possibility of wish and fantasy arising, then collapsing, out of this constitution is not itself necessitated by any fixed conceptual truths about the nature of the intellect, the will, rules, or dispositions. Nor is the possibility of continuing in that fantasy foreclosed by demonstrative conceptual argument. ("I shall remain obstinately attached to this idea, and if by this means it is not in my power to arrive at the knowledge of any truth, I may at least do what is in my power, and with firm purpose avoid giving credence to any false thing, or being imposed upon by this arch deceiver, however powerful and deceptive he may be.")[43] Rather, the possibility of this fantasy arising and the subsequent acceptance of its apparently necessary collapse—as they occur in and through the self-interrogations of this protagonist—*show* our character as subjects of the imperfect information of *Willkür* by *Wille.*

We *can* go on to talk of "wired-in rules," of "mental objectivity," of "transparent normativity," or "tendencies to group bits of data." We can go on repressing the importance of the understandings of persons as imperfect bearers of *Willkür* that are achieved, in manifold different ways, in and through the reading of what is expressed in conceptual performances: in conversation, in music, in teaching and learning, in reading, in painting, in all the ranges of acting as opposed to mere behaving. We can repress all this, and we can go on instead to seek a correct cognition or representation of "the essence of the human" independently of attentions to expressive performances. But as the protagonist's indulgences and foregoings of fantasies show, yet do not prove by appeal to "conceptual truths," that effort is empty, goes nowhere.

There is no *essential component* of understanding that stands behind conceptual performance and makes it both necessary and potentially perfect. There are, for example, no Forms, such that a partial grasp of them is constitutive of ordinary, imperfect conceptual performance (and integrity) and a full grasp of them is constitutive of perfect conceptual performance (and integrity). Nor will transparent normativity, the deliverances of mental objectivity, or natural tendencies do this job either. Or at least so the career of this protagonist shows.

---

43. Descartes, *Meditations,* in *Philosophical Works of Descartes,* trans. Haldane and Ross, Meditation I, 1:148.

Instead there are dialectical relations between natural power or capacity, shared public practice, and potential public practice (not yet or necessarily shared) in uses of concepts and language, dialectical relations that involve accommodation, resistance, and refiguration of the modes of the partial information of *Willkür* by *Wille* that are present in the ways of life of individuals in, or falling out of, community. Once we note the importance of these dialectical relations of accommodation, resistance, and refiguration, in and through which alone—does this show itself? can we accept it?—the articulation of natural capacity into explicit conceptual ability is possible, then we can see the importance of Pears' remark that Wittgenstein perhaps "did not mean to commit himself to the theory of a single decisive loss"[44]—is it other persons or public objects?—the occurrence of which would undo the possibilities of thinking, understanding, and using language. "We want to say: 'When we mean something, it's like going up to someone, it's not having a dead picture (of any kind).' We go up to the thing we mean. [Wir wollen sagen: 'Wenn wir meinen, so ist hier kein totes Bild (welcher Art immer), sondern es ist, als gingen wir jemand auf zu.' Wir gehen auf das Gemeinte zu.]" (§455). Here to go up to someone (*auf jemand zugehen*: to make an approach to someone, solicit someone, make an effort at a relationship with someone) is to engage with persons who have identities within practices that are laid down in public life. Doing this is part of the structure of the conceptual life of a person.

✳

Or so, at least, the protagonist of *Philosophical Investigations* shows himself, or allows himself to be read, through marking his progress. He represents *himself* as (1) given over to or caught up within an effort to go up to someone—to make sense to and with others (and to and with himself), by engaging with stable yet transfigurable linguistic practices, and (2) resisting this sense of being given over to engagement, with all its risks of repudiation, and wishing instead somehow to exercise a natural power of conceptualization immediately and perfectly. Can this wish lead anywhere? Can the necessity of engagement be simply accepted, in such a way that the wish disappears?

And so the protagonist asks himself: "Would it be thinkable for there to be a language in which one could write down or give vocal expression to his inner experiences—his feelings, moods, and the rest—for his private use?"

44. Pears, *The False Prison*, 2:364.

(§243). This is not to be merely an idiosyncratic way of noting and understanding what another person might note or understand. Only an in principle private and perfect conceptual performance would satisfy the wish for perfect authority. The referents of the terms of this private language, the objects of these putatively perfect conceptual performances, are to be inaccessible to—in principle, unknowable by—anyone else. "The individual words of this language are to refer to what can only be known to the person speaking; to his immediate private sensations. So another person cannot understand the language" (§243).

It immediately becomes clear that the issue for the protagonist is the nature and conditions of exercise of conceptual power at all. What makes linguistic and conceptual practice possible? Is it somehow the grounding of some words and concepts in a stream of sensory life? "How do words *refer* to sensations?" (§244). Is the reference of words somehow the result of the exercise of a power of conceptualization and recognition that is prior to and logically independent of training in the ways of a public practice?

The idea that this might be so is immediately rebuked, and the importance of training in the ways of a public practice is emphasized. "This question [How do words refer to sensations?] is the same as: how does a human being learn [wie lernt ein Mensch] the meaning of the names of sensations?—of the word 'pain' for example" (§244). "Ein Mensch," a human being—not "Einer," one—emphasizes the existence of a shared and public way of being that is worked out and displayed in public training, not the priority of a necessarily private power. What then happens in the learning of sensation language by a human being?

> Here is one possibility: words are connected with the original, the natural [ursprünglichen, natürlichen] expressions of sensation and are put in their place [an dessen Stelle gesetzt]. A child has hurt itself; it cries [Ein Kind hat sich verletzt, es schreit]; and then grownups talk to it and bring exclamations forward to it [ihm . . . beibringen] and, later, sentences. They teach the child new pain-behaviour [Sie lehren das Kind ein neues Schmerzbenehmen].
> . . . the verbal expression of pain replaces the crying [ersetzt das Schreien] and does not describe it.
>
> (§244)

The emphasis here is on something public, the learning by the child from grownups of a way of behaving, acting, or conducting oneself (*Schmerzbeneh-*

men). This, and not acts of inner recognition that are logically independent of public, practical life, is where the life of conceptual consciousness dawns and natural power is articulated into explicit ability.

Yet this claim is not simply asserted and is not presented as the conclusion of an argument. Instead, it is a conjecture, a way in which one might make sense of and come to accept the character of one's life as a possessor of conceptual consciousness: "Here is one possibility." As a conjecture, the suggestion is naturally disappointing. It does not *explain how* we, with our mental or physical nature somehow commanding us or us commanding it, do this thing somehow, enter into the exchange of verbal expressions and so into new ways of behaving. It simply denies that there is a level of the exercise of a natural power to recognize phenomenal objects that lies underneath our accommodations to public practice. The conjecture repudiates the fantasy of perfect authority and the perfect, because necessarily private, information of *Willkür* by *Wille.*

In the face of this repudiation by conjecture, the fantasy is then immediately re-expressed. "How can I then still want to step with language between pain and the expression of pain? [Wie kann ich denn mit der Sprache noch zwischen die Schmerzäußerung und den Schmerz treten wollen?]" (§245). This question does not mean, "I can't do it; it's impossible; there can't be a private language; there can't be an exercise of a conceptual power that is, in principle, private and perfect." Instead it asks: "How can I go on in the fantasy? How can I still think of a natural power of conceptualization as actualizable, as perfectly mine? I wish to do this. What about me, and in my life with language as it stands, leads me to have this want?" The question acknowledges the presence and force of the wish, however unappeasable, rather than dismissing it.

In order then to go on with this fantasy, there would have to be some sense in which my sensations, and hence my recognitions of them that I wish to be perfect, *are private,* not caught up in or constituted as what they are in relation to the ways of public practices. They would have to be either inalienable ("only I can have them") or incommunicable ("only I can know them") or, best of all, somehow both inalienable and incommunicable.

Is it true then that only I can have my sensations or only I can know them? Can I persist in this thought? In one sense, it is true that only I have my sensations. But in this sense, it is also true that only I sneeze my sneezes, only

I am married to my wife, and only I have my handwriting.[45] There is nothing necessarily private or hidden about any of these possessions. They do not stand for me as objects of private and perfect recognition or conceptualization. Is it then true that only I can know my sensations (really, directly, or with certainty), that only I can know whether I am in pain and what it is for me to be in pain? "In one way this is wrong, and in another nonsense" (§246), the fantasy-undoing voice replies. Others often do know when and whether I am in pain, and in one clear sense of "know" I don't. There is no distinction for me between the appearance and the reality of my pain. I cannot doubt whether this is pain, and where doubt is not possible, then neither is knowledge, *in any central and ordinary* sense of "know." " 'I know I am in pain' can only be conceived as an epistemic utterance if 'I do not know whether I am in pain' is held to be intelligible."[46] "I know I am in pain" is, in relation to ordinary uses of "know," at best a misleading paraphrase of "I am in pain." In saying "I know I am in pain," I express my pain but do not report the result of an inner observation or recognition. "It can't be said of me at all (except perhaps as a joke) that I know I am in pain" (§246). The grammar or shape of the concept of knowledge, as it is evident in ordinary uses of "knows," rules that out.

Then does the fantasy of discovering within oneself the nature and conditions of the absolute and perfect exercise of a natural power of conceptualization collapse? It has *not* been given content in terms drawn from ordinary usage. Its sense is *not* hit off by saying "Only I can (really, directly, or with certainty) *know* I am in pain"—so long, at least, as ordinary achievements of knowing (as opposed to "phenomenological knowing," say?) are kept in the foreground as establishing the appropriate uses of "know." "I cannot be said to learn of [my sensations]. I *have* them" (§246).

But what does this show? Is doubt about whether I have a sensation, and hence knowledge of my sensations, then necessarily impossible? Am I foreclosed by commitments to my conceptual life in relation to public practice from going on with fantasies of perfected phenomenological knowing? A voice enters, partly to deepen the criticism that the fantasy of perfected conceptualization is without content, that a private language is *not* thinkable, but partly also to hint that it might yet be thinkable by drawing on a *new* concept of

---

45. Cf. Hacker, *Wittgenstein: Meaning and Mind,* p. 52.
46. Ibid., p. 57. Cf. pp. 54–62 on epistemic privacy.

knowledge, invented for the purpose. I have my sensations, but I do not know
I have them in the ordinary sense of "know." "That is right [Das ist richtig]:
it makes sense [es hat Sinn] to say about others that they may be in doubt
about whether I am in pain; but not to say it about myself" (§246). Is this the
completion of the criticism, the final repudiation and dismissal of the fantasy of
perfect knowing, or also a hint that there might be a new concept of knowledge
("incorrigible knowledge") achievable in some cases in which doubt is senseless? What else should we expect than that a new concept will be needed to
characterize our achievements in a special realm of inner experience? "If we
are using the word 'to know' as it is normally used," then we can go nowhere—
"(and how else are we to use it?)" (§246). We cannot (or only do not yet
manage to?) by drawing on ordinary language give any content to the temptation to say only I know (intimately, uniquely) my own sensations. When we
say this, we mean something other than we thought (perhaps it's a joke), or we
mean nothing. Yet the idea of a special form of knowledge, hitherto unknown,
continues to tempt us. Perhaps the joke in saying "I know I am in pain" is
"something like an understatement, like saying of Newton or of Leibniz that
he knew calculus. Or like familiar passages in comedy, say the one in *As You
Like It* in which to Orlando's question 'But will my Rosalind do so?', Rosalind
(disguised) answers, 'By my life, she will do as I do.' "[47] Yet when we try to
unpack the joke, to give criteria for the special form of knowledge on the
model of ordinary criteria of knowledge ("I did the experiment"; "I saw him
put his hand in the cookie jar"), only criteria that are stricter and more absolute
than the ordinary, then we come to nothing. What then are we trying to say,
and why? "How can I then still want to step with language between pain and
the expression of pain?" (§246).

Can we then *conclude* that the fantasy of perfect authority in conceptual
performance *can't* be given content, that we *could not* discover objects of perfect
recognition in us, prior to and independently of our engagements with public
practices? We can emphasize that the fantasy has not yet been given content
and that as things stand now the criteria for saying "I know . . . " do not allow
us to say "I know I am in pain" as a report of a private, practice-independent
discovery. Within our present grammar, the inalienability of our sensations is
like the inalienability of our sneezes. It involves no impenetrable epistemic
or ontological privacy or interiority. That is our grammar. "The proposition

47. Cavell, *The Claim of Reason*, p. 100.

'Sensations are private' is comparable to: one plays patience by oneself"
(§248).

But what underpins and fixes that grammar? Only the history of criteria,
techniques, practices, and the interests they serve, together with the *seeming*
necessity—no other way has yet been found—of accommodation to *some*
standing, public criteria, techniques, and practices in order to recognize things
at all. But no absolute fact, no course of events or changes of states that are
determined independently by the essences of things—free of *Willkür* as it has
so far partially expressed itself in cognitive practices—either grounds our
grammar or upholds that seeming necessity. It is part of our grammar, for
example, that "the smile of an unweaned infant is not a pretence" (§248). The
ordinary criteria of *pretending* block the application of that concept there. But
why? The question is allowed to surface, is not stopped in the protagonist:
"And on what experience is our assumption based?" (§249). If the answer is
"none; grammar is autonomous from founding experiences, and it's not even
properly an assumption or belief, not something up for confirmation or in-
firmation, that unweaned infants do not pretend; rather 'the surroundings
which are necessary for this behavior to be real simulation are missing'"
(§250), then nonetheless the question of a ground, or a wish for a ground,
has been allowed to surface. We do change our concepts, or introduce new
ones, sometimes on the basis of crucial discoveries or experiences. *Why* should
such developments be limited to technical concepts within well-established
scientific research programs? Mustn't *something* about the way the world is
underlie our simplest and most basic concepts, techniques, and practices? Is
a wish to discover this unnatural?

But when we enter into this wish and try to give it content, then we treat
what are really rules or grammatical propositions as though they were fact-
stating propositions, justified by experience. "Sensations are private" has a
subject-predicate form, a "form through which it appears to us to be an experiential sentence, while in actuality it is a grammatical sentence [was uns durch
seine Form eine Erfahrungssatz vortäuscht, aber in Wirklichkeit ein grammat-
ischer Satz ist]" (§251). We remind ourselves of our grammar, of the existence
of grammatical propositions and the autonomy of conceptual practice from
any ultimate grounding in experience or in the nature of things in themselves,
as we continue to find ourselves failing to give experiential content to metaphysical claims, such as "sensations are private." In scrutinizing one's inner

life, or in looking anywhere for bases of criteria, techniques, and practices of conceptualization that are set in an order of things that is absolutely present to us, "however far you have gone . . . , you will find that what is common is there before you are."[48] "One does not define a criterion of identity by emphatic stressing of the word 'this' " (§253).

So "the philosopher *treats* [Der Philosoph *behandelt*—treats, attends to, manages] a question; like an illness" (§255). But what is the aim of this treatment? What is its conclusion? "We must be reminded of [a criterion of identity; wir aber daran erinnert werden müssen]" (§253). These reminders make it clear that it is only in engagement with ordinary, public criteria, practices, and techniques that we can articulately exercise our natural power of conceptualization, bring *Willkür* even to partial information by *Wille*. Yet among the criteria of which we remind ourselves are the criteria for "understanding" and "person." Only human beings (and what acts as they do) understand. They sometimes generate and understand deviant uses of expressions—metaphors and new pieces of terminology. Their doing so evinces a power of resistance to ordinary criteria. It is natural to wish to exercise this power absolutely. This wish—so far as our efforts to articulate modes of its pursuit come to nothing, so far as they collapse into either nonsense or grammatical claims, without recording discoveries—is unrealizable. It is a product of fantasy and a symptom of illness. It requires treatment, handling, attention, but not abandonment, denial, or repression. These latter modes of mistreatment themselves absolutize and circumscribe our exercises of a natural power, welding it too closely to ordinary conceptual practices as they stand. Abandonment, denial, and repression of the wish are then also informed by it. Instead of denial or repression, treating that wish must involve *acknowledging* it, accepting both its presence and its unsatisfiability as part of our condition. That acknowledgment and avoidance (either through repression or through its reconstrual into a project of discovery) are alternatives for us in relation to this wish is our condition. That a being is capable of, and fated to, these modes of response is among our criteria for the application of "person." To see persons in this way is to accept them as bearers of natural power, articulable and expressible only in relation to ordinary practice, but also in partial resistance to it. It is to see our relations with persons as involving an infinite task of "self-recognition in abso-

48. Ibid., p. 361.

lute otherness," as we must accept both the sharing and reflection of our own mindedness, which comes to exist only therein, in another, and the otherness of the other as a bearer of natural power.

"Now what about the language which describes my inner experiences and which only I myself can understand?" (§256). Either "I use words to stand for my sensations . . . as we ordinarily do. . . . In that case my language is not a 'private' one. Someone else might understand it as well as I do" (§256). So the wish goes unappeased. Or instead I pursue the wish. I make an effort. "And now I simply *associate* names with sensations and use these names in descriptions" (§256). Then I find I have done nothing. My effort is empty. Absent "a great deal of stage-setting in the language" (§257), without drawing on what "must already be prepared in language in order that the mere naming of a sensation have a sense [schon viel in der Sprache vorbereitet sein muß, damit das bloße Benennen einen Sinn hat]" (§257), my effort is a mere "ceremony" (§258), empty of cognitive achievement.

So I cannot "simply *associate* [assoziiere . . . einfach] names with sensations and use these names in descriptions" (§256). I cannot in that way appease my wish, under that account of what I do or might do. Insofar as I characterize what I undertake to do under that formula, my wish is betrayed. "For 'sensation' is a word of our common language, not of one intelligible to me alone. So the use of this word stands in need of a justification which everybody understands" (§261).

Is the wish then to be abandoned? What happens is that another formula to describe action in pursuit of this wish is groped for, in this protagonist. Perhaps one can "inwardly *undertake* to use the word in such-and-such a way" (§262). "But I can (inwardly) undertake to call THIS 'pain' in the future" (§263). Or perhaps my inner use of a term in a language only I can understand rests on "a subjective justification [eine subjektive Rechtfertigung]" (§265). But in these cases too the formulae betray us, and the pursuit of the wish is not effectively imagined. "The further practical consequences" (§268) of the efforts carried out under these formulae are not those of private, absolute understanding. Either justification for the use of terms and genuine recognizing and classification of my sensations under concepts are present, so that my act is intelligible to (and contestable by) others, or my act is empty.

Talk of absolute, ordinary-practice-independent *recognition* accomplished within comes to nothing. If it is genuine recognition and is achieved under ordinary criteria of application, then it is not absolute and inner. If it is absolute and inner, then it is not recognition, not a founding inner conceptualization of which public practice is the mere secondary derivative through conventional translation. "A wheel that can be turned though nothing else moves with it is not part of the mechanism" (§271).

Yet the failure of the wish to come to articulate expression under a formula describing its pursuit does not thereby adjust inner and outer (*Willkür* and *Wille*), so as to make the inner the secondary derivative of the outer, something that we construct or that does not exist in the absence of public techniques and practices. There is 'inner experience.' My sensations are grammatically mine. So is my natural power as a being capable of conceptualization. Yet I cannot exercise my power without taking up ordinary criteria. It is not easy to describe the relation between my sensations and public objects, when my sensations are both grammatically mine and yet objects of conceptual consciousness for me only insofar as I engage with public criteria, techniques, and practices. "What am I to say about the word 'red'?—that it means something 'confronting us all' and that everyone should really have another word, besides this one, to mean his *own* sensation of red? Or is it like this: the word 'red' means something known to everyone; and in addition, for each person, it means something known only to him? (Or perhaps rather: it *refers* to something known only to him.)" (§273).

No. Talk of something unique within me that I mean or refer to leads nowhere. Yet my sensations are mine. I have them. My uses of "red," for all that they are enabled and informed by training in public criteria, techniques, and practices, surely also have something to do with me, with the fact that, drawing on my training, *I* apply the word "red" when *I* have certain visual experiences. Despite the importance of training, something is left to me to do on the basis of my training and experience. Where we go wrong is in trying to theorize this performance as a univocal effect of a stable something, whether that something is taken to be the absolute and transparent presence to consciousness of "inner objects," or natural processes, or even ordinary practice itself. It is senseless to deny the importance of my powers and their contributions to my linguistic and conceptual performances; it is likewise senseless to deny the importance of training in public practice and to construe my performances as in their essence stemming from the concentration of "inner attention." The mistake is to try in any way to theorize about conceptual performance as an effect of an essence, no matter whether inner or in practice, to try to cast the inner either as a construction out of public practice or as the autonomous foundation of that practice. When I call something red, either to myself or to others, what I do is the result of the inextricable interfusion of inner and outer, of natural power and public practice, of nature and convention, together with all the temptations, wishes, fantasies, and anxieties about otherness involved in coming to be an articulate conceptualizer only within that interfusion.

"Only of a human being and what resembles (behaves like) a living human being can one say: it has sensations; it sees; is blind; hears; is deaf; is conscious or unconscious" (§281). Human beings are the kinds of beings who are capable of articulate conceptualization within that interfusion wherein natural power and public practice are brought into engagement with one another. Seeing this—not propounding a new theory of the inner, no matter whether intellectualist, naturalist, or constructivist—is what matters. It is not a biological claim about human beings that this is what we are like, not a claim to be grounded in neuroscience or computational linguistics. It is not a belief or opinion to be tested, supported, or discredited by any human-expression-independent experience of things. It is part of the grammar of "person."

> What gives us *so much as the idea* that living beings, things can feel?
> Is it that my education has led me to it by drawing my attention to feelings in myself, and now I transfer the idea to objects outside myself? That I recognize that there is something there (in me) which I can call "pain" without getting into conflict with the way other people use this word?
>
> (§283)

Do I "learn" from "attention" to my own inner experience what pain is? Or do I learn how to construct or experience what is in me as pain only as other people talk about it? That is, do I either infer, surmise, that some other beings have an "inner life" like mine, the one I "know" myself to have, or do I discover that what is in me, my sensations, are what others talk about? No. "I do not transfer my idea [of a thinking, feeling being] to stones, plants, etc." (§283). That idea—persons, in their likeness and otherness to me, as bearers of power and participants in practice—is primordial with my idea of a person and with my sense of myself as a person, as power and practice come into engagement in me. There is no question of transferring, justifying, or grounding that idea and its application to speaking human beings. "Only of what behaves like a human being can we say that it *has* pains. For one has to say it of a body, or, if you like of a soul which some body *has*. And how can a body *have* a soul?"

(§283). Ensouled body, discursive intelligence in human beings, is not merely an effect of natural processes, not for me a conjecture from my own case. It is in part projectible by analogy onto other animate beings. It "seems able to get a foothold" with "a wriggling fly," whose struggles to act according to its nature we can see, but not with "a stone" (§284). But that idea of ensouled body is not an inference from what I can see in the fly and in myself. That idea is primordially part of the way I experience human beings, as I come to have conceptual consciousness at all.

Our relations with persons—beings who have a natural power of conceptualization articulable only in and through some shared practice—are different from our relations with mere physical things. We see their animation directly and do not infer it from a prior recognition of a spatial configuration in a face, coupled with knowledge of a "law" correlating types of spatial configuration with types of emotion. "Think of the recognition of *facial expressions*. Or of the description of facial expressions—which does not consist in giving the measurements of the face" (§285).[49] To ask where pain is—is it in the body or in the mind? (cf. §286)—is to suppress the primitiveness of the concept of a person as embodied soul, alive through the interfusion of natural power and public practice. To ask that question is to seek for a measurable something to bear the pain—the hand and its measurably damaged nerves, or the brain and its neural firings, or the isolate mind and its transparent self-knowledge— and to deny the unity and life of the person, thereby casting persons as objects of explanation, not bearers of life. Doing this can be desperately important for the development of physical therapies that may repair the vehicles of a natural power. But explanations arrived at on the basis of this maneuver will neither capture the nature of that natural power itself nor explain its mode of life. "If we cast out human behavior, which is the expression of sensation, it looks as if I might legitimately begin to doubt afresh" (§288)—where the pain is (in the body or in the mind) or whether I am in pain. Such doubts may be fruitful for therapy. But they will not capture the place of pain in the life of a person; they will not ground in measurable or intellectible natural essences what *is* expressed in the expression of pain, a particular juncture in the life of an embodied soul.

Yet there remains a powerful temptation to repudiate the fact that the life of

---

49. Compare Hegel's criticisms of phrenology and physiognomy in the *Phenomenology*, chap. 5, part A, sec. c. See also Alasdair MacIntyre, "Hegel on Faces and Skulls," in *Hegel*, ed. MacIntyre (Garden City: Doubleday, 1972), pp. 219–36.

a person arises through the interfusion of natural power with public practice, a temptation that is not itself denied or cast by the protagonist as external to what he is. "That I am here tempted [Daß ich hier versucht bin] to say that one might take a sensation for something other than it is arises from this: if I assume the abrogation [Wenn ich . . . abgeschafft denke] of the normal language-game with the expression of a sensation, I need a criterion of identity for the sensation; and then the possibility of error also exists" (§288). I am here tempted to repudiate my dependence on public practices for my articulate life as a conceptually conscious being, tempted to envision my control and command of the perfect exercise of a natural power of mind. I seek a perfect justification for my perfected usages, in independence of the stable yet shifting criteria of usage that are laid down in public practice. I wish to be absolutely "justified *before myself* [*vor mir selbst* gerechtfertigt]" (§289), and so made sublime and whole in my intentionality and judgment, apart from the relation to public practice that I can experience as involving dependency and defeat.

Yet this relation is also one of the animation of conceptual consciousness. Such sublimity and wholeness in intentionality, judgment, and usage as there may be are to be found in engagement with public practice, not in its repudiation—or so, at least, this protagonist is coming to accept, as routes of temptation exhaust themselves and acknowledgment and gratitude begin to be possible. "To use a word without justification," without grounding its usage in perfected inner intentionality, "does not mean to use it without right. What I do is not, of course, to identify my sensation by criteria, rather I use the same expression. But this is not the *end* of the language-game: it is the beginning" (§§289–90). I cease—this protagonist ceases—to abstract or except myself as an articulate exerciser of a natural power from engagement with public practice. I consent to my own legibility in its terms, or in publicly accessible transformations of them, and I accept the joint dependence and animation of my life as a person, an intentional, conceptually conscious being, on others.

There is for me no describing the facts of my own case, no identification of my sensations, no achievement of intentionality, apart from my acceptance of that dependence and that animation. "Don't always think that *you* read off what you say from the facts [daß du deine Worte von Tatsachen abliest]; that you portray these in words according to rules" (§292). The objects or facts that we wish or fantasize might absolutely ground our intentionality and rule-applications by serving as perfect private samples within do not exist for us *as such objects of perfect conceptualization.* "If we construe the grammar of the expression on the model of 'object and designation' the object drops out of consideration as irrelevant" (§293).

Not that sensations are not objects of judgment: there is something there, and there may even be cases in which we can say, "I know that this is what I felt yesterday; it's the same dull ache, intensifying to a stab of pain when I turn my neck." Outside the context of whether knowledge of inner states as "private samples" might be achieved independently of training in public practice, it is clear that we can sometimes know our own sensations. "I say, 'I am afraid'; someone else asks me: 'What was that? A cry of fear; or do you want to tell me how you feel; or is it a reflection on your present state'—Could I always give him a clear answer? Could I never give him one?" (II, ix, p. 187). Supposing that the cases are murky and it is not clear when we can give a clear answer, still it seems that sometimes we can formulate descriptions of a state of mind. Sometimes we can observe, recognize, and report the occurrence of mental states or conditions, including both states of mind, such as fear or anxiety, and states of sensation.[50]

But the grammar of such claims is *not* that of a given object facing a private, perfect, concept-applying intelligence. The roots of conceptual consciousness, and of the lives of persons, are not to be found in such fantasized encounters of subject and object apart from or beneath practice. That is not the grammar of "sensation." "The thing in the box [Das Ding in der Schachtel] . . . cancels itself out [hebt sich weg], whatever it is" (§293). It does not found or ground our intentionality or conceptual consciousness. A fantasized perfectly present object of private conceptual consciousness fails to underlie and explain our coming to public conceptual consciousness, as natural power engages with public practice. Such an object remains a fantasy. It is in this sense—it fails to found our intentionality by standing as an inner, self-given sample—that pain is "not a *something*, but not a *nothing* either" (§304). When we try to characterize it, to say to ourselves of what we are conceptually conscious in independence of public practice, then either we speak to ourselves in terms that are—in principle—intelligible to all, therein revealing our dependence as conceptually conscious beings on public practice, or we say nothing, make a mere noise.

Yet there is something inner, a natural power which is brought to articulate

---

50. Cf. Alan Donagan, "Wittgenstein on Sensation," in *Wittgenstein: The Philosophical Investigations,* ed. Pitcher, pp. 326–27, 335–36.

life in its engagement with public practice. My sensations are grammatically mine. And so a fantasy arises of exercising that natural power on one's own, of achieving perfect conceptual consciousness, *Willkür* fully informed by *Wille,* on one's own. "The very fact that we should so much like to say [Daß wir gerne sagen möchten]: '*This* is the important thing'—while we point privately to the sensation—is enough to show *how much we are inclined* to say something which gives no information" (§298, emphasis added).

We do have this inclination. We remain tempted in fantasy to combine the fact of a natural power in us with the grammatical identity of sensations as peculiar to individuals. The protagonist finds this inclination persistently present in himself. Only a discovery of self-given, private samples would perfect one's exercises of a natural power and immunize them against criticism, through foreclosing the vertiginousness and anxiety of one's life in language with others. But the presence and power of this inclination do not mean that any object exists to satisfy it. "Being unable—when we surrender ourselves to philosophical thought [wenn wir uns philosophischen Gedanken hingeben— when we give ourselves over to philosophical thought]—to help saying such-and-such; being irresistibly inclined to say [unwiderstehlich dazu neigen, dies zu sagen]—does not mean being forced into an *assumption,* or having an immediate perception or knowledge of a state of affairs" (§299). When we say, for example, "I know my pain" in a metaphysical voice, announcing the existence of a discoverable, judgment-determining object present to oneself prior to and apart from public practice, it does not follow that there is any such object. Such an utterance voices a fantasy; it does not outline an epistemological research program. It is this persistent fantasy, woven, it seems, into the structure of our intentionality as it comes to articulate life through training in public practice, that is essential to us as human persons and possessors of conceptual consciousness.

Yes, there is pain. It can be expressed and talked about and known, only not as a practice-independent, consciousness-founding object. "The representation [Vorstellung] of pain certainly enters into the language game in a sense; only not as an image [Bild—not as a model or form or idea or pattern that grounds a practice-independent judgment or conceptualization]" (§300). The important thing is to remember that pain is something that is experienced in the life of a *person,* a being who comes to conceptual consciousness as natural power interfuses with public practice, within a resultant structure of standing fantasy, inclination, and temptation. It is such a being, a person, not a pure and primitive intentionality, who can say, "I am in pain; it hurts here." "The suffering person is the one who expresses pain [die leidende Person ist die, welche Schmerz aüßert]" (§302). To say this is to accept—or it is for this protagonist to accept—one's life as a person, however much one has wished, and wishes, to repudiate it.

Pain thus expressible in the life of a person is not pain as it is conceived of within the epistemological fantasy of the discovery of the perfect presence to oneself alone of a conceptual-performance-determining sample. What pain is is shown by the kinds of expressions, from screaming to articulate acknowledgment, of it that are possible for us in our lives as persons. Its essence is made manifest in these expressions. ("Essence is expressed by grammar" [§371].) "It is not a *something*, but not a *nothing* either" (§304). The important thing is to reject the grammar of perfect recognition under a perfect concept of a practice-independent object, a grammar that is forced on us when in the grip of a standing fantasy of perfect authority. It is not that the reality of sensations is denied; it is that the nature of that reality is reconstrued. It is seen as not simply given, but as a reality that is present in and expressible within the lives of persons who come to conceptual consciousness through engagement with public practice. ("Meaning something is like going up to someone; it's not like having a dead picture [Bild—model or pattern] of any kind" [§455].)

As Alan Donagan has usefully noted, the aim throughout these remarks about sensation is to locate the actual place and nature of sensations within human life so as to unseat misleading, humanity-distorting (but also, as fantasy, humanity-expressing) construals of inner and outer. Both Cartesianism and behaviorism (as well as various other naturalized epistemologies and conventionalisms that repudiate the interfusion of power and practice in conceptual life) rest on such construals. The effort is to get beyond them; it is, as Donagan puts it,

> to allow that the Cartesian grammatical facts are facts, that sensations are private, non-dispositional accompaniments of behaviour by which they are naturally expressed, but to refuse to recognize those accompaniments as processes that can be named and investigated independently of the circumstances that produce them, and the behaviour by which they are naturally expressed. Sundered from their external circumstances, such private accompaniments cannot even be named in a common language; *a fortiori*, they cannot be investigated in any way at all. But equally, should an investigation [intellectualist, behaviorist, cognitivist, connectionist, or conventionalist, as

may be] ignore such facts as that something accompanies a cry of pain, something which is important and frightful, then to describe it as an investigation
of *sensation* would be preposterous.[51]

"The decisive movement in the conjuring trick" (§308) is to sever pain
from either its circumstances and expressions or from its being given as something inner. We likewise play a conjuring trick upon ourselves when we sever
the existence of conceptual consciousness from either *its* circumstances and
public expressions or from *its* emergence out of inarticulate natural power.
Conceptual consciousness is described preposterously, when it is cast as a fact
of neural wiring, or as a disposition to behave, or as a matter of public convention. Such maneuvers are repressions of our lives as persons. No layer of pure
natural essences or processes (intellectual or neural-biological or transparently
conventional) underlies and explains how we understand, judge, talk, and act.
Understanding, judging, talking, and acting are things we do, in our lives as
persons with and against others, not things that are done in us by some power-
and-practice-independent essence or process. This is what we need to remember.

But we also need to remember that the structure of our intentionality in
our lives with and against others includes a structure of fantasy, a wish to
repudiate and overcome our entanglements and liabilities with others and with
ourselves. "We talk of processes and states and leave their nature undecided"
(§308). We hope to scrutinize these processes and states so as to explain,
ground, or perfect our intentionality. "That is just what commits us to a particular way of looking at the matter" (§308). But this talk then leads nowhere,
except into alienation from our lives as persons. "For us, of course, these forms
of expression are like pontificals which we indeed put on, but cannot do much
with, since we lack the effective power that would give these vestments meaning and purpose" (§426).

It is not just that there are qualia and that cognitivism and behaviorism
and conventionalism are silent about them. It is that persons lead lives, including both indulgences in fantasy and possibilities of acknowledging or repudiat-
ing one's intentionality with others, in ways that these programs distort or
repress or deny. "What we deny is that the picture of the inner process gives
us the correct idea of the use of the word 'to remember' ['erinnern']. We say
that this picture with its ramifications stands in the way of our seeing the use

51. Ibid., pp. 350–51.

of the word as it is" (§305)—and of our seeing our lives as they are. Programs for the analysis and explanation of conceptual consciousness, intentionality, and linguistic competence that seek an inner process through which such abilities are constituted fail to grasp the entanglements of these abilities with relations with others, with fantasy, and with possibilities of acknowledgment and avoidance. They misunderstand, for example, the nature of such intentional phenomena as remembering, which involves the exercise of those there-entangled abilities.

In thus misconstruing remembering and other intentional phenomena, they also suppress or deny the possibility of impersonal remembering, or acknowledgment, or recollection (*Erinnerung*), of our humanity. Among the correct uses of "remember" (*sich erinnern*) is its use to describe the acknowledgment or recollection of all that is entangled with one's life as a human person. ("There is no guilt in reverence for the dead.")[52] These entanglements mean that such impersonal remembering is not simply a neural or mental process of retrieving an item of information. It involves *Erinnerung*, not *Gedächtnis; anamnesis,* not *mneme;* acknowledgment and recollection of one's human life, not recalling what one ate for breakfast or when the Battle of Hastings occurred. Such acknowledgment and recollection are interwoven with senses of one's human expressive activity, arrived at imperfectly under training within social life, hence also a sense of the presence of others and of gratitude for their roles in enabling one's expressive life, wherein natural power is brought to articulate ability. It involves a sense of self-collection, of stillness or suspension within an open-ended process—without clear beginning in the given, without obvious end—of the articulation and exercise of expressive ability. In its location as a moment of suspension or stillness within such an open process of leading a life, such a remembrance also involves a sense of its own situatedness and transitoriness. It is a moment of self-recollection of one's impersonal, human identity as intentionally conscious, involving a natural power specifically articulated through engagement with public practice Such a moment is achieved in partial withdrawal from such engagements, but only partial, and only passing, since they structurally enable one's articulate, expressive, human life.

This kind of remembrance is repudiated, and our humanity is distorted, in programs that cast our intentionality as somehow a complex effect of given

---

52. Sophocles, *Antigone,* trans. Dudley Fitts and Robert Fitzgerald, in Sophocles, *The Oedipus Cycle* (San Diego: Harcourt Brace Jovanovich, 1976), scene II, p. 205.

substances or fixed phenomena of will, whose natures or essences somehow command, or might command, intentionality's motions. It is to this kind of remembrance that the progress of the protagonist of *Philosophical Investigations*, enacting it, fitfully, calls us. It is the kind of remembrance that Hölderlin describes in an essay fragment.

> You ask me why, even though the people, following their nature, elevate themselves above necessity and thus exist in a more manifold and intimate relation with their world, even though, to the extent that they elevate themselves above physical and moral needs, they always live a—in human terms—higher life, so that between them and their world there be a higher [and] more than mechanical *interrelation*, a higher destiny, even though this higher relation be truly the most sacred for them because within it they themselves feel united with their world and everything which they are [and] possess, you ask me why exactly they *represent* the relation between them and their world, why they have to form an idea or image of their destiny which, strictly speaking, can neither be properly thought nor does it lie before our senses?
>
> You ask me, and I can answer you only so much: that man also elevates himself above need in that he can *remember* his destiny, in that he can and may be grateful for his life, that he also senses more continuously his sustained relation with the element in which he moves, that by elevating himself above necessity in his efficiency and the experience connected to it, he experiences a more infinite [and] continuous satisfaction than is the satisfaction of basic needs, provided that, on the one hand, his activity is of the right kind, is not too far-reaching for him, for his strength and skill, that he is not too restless, too undetermined nor, on the other hand, too anxious, too restricted, too controlled. However, if man approaches it the right way, then there exists, in every sphere that is proper to him, a more than necessity-based, infinite satisfaction. Just as every satisfaction is a momentary standstill of *real* life, so, too, is an infinite satisfaction.[53]

In such a moment of remembrance, gratitude, and suspension, one will feel one's human life—natural power articulated within practice into expressive ability—to be achieved within a larger movement that it does not make sense

---

53. Friedrich Hölderlin, "On Religion," in *Essays and Letters on Theory*, trans. and ed. Thomas Pfau (Albany: State University of New York Press, 1988), p. 90. I am grateful to Eckhart Förster for calling my attention to both this passage from Hölderlin and the one from *Hyperion* that follows.

to break down or reduce to congeries of movements of physical nature or detached mind or transparent convention. One will feel oneself to be a halted traveler, lingering within the larger movement of Power in Nature, stopped but aware also of the onwardness of the movement. Hölderlin catches too this sense of lingering within a larger movement.

> We remembered the past May; never, we said, had we seen the Earth as it was then; it had been transformed, a silver cloud of flowers, a joyous flame of life, purified of all crude matter.
>
> "Oh! all was so full of pleasure and hope," cried Diotima, "so full of unceasing growth and yet so effortless, so blessedly quiet, like a child playing on and on without another thought."
>
> "In that," I cried, "I recognize the soul of Nature—in that still fire, in that lingering in its mighty haste."
>
> "And how dear it is to the happy, that lingering," cried Diotima; "do you remember? once at twilight we stood together on the bridge, after a hard storm, and the red mountain stream shot away under us like an arrow, but there beside it the forest stood in green peace and the bright leaves scarcely stirred. We felt so glad then that the living green did not flee from us too, like the brook, and that the beautiful spring stayed for us like a tame bird; yet now spring, too, is over the hills and away."
>
> We smiled at that, although sorrow was closer to us.
>
> So was our own bliss to depart, and we foresaw it.[54]

If such moments of personal-impersonal remembrance of one's human life in its entanglements are authentic—and do these examples, Hölderlin, Wordsworth, the protagonist of *Philosophical Investigations,* and others show that they are? what sort of showing of their authenticity do we need or can we receive?— then our responses to them and to expressions of them will properly involve not explanation, but acknowledgment, acceptance, and repetition. "We must do away with all *explanation,* and description alone must take its place" (§109). We will then have these moments and their expressions not to imitate or to explain, but to follow after, as we are provoked by them to remembrances and expressions of our own entangled, specifically articulated power, our own human life.[55] "The criteria for the truth of the *confession* that I thought such-and-such are not the criteria for a true *description* of a process. And the impor-

---

54. Friedrich Hölderlin, *Hyperion and Selected Poems,* ed. Eric L. Santner (New York: Continuum, 1990), p. 76.
55. Cf. Kant, *Critique of Judgment,* pp. 171, 181.

tance of the true confession does not reside in its being a correct and certain report of a process. It resides rather in the special consequences which can be drawn from a confession whose truth is guaranteed by the special criteria of truthfulness" (II, xi, 222). My confession, my remembrance of my humanity and its expression or its repudiation, is not something that happens in me; it is not the effect of mental or physical or social substance acting according to their fixed and given natures. It is something that I, animated through my life with others, do. "Tell them I've had a wonderful life."[56]

56. Wittgenstein, cited in Malcolm, *Ludwig Wittgenstein: A Memoir,* p. 100.

Bibliography

Abrams, M. H. *Natural Supernaturalism*. New York: W. W. Norton, 1971.

Augustine. *Confessions*. Translated by R. S. Pine-Coffin. Harmondsworth, England: Penguin Books, 1971.

Ayer, A. J. "Can There Be a Private Language?" In *Wittgenstein: The Philosophical Investigations,* ed. Pitcher.

Baker, G. P., and P. M. S. Hacker. *Language, Sense, and Nonsense*. Oxford, Basil Blackwell, 1984.

———. *Scepticism, Rules, and Language*. Oxford: Basil Blackwell, 1984.

———. *Wittgenstein: Rules, Grammar, and Necessity*. Oxford: Basil Blackwell, 1985.

———. *Wittgenstein: Understanding and Meaning*. Oxford: Basil Blackwell, 1980.

Baynes, Kenneth, James Bohmann, and Thomas McCarthy, eds. *After Philosophy*. Cambridge: MIT Press, 1987.

Beck, J. S. "Letter to Kant, June 24, 1797." In Kant, *Philosophical Correspondence,* edited and translated by Zweig.

Beiser, Frederick C. *The Fate of Reason: German Philosophy from Kant to Fichte*. Cambridge: Harvard University Press, 1987.

Bernstein, J. M. *The Fate of Art: Aesthetic Alienation from Kant to Derrida and Adorno*. University Park: Pennsylvania State University Press, 1992.

Bloor, David. *Wittgenstein: A Social Theory of Knowledge*. New York: Columbia University Press, 1983.

Bourdieu, Pierre. *Le sens pratique*. Paris: Minuit, 1980. Cited in Charles Taylor, "To Follow a Rule," in *Rules and Conventions: Literature, Philosophy, Social Theory,* edited by Mette Hjort (Baltimore: Johns Hopkins University Press, 1992), p. 180.

Bouveresse, Jacques. " 'The Darkness of This Time': Wittgenstein and the Modern World." In *Wittgenstein: Centenary Essays,* ed. Phillips Griffith.

Breazale, Daniel. "Fichte's *Aenesidemus* Review and the Transformation of German Idealism." *Review of Metaphysics* 34 (1981): 545–68.

Cavell, Stanley. *The Claim of Reason*. New York: Oxford University Press, 1979.

———. *Conditions Handsome and Unhandsome: The Constitution of Emersonian Perfectionism*. Chicago: University of Chicago Press, 1990.

———. *In Quest of the Ordinary: Lines of Skepticism and Romanticism*. Chicago: University of Chicago Press, 1988.

———. *Must We Mean What We Say?* New York: Charles Scribner's Sons, 1969.

———. "The *Philosophical Investigations*' Everyday Aesthetics of Itself." Lecture at the University of Pennsylvania, October 23, 1995.

————. *This New Yet Unapproachable America.* Albuquerque: Living Batch Press, 1989.

Chomsky, Noam. *Knowledge of Language.* New York: Praeger, 1986.

Coleridge, Samuel Taylor. *The Notebooks of Samuel Taylor Coleridge.* Vol 3. Edited by Kathleen Coburn. Princeton: Princeton University Press, 1989. Cited in Laurence S. Lockridge, *The Ethics of Romanticism* (Cambridge: Cambridge University Press, 1989), p. 85.

————. *The Portable Coleridge.* Edited by I. A. Richards. Harmondsworth, England: Viking Penguin, 1978.

Descartes, René, *Discourse on Method and Meditations on First Philosophy,* Translated by Donald Cress. Indianapolis: Hackett, 1980.

————. *Philosophical Letters.* Translated and edited by Anthony Kenny. Oxford: Clarendon Press, 1970.

————. *The Philosophical Works of Descartes.* Vol. 1. Edited by E. S. Haldane and G. R. T. Ross. Cambridge: Cambridge University Press, 1911.

Diamond, Cora. *The Realistic Spirit: Wittgenstein, Philosophy, and the Mind.* Cambridge: MIT Press, 1991.

Donagan, Alan. "Wittgenstein on Sensation." In *Wittgenstein: The Philosophical Investigations,* ed. Pitcher.

Drury, M. O'C. "Conversations with Wittgenstein." In *Recollections of Wittgenstein,* ed. Rhees.

Dummett, Michael. "Wittgenstein's Philosophy of Mathematics." In *Wittgenstein: The Philosophical Investigations,* ed. Pitcher. First published in *Philosophical Review* 68 (1959): 324–38.

Eagleton, Terry. "Wittgenstein's Friends." *New Left Review* 135 (September–October 1982).

Edwards, James C. *Ethics without Philosophy: Wittgenstein and the Moral Life.* Tampa: University Presses of Florida, 1982.

Eldridge, Richard. "Internal Transcendentalism: Wordsworth and 'A New Condition of Philosophy.'" *Philosophy and Literature* 18, no. 1 (April 1994): 50–71.

————. "Kant, Hölderlin, and the Experience of Longing." In *Beyond Representation: Philosophy and Poesis,* edited by Richard Eldridge (Cambridge: Cambridge University Press, 1996), pp. 175–96.

————. "The Normal and the Normative: Wittgenstein's Legacy, Kripke, and Cavell." *Philosophy and Phenomenological Research* 46, no. 4 (June 1986).

————, ed. *Beyond Representation: Philosophy and Poetic Imagination.* Cambridge: Cambridge University Press, 1996.

Elias, Norbert. *The Civilizing Process.* Vol. 1, *The History of Manners.* Translated by Edmund Jephcott. Oxford: Basil Blackwell, 1993.

Engelmann, Paul. *Letters from Ludwig Wittgenstein with a Memoir.* Edited by B. F. McGuinness. Oxford: Basil Blackwell, 1967.

Fichte, J. G. "Concerning Human Dignity." Translated by Daniel Breazale. In *Early Philosophical Writings,* edited by Breazale.

————. *Early Philosophical Writings.* Edited by Daniel Breazale. Ithaca: Cornell University Press, 1988.

———. *The Science of Knowledge.* Translated by Peter Heath and John Lachs. Cambridge: Cambridge University Press, 1982.

Fodor, Jerry A. *The Language of Thought.* New York: Thomas Y. Crowell, 1975.

———. *Psychosemantics: The Problem of Meaning in the Philosophy of Mind.* Cambridge: MIT Press, 1987.

Frye, Northrop. "The Drunken Boat." In *Romanticism Reconsidered,* edited by Northrop Frye. New York: Columbia University Press, 1963.

Hacker, P. M. S. *Insight and Illusion: Themes in the Philosophy of Wittgenstein.* Rev. ed. Oxford: Clarendon Press, 1986.

———. *Wittgenstein: Meaning and Mind.* Oxford: Basil Blackwell, 1990.

Hallett, Garth. *A Companion to Wittgenstein's "Philosophical Investigations."* Ithaca: Cornell University Press, 1977.

Hartman, Geoffrey. *Wordsworth's Poetry 1787–1814.* New Haven: Yale University Press, 1964.

Hegel, G. W. F. *Phenomenology of Spirit.* Translated by A. V. Miller. Oxford: Clarendon Press, 1977.

———. *Philosophy of Right.* Translated by T. M. Knox. Oxford: Clarendon Press, 1952.

Herzog, Patricia. "The Practical Wisdom of Beethoven's *Diabelli* Variations." *Musical Quarterly* 79, no. 1 (Spring 1995).

Hjort, Mette, ed. *Rules and Conventions: Literature, Philosophy, Social Theory.* Baltimore: Johns Hopkins University Press, 1992.

Hölderlin, Friedrich. *Essays and Letters on Theory.* Translated and edited by Thomas Pfau. Albany: State University of New York Press, 1988.

———. *Hyperion and Selected Poems.* Edited by Eric L. Santner. New York: Continuum, 1980.

Isenberg, Arnold. "Critical Communication." In *The Philosophy of Art: Readings Ancient and Modern,* edited by Alex Neill and Aaron Ridley. New York: McGraw-Hill, 1995. First published in *Philosophical Review* 58 (1949): 330–44.

Kant, Immanuel. *Critique of Judgment.* Translated by J. C. Meredith. Oxford: Clarendon Press, 1952.

———. *Critique of Practical Reason.* Translated by Lewis White Beck. Indianapolis: Bobbs-Merrill, 1956.

———. *Critique of Pure Reason.* 2d ed. Translated by Norman Kemp Smith. London: Macmillan, 1933.

———. *On History.* Edited by Lewis White Beck. Indianapolis: Bobbs-Merrill, 1963.

———. *Kritik der Urteilskraft.* Frankfurt: Suhrkamp, 1974.

———. *Philosophical Correspondence, 1795–99.* Edited and translated by Arnulf Zweig. Chicago: University of Chicago Press, 1967.

———. *Religion within the Limits of Reason Alone.* Translated by T. M. Greene and H. H. Hudson. New York: Harper and Brothers, 1960.

Kenny, Anthony. "Cartesian Privacy." In *Wittgenstein: The Philosophical Investigations,* edited by Pitcher.

———. *The Legacy of Wittgenstein.* Oxford: Basil Blackwell, 1984.

———. *The Metaphysics of Mind.* Oxford: Oxford University Press, 1992.

———. *Wittgenstein.* Cambridge, Mass.: Harvard University Press, 1973.

Kripke, Saul A. *Wittgenstein on Rules and Private Language.* Cambridge: Harvard University Press, 1982.

Lacoue-Labarthe, Philippe, and Jean-Luc Nancy. *The Literary Absolute: The Theory of Literature in German Romanticism.* Translated by Philip Barnard and Cheryl Lester. Albany: State University of New York Press, 1988.

Locke, John. *Essay Concerning Human Understanding.* Edited by Alexander Campbell Fraser. New York: Dover, 1959.

Lockridge, Laurence S. *The Ethics of Romanticism.* Cambridge: Cambridge University Press, 1989.

Lurie, Yuval. "Culture as a Form of Life: A Romantic Reading of Wittgenstein." *International Philosophical Quarterly* 32, no. 2 (June 1992).

MacIntyre, Alasdair, ed. *Hegel.* Garden City: Doubleday, 1972.

Malcolm, Norman. *Ludwig Wittgenstein: A Memoir.* Oxford: Oxford University Press, 1958.

———. "Wittgenstein on Language and Rules." *Philosophy* 64, no. 247 (January 1989): 5–28.

Marcuse, Herbert. *The Aesthetic Dimension.* Boston: Beacon Press, 1978.

Mill, John Stuart. *Autobiography and Other Writings.* Edited by Jack Stillinger. Boston: Houghton Mifflin, 1969.

Monk, Ray. *Ludwig Wittgenstein: The Duty of Genius.* New York: Macmillan, 1990.

Morton, Michael. *The Critical Turn: Studies in Kant, Herder, Wittgenstein, and Contemporary Theory.* Detroit: Wayne State University Press, 1993.

Nagel, Thomas. *The View from Nowhere.* Oxford: Oxford University Press, 1986.

Novalis [Friedrich von Hardenburg]. *Schriften.* Vol. 3. Edited by Paul Kluckholn and Richard Samuel. Stuttgart: Kohlhammer, 1960. Cited in Azade Seyhan, *Representation and Its Discontents: The Critical Legacy of German Romanticism* (Berkeley: University of California Press, 1992), p. 75.

Pears, D. F. *The False Prison.* Vol. 2. Oxford: Clarendon Press, 1988.

Phillips Griffith, A. *Wittgenstein: Centenary Essays.* Cambridge: Cambridge University Press, 1991.

Pitcher, George, ed. *Wittgenstein: The Philosophical Investigations.* Garden City: Doubleday, 1966.

Rhees, Rush, ed. *Recollections of Wittgenstein.* Oxford: Oxford University Press, 1984.

Rorty, Richard. *Consequences of Pragmatism.* Minneapolis: University of Minnesota Press, 1982.

———. *Contingency, Irony, and Solidarity.* Cambridge: Cambridge University Press, 1989.

Rowe, M. W. "Goethe and Wittgenstein." *Philosophy* 66 (1991).

Rubinstein, David. *Marx and Wittgenstein: Social Praxis and Social Explanation.* London: Routledge and Kegan Paul, 1981.

Schiller, Friedrich. "On Naive and Sentimental Poetry." Translated by Julius A. Elias. In *The Origins of Modern Critical Thought,* edited by Simpson.

———. *On the Aesthetic Education of Man in a Series of Letters.* Translated by Elizabeth.

M. Wilkinson and L. A. Willoughby. In *The Origins of German Critical Thought*, edited by Simpson.

———. *On the Aesthetic Education of Man in a Series of Letters*. Translated by Reginald Snell. New York: Frederick Ungar, 1965.

Schlegel, Friedrich. *Friedrich Schlegel's "Lucinde" and the Fragments*. Translated by Peter Firchow. Minneapolis: University of Minnesota Press, 1971.

Schulte, Joachim. "Chor und Gesetz: Zur 'Morphologischen Methode' bei Goethe und Wittgenstein." *Grazer Philosophischer Studien* 21 (1984).

Searle, John. *The Rediscovery of the Mind*. Cambridge: MIT Press, 1992.

Seyhan, Azade. *Representation and Its Discontents: The Critial Legacy of German Romanticism*. Berkeley: University of California Press, 1992.

Shields, Philip R. *Logic and Sin in the Writings of Ludwig Wittgenstein*. Chicago: University of Chicago Press, 1993.

Silber, John. "The Ethical Significance of Kant's *Religion*." Introduction to *Religion within the Limits of Reason Alone*, by Immanuel Kant. Translated by T. M. Greene and H. H. Hudson. New York: Harper and Brothers, 1960.

Simpson, David, ed. *The Origins of German Critical Thought*. Cambridge: Cambridge University Press, 1988.

Sophocles. *The Oedipus Cycle*. Translated by Dudley Fitts and Robert Fitzgerald. San Diego: Harcourt Brace Jovanovich, 1976.

Stern, David G. "The 'Middle Wittgenstein': From Logical Atomism to Practical Holism." *Synthese* 87 (1991).

———. *Wittgenstein on Mind and Language*. Oxford: Oxford University Press, 1994.

Strawson, P. F. "Review of Wittgenstein's *Philosophical Investigations*." In *Wittgenstein: The Philosophical Investigations*, edited by Pitcher. First published in *Mind* 63 (1954): 70–99.

Stroud, Barry. "Wittgenstein and Logical Necessity." In *Wittgenstein: The Philosophical Investigations*, edited by Pitcher.

Taylor, Charles. "Overcoming Epistemology." In *After Philosophy*, edited by Baynes, Bohmann, and McCarthy.

———. *Sources of the Self: The Making of the Modern Identity*. Cambridge: Harvard University Press, 1989.

———. "To Follow a Rule." In *Rules and Conventions: Literature, Philosophy, Social Theory*, edited by Hjort.

von Wright, G. H. *Wittgenstein*. Minneapolis: University of Minnesota Press, 1982.

Wittgenstein, Ludwig. *Culture and Value*. 2d ed. Edited by G. H. von Wright with Heikki Nyman. Translated by Peter Winch. Chicago: University of Chicago Press, 1980.

———. *Lectures on Aesthetics, Psychology, and Religious Belief*. Edited by Cyril Barrett. Berkeley: University of California Press, 1967.

———. *Ludwig Wittgenstein and the Vienna Circle: Conversations Recorded by Friedrich Waismann*. Edited by B. F. McGuinness. Translated by J. Schulte and B. F. McGuinness. Oxford: Basil Blackwell, 1979.

————. *Notebooks 1914–1916.* Translated by G. E. M. Anscombe. Oxford: Basil Blackwell, 1961.

————. *On Certainty.* Edited by G. E. M. Anscombe and G. H. von Wright. Translated by Denis Paul and G. E. M. Anscombe. Oxford: Basil Blackwell, 1969.

————. *Philosophical Grammar.* Edited by Rush Rhees. Translated by Anthony Kenny. Oxford: Basil Blackwell, 1974.

————. *Philosophical Investigations.* 3d ed. Translated by G. E. M. Anscombe. New York: Macmillan, 1958.

————. *Philosophical Occasions 1912–1951.* Edited by James Klagge and Alfred Nordmann. Indianapolis: Hackett, 1993.

————. *Philosophical Remarks.* Edited by Rush Rhees. Translated by Raymond Hargreaves and Roger White. Oxford: Basil Blackwell, 1975.

————. *Remarks on the Philosophy of Psychology.* Vol. 1. Oxford: Basil Blackwell, 1980.

————. *Tractatus Logico-philosophicus.* 2d ed. Translated by D. F. Pears and B. F. McGuinness. London: Routledge and Kegan Paul, 1971.

Wood, Allen. "Unsocial Sociability: The Anthropological Basis of Kantian Ethics." *Philosophical Topics* 19, no. 1 (Spring 1991): 325–51.

Wordsworth, William. *Selected Poems and Prefaces.* Edited by Jack Stillinger. Boston: Houghton Mifflin, 1965.

Index